USA BY RAIL

Plus Canada

USA BY RAIL

Plus Canada

John Pitt

BRADT PUBLICATIONS, UK
HUNTER PUBLISHING, USA

First published in 1992 by Bradt Publications, 41 Nortoft Rd, Chalfont St Peter, Bucks SL9 0LA, England.
Distributed in the USA by Hunter Publishing Inc., 300 Raritan Center Parkway, CN94, Edison, NJ 08810.

Updated reprint November 1992

British Library Cataloguing-in-Publication data

A catalogue record for this book is
available from the British Library

Illustrations by Emma Hill
Cover illustration from the Amtrak calendar, courtesy of Amtrak, Washington
Maps courtesy of Amtrak
Route maps by Patti Taylor
Typeset from the author's disc by Patti Taylor, London NW8 0RJ
Printed in Great Britain by Guernsey Press

ACKNOWLEDGEMENTS

The author would like to thank Patricia Kelly (Manager, Amtrak Travel Communications), Mark Smith (Editor, Locomotive & Railway Preservation) and Marjorie and Wayne Preston of Florida.

Travellers' Tales
The publisher would like to thank the following members of the Globetrotters Club who sent in their Amtrak stories: John Ainsworth, Laila Allen, Susan Bishop, Molly Elliot, William Hughes, and Kenneth Wescott-Jones.

The prize of £50 for the best contribution is shared by John Ainsworth and William Hughes for their varied and informative pieces.

We expect this guide to be updated regularly so if you have a traveller's tale you would like to share, do write to us. "USA by Rail", Bradt Publications, 41 Nortoft Rd, Chalfont St Peter, Bucks SL9 0LA.

Contents

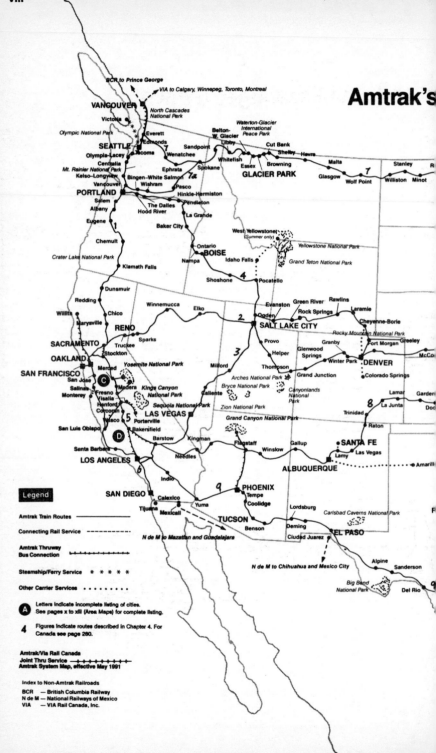

Amtrak's

tional Rail Passenger System

VIA to Halifax, Sydney and Quebec

VIA to Quebec

VIA to Halifax

VIA to Ottawa

MONTREAL

St. Albans
Plattsburgh
Burlington-Essex Jct.

VIA to Winnipeg and Vancouver

Lake

Duluth

Detroit Lakes

Staples

St. Cloud

MINNEAPOLIS

Red Wing

Winona

Grand Rapids

MILWAUKEE

Madison

Battle Creek

Rockford

CHICAGO

TORONTO

Burlington

Niagara Falls

London

Hamilton

BUFFALO

Schenectady

Albany-Rensselaer

Springfield

BOSTON

NEW YORK

DETROIT

Toledo

Akron

CLEVELAND

Harrisburg

PHILADELPHIA

Atlantic City

PITTSBURGH

BALTIMORE

WASHINGTON, DC

OMAHA

lcoln

Ottumwa

Galesburg

West Quincy

Springfield

INDIANAPOLIS

CINCINNATI

Shenandoah
National Park

Lorton

Charlottesville

Richmond

NORFOLK

KANSAS CITY

Lawrence

St. Joseph

Independence

Lees Summit

Topeka

Emporia

Warrensburg

Sedalia

Newton

tchinson

ST. LOUIS

Belleville

Kirkwood

Jefferson City

Centralia

Carbondale

Louisville

Clifton Forge

Roanoke

Danville

Lynchburg

Greensboro

High Point

Salisbury

Kannapolis

Charlotte

Gastonia

Southern
Pines

Burlington

Durham

Hamlet

Rocky Mount

Wilson

Raleigh

Selma

Fayetteville

Poplar Bluff

Fulton

Great Smoky Mountains
National Park

Nashville

Greenville

Clemson

Toccoa

Spartanburg

Camden

Columbia

Dillon

Florence

Kingstree

Walnut Ridge

Newport

Dyersburg

MEMPHIS

Gainesville

Denmark

Charleston

Hot Springs National Park

Little Rock

Malvern

Arkadelphia

Batesville

Grenada

Winona

Durant

Canton

Anniston

Birmingham

Tuscaloosa

ATLANTA

Yemassee

Savannah

DALLAS

Texarkana

Marshall

Longview

Corsicana

Hazlehurst

Brookhaven

McComb

Jackson

Laurel

Hattiesburg

Picayune

Meridian

Bay Minette

Montgomery

Greenville

Atmore

Evergreen

Pensacola

Jesup

Lake City

JACKSONVILLE

College Station-Bryan

Lake Charles

Beaumont

HOUSTON

Lafayette

New Iberia

Hammond

Baton Rouge

Schriever

Slidell

Gulfport

Biloxi

Mobile

Pascagoula

Tallahassee

Waldo

Palatka

DeLand

Sanford (Station and Auto Train Terminal)

Ocala

Wildwood

Dade City

Winter Park

Orlando

Kissimmee

Sebring

Okeechobee

West Palm Beach

Delray Beach

Deerfield Beach

Fort Lauderdale

NEW ORLEANS

Walt Disney World

Clearwater

ST. PETERSBURG

TAMPA

Bradenton

Sarasota

Winter Haven

Lakeland

Hollywood

MIAMI

Everglades National Park

NTONIO

SANTONIO

Area maps

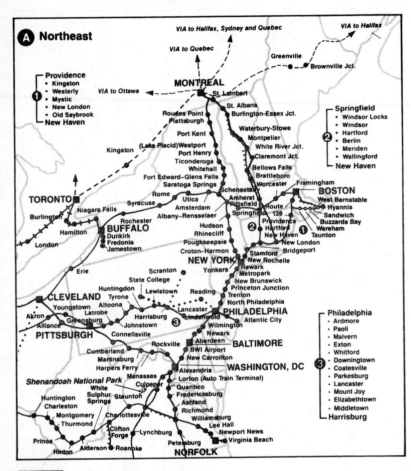

A Northeast

VIA to Halifax, Sydney and Quebec

VIA to Halifax

VIA to Quebec

Greenville

Brownville Jct.

① Providence
- Kingston
- Westerly
- Mystic
- New London
- Old Saybrook

New Haven

VIA to Ottawa

MONTREAL   St. Lambert

St. Albans

Burlington-Essex Jct.

Roudes Point

Plattsburgh

Port Kent

Kingston

(Lake Placid) Westport

Port Henry

Ticonderoga

Whitehall

Fort Edward–Glens Falls

Saratoga Springs

Waterbury-Stowe

Montpelier

White River Jct.

Claremont Jct.

Bellows Falls

Brattleboro

Worcester

Springfield
- Windsor Locks
- Windsor
- Hartford
- Berlin
- Meriden
- Wallingford

New Haven

② Framingham

TORONTO

Rome

Utica

Amsterdam

Albany–Rensselaer

Schenectady

Amherst

Pittsfield

Springfield

Route
128

BOSTON

West Barnstable

Hyannis

Sandwich

Buzzards Bay

Wareham

Taunton

Burlington

Niagara Falls

Syracuse

Rochester

Providence

Hartford

New Haven

New London

Bridgeport

① ②

Hamilton

BUFFALO

Dunkirk

Fredonia

Jamestown

Hudson

Rhinecliff

Poughkeepsie

Croton-Harmon

London

Erie

Scranton

State College

Huntingdon

Stamford

New Rochelle

NEW YORK

Yonkers

Newark

Metropark

New Brunswick

Princeton Junction

Trenton

North Philadelphia

CLEVELAND

Youngstown

Tyrone

Lewistown

Reading

Akron

Altoona

Alliance

Greensburg

Latrobe

Harrisburg

Johnstown

Lancaster

Lindenwold

PHILADELPHIA

Atlantic City

PITTSBURGH

Connellsville

Wilmington

Newark

Philadelphia
- Ardmore
- Paoli
- Malvern
- Exton
- Whitford
- Downingtown
- Coatesville
- Parkesburg
- Lancaster
- Mount Joy
- Elizabethtown
- Middletown

Harrisburg

Rockville

Aberdeen

BALTIMORE

Cumberland

Martinsburg

Harpers Ferry

BWI Airport

New Carrollton

③

Shenandoah National Park

Manassas

Culpeper

Alexandria

Lorton (Auto Train Terminal)

WASHINGTON, DC

Huntington

Charleston

White
Sulphur
Springs

Staunton

Quantico

Fredericksburg

Ashland

Richmond

Montgomery

Thurmond

Charlottesville

Williamsburg

Lee Hall

Prince

Clifton
Forge

Lynchburg

Newport News

Virginia Beach

Hinton

Alderson

Roanoke

Petersburg

NORFOLK

Legend

Amtrak Train Routes	———————
Connecting Rail Service	– – – – – – –
Amtrak Thruway Bus Connection	⊢⊢⊢⊢⊢
Other Carrier Services	••••••••••••
Seasonal Train Service	–o–o–o–o–o–
Amtrak/Via Rail Canada Joint Thru Service	┼┼┼┼┼┼

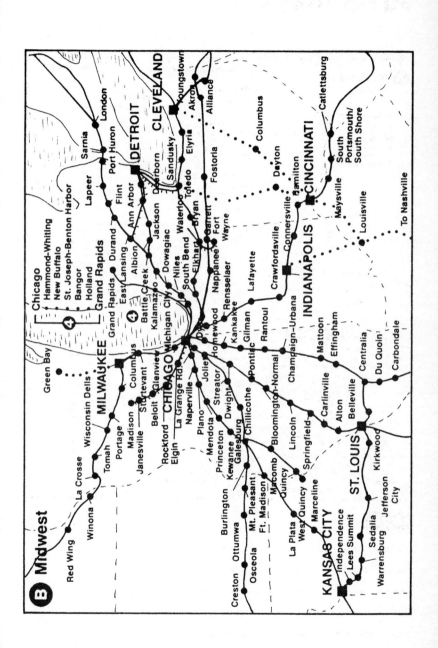

C Northern California

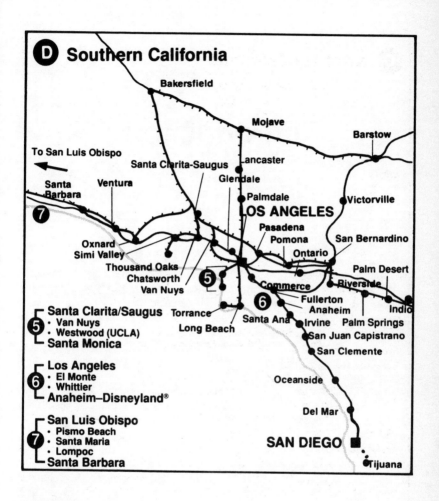

D Southern California

Legend

Amtrak Train Routes ——————

Connecting Rail Service ————————

Amtrak Thruway Bus Connection ┌──┬──┬──┬──┐

Introduction

All Aboard!
The rhythm of wheels on the track. The hoot of a lonesome whistle. America's long love affair with trains is on again after all seemed lost. Every day more people are rediscovering the experience of seeing this diverse country from the last true means of luxury transport. Computerised ticketing, baggage check-ins, club class seats and electrification have brought environmentally-benign railroads back into fashion. New lines are opening up and Amtrak now carries more passengers than ever, to over five hundred destinations.

Less expensive than flying — and more comfortable than the bus — trains are clean, spacious, energy-efficient and incorrigibly romantic. A unique blend of nostalgia, excitement and practicality. Besides, no airport can match the grandeur of Chicago's Union Station or the ornate masterpiece in Washington, DC.

As a passenger you can go for a stroll, get a meal or drink, sleep in comfort, watch a movie or just absorb the passing scene. You'll see mountains and cities, cross deserts and lakes, and travel next to two oceans. Sometimes the only practical way of seeing these things is to go by rail, and though trains may sometimes take a little longer they are not just a way of getting from one place to another. The slower pace is part of the pleasure.

Chapter 1

History: From horsepower to Amtrak

The Iron Horse

US history mostly coincides with the story of its railroads. They created a sense of national identity, symbolising strength, optimism, unity and the pioneering spirit. Americans have been 'locomotive people' for more than 160 years.

In 1826 Gridley Bryant's Granite Railway operated over three miles of track at Quincy, Massachusetts, using horse-power to haul granite for the Bunker Hill Monument. America's first steam locomotive was the English-built *Stourbridge Lion*, inaugurated in August 1829 on the Delaware & Hudson Canal Company's line at Honesdale, Pennsylvania. On February 19 1827 a group of Baltimore citizens decided to build the country's first public railway on a track from their city to the Ohio River. Charles Carroll, sole surviving signatory to the Declaration of Independence, laid the cornerstone on July 4 1828. Two years later the experimental engine *Tom Thumb* (weighing less than a ton) reached 18mph on 13 miles of Baltimore & Ohio track.

America's first (and the world's second) regular steam train service went into operation on Christmas Day 1830 on the South Carolina Canal & Railroad. The *Best Friend of Charleston* took a passenger train out of Charleston on a line built to transport cotton from central Georgia. When completed three years later the Charleston & Hamburg was the world's longest railway (135 miles).

Others soon followed — notably the New York Central (from Albany to Buffalo) and the Philadelphia & Columbia (the first to be government-sponsored). Like most early lines, they served local needs and few people foresaw their full potential. Canal owners and road transport companies opposed them, partly on safety grounds, and doctors warned of the dangers inherent in such reckless speeds. Accidents often did happen, since rights-of-way were not usually fenced off and railroad cars were little more than stage-coaches with flanged wheels.

Despite objections, total trackage increased to 3,000 miles by the early 1840s and to 9,000 miles by 1850 (three times that of canals). Greater speeds and improved reliability encouraged expansion so that railroads became big business, though most were still in New England and the Atlantic states.

Early locomotives like *Tom Thumb* and the *Best Friend of Charleston* had upright boilers. These were replaced by engines using horizontal English-style boilers, allowing greater capacity. By mid-century locomotives were mostly American-type (4-4-0) wood-burners, brightly painted and decorated with brass. Innovations included a bell, whistle, headlight and pilot (or 'cowcatcher') to remove obstacles ahead. A cab gave protection from the weather and a sandbox improved traction. Typical examples appear in the 1903 silent film *The Great Train Robbery* and in D W Griffith's *Intolerance*.

In the Northeast the New York Central brought together ten smaller railroads, running parallel with the Erie Canal and later extending to St Louis. The Erie Railroad ran from the Hudson River north of New York City to Lake Erie (and eventually Chicago). New York was able to enjoy fresh milk and consume more strawberries than anywhere else in the world. Chicago had 11 railways, with 70 trains a day, and in 1856 the Illinois Central linked the city to Cairo, at the junction of the Mississippi and Ohio Rivers. Federal land grants assisted the line's construction through 700 miles of thinly populated country.

The Far West's first railroad (the Sacramento Valley) opened in 1856 between Sacramento and the gold mines around Folsom. Southern railways made slower progress than those in the North, but by the time of the Civil War a thousand miles of track existed in each of Georgia, Tennessee and Virginia. A network served all states west of the Mississippi and this proved vital to both sides during the war. In 1862 General Bragg's army of 30,000 men travelled nearly 800 miles to Chattanooga by Confederate railway from Mississippi. The following year, 23,000 government troops (plus equipment) covered 1,200 miles from Virginia to relieve Chattanooga. The journey took 12 days, using 30 trains and 600 coaches. Without its rail network the North might never have broken Confederate resistance.

The Golden Age

Even before the war, railroads had come to represent unity for a country divided by geography and culture. In 1862, at a crucial time for the Union, President Lincoln signed the Pacific Railway Act making possible America's first trans-national route. The Central Pacific set out to build a line eastwards from Sacramento, California. The Union Pacific would go west from the Missouri River. Each company received federal loans and 10 sections of land for each completed mile.

Track was laid at a phenomenal rate, using mostly Irish labour on the Union Pacific and Chinese on the Central Pacific. Charles Crocker's CP team won a $10,000 bet from Dr Durant of the Union Pacific when workers laid 10 miles in a single day (still a record). It's estimated that each track layer lifted more than a hundred tons of steel in the process.

Over 1,780 miles had been constructed when the lines met at Promontory Point to the north of Utah's Great Salt Lake. Half a million people gathered to watch the Golden Spike ceremony on May 10 1869 between the Central

Pacific's *Jupiter* and the Union Pacific's *No. 119*. The latter featured in the final scenes of John Ford's film *The Iron Horse*. Cecil B De Mille retold the story less persuasively in *Union Pacific*.

As the Iron Horse began to conquer a continent, the West opened up and rapid development took place in cities along the way. In 1883 the Southern Pacific linked southern California to New Orleans and two years later the Atchison, Topeka & Santa Fe ran from Kansas City to Los Angeles (via the Southern Pacific). Cross-country travel took five days instead of a month. When the Santa Fe first reached Los Angeles only 10,000 people lived in southern California. Competition soon brought the fare from New York down as low as one dollar, and migration was further encouraged by promises of cheap land and constant sunshine.

The Northern Pacific opened up the Northwest in the 1880s, and James J Hill built a similar transcontinental route (the Great Northern) between St Paul and Seattle. Most construction west of the Mississippi received federal land grants, with 131 million acres eventually being handed over. In return the railways charged reduced rates for government traffic. Almost all Americans soon lived less than 25 miles from a railway and new Union stations opened at South Street, Boston (1890), St Louis (1894), Washington, DC (1907) and New York (Pennsylvania 1910, Grand Central 1913).

Standard gauge track and Standard Time (adopted in 1883) helped integration. Safety improved with innovations such as air brakes and automatic coupling. Trains became longer, faster and more efficient as coal-burning locomotives replaced the less powerful wood-burners, and American-types gave way to heavier Atlantics (4-4-2) and Pacifics (4-6-2). Refrigerated wagons began to ship beef from Chicago and oranges from Florida.

Compressed gas and electricity superseded candlelight in passenger cars, and hot-water heating replaced wood stoves after the Civil War. Corridors and steam heat arrived by the end of the century. Sleeping and dining cars, rarely seen before the war, became more common afterwards. George Pullman's $20,000 *Pioneer* sleeper boasted carpets, chandeliers, crimson plush, polished walnut and marble wash-stands.

Delmonico dining cars, introduced in 1868, meant that passengers no longer had to snatch hurried meals at scheduled stops along the way. Parlor cars, forerunners of present day lounge and club cars, also came in at this time. The rich could buy lavish private vehicles, or a group might hire an entire 'hotel train' with barber shop and space for dancing. Some lines began to operate express services for both passengers and freight.

Unfortunately the golden age also had its less appealing side. Strong unionisation brought better pay, at least for train crews, but a dispute on the Baltimore & Ohio in 1877 spread to other states and resulted in violent riots. A strike at the Pullman Company in 1894 led to sympathy action throughout the Midwest until it was broken by federal troops. Union leader Eugene Debbs was subsequently jailed.

Fraud, corruption and violence became commonplace as the vast sums of money involved attracted crooks. Cornelius Vanderbilt ('the public interest be damned') and the Central Pacific's 'scrupulously dishonest' Collis Huntington were notorious. Jim Fisk defrauded Erie Railroad stockholders of $64 million and railways often exploited their monopoly, but on balance the country still had reason to be grateful. Railways united the nation, brought prosperity, opened up the West and helped turn the USA into a world power.

The Twentieth Century

In 1902 the New York Central's Twentieth Century Limited was inaugurated on the 'water level route' between New York and Chicago. It became a national institution, its name redolent of luxury and prestige. By the late 1920s more than 15,000 passenger trains ran every day over 254,000 miles of track, but the 20th Century brought changes, some of them traumatic.

When the First World War imposed heavy demands on the movement of freight and people, President Wilson put the rail network under government control for the duration. Diesel power began to replace steam locomotives, which reached their peak of 72,000 just after the war. No more were put into service after 1953 and the last Norfolk & Western steam train ran on April 4 1960. The first successful diesel service was the streamlined Pioneer Zephyr, which in 1935 averaged 77½mph on its inaugural run from Denver to Chicago.

By then the railways were suffering from the Depression as well as from increased competition. Mass car ownership, interstate highways and the spread of air travel took away traffic and reduced revenues. Improvements such as air-conditioning and all steel coaches failed to keep passenger services sufficiently profitable. Almost 98% of inter-city passengers went by train in 1916 but by 1975 the figure was down to 6%.

Freight traffic suffered too, though not so dramatically. Greater efficiency and lower wages could not prevent railways running into deficit, and for many the Second World War proved only a temporary respite. After the war other streamlined trains came in, as did domed observation cars, high level seating and economy sleepers, and for a while the railways still carried more traffic than all other means of transport put together. The Interstate Commerce Commission insisted they operate passenger services, but by 1970 only 500 inter-city trains continued to run.

Railroads merged or were forced into bankruptcy, the biggest collapse being that of the Penn Central in 1970 (formed only two years earlier). Something clearly had to be done and the federal government was pressured to step in to save America's trains by passing the 1970 Rail Passenger Service Act. In 1971 the National Railroad Passenger Corporation set up Amtrak (short for 'American Trackage') to take over most long-distance routes.

Prospects today are much brighter. Oil crises, environmental concern and the need for energy conservation have caused people to look more favourably on eco-friendly trains. They continue to be one of the safest and most enjoyable ways to travel.

Chapter 2

Amtrak

Trains Today

The system Amtrak inherited in 1971 was dilapidated after being starved of investment for so many years. Rolling stock was run down, staff demoralised and losses seemed inevitable. Amtrak initially served just 340 cities, with only 21 routes over 20,000 miles of track. Things gradually improved as more trains were scheduled, new equipment bought and better services provided. Stations got spruced up, staff became more cheerful, and running times and reliability improved. The public began returning to such trains as the California Zephyr and Sunset Limited.

In 1976 Conrail (the Consolidated Rail Corporation) took over six bankrupt railroads in the Northeast and Amtrak acquired its first tracks — the electrified Boston-New York-Washington route. The number of Amtrak employees has risen from 1,200 in 1972 to 23,000. The corporation today owns 300 locomotives and 1,700 passenger cars, along with 700 miles of track. In co-operation with contract railroads and local government, 30 new stations have been built and 35 others completely renovated.

Each day, 220 trains use a 25,000-mile network serving most major cities in 45 states and the District of Columbia. Around 40 million people travel every year, including 18 million commuters, and in 1990 inter-city passengers travelled six billion miles. Only shortage of capital limits further progress, but Amtrak has more locomotives and Superliner coaches on order. For a copy of *Amtrak's USA*, which includes timetables and tours, contact any Amtrak agent or write to Amtrak International Sales, Amtrak Distribution Center, PO Box 7717, Itasca, IL 60143, USA.

Note that many large cities operate their own suburban and commuter services, either independently or in association with Amtrak. These trains may provide a more frequent or cheaper alternative to Amtrak for shorter journeys. Check at the station or local information bureau.

Equipment

Superliner: Introduced in 1979, these spacious, twin-decked coaches operate on all long-distance routes west of the Mississippi. Big windows give an excellent view, especially on the upper level. Reclining seats have leg and foot rests, folding trays and personal reading lights. Rest-rooms (toilets) are on the lower level, with at least one accessible to disabled passengers. Facilities include toilet, wash basin, mirror, infant changing table, soap, tissues and 120V AC electric point. Luggage can be left at the lower level on entry or stored on overhead racks. Dining cars cater for up to 72 people and are on the upper level, above the kitchen. Superliners have sightseer lounge cars and most kinds of sleeping accommodation.

Amfleet: Designed for short and medium journeys, Amfleet coaches have reclining seats, fold-down trays, overhead luggage racks and personal reading lights. Amfleet II coaches, intended for longer distances, have leg rests and more space. At least one rest-room caters for disabled passengers. Club cars have a double seat on one side of the aisle and a single seat on the other, with at-your-seat food and drinks service. Dinette and lounge cars provide light meals which you can take to a table or back to your coach.

Horizon Fleet: The latest short distance coaches, these operate on trains out of Chicago and in the San Joaquin valley. In addition to all the Amfleet facilities, Horizon cars give easier access for disabled passengers.

Heritage: Predating Amtrak, these fully refurbished coaches are often preferred for their smooth ride. Reclining seats have leg and foot rests. There are overhead luggage racks, and rest-rooms are located at one end of the coach. Full dining car service is normally available, as well as lounge and sometimes dome cars. Sleeping accommodation consists of bedrooms and roomettes, with slumbercoaches (see next section) on a few routes.

Sleeping

Reclining seats, dimmed lights, a free pillow (courtesy of the attendant), gentle rocking and the hypnotic rumble of the wheels: getting a comfortable night's sleep is reasonably easy even when travelling coach, given a certain amount of practice. And you save money. For best results choose a seat in the middle of the car, well away from the doors. Take a blanket or coat to ward off the over-enthusiastic air-conditioning.

Travellers' Tales
Sleeping compartments

Mrs Laila Allen, a senior citizen travelling with her sister, decided to take two single compartments. "They were the tiniest rooms I have ever seen but with all mod cons. The corridor runs through the middle of the carriage and the compartments are on either side. They were about 5ft by 4ft with a toilet, and above that a small washbasin that folded into the wall. A seat was easily converted into a bed. In my cabin there was a high step up onto the seat and to get into bed I had to put one foot on the toilet and jump up. Not easy at 60 plus. During the journey we asked the attendant to find us a double cabin, since the single ones were too tiny for us both to sit together."

John Ainsworth and his friend took a double compartment: "Our steward showed us to the cabin and explained how everything worked. I was struck by its compactness. The two individual seats facing each other pulled down into one bed and the other pulled down from the ceiling. I expected the foldaway washbasin but not the toilet neatly located next to one of the chairs. This was the one thing that put us off. Most people, however intimate their relationship, don't go to the toilet in front of each other. We either made the trek to the "public" washroom in coach class or one of us would leave."

Economy Bedroom (Superliner):   Sleepers have ten economy bedrooms on the upper level and four on the lower, each accommodating two adults. Two seats face each other and slide together to form the lower berth, with a second berth folding out from the wall. Features include a picture window, narrow closet (wardrobe), fold-down table, mirrors and an aisle window with curtains. Individual controls regulate heating, air-conditioner and reading lights. Rooms are compact, so leave most of your luggage in the lower level storage area and only take a small bag of essential items into the bedroom. Accommodation includes all meals in the dining car. There is no individual rest-room, so you use facilities provided on the lower or upper level.

Deluxe Bedroom (Superliner):   Five deluxe bedrooms are on the upper level, each sleeping two adults on berths which fold down. Daytime seating consists of a large sofa and a swivel chair. Features include a closet (wardrobe), fold-down table and an aisle window with curtains. Individual controls regulate heating, air-conditioner and reading lights, and there is space for two medium-sized suitcases. Complimentary tea, coffee or fruit juice (plus newspaper) are served 0630-0930, and accommodation includes all meals in the dining car. Rest-room facilities include a shower, wash basin, toilet, mirror and 120V AC electric point.

Family Bedroom (Superliner):   One family bedroom on the lower level sleeps two adults and two children. Daytime seating consists of two seats and a sofa. Upper and lower berths are for adults, with two short berths for children. Features include a closet and fold-down table. Family bedrooms extend the full width of the car, allowing two windows on each side. Individual controls regulate heating and air-conditioner, and there is space for up to three suitcases. Complimentary tea, coffee or fruit juice (plus newspaper) are served 0630-0930, and accommodation includes all meals in the dining car. There is no individual rest-room, so you use facilities provided on the lower level.

Special Bedroom (Superliner):   Each sleeping car has one special bedroom on the lower level, intended for use by a disabled passenger and companion. Features include an attendant call button. Two berths fold down for sleeping, and daytime seating consists of two reclining seats. Individual controls regulate heating and air-conditioner, and there is space for two suitcases. Accommodation includes all meals and drinks served in your room by the car attendant. Rest-room facilities (curtained off) include a toilet, wash basin, handgrips, mirror and 120V AC electric point.

Bedroom (Heritage):   For two adults, or one adult and two children. Daytime seating consists of either a long couch or two seats, and two berths fold down for sleeping. There is space for three medium suitcases. Complimentary tea, coffee or fruit juice (plus newspaper) are served 0630-0930, and accommodation includes all meals in the dining car. Rest-room facilities include toilet, wash basin and 120V AC electric point.

Roomette (Heritage):   Intended for one adult. During daytime there is a single seat and a berth folds down for sleeping. Individual controls regulate heating and air-conditioner, and there is space for two medium suitcases. Complimentary tea, coffee or fruit juice (plus newspaper) are served 0630-0930, and accommodation includes all meals in the dining car. Rest-room facilities include toilet, wash basin and 120V AC electric point. These facilities can not be used when the bed is in position.

Special Roomette (Heritage):   For use by a disabled passenger, with an attendant call button provided. A berth folds down for sleeping. Individual controls regulate heating and air-conditioner, and there is space for two suitcases. Accommodation includes all meals and drinks served in your room by the car attendant. Rest-room facilities (curtained off) include a toilet, wash basin, handgrips, mirror and 120V AC electric point. (See page 7)

Single Slumbercoach (Heritage):   Intended for one adult. During daytime there is a single seat, and a bed folds down for sleeping. Individual controls regulate heating, air-conditioner and reading light. There is space for two small suitcases. Rest-room facilities include toilet, wash basin and 120V AC electric point. (See page 7 for travellers' comments.)

Double Slumbercoach (Heritage):   For two adults, with facing seats during daytime and two beds that fold down for sleeping. Individual controls regulate heating, air-conditioner and reading lights, and there is space for two small suitcases. Rest-room facilities include toilet, wash basin and 120V AC electric point.

Dining

Most long-distance trains have a complete meals service in the dining car, providing breakfast, lunch and dinner. Regional specialities like barbecued spare ribs join such standards as steak, chicken and lasagne, and there are special meals for vegetarians and children. For kosher or low-sodium diets you should let Amtrak know your requirements at least 72 hours before travelling. Call 1-800-USA-RAIL and ask for the Special Services Desk.

Advance dinner reservations are normally taken by the chief of on-board services or dining car attendant moving through the train. This minimises waiting time, so that on arrival you are seated by the steward and presented with a menu. Amtrak uses china dishes and linen tablecloths on the Capitol Limited, Coast Starlight and Southwest Chief, and plans to extend these to other long distance trains. Buffet-style dining cars operate on Florida routes, but first class Auto Train passengers get a full dining car service.

On shorter journeys you can buy snacks to take back to your seat or to tables in dinette and cafe cars. Sandwiches, drinks and sweets are also available. Club cars on the Northeast Corridor provide a meal service to your seat.

Lunch is usually a better buy than dinner for anyone on a tight budget. You can also bring your own food on board, though this isn't encouraged.

Lounge and Dome Cars

Superliners have a sightseer lounge car, giving views through wide windows that extend part way over the roof. Here you can meet fellow passengers, see a film, have a drink at the bar, enjoy a sandwich or coffee, or simply watch America pass by. Hospitality hour is a good way to break the ice, and most Americans seem happy to tell you their life story. Smoking is permitted only on the lower level.

Amfleet and Heritage lounge cars provide most of the services offered by Superliners. Dome cars present more 'land cruise' experience, with wide-angle viewing on some eastern and mid-western trains.

Timetables

Amtrak ticket offices and travel agents have free timetables covering individual routes or the whole network. The times shown are local, taking full account of zone changes en route. In autumn, on the day clocks go back, trains may be deferred an hour in order to arrive 'on time'. On the day clocks go forward in spring, the new timetable comes into effect.

Timekeeping is reasonably good but circumstances beyond Amtrak's control can lead to delays. Allow at least an hour between trains when planning connections, especially on long distance routes. Note that some cities have more than one station. Trains do not always stop as long as the timetable indicates, so listen for announcements or ask the attendant before deciding to stretch your legs on the platform. Stay within sight and hearing of your train so you don't get left behind.

Anyone intending to meet a train can check times of arrival and departure by calling 1-800-USA-RAIL.

Travellers' Tales
Getting it together
by William H Hughes

During the summer of 1989 I was living in American Samoa when a business trip brought me to Seattle, Washington. I completed my business and found that I had three weeks to do what I wanted, so I decided to take a round trip to Tennessee, Louisiana and Arizona before heading back to the tropics.

It's hard to get information about Amtrak in the South Pacific, and I wasn't sure where to go for current information in Seattle. So I let my fingers do the walkin' through the yellow pages. I called the 800 number and explained my itinerary. The agent told me that there were several package deals — you can still get a bargain even if you buy the ticket in the USA. Amtrak markets various packages at different times of the year. I purchased a "See America" package (30 days with five stops) for around $275. My stops of one week each included Memphis (Tennessee), Jackson (Mississippi) and Flagstaff (Arizona). I was allowed to change departure dates as long as I continued in the same pre-planned direction.

The cars used in the western routes are much nicer and more comfortable than those I rode in between Chicago and Jackson. I heard that the older coaches were used on the Eastern tracks (east of the Mississippi). The seats were the old leather type which were set at a very uncomfortable angle, unless completely reclined. Fortunately this leg of the trip was not too long and the majority of it was at night.

Although a certain number of tickets are sold, it still is run and grab the seat you want. Travelling as a single passenger can be a disadvantage. After everyone, or nearly everyone, has found a seat, and the happy couple with two kids comes struggling in 10 minutes before departure, the attendant requests for single occupants to double up so that families can sit together. So if anyone showed up early to get a good window seat it may turn out in vain. The plea is made by the attendant in such a manner that only a discompassionate, un-American, and all round louse would not change. Maybe Amtrak will remedy this deficiency in their system soon by offering reserved seats.

Boarding

You should arrive at least half an hour before departure time (two hours for the Auto Train). Tell the gate attendant your destination and he will direct you to the appropriate coach. Red Caps (porters) are there to assist with luggage if required.

Reservations

Club service and sleeping car accommodation, as well as coach travel on 'all reserved' trains, require reservations. Make these well in advance, particularly during summer. You can obtain reservations through any ticket office or designated travel agent, including those abroad.

Alternatively, call 800-USA-RAIL or 1-800-872-7245. You will be given a reservation number and a hold date by which you must collect your tickets. Reservations are cancelled if collection is not made by then. Coach seating on unreserved trains is not guaranteed.

Tickets

Fares depend on the distance travelled and standard of service provided. Special offers, seasonal rates and excursion deals can mean big reductions. Children aged 2-15 pay half fare. Sleeping accommodation is always charged for in addition to coach fare.

The All Aboard America scheme allows you to make a one-way or round-trip journey for a set fare in any of three regions — Central, Eastern or Western. For an additional fee you can make a trip in two adjacent regions or throughout the USA. Current (1991) prices are $189 for one region, $269 for two and $339 for three. One stopover is permitted in both directions. The rates are lower during autumn, winter and spring (excepting holidays). (See *Travellers' Tales* on page 10.)

You can buy one-way standard rate tickets on board the train, subject to a surcharge if the ticket office was open at the time of departure. You can also upgrade accommodation on board (including sleepers) where space is available. Ask the conductor or chief of on-board services.

Tickets can be sent to you through the mail if paid for by credit card. Amtrak accepts no responsibility for lost, stolen or destroyed tickets.

USA Rail Pass

Anyone other than Americans and Canadians can buy a 15 or 30-day pass giving unlimited coach travel. In peak season (from the end of May to the end of August), a 15-day national pass, covering the entire system, costs $308. The eastern pass (for routes from the Atlantic as far west as Chicago and down to New Orleans) and the far western pass (from the Pacific inland to Salt Lake City, Albuquerque and Reno) cost $178. The western pass (from the Pacific across to Chicago and down to New Orleans) is $228. Off-peak prices are $208 (national), $158 (eastern or far western) and $188 (western).

For 30 days travel during peak season the prices are $389 (national), $199 (eastern or far western) and $289 (western). Off-peak prices are $309 (national), $179 (eastern or far western) and $259 (western).

All passes allow unlimited stop-overs and must be purchased outside the USA or Canada, through Amtrak-appointed agents (see Appendix).

Metroliner services, club class and sleeping accommodation all require a supplement. Rail pass prices for children aged 2-15 are half the adult fare, and children under two ride free.

Payment

You can pay for tickets or dining car meals by credit card or personal cheque (US bank only, minimum $25). Two pieces of identification are required, including one with your photograph and signature.

Refunds

A refund will be made on the unused value of a coach ticket cancelled before departure (at least one hour before in the case of the Auto Train). Refunds on sleeping accommodation cancelled less than 48 hours before the train's departure will be assessed a penalty. Partly used special fare and excursion tickets may have limited refunds.

Reimbursement is obtainable at ticket offices or by mail from Amtrak

Customer Refunds East, 30th and Market Streets, Philadelphia, PA 19104 (for passengers living east of Ohio and north of Virginia). Passengers elsewhere should apply to Amtrak Customer Refunds West, Chicago Union Station, 210 South Canal Street, Chicago, IL 60606.

Travel agency-sold tickets must be refunded through the travel agent.

Baggage

Trains can accommodate up to two items of carry-on luggage per passenger, and bags may be stored in overhead racks or at the end of the car. In sleeping accommodation you can bring as much as will safely fit in your room. For some Superliner bedrooms this will not be very much, but bags can also be left in the storage area. Missing items should be reported as soon as possible, though Amtrak does not accept liability for loss or damage to carry-on luggage.

Where a check-in service is provided you can check up to three items of baggage, weighing no more than 75lbs each or 150lbs altogether. You pay a surcharge if this allowance is exceeded. Well-secured boxes or cartons must weigh less than 50lbs. If you need special assistance with baggage you should let Amtrak know when you make your reservation. Some stations have luggage trolleys for which a small charge may be made. This is partly refunded when you return your trolley to the vending machine.

Baggage should be labelled with your name and address and checked in at least half an hour before departure. Amtrak's liability for checked baggage is limited to $500 per passenger, though you can buy additional insurance if required.

Red Caps (Porters)

Assistance with baggage is provided free by uniformed Red Caps at most big stations. Make sure you get a receipt in case your bags are mislaid. Amtrak recommends you accept help only from a Red Cap.

Smoking

Cigarette smoking is permitted only in designated coaches (or sections of coaches), sleeping accommodation, and some parts of club cars and lounges. Pipes and cigars are prohibited and no smoking is allowed in diners, dinettes or cafes.

Tipping

Tipping of Amtrak personnel is not required, though most people reward bar staff and waiters, as well as the sleeping car attendant where extra services have been provided. Red Caps may also be tipped.

Alcohol

Except in sleeping cars, you are not supposed to consume your own supplies of alcoholic drinks.

Radios

Earphones or headphones must be used when listening to radios, tape-players or portable TVs. Keep the volume down to avoid 'leakage'.

Pets
The only animals permitted on board are guide dogs accompanying blind or deaf passengers.

Unaccompanied Children
Children under eight years old are not allowed to travel unaccompanied. Those aged between eight and eleven can travel during daylight hours provided there are no train connections. Prior written permission is required from the person in control at the boarding station, and full adult fare will be charged. Call 1-800-USA-RAIL for details.

Senior Citizens
Senior citizens (those over 65) get 25% discount off a full, one-way coach fare. Some blackout dates and times apply and discounts are not available on Metroliners, the Auto Train or sleepers.

Passengers with Disabilities
Except for the Auto Train and Metroliners, disabled passengers get a 25% reduction off regular one-way coach fares. Disabled children pay half the disabled adult fare. Personal companions don't qualify for this discount. Guide dogs accompanying blind or deaf passengers travel free.

Wheelchair passengers can receive special assistance at the station and on board. Call 1-800-USA-RAIL for details and explain your needs when making reservations. Most trains have special rest-rooms and sleeping accommodation, and meals can often be served to a passenger's seat. Ask for a copy of *Access Amtrak*, a guide to services provided for the elderly or handicapped. Remember to bring with you any medication you require.

Amtrak Thruway and other bus connections are not accessible by wheelchair. Folding wheelchairs can be stored on most buses but you must occupy a standard seat and be able to board unassisted.

Deaf people can use a teletypewriter to obtain information or make reservations. The service operates between 0830 and 2000 Eastern Time on weekdays, when you should call 1-800-523-6590 nationwide or (in Pennsylvania only) 1-800-562-6960.

Potomac Tours, 1919 Pennsylvania Ave NW, Washington, DC 20006 (800-424-2969) offers escorted rail tours for groups of people with disabilities. Many states supply access information in their brochures and the major rental companies have a few hand-controlled cars (call their toll-free numbers to check).

Entertainment
Video movies and travelogues often feature in the lounge car, as do card games, quizzes and games of trivia. On some routes a guide will board to talk about the landscape through which you travel. Games of bingo, with modest prizes, may be held in the dining car.

On-board Service
The conductor is in charge of the train's crew. He is responsible for collecting tickets as well as for train safety.

The chief of on-board services supervises service personnel on overnight long distance trains.

The car attendant looks after a particular car. He or she will help in boarding, detraining, arranging seats, answering questions, bringing pillows and generally making your journey more comfortable. You will be assigned a seat when you board and should not change without consulting the attendant.

A sleeping car attendant will help with luggage, make up rooms for day or night use, and bring room service orders from the lounge car. In the morning he delivers complimentary tea, coffee or fruit juice, along with the newspapers.

Travellers' Tales
Arriving at your destination

The excellent service found on board does not always extend to stations. Bill Hughes writes: "Once a passenger arrives at the train terminal, the railroad company evidently assumes that their responsibility is over. There are abundant taxis, but economy-minded travellers will have to look hard to find out about limousines and small buses for connections to other modes of transport". Even going from one station to the other can be difficult for the uninitiated: "Upon arriving at New York's Grand Central Station we were offered a complimentary bus ride to Penn Station to catch our train to New Jersey. When we got there we found the trains no longer leave from Penn. We waited in a queue to take a taxi but when we tried to put our cases in, the driver turned nasty and wanted to take the people behind us. We found out later that there was a man allocating taxis on payment of $1. You live and learn!" (Laila Allen)

Chapter 3

For The Visitor From Overseas

Documents

Travellers to the USA must have a full passport valid for at least six months after the intended date of return. Children should have their own passport or be included in that of a parent or guardian.

Apart from Canadians and permanent legal residents of the USA, visitors may need a visa — either B-1 (for business) or B-2 (pleasure). Application forms are available from travel agents, airlines, US embassies and consulates. Applications must be made by post or through a travel agent or courier, and you should allow two weeks (preferably a month) before departure. No charge is made to UK citizens.

Visas for Europeans are usually valid for an indefinite period, allowing multiple entries, and a visa is still valid in an expired passport provided you also have a current valid one.

Visas are no longer required by citizens of the UK, France, Germany, Italy, Japan, the Netherlands, Switzerland or Sweden who intend to stay no more than 90 days, possess an unexpired passport and have a return ticket issued by a participating airline. UK travellers to Canada planning to cross the land border no longer need a visa. If in doubt, contact a US embassy.

Where appropriate you should obtain in advance an International Student identification card and an American Youth Hostel card.

Immigration

Before passing through immigration control you will be given a form to complete, asking where you are going to stay and the date you intend to leave. This is attached to your passport and must be shown on departure. If you lose the certificate or wish to extend your stay, contact the nearest Immigration and Naturalisation office. More details can be had from the INS Information Unit, No 5044, 425 I Street NW, Washington DC, 20536 (202-633-1900).

Immigration officers may ask for evidence that you can support yourself during your visit, usually reckoned on the basis of $150 per week. Take plenty of travellers cheques.

Customs

As well as personal belongings you can bring in 200 cigarettes, 50 cigars or 2kg of tobacco. Plus, if over 21, one litre of wine or spirits. It is forbidden to bring in food, illegal drugs or firearms. For more information contact the US Customs Service, 1301 Constitution Ave NW, Washington, DC 20229 (202-566-8195) or write to PO Box 7407, Washington, DC 20044 for a copy of *Know Before You Go.*

Health Regulations

No inoculations are required for visitors from Europe. Visitors from elsewhere should check with their US embassy.

When To Visit

Most people opt for summer, when the weather is warmest and more attractions are open. This can create problems. Hotels are expensive, restaurants crowded and train reservations harder to come by. Large numbers of people, many as regrettably foreign as yourself, form around everything you want to see. Sometimes it just gets too hot for comfort. Usually the weather's fine though, and it can be invigorating to travel when half the country seems on the move.

Flights and accommodation are more readily available during winter, often at reduced prices. You see fewer tourists and more of the real America, and you only have to wait an hour (instead of all day) for the Washington Monument elevator. The sun still shines, at least in the south, and the Rockies are even more spectacular covered in snow.

Spring and fall are probably best. During spring, flowers bloom in the mountains and the land is at its greenest (but watch out for storms, particularly in the south). New England's forests always put on a dazzling show for autumn 'leaf peepers'.

Weather

This is a big country with a diverse geography so the climate varies accordingly. Temperatures through the year can get well above 100°F or as cold as 40 below. Some places see dramatic differences between summer and winter while others scarcely change at all.

Northern areas have a European-type summer but other regions, especially the Southwest, get much hotter. The South and Midwest are likely to be humid. In winter the Northwest continues to follow a European pattern, but the Northeast and Midwest get considerably colder. Florida, southern California and the Southwest stay mostly warm.

Though spring and fall may be best for a vacation these seasons can be quite short. In the Midwest, summer and winter often swap places in a few days. Autumn is the hurricane season along the Gulf of Mexico, and spring can bring tornadoes to central regions.

Getting There

Competition has brought down the cost of flights, particularly on North Atlantic routes. It's usually cheaper to fly into one of the gateway airports such as Boston, Los Angeles and New York (John F Kennedy and Newark). For the latest bargains look for flight-only advertisements in the press.

Council Travel sells Amtrak passes and specialises in student and budget travel, with flights to all major North American cities. Offices world wide include 28A Poland Street, London W1V 3DB (071-437 7767) and 205 East 42nd Street, New York, NY 10017 (212-661-1450).

Money

The American dollar (or buck) is worth 100 cents. Coins are one cent (penny), five cents (nickel), 10 cents (dime), 25 cents (quarter), 50 cents (half dollar) and one dollar. Dollar and half dollar coins seem as rare as two dollar bills (no longer printed). Most common denomination banknotes (confusingly similar in size and colour) are for 1, 5, 10, 20 and 50 dollars. You'll need plenty of coins for telephones, buses, vending machines and tips, so carry enough cash on arrival to last for two or three days.

American dollar travellers cheques are the safest and most convenient currency — American Express and Thomas Cook being the most widely recognised. You can use them as cash in hotels, restaurants and shops (take your passport for identification). Signs saying 'no checks' generally refer to personal cheques.

Lost or stolen cheques can be replaced by contacting the issuing company (American Express 800-221-7282; Thomas Cook 800-223-7373; Visa 800-227-6811). Keep a note of your cheque numbers separately from the cheques.

Charge and credit cards (such as American Express, Visa and Access) are accepted throughout the USA. Handy when paying for hotels, car hire or tickets by phone, they can also be used for obtaining cash at banks and bureaux de change. Make a note of the card number and keep it separately. In case of loss or theft you should notify the police straight away and call the card company's emergency number.

Banks generally open at 0900 on weekdays, closing at 1500 (Mon-Thurs) or 1700 (Fri). Some will change foreign currency and travellers cheques but the commission may be high.

In an emergency you can have money transferred from your bank account at home to an associated US bank or to an office of Thomas Cook. International money orders take about a week to arrive by airmail. If you are really desperate, consulates will reluctantly help you get money from home.

Prices

Unless you are feeling extravagant you should save the uptown streets for window-shopping and look for better bargains where tourists are less in evidence. Books and records are always a good buy, frequently discounted, and clothing is also inexpensive. New York's garment district has many bargain stores and factory outlets. American clothing and shoe sizes are different from British or European, so try on things before buying.

Car hire, gas (petrol) and cigarettes are often sold at much lower prices than you've been used to. You can save even more on gas by using a self-service station and paying cash. US gallons are five-sixths the volume of Imperial gallons.

Local buses and subways are often excellent value, especially with a travel pass. Tourist bureaux should have the details. Taxis can be expensive but sometimes there is no alternative.

In most states a sales tax of 5-8% is added to retail prices, except for some foods and other goods. Municipalities can impose further taxes, so prices displayed are almost always less than you actually have to pay.

Food

Americans dine out more than most so finding somewhere to eat is no problem. New York City alone boasts 15,000 places, from unpretentious hamburger bars to some of the best restaurants in the world. Hot dogs, burgers, pizzas and ice cream come in endless varieties. Kentucky Fried Chicken and McDonalds are there to make you feel at home, though the American version tends to be superior.

Look for the increasingly rare 1940s-style diners. An authentic place should have chrome fittings, a juke box, ornate mirrors, counter seats and booths. Like coffee shops, diners are good for sampling the traditional American breakfast of eggs (cooked your way), crispy bacon, pancakes (with maple syrup), sausage, toast (ready buttered) and hash browns (fried grated potato). All washed down with coffee (free refills), tea (for the adventurous) or ubiquitous Coke and Pepsi. Some places serve breakfast 24 hours a day.

Sweets are a major temptation — from apple pie to chocolate fudge brownies — and no country has a greater choice of doughnuts or better Danish pastries. Not to mention frozen yoghurt.

America's diverse population produces an unlimited range of cuisine, and some of the world's best Chinese food can be had in the Chinatowns of cities like San Francisco and Los Angeles. Mexican food is filling and cheap, and tastes better than it looks. You can sample black-eyed peas and grits in the South, or lobster, crabs and clam chowder in New England. Steaks are big in Chicago and Texas. Creole cooking around New Orleans is legendary.

Whether looking for quality or getting by on a budget you should be able to find what you need. Some restaurants offer all you can eat for a fixed charge or 'two for the price of one' deals. Lunch (eaten around noon) is usually better value than dinner (taken around six in the evening). Salad bars, delis and supermarkets provide the basis for an inexpensive picnic, and sandwich bars offer any filling or bread you can think of. Don't miss bagels with cream cheese, or the kind of fresh sourdough bread that melts in your mouth.

Drink

The water is safe and Americans prefer it iced. If a glass isn't delivered with your meal you only have to ask. Any soft drink is a soda, with Pepsi and Coca Cola coming in small, medium and large (enormous) sizes. Sprite and 7-Up may be familiar but most people find root beer an acquired taste.

Cocktail bars cater for every fantasy and their bartenders are the smoothest operators anywhere. Try a genuine margarita, tequila sunrise or mint julep. Drinks 'on the rocks' have ice added, whereas those served 'straight up' don't. Bourbon is American whisky (such as Old Grandad) made from maize. Rye whiskies include Seagrams and Canadian Club. Measures tend to be generous and the spirits often 80 or 90 proof, so do not underestimate your consumption.

Bars range from seedy to glamorous and from cheerful to gloomy. The clientele might be businessmen, gays, singles, TV addicts or any other all American type. Look for cut-price drinks during the happy hour, often stretching much further than 60 minutes. Go between five and seven on weekday evenings and you can often fill up with free hors-d'oeuvres (provided you look respectable).

Beers usually come in cold cans and are of the Budweiser type. Canadian or Mexican beers, when available, are superior. Groups can save money by ordering a 'pitcher' or half-gallon jug. Wines — especially those from California — can be excellent.

Some states, including Utah, have laws prohibiting the sale of alcohol. All states have a minimum age (usually 21) and you may be asked for identification.

Accommodation

Major cities have international-type hotels where you can expect the highest standards of service, with air-conditioning, colour TV and room telephones. Hilton and Hyatt Regency are among those most often found. Many hotel chains have a toll-free reservation number, available by calling 800-555-1212. Prices vary with season but a double room is likely to cost $90 upwards per night. Single rooms cost almost as much as doubles or triples so it pays to travel in company. Hotels may offer American plan (meals included) or European (without meals).

Smaller hotels tend to be more individual and charge $25-50 per night for a single room. Local tourist bureaux should help you choose a place in a safe area, convenient for the sights. Rates are lower if you book for a week or more and some chains offer discounts with prepaid vouchers.

Bed & breakfast is becoming easier to find, especially in rural areas, and prices range as low as $30. Check with the tourist bureaux or contact one of the agencies for details. Those covering the whole country include the Bed & Breakfast Registry, PO Box 80174, St Paul, MN 55108; American Bed & Breakfast Association, PO Box 23486, Washington, DC 20024; National Network, PO Box 4616, Springfield, MA 01101; Tourist House Association of America, PO Box 355A, Greentown, PA 18426 (717-857-0856).

Motels cost less — down to $25 — but vary in quality and service. Always ask to see the room before accepting. The best motels will have a restaurant, a shop and possibly a swimming pool. Major chains include Holiday Inn, Travelodge, Sheraton, Marriott, Ramada and Best Western, all of which have toll-free reservation numbers (call 800-555-1212). Regal 8 Inns (800-851-8888) are particularly good for those on a limited budget. Unfortunately, motels tend to be situated a long way from downtown, making them less convenient for rail travellers.

An alternative, particularly for young people, are the YMCA centres found in most big cities. Some have swimming pools, cafes, a library and sports facilities. Single and double rooms are usually available to both men and

women. YWCA centres are for women only. For information write to the
National Council, 356 W 34th Street, New York, NY 10001 (212-760-5856) or
to the YWCA, 726 Broadway, New York, NY 10003 (212-614-2700).

More than 200 youth hostels provide some of the best value and friendliest
accommodation of all. They are often located in historic buildings, including
three coast guard lighthouses, and some have family rooms. Most close
during the day and operate a midnight curfew. Cooking facilities are provided
but alcohol and drugs are forbidden. For about $10 per night you get a bed
in a dormitory (segregated by sex) but must bring your own sleeping bag. No
age restrictions apply, though you'll enjoy your stay more if you are young
at least in spirit. Take out IYHF membership before travelling, or purchase
guest membership on arrival. The International Youth Hostel handbook has
a full list of addresses and more information is available from American Youth
Hostels, PO Box 37613, Washington, DC 20013-7613 (202-783-6161).

Camping sites both public and private are found in most parts of the
country, and unrestricted camping opportunities still exist in wilderness areas.
You should obtain a permit (often free) from the nearest park rangers' office.
Reservations are recommended for state sites and national park areas. You
can get information from the National Campers and Hikers Association, Box
451, Orange, NJ 07051. Kampgrounds of America is a private organisation
with 600 sites throughout the country. Contact KOA, PO Box 30558, Billings,
MT 59114 (406-248-7444). Some youth hostels also allow camping.

If staying in one place for long it is worth checking the price of apartments
and rooms, though usually you need to rent for at least a month. Ask around
and check newspapers (under 'furnished rooms'). For college rooms let
during summer you should enquire at the housing office or visitors bureau.

Telephones

The US telephone system is famous for efficiency and economy. Public
phones are found in train and bus stations as well as in stores, hotels,
restaurants and bars. You needn't be a customer to use one. Read the
instructions before making your call and have plenty of change handy. Local
calls usually cost 25 cents. Dial the area code first when calling from out of
town, and '1' before the code for long distance. For assistance call '0'.

If you need to know a number and have no directory call 1-555-1212. For
long distance information call 1-(area code)-555-1212. Directory inquiries are
free from pay phones. Calls prefixed 800 or 1-800 are toll-free and any toll-
free number can be obtained by calling 1-800-555-1212.

Calling home is cheaper from a public phone than from your hotel, which
may add a surcharge. The international prefix is 011. This must be followed
by the country's code (44 for the UK). It's easiest to call collect (reverse
charges) and you can contact the international operator on 1-800-874-4000.
The lowest rates for non-local calls are between 1800 and 0800 or at
weekends. It is more economical to use a private telephone and to dial direct
if possible. Sending a telegram generally costs more.

In most places the emergency number for police, fire or an ambulance is
911. No coin is required. If in difficulty call the operator on '0' or '01'.

Postal Service

Not as wonderful as the telephones, so when you send postcards home by airmail allow a week for delivery. Either put them in the appropriate box or hand them over the counter at a post office, where you will find information on mailing rates. Post offices open between 0900 and 1700 on weekdays, 0900 to 1200 on Saturdays. Big cities usually have one branch open 24 hours. You can also buy stamps from shops or vending machines (at 25% extra cost).

Street corner mail boxes are dark blue and easily mistaken for litter bins. Allow between two and four days for letters to be delivered within the USA, and another day or so without the zip code. The correct code can be obtained from a local telephone directory or at post offices.

You can have mail delivered c/o General Delivery to a main post office anywhere in the USA, which will keep it for up to a month. To collect it you'll need identification, such as your passport.

Newspapers

America has more daily papers than any other country, but no nationals apart from the *Wall Street Journal* and tabloid *USA Today*. The *Los Angeles Times* and *New York Times* are fairly widely distributed to other cities. Local papers are inexpensive (some only 25 cents) and heavy (especially at weekends), making them good value for the funny pages alone. Station shops have a selection and there are usually street corner vending machines. The local press gives an insight into a town's character as well as providing information on clubs, hotels, shops and theatres. Look for restaurants and cinemas offering special deals.

Foreign newspapers are hard to find even in big cities, but if you become desperate the local public library should have a week-old copy of something reassuring.

Tipping

You may think tipping is a class-conscious anachronism inappropriate for a country where everyone has been proclaimed equal. This isn't a good line to take with the average cab driver. He expects 10 or 15%, as do bartenders and hairdressers. In restaurants 20% is more usual. Follow the practice of other customers or you will notice an abrupt change in the service. There's no need to tip in self-service cafes or fast food places.

Most hotels do not include a service charge so a tip is appreciated. Hotel, airport and railway porters get around one dollar per bag. You don't have to tip someone who is rude or unhelpful. Amtrak service is free but you should reward staff for exceptional help.

Car Travel

Trains and buses won't take you everywhere, so you may need to hire a car. You are allowed to drive in the US if you hold a valid licence in a country (such as the UK) which has ratified the Geneva Road Traffic Convention. An international driving licence isn't necessary but would be more readily accepted by a traffic cop. Always carry your licence when driving.

Rental companies have a minimum age restriction (usually 21) and sometimes a maximum. Check the limits when booking and take your passport. National firms have offices in most cities and can be reached on the following toll-free numbers. Hertz 800-654-3131; Avis 800-331-1212; Budget 800-527-0700; Dollar 800-421-6868; Thrifty 800-367-2277. For cheap transport, companies with names like Wrent-A-Wreck hire out battered but roadworthy cars past their prime.

Local companies may be less expensive or more convenient, but the national ones allow you to rent a car in one place and leave it in another. Prices depend on location, size of vehicle and rental period. Economy cars are smallest, followed by compact and standard (the normal American size). Almost all have automatic gears.

Make certain you get third party insurance of at least half a million dollars and ask for the collision damage waiver (CDW). This should include protection against vandalism and theft. If you plan to drive a lot you could find it more economical to buy car insurance before leaving home. American policies don't automatically include third party protection and in some states insurance is not compulsory. Good reasons for having full medical cover (see next section).

Members of affiliated organisations can get free assistance and maps from the American Automobile Association, 8111 Gatehouse Road, Falls Church, VA 22047 (800-336-4357).

Medical Insurance

The US has no free health service and a hospital room alone can cost $300 per night. Horror stories about people being financially ruined by illness or accident are not apocryphal. Take out enough insurance to cover the whole of your stay, including provision for being flown home for treatment. Airlines and travel agents will try to sell you their version when you book your trip, but check the small print and compare prices.

Hospital clinics often provide simple treatment on the spot and some have a 24-hour emergency room. Most towns have a late-opening pharmacy where a wide range of medicines can be bought. If you need regular medication you should take sufficient for your visit. For prescribed drugs it's best to get a letter from your doctor explaining why you need them. If you wear glasses carry an extra pair.

Other Insurance

Make sure your policy protects against cancellation or delays, loss of baggage and claims for negligence. For motor insurance, see *Car Travel*.

Crime

Contrary to legend, most people survive a visit to the United States without being mugged, assaulted or robbed. Even so, sensible precautions should be taken. Don't keep all your valuables in one place, then if some get stolen you still have an emergency fund. Stick to downtown or well-lighted areas and avoid going to secluded places alone, especially at night. Your hotel desk clerk will advise on safety for the part of town you are staying in.

Don't flash money around in public. Lock your hotel door, watch over your belongings, know where your wallet is and don't leave valuables in your room. Be wary of pickpockets and bagsnatchers in crowded places such as train and bus stations. Don't ask total strangers to keep an eye on your things. At stations, only trust your bags to a uniformed member of staff. Report any theft to the nearest police station and get a reference number you can show to your insurance company.

When leaving a car, lock any bags and packages in the trunk (boot) and park in a busy place.

Many cities have residential areas segregated by race, so ask advice before venturing where your presence might be too distinctive. All policemen and some private security guards carry guns. Do not run away if challenged.

Drugs

The authorities take a dim view of illegal drug use even in California, where possession of small amounts of cannabis is condoned. Apart from the inherent dangers of dealing with shifty characters on street corners, you are likely to get ripped off. If caught with drugs the best you can hope for is to be put on the next flight home, and you won't find it easy getting back into the USA.

If you do run into trouble you should contact your nearest consulate, which will recommend a suitable lawyer. Or notify the International Legal Defence Counsel, Suite 315, 1420 Walnut Street, Philadelphia, PA 19102 (215-545-2428).

Sex

Casual sex isn't recommended. The dangers are more prevalent away from home and sexually transmitted diseases may be more common than in your own country. AIDS is a growing problem, with upwards of 1½ million people thought to be HIV positive. In many cities most prostitutes carry the virus. Enjoy the bars and nightlife but save your affections for those you can trust.

Some states, particularly in the South and Midwest, have laws restricting certain kinds of sexual behaviour. In most places the age of consent for males and females is 16, but may be up to 18. Statutory rape (sex with a minor) is treated legally in the same way as any other rape. Nevada is the only state where prostitution is legal.

Time Zones

Mainland USA has four time zones. Seattle (Pacific Time) is an hour behind Denver (Mountain Time), two hours behind Chicago (Central Time) and three hours behind New York (Eastern Time). Amtrak's timetables take account of this and show local times for arrival and departure.

Most states other than Arizona and parts of Indiana observe Summer Time (or Daylight Saving Time). Clocks are set ahead an hour at 0200 on the first Sunday in April. Standard Time returns when clocks go back an hour on the last Sunday in October.

Public Holidays

Banks, businesses, museums and government agencies are likely to be closed on the following dates —

New Year's Day	— January 1
Martin Luther King's Birthday	— January 15 (or third Monday in month)
Lincoln's Birthday	— February 12 (or first Monday in month)
Washington's Birthday	— February 22 (or closest Monday)
St Patrick's Day	— March 17
Memorial Day	— May 30 (or closest Monday)
Independence Day	— July 4
Labor Day	— first Monday in September
Columbus Day	— second Monday in October
Election Day	— November 4
Veteran's Day	— November 11
Thanksgiving	— fourth Thursday in November
Christmas Day	— December 25

Travelling on these days, even where possible, is sure to be crowded. If it can't be avoided, remember to reserve your tickets and accommodation well in advance.

Working

Working illegally in America can result in stiff penalties, including being deported and banned from the country for up to five years. To work legally you must obtain a special visa (J-1 or H-2) prior to departure. Forms are available from US employer sponsors and more information can be had from the Consumer Center, Department 455W, CO 81009 (719-948-3334).

If you get on well with children and are aged 18-35 you could apply to work at one of America's 12,000 summer camps. Most are in the northeast but some are located as far west as California and Oregon. Work starts in June and lasts for about nine weeks. You receive a return flight plus the necessary work permit, pocket money and six weeks independent travel time. Contact Camp America, 37a Queens Gate, London SW7 5HR (071-589 3223).

BUNAC (the British Universities North America Club) also has summer camp jobs as well as other work programmes in the US and Canada (students only). Early application is strongly advised. Visas are valid from June to October and support and advice is provided during summer from a New York office. Good travel deals, loan plans and free job directories are available. BUNAC is at 16 Bowling Green Lane, London EC1R 0BD (071-251 3472).

Chapter 4

The Trains

How to use this section

Each of the following sections gives details of a different long distance Amtrak train. Scheduled stops are designated in CAPITALS. These and other places en route are followed by figures in parentheses, eg 'Kent (20/32)'. This shows that, when travelling south, Kent will be reached 20 minutes after you leave the previous scheduled station, SEATTLE. Going north, Kent is 32 minutes from TACOMA. Routes can therefore be read in either direction, changing left for right and arrival for departure as appropriate. Some places can only be seen in daylight when travelling in one direction.

Accommodation has been selected wherever possible for easy access either from the station or from downtown. Consideration is also given to safety and value for money, hotels being listed in descending order of price per room.

The maps

The strip maps that illustrate the routes are inevitably schematic. They are not to scale and curves have been somewhat straightened, although the North indicator will show you roughly which direction you are travelling in. Occasionally stations have been omitted for lack of space; refer to the Area Maps on pages x to xiii for a more accurate view of the routes.

1 The Coast Starlight

Seattle—Los Angeles

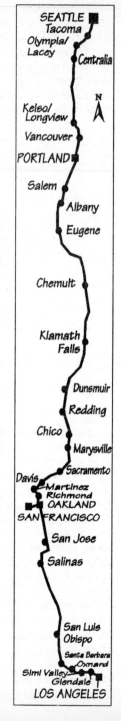

This is the most popular of Amtrak's long distance routes and a particular favourite with young people. Not surprisingly, a party atmosphere can develop, starting in the lounge car and spreading throughout the train. On a 33-hour journey you see snow-covered mountains, seascapes, forests, valleys and long stretches of Pacific shoreline. When travelling south be sure to sit on the right of the train for the best views.

Frequency: Daily. The southbound service leaves Seattle mid-morning to arrive in Portland mid-afternoon, Oakland (for San Francisco) early next morning, Santa Barbara late afternoon and Los Angeles mid-evening.
  Travelling north, trains leave Los Angeles mid-morning, reaching Santa Barbara by midday and Oakland mid-evening. Arrive Portland the following afternoon and Seattle by early evening.

Reservations: All reserved. Book well ahead, especially during summer and at weekends. Passengers for San Francisco get bus transport from Oakland included.

Equipment: Superliner coaches.

Sleeping: Superliner economy, de luxe, family, special bedrooms.

Food: Complete meals, snacks, sandwiches, drinks.

Lounge Car: Video movies, games, hospitality hour.

Baggage: Check-in service at most stations.

SEATTLE

The Emerald City, named after Indian chief Sealth, was the birthplace of guitarists Jimi Hendrix and Robert Cray. It's Washington's biggest city, surrounded by mountains, Lake Washington and Puget Sound. Seattle only gets 56 days of sun per year but is ranked 44th in the country for rainfall, so it's not as wet as outsiders imagine. Countless marinas allow two boats for every three people.

Although this is one of America's safer cities you should take sensible precautions after dark, particularly in the Pioneer Square district.

Transport: King Street Station at 303 S Jackson was built by the Great Northern Railway in 1905. Note the distinctive clock tower. Ticket office open 0510-1730. Waiting room 0500-2200. Lockers, vending machines, newspapers, luggage trolleys, Red Caps, taxi stand.

Trailways Northwest buses connect incoming Coast Starlight trains with Vancouver, BC (604-875-1307).
Metro buses (447-4800) are free in the downtown area.
Taxis: Yellow (622-6500) and Farwest (622-1717).
Car Rental: Rent-A-Car, 804 N 145th (364-1995).
Greyhound: 8th Ave and Stewart (624-3456).
Seattle-Tacoma Airport (433-5217) is 12 miles south by Airport Express bus (626-6088), taxis and Metro bus No 174.

Tours: Coach and boat trips from Gray Line (626-5208).

Visitors Bureau: 666 Stewart (461-5840). Open Mon-Sat.

Telephone Code: 206.

Accommodation: Contact Pacific Bed & Breakfast, 701 NW 60th (784-0539) or the B & B Inn Association, Box 95853, Seattle, WA 98145 (547-1020).
YMCA: 909 4th Ave (382-5000). Over 200 rooms for men or women. Incorporates the Traveller's Aid office. Singles $38, doubles $44.
YWCA: 1118 5th Ave (461-4888). Women over 18 only. Singles $24, doubles $35.
AYH Youth Hostel: Western Ave and Union (622-5443). Dormitory rooms. Members $10, non-members $14.
Hotels include the Four Seasons Olympic at 411 University (621-1700); Sorrento, 900 Madison (622-6400); Sixth Avenue Inn, 2000 6th Ave (682-8300); Town Center Inn, 2205 7th Ave (622-3434); Cosmopolitan, 2106 5th Ave (682-8833); Bush, 621 S Jackson (623-8079) — singles $17, doubles $20.

Seattle Center: This legacy of the 1962 World's Fair, one minute from downtown by monorail (625-4234), has over 70 acres of parkland and entertainments dominated by the 605ft Space Needle. Take an elevator to the observation deck for views of the city, Puget Sound and Mount Rainier.

Pike Place Market: Above the waterfront between First and Western Ave, the market began in 1907. It's a warren of shops, restaurants, galleries and stalls selling every kind of fish, fruit and vegetable. Good street entertainment.

The Waterfront: Where gold arrived during the 1897 Klondike gold rush, former Australian streetcars now run along waterfront tracks. Ferries to Canada and Alaska go from Pier 48, and to Bremerton and Bainbridge Island from Pier 52. Ye Olde Curiosity Shop at Pier 54 sells souvenirs alongside its bizarre museum of relics. Pier 55 is the base for Seattle Harbor Tours (623-1445). Excursions from Pier 56 go to Tillicum Village on Blake Island. Pier 59 has the Seattle Aquarium.

Pioneer Square: Covering 12 blocks from the waterfront to 2nd Ave. Seattle began here in the 1850s with the setting up of a sawmill, and logs were skimmed along Skid Road. During the gold rush this was a dangerous place and in the Depression it became a refuge for down-and-outs ('Skid Row'). Art galleries, restaurants and shops occupy restored buildings and an Underground Tour (682-4646) takes in the basements of old Seattle.

Klondike Gold Rush National Historic Park: 117 S Main (442-7220). Portraying the excitement and hardship. Chaplin's film *The Gold Rush* shows on weekend afternoons. Open daily, free.

The Coast Starlight departs King Street Station with Smith Tower, once one of Seattle's tallest buildings, on the right. You pass the Kingdome stadium on your right and for the next few miles travel through industrial territory with factories owned by the likes of Westinghouse, Nabisco and Ford.

Boeing Field (7/45)
Seattle's biggest company, Boeing, is on the right. The airport is used for testing and sometimes by private planes. Boeing's original factory — the red building across the runway — is now the Flight Museum.
   Continue through residential areas, with the Green River on your right and Longacres racetrack to your left.

Kent (20/32)
An interesting old station building and town park are on the left.
   Across the Green River, half an hour from Seattle, the urban landscape gives way to small farms and dairies. After crossing the White River you begin a right turn towards the east, crossing the Puyallup River.

Puyallup (40/12)
Named after an Indian tribe. The train proceeds through downtown and the western suburbs, then crosses Clark's Creek and travels through tall forest.

TACOMA (52/42)
Note the eccentric domed station. Tacoma is the third largest city in Washington. Called the City of Destiny because this is where much of the state's lumber reached the sawmills. Timber remains an important industry, alongside shipbuilding. Amtrak is at 1001 Puyallup Ave. Information: 627-

8141. Ticket office open 0600-2130.

The city overlooks Commencement Bay in the east and the Tacoma Narrows Bridge to the west. Point Defiance Park has beaches, forest walks and an aquarium famous for octopuses. The State Historical Society Museum is at 315 N Stadium Way. Gig Harbor on the waterfront is the place for seafood. For more information contact the Chamber of Commerce, 950 Pacific Ave (383-2459).

You leave and travel beside the City Waterway. Old City Hall with its elaborate clock tower perches on cliffs to your left next to the Northern Pacific Railroad building.

Ten minutes later you go through a tunnel and turn south, emerging on the shoreline of Puget Sound with the Olympic Mountains beyond. This idyllic coast has fishing coves, herons, bald eagles and rivers with Indian names like Nisqually and Skookumchuck.

Stellacoom (26/16)
A ferry terminal serves Anderson and McNeal Islands, seen to the right.

OLYMPIA/LACEY (42/20)
Olympia is Washington's state capital on Puget Sound and Amtrak's station is at 6600 Yelm Hwy SE. The 900,000-acre Olympic National Park is accessible via US 101.

The train crosses the Skookumchuck River.

CENTRALIA (20/45)
A centre for food processing and logging, Centralia was founded in 1875 by a former slave called George Washington. Early settlers built the blockhouse in Fort Borst Park as a defence against Indians. Amtrak's brick station at 210 Railroad Ave opens 0730-2000.

As you leave you glimpse Mount St Helens across fields to your left. Traces of grey ash from the volcano's 1980 eruption can still be seen, though grass has begun to sprout on 'pumice plain'. The explosion killed 57 people as well as thousands of birds, animals and fish.

You continue through Chehalis and cross the Newaukum River.

Winlock (18/27)
Winlock claims to be 'the egg capital of the world' and its chicken industry is celebrated by an annual festival. The 'world's largest egg' nestles in a monument on the right.

Castle Rock (35/10)
The Cowlitz River is to the right. Mud reached this far from the St Helens blast 40 miles away, and the volcano is now a 110,000-acre monument. You can take a flight over the summit and buy souvenirs sculpted from debris.

KELSO-LONGVIEW (45/40)
'Smelt capital of the world', where vast numbers of these small fish return every year to spawn. The town also has a lumber industry and deepwater port.

As you leave, three of America's most impressive mountains can be seen on a clear day. Mount St Helens (10,165ft) and Mount Adams (12,307ft) are on the left, with Mount Rainier (14,410ft) to the right. Between May and October Gray Line buses run from Seattle to Rainier National Park.

Columbia River (8/32)
Joined on the right. The Columbia was once the border between the USA and Canada and you follow it all the way to Vancouver, with Oregon on the opposite shore. Watch for rafts of logs moving downstream.

Trojan Nuclear Power Plant (12/28)
On the Oregon side.

Kalama (15/25)
Look for a giant totem pole on the right. The land turns marshy as you approach Lake Vancouver and meet its shoreline to the right.

VANCOUVER (40/25)
The oldest non-Indian settlement in the Northwest and not to be confused with Vancouver, Canada. The Hudson's Bay Company built Fort Vancouver as a trading post in 1824. A museum here is dedicated to Ulysses S Grant. Amtrak's station at the foot of W 11th opens 0730-2030.

You leave Vancouver, crossing the Columbia into Oregon via Hayden Island, then cross the Willamette River.

As you near Portland look for the *River Queen*, an old steamboat converted into a restaurant.

PORTLAND (25/65)
Some consider the City of the Roses America's most beautiful, spread out along the Columbia between the Cascade Mountains and the Pacific. Oregon's only metropolis is a seaport with gardens, fountains and parks enough to make it rival Seattle as 'America's most livable city'.

Transport: Union Station is at 800 NW 6th Ave, constructed in 1890 on a former lake in an old part of the city. Ticket office open 0730-1730. Waiting room 0730-2130. Vending machines, newspapers, luggage trolleys, Red Caps, restaurant, left luggage room, taxi stand.

Portland is best explored on foot. It's well served by Tri-Met buses and the MAX light railway (233-3511). Both are free downtown.

Taxis: New Rose City (282-7707) and Broadway (227-1234).
Car Rental: Budget, 2033 SW 4th (222-9123).
Greyhound: 550 NW 6th (243-2323).
The airport is eight miles northeast by taxi and Tri-Met bus No 12.

Tours: Rose-Smith (201-1921).

Visitors Bureau: 26 SW Salmon (275-9750). Open Mon-Sat.

Telephone Code: 503.

Accommodation: Contact Bed & Breakfast Oregon Plus, 5733 SW Dickinson, Portland 97219 (245-0642) or Northwest B & B, 610 SW Broadway, Portland 97205 (243-7616).
YMCA: SW Main and 11th (241-6331).
YWCA: 1111 SW 10th (223-6281). Women only. Singles $20.
AYH Youth Hostel: 3031 SE Hawthorne Blvd (236-3380). Members $8, non-members $12.
  Hotels include the Imperial at 400 SW Broadway (228-7221); Caravan, 2401 SW 4th (226-1121); Corsun Arms, 809 SW King (226-6288); Saharan, 1889 SW 4th (226-7646); Cabana, 1707 NE 82nd (252-0224); Jack London, 415 SW Alder (228-4303) — singles $14, doubles $20.

Rose Festival: A week of parades, concerts, sporting events and bands in early June to honour the city's favourite flower (248-7923). Mostly free.

Washington Park: 4001 Canyon Rd (248-4302). With Douglas firs, a Japanese garden, statues and 400 types of rose.

Washington Park Zoo: Two miles from downtown on Highway 26 (226-1561). Take Tri-Met bus No 63. This is a natural setting for beavers, otters and nocturnal cats. Steam and diesel trains operate around the zoo and through forested hills to Washington Park. Open daily, admission.

Pioneer Court-house: 5th Ave and Morrison (221-0282). The oldest public building in the Northwest dates from the 1870s. You can tour the courtroom and judge's quarters. Open daily, free.

  Departing Portland, the Coast Starlight leaves the Burlington Northern route followed this far and travels via Southern Pacific's line to Los Angeles.
  You cross the Willamette on a steel bridge then go through Milwaukie and Gladstone suburbs. As the train heads into the Willamette Valley the Cascades and Mount Hood (11,235ft) are seen on your left, the Coast Range to your right.

Oregon City (30/35)
This was the original capital of Oregon territory and the end of the Oregon Trail. Look for waterfalls to the right, with lumber factories and logs on the river. The Oregon Trail Centre has films and exhibits commemorating this pioneer route.

Aurora (45/20)
Reached after crossing the Pudding River. Aurora was America's first commune, founded by Germans in the 19th Century.

Woodburn (50/15)
A Southern Pacific steam engine is on the left.

SALEM (65/28)
Oregon's capital and second largest city is the home of Willamette University, the oldest in the West. On your right the white marble capitol is topped by a gold-plated statue of a man with an axe (the Spirit of Oregon).

Leave with the city airport to your left. Between the towns of Turner and Marion, fifteen minutes later, is a llama farm. Formerly kept for wool, the llamas are used as pack animals on expeditions into the mountains.

Jefferson (20/8)
Cross the Santiam River.

ALBANY (28/40)
Founded in 1845, Albany was eventually connected by railroad in 1870 after citizens paid the O & C company 50,000 dollars to be included in the line. This agriculture and lumber centre supplies almost all the grass seed produced in America. It also hosts the world championship timber carnival, with everything from tree climbing to axe throwing. Visitors bureau: 435 W First Ave. Amtrak at 110 W 10th opens 0900-1715. Corvallis is ten miles southwest.

The train leaves Albany and crosses the Calapooia River.

Tangent (15/25)
So named after this long straight stretch of track. Buttes on the right, created by volcanoes in prehistoric times, contain fossils and mammoth bones. To the left are fields of grass seed.

Between here and Eugene look for farms growing mint — another local speciality.

Harrisburg (25/15)
The snow-covered Three Sisters Mountains are visible in the left distance before you cross the Willamette River.

Southern Pacific rail yards and Lane County jail appear to your right as the train nears Eugene.

EUGENE (40/165)
This 'lumber capital of the USA' is the most western city served by Amtrak. It was named after Eugene Skinner, one of the first settlers in the 1840s. It's the home town of Mary Decker Slaney as well as a centre for fishing and boating on the McKenzie River. Visitors bureau: 307 W 7th Ave (484-5307). Amtrak's station at 433 Willamette opens 0930-1800.

Leaving town you pass the University of Oregon on your right before crossing the Willamette into Springfield, sister city to Eugene.

For the next 70 miles the train climbs slowly into the Cascades, winding through 22 tunnels and a number of snowsheds towards the source of the Willamette. Snowsheds are wooden or concrete structures built over the track to protect it from avalanches and accumulating snow. Spectacular waterfalls and dense vegetation feature in Willamette National Forest, but this part of the route is travelled in darkness going south.

Lookout Point Reservoir (30/135)
The dam and reservoir are on your left, with Diamond Peak (8,750ft) to the south and the Three Sisters Mountains in the distance.

Westfir (60/105)
Spanning the Willamette on your right is one of the covered bridges common in this area.

Oakridge (65/100)
Start to climb 'the hill', an ascent of 3,600ft in 44 miles to Cascade Summit. You cross Salmon Creek then follow Salt Creek on the right.

Salt Creek Canyon (80/60)
Views of the tracks above and below show the train's steep climb. There is still another 2,700ft to go to the summit along 30 more miles of track.

Willamette Pass (100/55)
This is the source of the Willamette River, and Willamette ski resort is seen ahead.

Cascade Summit (120/35)
At 4,800ft above sea level. Maiden Peak (7,811ft) overlooks deep blue Odell Lake to the left. Other Cascade mountains are all around as you gently descend towards the Oregon/California border.

CHEMULT (165/70)
Diamond Peak (8,750ft) is on the right. Buses connect with Bend, a resort 60 miles northeast.

  After Chemult you pass Mount Thielsen and Mount Scott (both over 9,000ft) on the right. Diamond Lake appears five minutes later, also on the right. You enter the Winema National Forest, with more logging facilities, then continue to Klamath Marsh.

  Half an hour from Chemult you join the Willamette River on the right and intermittently follow it for 15 miles through a canyon.

Chiloquin (55/15)
America's largest museum of logging is in nearby Collier State Park.

Upper Klamath Lake (60/10)
One of the biggest fresh-water lakes in the country, where in summer you might see the rare white pelicans. Mount McLaughlin (9,760ft) is on the right.

KLAMATH FALLS (70/160)
Sawmills appear to your left as you near the station. Geothermal springs used by Klamath Indians for cooking are now harnessed to heat homes. Klamath County Museum explains this underground activity along with pioneer history.

Visitors bureau: 125 N 8th (884-5193). Amtrak at 1600 Oak opens 0600-1000 and 2100-2300.

Leave with the Klamath River on your right and cross the state line, 20 miles south, into California. As you approach Dunsmuir you see the Cascades' highest peak, Mount Shasta (14,380ft). This snow-covered mountain is equally impressive by moonlight.

DUNSMUIR (160/100)
Once a base for the Southern Pacific, Dunsmuir is now an all-year recreation centre.

REDDING (100/70)
Located at the north end of the Sacramento valley close to Lake Shasta and Lassen National Park. Visitors bureau: 777 Auditorium Drive (225-4100). Amtrak's station is at 1620 Yuba. Nearby Shasta Dam (three times the height of Niagara Falls) backs up the Sacramento, McLoud and Pit Rivers.

CHICO (70/40)
The home of California State University, Chico was originally settled by gold miners. Larger fortunes were later made by those who came to farm. Most things can grow here, including rice, peaches and olives. General John Bidwell founded the town and his mansion forms part of a state park. Nearby to the south is Oroville Dam — the biggest earth-filled dam in America.

MARYSVILLE (40/70)
This former gold prospectors' town is now a centre for agriculture. Yuba City is adjacent to the west.

SACRAMENTO (70/20)
California's capital, to the scorn of some who live in more famous and glitzy cities further south. The 1849 gold rush started here at Sutter's Mill and many 19th Century houses are preserved. A reconstructed Sutter's Fort is on the east side of town. The 1869 Capitol has oak staircases and elaborate plasterwork.

Sacramento visitors bureau is at 1421 K (442-5542). Amtrak's vast terminal at 401 I opens 0515-2300. The Pony Express ended its inaugural run here in 1860 and a rail link over the Sierra Nevada brought the first trains across country. Sacramento today forms the hub of an extended food producing region.

Close to Amtrak's station is the California State Railroad Museum at 111 I Street (448-4466). Among 30 locomotives is the *Governor Stanford*, present at Promontory Point for the transcontinental link-up. Passenger cars include a 1929 *St Hyacinthe* Pullman sleeper. The Central Pacific depot and passenger station at 1st and J are also part of the museum. Open daily, admission. On summer weekends trains travel on the Southern Sacramento Railroad beside the river.

More nostalgia is on hand at the hardware store where the Central Pacific and Southern Pacific were planned by the big four financiers — Leland Stanford, Charles Crocker, Mark Hopkins and Collis Huntington, together with designer Theodore Judah. The store museum recreates the boardroom and features archive material. Southern Pacific eventually came to own a fifth of California's land.

The Capitol's gilded dome appears on the left as you leave. You cross the Sacramento River with a drawbridge to your left.

DAVIS (20/40)
The Spanish adobe-style station on the right dates from 1913. Part of the University of California (specialising in wine research) is based in Davis. Enlightened policies promote energy conservation, recycling and bicycle pathways through the city.

Leave past the university campus on the right.

Suisun-Fairfield (25/15)
The white pillars of Solano County court-house are to the right at the end of Union Ave.

Mothball Fleet (30/10)
On your left near the shoreline of Suisun Bay lies a fleet of merchant ships kept in 'mothballs'. Some date from the Second World War, and many saw action in Vietnam. Also on the left are docks through which countless Japanese cars are imported.

In the right distance is Mount Diablo. The beacon on top was extinguished after Pearl Harbor but is lit once a year by war veterans. You cross the Martinez-Benicia Bridge spanning the Carquinez Strait. Before they built this bridge in 1930 trains had to be ferried across in sections.

MARTINEZ (40/25)
Named after the area's Spanish governor, Ignacio Martinez. Amtrak's station at 401 Ferry (open 0630-2230) is the connecting point for services along the San Joaquin valley. Martinez was the birthplace of Joe Di Maggio and the home of John Muir, an early conservationist. The city museum occupies an old framehouse to the left of the station.

You leave Martinez and travel along the Carquinez Strait, with the Carquinez Bridge on your right and California's Maritime Academy across the water.

RICHMOND (25/15)
More than 100,000 people worked at the Kaiser Shipyards during the Second World War. These days Richmond is a San Francisco suburb, its station at 1700 Nevin Ave linked to the Bay Area Rapid Transit system. BART trains can be seen on your left.

Look for San Francisco's skyline across the bay to your right as you leave. The Golden Gate Bridge is to the north and Oakland Bay Bridge (eight miles long) to the south.

Golden Gate Race Track (5/10)
On the right, alongside an aquatic park for waterskiing.

OAKLAND (15/70)

'The place where the trains stopped', and the Coast Starlight is refurbished at Southern Pacific's depot before continuing. Amtrak's station at 17th and Wood is in a seedy area but has an interesting interior. Information: 982-8512. Ticket office open 0645-2145. Waiting room 0630-2230. Passengers for San Francisco disembark and transfer to the Amtrak shuttle bus connecting with Transbay Terminal.

Oakland may lack San Francisco's glamour but it's still California's fifth largest city, and the cheap accommodation here is less easy to find across the bay. Visitors bureau: 1000 Broadway (839-9000). YMCAs can be found at 2101 Telegraph Ave (451-5711) and on the corner of Alliston and Milvia (848-6800). The French Hotel is at 1538 Shattuck Ave (548-9930).

Oakland is the home town of rap artist MC Hammer. Other residents have included Jack London, Gertrude Stein, the Black Panthers and the Symbionese Liberation Army. A museum on Oak Street has Californian art and a simulated journey from sea level to the Sierra Nevada. Ferry tours around the harbour are free on some weekends. Lake Merritt in the centre of the city features a wildlife refuge and boating.

SAN FRANCISCO

The Golden Gate Bridge, fog in the morning, vertiginous streets, elegant houses, Chinatown and Alcatraz Island. 'Baghdad by the bay' was the home of Dashiell Hammett and Sam Spade. Birthplace of hippies and the first topless bar, San Francisco is a relaxed, cosmopolitan centre for finance and the arts.

The Spanish founded San Francisco in 1776 but the city didn't really take off until it became part of the USA and gold was discovered. Transcontinental railroads soon brought settlers, and the 1906 earthquake and 1989's tremors haven't stopped three quarters of a million people making this their home.

Daytime temperatures average mid-50s to mid-60s so a sweater is sometimes necessary, especially when fog blankets the city.

Transport: Amtrak services are at the Transbay Terminal, 425 Mission. Ticket office open 0630-2200. Waiting room 24 hours. Newspapers, restaurant, taxi stand. A Caltrain service operates to San Jose from the Southern Pacific station at 4th and Townsend (557-8661).

The best way to see San Francisco is on foot or by cable car. Or use buses and the MUNI Metro — a light railway running partly underground. For information on buses, cable cars and Muni trains call 673-6864. BART trains (778-2278) which leave from Market Street are a fast, inexpensive way to explore Oakland, Berkeley and Concord.

Taxis: Luxor (282-4141) and De Soto (673-1414).
Car Rental: Rent-A-Wreck, 555 Ellis (776-8700).
Greyhound: 7th and Market (558-6616).

The airport is 14 miles south on US 101. Airporter buses connect to a downtown terminal at Taylor and Ellis (495-8404), or you can take SamTrans bus No 7F (761-7000).

Tours: Gray Line (558-9400) has a 3½-hour city tour leaving from Transbay

Terminal. Cruises of the bay are available from the Blue and Gold Fleet (781-7877) at Pier 39. Air tours from Commodore Helicopters (332-4482) and Skycruise (568-4101).

Visitors Bureau: Hallidie Plaza, Market and Powell (391-2000). Open daily. Call 391-2001 for the latest events.

Telephone Code: 415.

Accommodation: Everything from expensive, classic hotels to downbeat rooming houses, with budget accommodation in Japantown and Oakland. Contact Bed & Breakfast International, 151 Ardmore Rd, Kensington, CA 94707 (525-4569) or American Family Inn/B & B, Box 349, San Francisco, CA 94101 (931-3083).
YMCA Chinatown: 855 Sacramento (982-4412). Singles $22, doubles $30.
Central YMCA: 220 Golden Gate Ave (885-0460). For men and women. Singles $29, doubles $40.
International Hostel: 240 Fort Mason (771-7277). Midnight curfew. Mostly dormitory rooms, $10.
   Hotels include the Kensington Park at 450 Post (788-6400); Carlton, 1075 Sutter (673-0242); Amsterdam, 749 Taylor (673-3277) — singles $38, doubles $42; Willows Inn, 710 14th (431-4770); Mark Twain, 345 Taylor (673-2332); Olympic, 140 Mason (982-5010) — singles and doubles $28.

Golden Gate Bridge: Linking the city with Marin County to the north is one of the world's most famous landmarks, which never ceases to inspire and charm. Over two miles long — seven including approaches — it incorporates 80,000 miles of cable and is painted orange rather than gold. Great views of San Francisco from the Marin County side.

Golden Gate Park: Between Fulton and Lincoln Way is the country's largest man-made park. Designed by Frederick Olmsted, who created New York's Central Park, it features many museums among its lakes, redwoods and eucalyptus (plus the occasional buffalo). Information: Fell and Stanyan (558-3706).

North Beach: Around Broadway and Washington Square. Scene of hectic neon nightlife and Little Italy, where beat poets once hung out. Now you are more likely to find naked dancers than coffee shops or bohemian conversation. Happily, Lawrence Ferlinghetti's *City Lights* bookstore still stands at 261 Columbus.

Cable Car Barn and Museum: Washington and Mason (474-1887). See this unique system in operation. The cars travel nine miles of track at up to nine miles an hour and are America's only historic landmarks with wheels. Old cable cars are on show along with other exhibits and a film. Open daily, free.

Fisherman's Wharf: On the waterfront between Taylor and the Embarcadero, with gift shops, salt air, cruise boats and tourists. Open-air stalls tempt the hordes with freshly cooked seafood. Sealions bark for fish in the water as gulls glide above. Downmarket delights include a wax museum, the Guinness collection of world records and Ripley's *Believe It Or Not*.

Alcatraz: The isle of pelicans was formerly the residence of Al Capone, 'Machine Gun' Kelly and the 'Birdman'. A million visitors each year come on boats from Pier 41 (546-2805). Make your reservations early and dress warmly. 'The rock' closed as a federal prison in 1963 but still has power to freeze the spirit. Tours are by national park rangers.

From Oakland the Coast Starlight gathers speed through industrial suburbs, with the Bay Bridge to your right.

Jack London Square (10/60)
Oakland's main tourist attraction is on the right, named after the author of *The Call of the Wild*. The waterfront area has restaurants, shops and hotels. Also on the right is the Alameda naval base.

Oakland Coliseum (20/50)
This massive circular construction on your right is home to the Oakland A's baseball team, shock losers of the 1990 world series.

Alameda County Stadium (25/45)
On your right.

Moffett Field (50/20)
Beyond the lower end of San Francisco Bay are the giant hangars of Moffett Field naval air station.

Marriotts Great America Park (60/10)
Roller-coasters and other rides can be glimpsed to the right.

Santa Clara (65/5)
The computer industry centre of Silicon Valley. An enclosed sports stadium of Santa Clara University is on the right.
   South of Santa Clara you pass extensive Southern Pacific yards and an old brick roundhouse.

SAN JOSE (70/70)
California's oldest city was founded in 1777 as Pueblo de San Jose de Guadalupe, and it became the first state capital in 1849. Now bigger than San Francisco in area and population, San Jose has fruit and wine industries as well as computer technology. The Mission of Santa Clara de Assisi is a reminder of earlier days. Amtrak's station at 65 Cahill opens 0630-2200. Caltrain commuter services operate between here and San Francisco.
   You leave and travel through the Santa Clara Valley, one of the richest farming regions in the country. On the left are Mount Hamilton (4,430ft) and the Diablo Mountains, with the Santa Cruz Range to the right.

Gilroy (30/40)
'Garlic capital of the world', where at the August festival tons of garlic-laden food are cooked and eaten by devotees from around the globe. See (and often smell) garlic plants near the tracks. On your right is St Mary's church with its gold bell, then the City Hall clock tower.

Pajaro Gap (40/30)
Cross the Santa Cruz Mountains into the Pajaro valley — 'valley of the birds'. Look for herons, divers and buzzards. More of the Santa Cruz Range features on your right, and exotic eucalyptus trees grow beside the track.

Watsonville (45/25)
Originally settled during the gold rush, this town has some attractive Victorian houses. Spanish explorer Don Gaspar de Portola discovered the first redwoods near here, and this area specialises in apples and strawberries. .

Castroville (60/10)
'Artichoke capital of the world'. Tall, bushy plants grow in fields of black earth to the right, making a change from garlic.

SALINAS (70/165)
The country's salad bowl, where vegetables grow fat beneath a benevolent sun. It was the birthplace of John Steinbeck, who described his home town in *East of Eden*. Steinbeck's house at 132 Central Ave is now a restaurant and museum, and the public library has some of his manuscripts. Information from the Chamber of Commerce at 119 E Alisal (424-7611). Amtrak's Railroad Ave station opens 1000-1330 and 1500-1800. Monterey and Big Sur are on the coast, 15 miles west.

Leave Salinas past an incongruous Firestone factory in fields to the right. San Benito Mountain (5,258ft) is the highest peak of the Diablo Range on the left, and the Santa Lucia Mountains are to the right.

Soledad (20/145)
This began as a mission town in 1791. On the left is the prison which once held Black Panther leader Eldridge Cleaver.

Continue along the Salinas River valley with Pinnacles National Monument to your left. Just before Rocky Point tunnel (1,305ft long) look left for an airfield. The light planes are used for spraying crops.

King City (45/120)
'The most metropolitan cow town in the West'. Crates of agricultural produce await transport on the right. Steinbeck's father was once the local railroad agent.

San Lucas (65/100)
A statue of Christ protects the cemetery to your right.

Camp Roberts (85/80)
The home of California's national guard.

San Miguel (95/70)
On your right is the 18th Century Mission San Miguel Arcangel, its two-storey adobe structure having the best-preserved interior of all California's missions. Coast Starlight tracks from Oakland to Los Angeles follow closely the Spanish mission path, El Camino Real. Between 1769 and 1823 Franciscan Father Junipero Serra founded 21 missions and four chapels along Camino Real, the Royal Road from San Diego to Sonoma. Each was a day's journey apart.

Atascadero (120/45)
A golf course on the right is bounded by Santa Lucia foothills. Atascadero's redbrick City Hall includes a history museum.

Cuesta Pass (145/20)
A quintessential railroad experience as for half an hour your train climbs the Santa Margarita Mountains, negotiating five tunnels and giving magnificent views of the Santa Lucias. Los Oros valley is below and Highway 101 opposite. Look for rocky outcrops, sheep, pine trees, eucalyptus and scrub oak. The descent from Cuesta Grande represents more than a thousand feet in 11 miles. An old wooden trestle can be seen ahead.

Horseshoe Curve (160/5)
As the Starlight winds down to San Luis Obispo it takes two sweeping curves that bring the whole train into view. On your right is the state penitentiary from which Timothy Leary escaped.

Cross Stenner Creek by means of the trestle seen earlier. On your left is the campus of California Poly State University.

SAN LUIS OBISPO (165/125)
An oasis of palm trees, sunshine and Spanish-style architecture that began in 1772 as the Mission San Luis Obispo de Tolosa. Many of the buildings on Marsh Street were built for rail workers' families when this was a railroad town. San Luis County Historical Museum is in the Carnegie Library building, and more information is available from the Chamber of Commerce, 1039 Chorro (543-1323).

Amtrak's station at 1011 Railroad Ave opens 0930-1730. Buses leave for the amazing Hearst Castle at nearby San Simeon, California's main tourist attraction after Disneyland. This was the home of William Randolph Hearst, on whom Orson Welles based *Citizen Kane*. Former guests have included Charlie Chaplin, George Bernard Shaw and Winston Churchill. Reservations are essential for the tour (800-446-7275).

As you leave, note the locomotive turntable to your right.

Grover City (15/110)
Obsolete rail coaches on the right house a restaurant.

The train crosses the Santa Maria River.

Pismo Beach (20/105)
Eucalyptus trees and dunes to the right conceal the resort of Pismo Beach.

Vandenberg Air Force Base (50/75)
For half an hour you travel through the Strategic Air Command western missile test range — home of the B-52 and launching site for Minuteman missiles. Further south are a number of satellite launch pads. This is military territory, and photography is not allowed.

Pacific Ocean (51/74)
More peaceful scenes appear to your right as the Coast Starlight continues beside the ocean.

Scurf (60/65)
As you cross the Santa Ynez River watch for oil rigs out to sea.

Space Shuttle (65/60)
The white building on the left was used during the launch programme.

Point Arguello (70/55)
Site of many shipwrecks, where an automatic lighthouse on the cliffs warns navigators of danger. Look for migrating grey whales in spring and autumn.
   The train's tracks run over a trestle above Jalama Beach Park at the southern end of Vandenberg base.

Point Conception (80/45)
The lighthouse on the bluff is still in use.
   You continue along clifftops, with ocean views shared by grazing cattle in an area accessible to the public only by train. The Santa Ynez Mountains begin in the left distance and will continue south beyond Santa Barbara.

Gaviota (95/30)
Cross on high trestles above Gaviota Pass and Tajiguas Creek.

Refugio State Beach (100/25)
On the right and dotted with picnic tables.
   Oil rigs and production platforms are common as you accompany the Santa Barbara Channel, which the Portuguese explorer Juan Cabrillo discovered in 1542. He was buried on San Miguel Island out to the right.
   Your train leaves the coast and travels inland towards Santa Barbara, passing on the right the bell tower of the University of California.

Santa Barbara Mission (123/2)
The 'queen of the missions' on your left was founded in 1786 and has been in use ever since. It's the only one with twin towers and a fountain fed by aqueduct.

SANTA BARBARA (125/45)

A resort and retirement area situated between a palm-lined beach and the Santa Ynez foothills, Santa Barbara was discovered by Sebastian Vizcaino on St Barbara Day in 1602. Here in 1782 Spain built its last New World fortress, the Presidio Real, and the Spanish influence persists. Much of the white adobe and red-tiled architecture had to be reconstructed after a 1925 earthquake. Visitors bureau: 1 Santa Barbara (966-9222). Amtrak's station at 209 State opens 0715-2130.

To the left of the station is the Moreton Bay fig tree — planted in 1877 and the biggest in the country. Branches spread 160ft to provide shade. The Museum on State Street has American, classical and impressionist art, and a thousand vintage cameras feature at the Museum of Photography.

The Goleta Railroad Museum is seven miles west at 300 N Carneros Rd (805-964-3540). This 1901 Southern Pacific depot has been relocated in Lake Los Carneros Park and restored. Model trains, rare photographs and miniature train rides. Open Wed-Sun, admission.

Leave Santa Barbara via some of its finest residential areas.

Andree Clark Bird Refuge (4/41)

This wildlife sanctuary next to the freshwater lagoon on your right is the home of herons, egrets and cormorants.

Miramar (5/40)

The station house on the left has become a restaurant.

Summerland Beach (6/39)

Nude bathers sometimes appear on the right. Bates Beach, a similar venue to look out for or recoil from, is 15 minutes further on.

From here to Ventura the Coast Starlight, like Highway 101, travels directly along the beach. Watch for surfers and (on a clear day) the Channel Islands. At Mussel Shoals a causeway leads to the island where oil production began in 1964. More platforms appear in the channel before you cross the Ventura River and head inland.

Ventura (30/15)

The county fairgrounds are to your right. The Spanish expedition of 1542 discovered Ventura, and San Buenaventura Mission on the left dates from 1809. Its unique wooden bells are preserved in the museum.

Cross the Santa Clara River.

OXNARD (45/20)

Founded in 1897 by the brothers Oxnard, who made their fortune from sugar beet. Now Oxnard is a centre for citrus fruit production and home of the state strawberry festival.

You continue east into the beautiful Simi valley, with the Simi Hills to the left and Santa Susanna Mountains on the right.

Camarillo (10/10)

A mission-type church stands on the hill to your left.

SIMI VALLEY (20/45)

Ronald Reagan's Presidential Library is located in this suburb of Los Angeles.

   After Simi Valley the Coast Starlight tackles the imposing Santa Susanna Hills, where tunnels and passes take you through a landscape of rocks and cacti. This was a film set for the *Lone Ranger* TV series as well as Cagney's *White Heat* and Hitchcock's *North by Northwest*.

Chatsworth (20/25)

On the border of Los Angeles County, this is the San Fernando valley — land of the swimming pool. Millions of Angelinos live the good suburban life in an area the size of Chicago.

Van Nuys (30/15)

Watch for factories belonging to General Motors and Schlitz as the scene becomes industrial. Van Nuys Airport is on the right before you pass beneath the awesome San Diego Freeway.

Hollywood-Burbank Airport (35/10)

A testing area for Lockheed, whose factory is beyond runways to the left.

Burbank (40/5)

The city of Burbank is on the left. Film studios of Disney, Warners and Columbia, plus NBC Television, are located among the Santa Monica Mountains to your right. TV's *MASH* helicopter scenes were shot here.

GLENDALE (45/15)

The ornamental, Spanish-style 1920s depot, lovingly restored at 400 W Cerritos Ave, has featured in many movies. Open 0700-2100.

   As you leave you see Forest Lawn memorial park on the left. Made famous by Evelyn Waugh's *The Loved One*, it's the burial place of Disney, Gable, Lombard, Harlow, Ladd, Flynn, and Chico and Gummo Marx. Tasteful highlights include a stained glass version of Leonardo's *Last Supper*.

   The train enters Los Angeles City.

Los Angeles River (8/7)

The concrete channel on the right remains dry most of the year but at times of flood becomes a river. This is another favourite film location, notably for *Point Blank* and *Repo Man*. You cross the river then pass beneath the Golden State and Pasadena Freeways.

Dodger Stadium (10/5)

Perched on a bluff to your right is the home of legendary baseball. An impressive Los Angeles skyline appears on the right as you pass Los Angeles County jail to the left.

LOS ANGELES

Palm trees, beaches, blondes, surfing, Mickey Mouse, freeways, smog and David Hockney swimming pools — Los Angeles is a sprawling place with a charm all its own. Founded by the Spanish in the 18th Century as 'the city of our lady queen of the angels', its name got shorter as the town grew bigger. The completing of the transcontinental railroad in 1869, together with oil, Hollywood and the climate, brought millions in search of a better life. True Angelinos wouldn't live anywhere else.

America's second largest city spreads 13 million people over an area the size of Rhode Island. The sun really does shine most of the time, though smog gets worse during summer.

Transport: The Union Passenger Terminal at 800 N Alameda is one of America's prettiest railway stations, built in Spanish style and lately restored. Information: 624-0171. Ticket office open 0545-2330. Waiting room 24 hours. Vending machines, newspapers, luggage trolleys, Red Caps, restaurant, left luggage room, shop, taxi stand. Amtrak Thruway buses go to Santa Barbara, Long Beach and Santa Monica.

RTD buses take in most of the Los Angeles attractions. Ask for a free map at the customer service centre in ARCO Plaza or write to RTD Marketing, Los Angeles, CA 90001 for a tourist kit. For transit information call RTD on 626-4455. DASH shuttle buses operate Mon-Sat, connecting Union Station with Chinatown and the downtown area. RTD bus No 1 leaves from the corner of Broadway and Arcadia for Hollywood.

Taxis: Checker (482-3456) and Yellow (481-2345).
Car Rental: Avon, 8459 Sunset Blvd (654-5533). This is the city of the automobile, with 6,500 miles of road and freeway, so renting a car is easy. The hard part is finding your way around. If you have the time and inclination, the Automobile Club can provide maps. Or buy *Thomas' Road Guide*.
Greyhound: 208 E 6th (620-1200) and 1409 N Vine, Hollywood (466-6381).

LAX Airport is 16 miles southwest of downtown by taxi, RTD bus No 42 and the Super Shuttle (338-1111).

Tours: Gray Line, 6541 Hollywood Blvd (856-5900) visits Hollywood, Beverly Hills and the film studios. Other companies include Starline (463-3131) and Hollywood Fantasy (469-8184). The Los Angeles Conservancy at 849 S Broadway has walking tours (623-2489). Grave Line Tours (876-0920) take you to places of morbid interest by chauffeur-driven hearse.

Visitors Bureau: 695 S Figueroa (689-8822) and 6541 Hollywood Blvd (461-4213). Open Mon-Sat.

Telephone Code: 213.

Accommodation: Los Angeles has more than 12 million visitors a year so there are plenty of places to stay. Consult the press for weekend rates and special offers. For bed & breakfast contact 32074 Waterside La, Westlake Village, CA 91361 (818-889-8870).
Hollywood YMCA: 1553 Hudson Ave (467-4161). For men and women. Singles $30, doubles $40.
International Youth Hostel: 3601 S Gaffey, San Pedro (831-8109).
Hollywood (AYH) Hostel: 1553 Hudson Ave (467-4161). Midnight curfew. Members $9, non-members $11.

Hotels include the Biltmore at 506 S Grand Ave (800-421-8000); Figueroa, 939 S Figueroa (800-421-9092); Hollywood Premier, 5333 Hollywood Blvd (466-1691); Milner, 813 S Flower (627-6981) — singles $35, doubles $45; Orchid, 819 S Flower (624-5855); Stillwell, 838 S Grand (627-1151); Park Plaza, 607 S Park View (384-5281) — singles $35, doubles $45, weekly $135.

El Pueblo de Los Angeles State Park: Next to Amtrak's station (680-2525). Los Angeles began here and Avila Adobe, the city's oldest house, can be visited at 10 E Olivera. This street also has Mexican restaurants and cheerfully tacky souvenir shops. There are free walking tours from 130 Paseo de la Plaza (628-1274).

Mann's Chinese Theater: 6925 Hollywood Blvd (464-8111). Match your favourite actor's cement prints outside this extravagant pagoda. More than 2,500 bronze stars in the sidewalk celebrate the great days of Tinseltown.

La Brea Tar Pits: 5801 Wilshire Blvd (936-2230). Bubbling black deposits contain many fossils, seen at the museum and observation pit. Closed Mon, admission.

Griffith Park: Los Feliz Blvd (665-5188). Includes a planetarium and zoo (both open daily, admission). The 4,500-acre park also has a miniature railway and an observatory.

Travel Town: In the northwest corner of Griffith Park (662-5874), featuring 16 steam locos plus passenger cars, freight wagons and cabooses (brake cars). Open daily, free.

Forest Lawn Memorial Park: 6300 Forest Hills Drive, near Griffith Park (254-7251). The last resting place of Buster Keaton, Stan Laurel and Charles Laughton. Open daily.

Lomita Railroad Museum: Just south of Los Angeles at 2135 250th, Lomita (326-6255). The museum has live steam engines, memorabilia and a replica of the Boston & Maine station at Wakefield, Massachusetts. Open Wed-Sun, admission.

2 The California Zephyr

Chicago—San Francisco

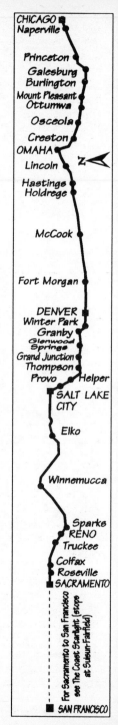

One of the world's great trains, the California Zephyr travels for two days and nights via farmland, prairie, deserts, rivers and mountains. Many catch the Zephyr just to see the Rockies. Pioneers came west this way, as did gold prospectors, the pony express and the telegraph. The Zephyr keeps to the first transcontinental railroad line for much of its 2,422-mile journey.

Frequency: Daily. The westbound service leaves Chicago mid-afternoon to arrive in Omaha late evening and Denver early next morning. You reach Salt Lake City late on the second day, Reno the following morning and Oakland (for San Francisco) mid-afternoon.

Travelling east, you leave San Francisco late morning to arrive in Reno early evening. You reach Salt Lake City next morning, Denver by evening and Omaha early on the second day, arriving in Chicago late afternoon.

Reservations: All reserved.

Equipment: Superliner coaches.

Sleeping: Superliner economy, de luxe, family, special bedrooms.

Food: Complete meals, snacks, sandwiches, drinks.

Lounge Car: Video movies, games, railroad history guide (Reno-Sacramento).

Baggage: Check-in service at major cities.

CHICAGO

The most American of cities, with more than 80 ethnic groups and three million people (plus four million in the suburbs) making for a vibrant mix of cultures. Writers Saul Bellow, Nelson Algren and 'Studs' Terkel have lived here, as have Al Capone (gangster) and Mother Cabrini (first US saint).

Chicago was created in 1833, destroyed by fire in 1871, then rebuilt to become a world centre for business, finance and the arts. A hard-headed commercial spirit makes the city more workable and less pretentious than New York or Los Angeles.

The first (11-storey) skyscrapers here led to the Chicago school of architects from Frank Lloyd Wright to Mies Van der Rohe. Superb buildings exist in every modern style, alongside an uncompromising elevated railway and the Chicago River. Down on the lakefront are parks, beaches and the harbour, where joggers and sunbathers take over. In winter, ice floats on the water.

Like any big city Chicago has its share of crime, but stay with the bright lights and you should have no problems.

Transport: This has long been a transport centre for ships arriving on Lake Michigan via the St Lawrence Seaway. Union Station at 225 S Canal is the hub of America's rail network, with 40 Amtrak and 160 commuter trains daily. The magnificently restored building retains its marble pillars and original wooden seats in the cathedral-like waiting room (as seen in Brian de Palma's *The Untouchables*). A separate waiting room is for Amtrak passengers only. The Metropolitan lounge, complete with large screen TV, is for first class passengers and opens 0800-2100. Ticket office open 0600-2200 (Mon-Fri) and 0700-2200 (weekends). Main waiting room 24 hours. Information: 558-1075. Lockers, vending machines, newspapers, luggage trolleys, Red Caps, restaurants, shops, taxi stand. Amtrak has other offices at 203 N LaSalle and 500 N Michigan Ave.

RTA buses cover the whole city (with a stop outside the Adams Street exit of Union Station) and a subway system augments the El railway. Call 836-7000 for information on all three.

Taxis: Flash (561-1444) and Yellow (829-4222).
Car Rental: Benders, 1545 N Wells (280-8554).
Greyhound: 630 W Harrison (781-2900).

O'Hare Airport is 20 miles northwest by coach, taxi or El train. Continental Air Transport (454-7800) runs every half hour between downtown and the airport.

Tours: Culture Bus (836-7000) and Gray Line (346-9506). The Architecture Foundation organises tours to Chicago's best buildings (326-1393). Views of the city and Lake Michigan are available from Mercury Sightseeing cruises at Michigan and Wacker (332-1353).

Visitors Bureau: 310 S Michigan Ave (793-2094). Open weekdays. An information centre opens daily at 163 E Pearson (280-5740) in the Water Tower, sole survivor of the great fire. For the latest events call 225-2323.

Telephone Code: 312.

Accommodation: Contact Chicago Bed & Breakfast, 1704 Crilly Court, Chicago, IL 60014 (951-0085). Some hotels offer weekend and summer packages. Call the Tourist Council (793-2094) or write to the Hotel Association, 100 W Monroe, Chicago, IL 60603.
YMCA and YWCA: 33 W Chicago Ave (944-6211). Over 18s only. Singles $25, doubles $35.
International (AYH) Youth Hostel: 6318 N Winthrop (262-1011). Members $10, non-members $13.
Hotels include the Drake at 140 E Walton Place (787-2200); Allerton, 701 N Michigan (440-1500); Blackstone, 636 S Michigan (427-4300); Bismarck, 171 W Randolph (236-0123); Ascot House, 1100 S Michigan (922-2900); Cass, 640 N Wabash (787-4030) — singles $35, doubles $40.

Sears Tower: Wacker and Jackson, near the station (875-9696). This is the tallest building in the world at 110 storeys and 1,454ft (1,707ft including antennae). Ear-popping elevators shoot you to the 103rd floor Skydeck for views of the city, Lake Michigan and four states. Go before sunset and watch the city light up. Open daily, admission.

John Shedd Aquarium: 1200 Lake Shore Dr (939-2438). The biggest collection of marine life anywhere, with more than 6,000 species of fish, whales, seals and dolphins. Open daily, free Thurs.

Art Institute: Michigan and Madison (443-3500). One of the world's great galleries, showing impressionist and renaissance works alongside major exhibitions. Very crowded at weekends. Open daily, free Tues.

Museum of Science and Industry: 57th and Lake Shore Drive (684-1414). Featuring a German U-boat, a British Spitfire and the Apollo 8 spacecraft, plus automobiles and train locos. The Santa Fe miniature railroad operates over 1,000ft of track. Open daily, free.

Pullman Community: 614 E 113th (785-8181). On the first Sunday in the month, tour America's first company town of railroad sleeping car fame.

20th Century Railroad Club: 509 W Roosevelt Rd, Chicago, IL 60607 (829-4500). Visits can be arranged to the club's library in the Amtrak yards.

You depart Chicago, its skyline diminishing to your right, and pass the eastbound Zephyr a few minutes out of Union Station. The westbound train continues through industrial scenes.

NAPERVILLE (30/60)
Chicago's main western suburb offers commuter connections to Aurora, La Grange and Cicero. It has attractive restored buildings and a riverwalk.

Aurora (10/50)
A stone roundhouse and other early railway buildings are on your right,

double-decked commuter trains to your left. Aurora has been a transport junction since stage-coach days, with the Chicago, Burlington & Quincy Railroad formed here in 1849. It was the first American city to have electric street lights. You leave and cross the Fox River.

PRINCETON (60/60)
The 'pig capital of the world' began as a New Englander settlement in 1833 and was the home town of John Bryant, one of the Republican party's founders. The Underground Railroad freedom trail for escaped slaves had a station here. Look for A-frame buildings housing the local pig population.

Kewanee (30/30)
Another New Englander settlement.

Galva (40/20)
In the 19th Century Swedish dissidents here set up the utopian community of Bishop's Hill.

GALESBURG (60/50)
Once the home of Olmstead Ferris, who invented popcorn and was related to the builder of the first Ferris wheel. On your right is the copper spire of Knox College. Galesburg was a station on the Underground Railroad and has an annual Railroad Days gathering. Amtrak's station at 225 S Seminary opens 0700-2100. A 1930s Hudson loco features on the right. Thruway buses connect with Peoria and with Texas Eagle trains stopping at Springfield.

Monmouth (20/30)
This was the birthplace of Wyatt Earp. The railroad brought here a block of granite for his monument. The region produces mostly cattle and corn.

Mississippi River (45/5)
You cross on a 2,000ft long bridge giving views of Burlington and this great river. The Mississippi travels 2,350 miles to the Gulf of Mexico, draining a third of the USA. Before the bridge opened in 1868 passengers crossed by ferry, and during winter they went over the ice on foot. Crossing takes you from Illinois into Iowa.

BURLINGTON (50/30)
Nearby hills were one of the few places where flint could be found, so Indians regarded them as neutral territory. Strategically placed on the river, Burlington became a natural railroad centre and capital of both Wisconsin and Iowa. Amtrak at 300 S Main opens 1100-1900. Note the steam engine to your left. Rail technology advanced here in 1887 when Westinghouse developed the air brake on Burlington Hill.

Leave through the older part of town, with a shopping area to your right and an ammunition plant on your left.

Danville (15/15)
This was a stop for stage-coaches and the pony express.

MOUNT PLEASANT (30/40)
A typical mid-western town in style and architecture, where the Old Settlers and Threshers Association celebrates frontier heritage. America's first toll roads with plank surfaces were laid between here and Burlington. Iowa Wesleyan College on the right dates from 1842.

Soon after leaving town you cross the Skunk River.

OTTUMWA (40/70)
On banks above the Des Moines River, Ottumwa was named after an Indian tribe. From a trading post in 1838 it's become an important business centre and home town of *MASH*'s Radar O'Reilly.

You leave Ottumwa and cross the Des Moines River on its way to join the Mississippi.

OSCEOLA (70/30)
Settlers in the early 1800s discovered the first Delicious apple tree 30 miles to the north. Osceola was named after a Seminole warrior chief whose wooden statue appears on your left beyond the station. Des Moines is 50 miles north.

CRESTON (30/105)
This railroad town's depot is a national landmark. Creston perches on a ridge between the Des Moines and Missouri valleys — the California Zephyr's highest point east of the Missouri. Farmers' co-operative silos on the right provide the town's best viewing platform.

Stanton (40/65)
Stanton is famous for its water tower on the right, shaped like a coffee pot. Also on the right is a red court-house.

Council Bluffs (75/30)
This was a pioneer trading post and the eastern end of the Union Pacific Railroad leading to California.

Missouri River (80/25)
From its source in the Montana Mountains — where the Gallatin, Jefferson and Madison Rivers converge — the Missouri journeys through here to join the Mississippi at St Louis. Crossing takes you from Iowa into Nebraska.

Offutt Air Force Base (90/15)
The airfield and Strategic Air Command museum are on the left.

OMAHA (105/60)
Nebraska's biggest city was the birthplace of Fred Astaire, Marlon Brando, Henry Fonda, Malcolm X and President Ford. Mormons wintered here in 1846 on their way to Utah, and Omaha played a vital part in westward migration when it was a stop on the first transcontinental railroad. The city now markets grain and cattle raised on the prairies, and its Union Stockyards have been in business since 1884.

Transport: Amtrak is at 1003 S 9th, a mile from downtown. Information: 342-1501. Ticket office open 0730-1530 (Mon-Fri) and 2230-0730 (daily). Vending machines, luggage trolleys, taxi stand. Thruway buses connect with Kansas City.

   MAT bus information and maps are available at the Park Fair Mall, 16th and Douglas (341-0800).

Taxis: Happy Cab (339-0110).

Car Rental: Rent-A-Wreck, 501 N 17th (344-2001).

Greyhound: 1601 Jackson (341-1900).

   The airport is reached by taxi and MAT bus No 28 from 10th Street.

Visitors Bureau: 1212 Deer Park Blvd (554-3990). Open daily. For the events hotline call 444-6800.

Telephone Code: 402.

Accommodation: For bed & breakfast try the Offutt Mansion, 140 N 39th (553-0951).

   Hotels include the Red Lion Inn at 1616 Dodge (346-7600); Best Western Immanuel Plaza, 6901 N 72nd (571-6161); Oak Creek Inn, 2808 S 72nd (397-7137); Days Inn, 3001 Chicago (345-2222); Thrifty Scot, 7101 Grover (391-5757); Super 8, 7111 Spring (390-0700) — singles $32, doubles $37.

Union Pacific Museum: 12th and Dodge (271-3530). Reviewing a long and sometimes controversial history, the museum features a railroad auditor's office and a model of Abraham Lincoln's funeral car. Open Mon-Sat, free.

Omaha History Museum: 801 S 10th (444-5071). Located in the 1929 Union Pacific depot, not far from today's Amtrak station. Open daily, admission.

Henry Doorly Zoo: 10th and Deer Park Blvd (733-8400). Gorillas, orangutans and white tigers live beside the Missouri River. Steam trains operate through the grounds on a 30in-gauge line. Open daily, admission.

Boys Town: Situated 10 miles west of the city, Boys Town was founded in 1917 as a home for underprivileged boys by Father Flanagan, played in the 1938 film by Spencer Tracy. Open daily.

Strategic Air Command Museum: At Bellevue, south of Omaha. Aircraft and missiles demonstrate the development of military aviation. Open daily, admission.

LINCOLN (60/90)

As you approach the station at 201 N 7th the University of Nebraska is to your left. Amtrak occupies the north end of a former Burlington & Northern building with a renovated waiting room (the Great Hall). Lincoln's 400ft high Capitol is on your left. The 'tower of the plains' is the only unicameral (single house) legislature in the USA, and a statue on its gold dome represents *The*

Sower broadcasting seed. Visitors bureau: 1221 N (477-6300).

HASTINGS (90/50)
A centre for trade and manufacturing, especially of farm machinery. The House of Yesterday Museum features pioneer life. Grand Island is 30 miles due north.
   The country becomes dryer as you head west, moving from farmland into cattle country.

Kenesaw (15/35)
Cross the Oregon Trail once used by wagon trains.

HOLDREGE (50/70)
Named after George Holdrege, who was manager of the Chicago, Burlington & Quincy Railroad.

MCCOOK (70/115)
Began in 1852 as a division point on the railway before becoming an oil town.

Nebraska/Colorado State Line (70/45)
As you change from Central to Mountain Time, watches go back an hour (forward when travelling east).
   The Zephyr leaves Nebraska and travels towards Denver over the high plains of east Colorado — former buffalo country.

FORT MORGAN (115/80)
The fort dates from 1864, since when the town has grown rich on oil and cattle.

Pike's Peak (60/20)
This 14,110ft mountain is just visible on the far left horizon. The Rockies are 80 miles to your right.

Commerce City (65/15)
Denver's main industrial suburb, with America's biggest sheep market and sugar beet factories. Cattle yards appear beside the track.

Riverside Cemetery (70/10)
The pioneer graveyard on your right was started in 1876.
   You pass beneath Interstate 70 and see Denver's skyline to your left. The front of the train comes into view on the right as it turns north before reversing into the station.

DENVER (80/120)
The Mile High City was a gold rush town founded in 1858 between barren plains and the Rocky Mountains. As Colorado's capital it has boomed thanks to oil, mining and high-tech industry, and the population is now almost two million (not counting the Carrington family). New skyscrapers glitter and older parts of the city have been restored.

Altitude and a dry, sunny climate make Denver unique among US cities, so treat the pure sunlight with respect. Allow a day or two to become accustomed to the thin air before undertaking strenuous activities. Many ski resorts are close by and you can hire equipment easily.

Transport: Union Station is at 1701 Wynkoop. Information: 534-2812. Ticket office open 0700-2130. Waiting room 0630-2230. Lockers, newspapers, luggage trolleys, snack bar, shop, taxi stand.

RTD buses serve downtown and the suburbs, with maps and schedules at the station (or call 778-6000). A free shuttle service runs along 16th Street. For buses to the resorts contact Colorado Ground Transportation (388-5669). *Taxis:* Metro (333-3333) and Yellow (777-7777).
Car Rental: Alamo (321-1176).
Greyhound: 1055 19th (292-6111).

Stapleton Airport is six miles from downtown by taxi, Airport Limousine (398-2284) and bus No 32.

Tours: Gray Line (289-2841) city and mountain excursions leave from the Greyhound depot. Walking tours with Historic Denver, 1330 17th (534-1858).

Visitors Bureau: 225 W Colfax (892-1505). Open weekdays. Free guide.

Telephone Code: 303.

Accommodation: Write to Rocky Mountain Bed & Breakfast, Box 804, Colorado Springs, CO 80901.
YMCA: 25 E 16th (861-8300). For men and women. Singles $15, doubles $25.
International Youth Hostel: 630 E 16th Ave (832-9996). Dormitory rooms $6.

Hotels include the Brown Palace at 321 17th (297-3111); Broadway Plaza, 1111 Broadway (893-3501); Relax Inns, 1680 Colorado Blvd (691-2223); Colburn, 980 Grant (837-1261); Regal 8, 12033 E 38th (371-0740); Standish, 1530 California (534-3231) — singles $14, doubles $16.

Larimer Square: Historic Denver, this was formerly the haunt of outlaws. It now has Victorian houses, gaslights, courtyards, craft shops, restaurants and nightclubs.

US Mint: 320 W Colfax (844-3332). The Mint produces five billion coins a year and has more gold than anywhere outside Fort Knox. Souvenir coins are on sale. Open weekdays, free.

State Capitol: E Colfax and Sherman (866-2604). Murals, rare onyx and a dome covered with gold leaf, plus balcony views towards the Rockies. The 13th step at the entrance is exactly one mile above sea level. Open Mon-Sat, free tours.

Colorado Railroad Museum: 17155 W 44th in Golden, 12 miles west of Denver (279-4591). Featuring the oldest locomotives and rail cars in the state. Open daily, admission.

Forney Transportation Museum: 1416 Platte (433-3643). More rail locos, including a 1941 Union Pacific *Big Boy*, as well as horse-drawn vehicles and antique cars. Open daily, admission.

_____

The Zephyr departs on Rio Grande Railroad tracks, having arrived on the Burlington Northern from Chicago. Pioneer through coaches to Portland and Seattle continue via Wyoming. Look back on your right for views of Denver.

Arvada (20/100)
Another large suburb, with the Front Range of the Rockies ahead. Mount Evans (14,264ft) is to the left and Long's Peak (14,255ft) on the right.

Rocky (40/80)
The train takes an S-shaped curve to gain height among the foothills. Winds here sometimes reach 100 mph so trains are protected at Big 10 Curve by railroad cars anchored with sand. The Zephyr climbs a 2% gradient, entering the first of 29 tunnels.

Plainview (50/70)
You get spectacular views of the Colorado plains 1,500ft below and the whole of Denver back to your right. Rocky Flats nuclear weapons factory is in the foreground. On your right are Colorado University and the city of Boulder as you travel into the Rockies via South Boulder Canyon.

Gross Reservoir (60/60)
A 340ft-high dam provides Denver with 14 billion gallons of water.
   Look for deer and elk as you enter Roosevelt National Forest, with the continental divide ahead.

Moffat Tunnel (100/15)
Six miles long and the highest point on Amtrak's network (9,239ft). Before the tunnel opened in 1928, reducing the distance between Denver and Salt Lake City by 65 miles, trains took five hours crossing the continental divide around James Peak (13,260ft). Now the journey takes 10 minutes before you emerge from complete darkness into brilliant light.

Winter Park Ski Resort (115/5)
Close on the left.

WINTER PARK (120/20)
This is one of Denver's many mountain parks, famous for tourism and ranching. The train station is actually in Fraser — called the 'icebox of America' because temperatures can get down to minus 50°F. On a ridge to your right is the Devil's Thumb rock formation.

Tabernash (5/15)
Named after an Indian chief. Before the Moffat Tunnel opened 'helper' locomotives would be added here to get trains over the pass.

Fraser Canyon (10/5)
The Zephyr accompanies a clear, trout-laden Fraser River where President Eisenhower came to fish.

GRANBY (20/180)
In the region of meadowlands known as Middle Park, with Trail Ridge Road — the world's highest car road — running through Rocky Mountain National Park to your right. Evidence has been found locally of a people who predate the Indians.

After Granby you join the Colorado River near its source and follow it for more than 200 miles.

Hot Sulphur Springs (15/165)
Thermal springs heat an indoor swimming pool on the right.

Byers Canyon (16/164)
Spiky rocks tower above the track and Highway 40 is to your left.

Watch for herds of deer and the odd buffalo as the train picks up speed through prime cattle country.

Kremmling (35/145)
Mount Powell (13,534ft) is on the left.

Gore Canyon (40/85)
Sheer rock walls reach 1,500ft, making the canyon accessible only by train. The Gore Range to your left is 13,000ft high.

Coming out of the canyon you travel through meadows and ranchland. Just before Bond look out for the old State Bridge on the left.

Bond (100/80)
A historic railroad town, where the Rio Grande branch line to Steamboat Springs is seen above on the right.

Red Canyon (110/65)
Spaniards called this area Colorado (meaning red) after seeing these vivid colours and strange rock formations.

Dotsero (140/40)
An 1885 survey of the Colorado River marked this point '0' or 'dot-zero' on its maps, and this is the midpoint of the California Zephyr's journey. To your left the Eagle River joins the Colorado.

Glenwood Canyon (155/10)
Coloured rocks, cliffs, aspen trees and evergreens proliferate as you follow the river. Interstate 70 is on the far side.

GLENWOOD SPRINGS (180/100)
A centre for fishing and hiking, where white-water rafters dice on the rapids. The ski resorts of Aspen and Snowmass are close by. On the right is one of

the world's largest outdoor swimming pools, heated year-round by Yampa Hot Springs. Beyond it is Theodore Roosevelt's favourite Colorado Hotel. Doc Holliday of OK Corral fame lived and is buried near here. Amtrak's station at 413 7th opens 0930-1645.

Leave along a typical Rocky Mountain valley, with the Roaring Fork River joining the Colorado on your left.

New Castle (30/70)

Huge oil shale deposits occur here, some of them in cliffs to the right. Also to the right is Mount Baxter (11,188ft). In 1896, 54 men died in a vulcan mine explosion and another disaster in 1931 killed all 37 workers. The mine continues to burn.

Travellers' Tales
The Amtrak Experience
by Molly Elliott

Everyone has a favourite travel season. I like autumn; cooler temperatures, fewer people. I couldn't have picked a better time for crossing America via Amtrak: Lakeshore Limited, New York-Chicago; California Zephyr, Chicago-Sacramento.

On the first leg I occupied a roomette, spacious and comfortable. I appreciated the giveaways: folder of stationery, pen, postcards — and a small bottle of wine served with supper although liquor is not otherwise available. At mealtimes I shared tables with interesting folk: a couple from Washington bound for a conference in San Francisco where the wife, blind and an authority on aids for the sightless, would lecture; an antique dealer from Boise, like me, kept a detailed diary, and a woman from Trinidad who belonged to a choir that, every two years, travelled overseas to perform.

Looking through my diary, I note the enormous variety of scenery: cities, farmland, lake ports, mobile home parks. With its height allowing wide views, the California Zephyr ran smoothly and quietly. Downstairs heavy baggage stowage meant a little more elbow room in the restricted couchette. Beyond Chicago, isolated small settlements in vast sweeps of country fascinated me. Everywhere residents had already put up Christmas decorations. In the darkness, the lights looked friendly and festive especially to one from a land where Christmas falls in midsummer. Hence my excitement when waking in the small hours and seeing moonlight shining on a limitless white vista of snow.

The Denver stop allowed passengers off for a leg stretch round the station with its souvenir and newspaper stall and Grandpa's Depot, full of railway memorabilia. We could have taken a breather at the second service stop at Salt Lake City but, as we arrived round midnight, I stayed in my comfortable berth.

Beyond Denver, we spent almost the entire day snaking through the Rockies' awesome scenery. On the serpentine track, the double-headed train ran fairly slowly and almost silently through tunnels and beside the Colorado River with ice forming on its edges. The Sierra Nevada also provided spectacular views and magnificent autumn colour as we negotiated the Donner Pass and looked down on Donner Lake. I had read about snow sparkling in sunlight and felt as thrilled as a child when I actually saw this as we clicked through Reno and Truckee.

And so into Sacramento — and I could have jumped right back on to see what I had missed during the hours of darkness.

Grand Valley (70/30)
The aptly named Parachute Mountains are on the right.

Dubeque-Palisade (80/20)
The beautiful Grand Mesa to the left is the world's largest flat-top mountain (over 10,000ft). This region produces great quantities of fruit, especially peaches and apricots.

GRAND JUNCTION (100/60)
Where the Gunnison and Colorado Rivers meet, Grand Junction is a centre for agriculture and the coal industry. Amtrak at 2nd and South Ave opens 1030-1745. Nearby are Mesa Verde National Park, Grand Mesa Forest and Colorado National Monument, whose red cliffs appear to the left as you leave.

Ruby Canyon (20/40)
Another photo opportunity arises as the train winds through brightly coloured rocks carved by the Colorado out of the Uncompahgre Plateau. A mark on the right canyon wall signifies the Colorado/Utah border.

At Westwater the Colorado goes south and you enter an entirely different landscape, travelling 150 miles through desert. The eroding mesas to your right are the Book Cliffs made from sandstone and shale. La Sal Mountains are in the left distance.

THOMPSON (60/95)
Rich in uranium, this part of Utah has dramatic and sometimes desolate scenery. Nearby are Arches National Monument, Dead Horse Point, Canyonlands National Park and Monument Valley (star of John Ford westerns).

Green River (25/70)
Famous for cantaloupes and watermelons. Green River Bible Church is on the right. An altitude of 4,075ft makes this the lowest point on the line between Denver and Salt Lake City.

HELPER (95/120)
Named after the extra locomotives attached to westbound freight trains, enabling them to climb the mountains. It's still a busy rail centre for coal, of which this region has enough to supply the US for 300 years.

Leave past the western downtown area to your left, where a big brick building on the hillside belongs to the Utah Railway.

As it heads into the Wasatch Mountains via Soldier Summit the Zephyr is joined on the left by the Price River. The conglomeration of machinery to your right 10 minutes from Helper is a coal processing plant.

Castle Gate (15/105)
This unusual rock formation protrudes above the track on the right.

Soldier Summit (60/60)
The 7,440ft peak's name commemorates Union soldiers buried here in 1860. Look for an abandoned mine on the right.

Your train descends into the Spanish Fork River Canyon in a series of horseshoe curves.

Thistle (100/20)
In 1983 heavy rains caused a mudslide which deluged the village of Thistle, along with the Rio Grande tracks. This route closed for three months while a 3,000ft tunnel was built beneath Billies Mountain to provide an alternative. Remnants of the village can be seen to your left.

Springville (115/5)
The colonial building on the right was once a school.

PROVO (120/55)
Utah's third largest city was founded by Mormons in 1849 between the Wasatch Mountains and Utah Lake. It's the home of Brigham Young University — America's largest private college — and the Osmond family. La Sal National Forest is close by.

You leave Provo and cross the Provo River. US Steel's Geneva works is on the right, Mount Timpanogos (11,750ft) is behind and Mount Nebo to the left.

Utah Lake (15/40)
On the left, with the Tintic Mountains visible in the distance.

Riverton (25/30)
The Kennecott copper mine, once the biggest in the world, is among the hills to your left.

Nearing Salt Lake City, Salt Lake Temple and the domed capitol appear on the right.

SALT LAKE CITY (55/250)
Founded in 1847 by Brigham Young and other pioneers seeking to practise their beliefs in freedom, Mormon influence here remains strong. Mining and electronics prosper in this pretty valley between the Wasatch Mountains and the Oquirrh Range.

Salt Lake City has clean air, wide streets and downtown crossing signals that chirrup endearingly. Promontory Summit, where the golden spike ceremony completed the first transnational route, is 40 miles north of here.

Ski resorts nearby include Alta (America's second oldest) and Sundance (proprietor Robert Redford). Five national parks featuring dramatic rocks and outdoor activities are within a day's drive.

Transport: The station used by Amtrak is at 320 S Rio Grande. Information: 364-8562. Ticket office open 0500-1400 and 1615-2400. Lockers, vending machines, luggage trolleys, restaurant, taxi stand.

UTA buses (287-4636) visit most tourist attractions and serve the ski resorts.
Taxis: City (363-5014) and Yellow (521-2100).
Car Rental: Payless, 1974 W North Temple (596-2596).
Greyhound: 160 W South Temple (355-4684).

The airport is six miles west by bus No 50.

Tours: Gray Line (521-7060) and Lewis Bros (359-8677).

Visitors Bureau: 180 S West Temple (521-2868). Open daily.

Telephone Code: 801.

Accommodation: For bed & breakfast contact Inn Tour Link, PO Box 7812, Murray, UT 84107 (534-8797). Eller Bed & Breakfast is at 164 S 9th East (533-8184).
*Avenues (AYH) Youth Hostel:*107 F (363-8137). Members $10, non-members $14. Singles $19, doubles $22.
   Hotels include the Brigham Street Inn at 1135 E South Temple (364-4461); Orleans, 352 S 300 East (521-3790); Desert, 50 W 5th South (532-2900); Friendship Skyline, 2475 E 1700 South (582-5350); Regal, 1025 N 900 West (364-6591); Carlton, 140 E South Temple (355-3418) — singles $20, doubles $30.

Temple Square: 50 W South Temple (531-2534). Heart of the Church of Jesus Christ of Latter-day Saints — the Mormons. The six-spired Temple can only be entered by believers but there are film shows and tours elsewhere. The Tabernacle has public recitals on its 10,000-pipe organ, complete with light effects. Many buildings of interest are within walking distance. The 1853 Beehive House which belonged to Brigham Young has free tours and traditional candy (closed Sun).

Family History Library: 35 N West Temple (240-2231). Otherwise known as the Genealogical Library, this is the largest of its kind in the world. Trace your family line among 800,000 rolls of microfilm. Closed Sun, free tours.

The Capitol: At the north end of State Street (538-1030). This impressive statehouse was built from marble and granite beneath a copper dome. Closed Sun.

Pioneer Memorial Museum: 300 N Main (533-5759). Pioneer artifacts include clothes and vehicles, looked after by ladies every bit as formidable as those in the photographs. Closed Sun, free.

Great Salt Lake: About 20 miles west on Interstate 80 (533-4080). Formerly part of Lake Bonneville, its high salt content makes swimming a buoyant experience.

The Zephyr departs Salt Lake City on Union Pacific tracks, having parted company with coaches of the Desert Wind (which continue to Los Angeles). After touching the edge of the Great Salt Lake the Zephyr crosses Bonneville Salt Flats.
   The run between here and Elko is Amtrak's longest without a scheduled halt. As you pass from Mountain to Pacific Time, watches go back an hour (forward when travelling east).

ELKO (250/120)

Now a base for the region's sheep and cattle ranches, Elko was once a stop for wagon trains on the Humboldt River Overland Trail. Each spring it holds the world championship chariot races. The Ruby Mountains are to your left.

WINNEMUCCA (120/165)

The town changed its name from French Ford to that of a Paiute chief. Formerly a trading post where wagons crossed the Humboldt, it's today a distribution point for agriculture and livestock. In 1900 Butch Cassidy's gang robbed Winnemucca's First National Bank, full of cash for local gold and silver mines.

Your train changes to Southern Pacific tracks then follows the Humboldt River. The Trinity Range is on the right, with the Humboldt Mountains left.

Fernley (140/25)

The Truckee River joins on the right as you begin tracing it back to the High Sierras.

Mustang Ranch (145/20)

Nevada's best-known little whorehouse appears on the right.

SPARKS (165/10)

The Zephyr takes a servicing stop at this railroad town, a major distribution centre since the introduction of Nevada's tax-free warehousing scheme. On your right is the Nugget casino. Pyramid Lake bird sanctuary, famous for pelicans, is 30 miles north.

As you leave Sparks and approach Reno look left for MGM's Grand Hotel, boasting the world's largest casino.

RENO (10/50)

'The biggest little city in the world' tries hard to be Las Vegas but can't quite lose its charm. What began as a Mormon settlement became more riotous when silver was discovered. Gambling became legal in 1931 and Reno started accumulating the neon-clad casinos and hotels that draw fun seekers to Virginia Street, near Amtrak's Spanish-style station at 135 E Commercial Row. Ticket office open 0710-1830.

If you plan to gamble or want to see what goes on behind the mirrors, take a Learn to Win tour from next to the visitors bureau at 135 N Sierra (329-3558). Harrah's Hotel has the world's biggest collection of antique cars and the Liberty Belle Saloon features old slot machines. *Bonanza's* Ponderosa ranch is nearby, with Lake Tahoe 35 miles southwest.

Leave with the dome of St Thomas Aquinas Catholic Church a calming presence on your left and continue through ranch country into Tahoe National Forest. You cross the Sierra Nevada, which climb to 7,000ft. Gold prospectors followed this route and it's a remarkable feat of rail construction. On weekends (daily during summer) a guide from the California Railroad Museum rides this train across the Sierras to describe sights en route.

Nevada/California State Line (20/35)
Look for a marker on the right. Wooden flumes on cliffs to the left are relics of the mining industry.

Floriston (30/20)
A yellow mansion can be seen on the left.

Boca (40/10)
A small dam to your right is all that remains of the town drowned beneath a reservoir. Boca formerly earned its living supplying ice to San Francisco.

TRUCKEE (50/125)
A holiday place on the banks of the Truckee River, this is the gateway to Lake Tahoe and numerous ski resorts. It was originally a logging town named after Paiute Winnemucca's father, Chief Tro-Kay. Chaplin filmed some of the wooden buildings on Main Street for *The Gold Rush*. Tourist information: 800-548-8388. Amtrak's station is at Railroad and Commercial Row.

After Truckee you start to ascend the Donner Pass in a sequence of horseshoe curves.

Donner Lake (15/110)
In 1846, blizzards here trapped 89 Illinois settlers travelling to California. Half froze to death or died of starvation and some were reduced to cannibalism. The lake is now a vacation area.

Mount Judah (25/100)
As you near Judah's summit the slopes of Sugar Bowl ski resort feature on both sides of the track, joined by an overhead chairlift.

Your train enters a tunnel through Mount Judah, named after the Central Pacific's Theodore Judah.

Norden (35/90)
Snowfall averages 34ft a year so building and maintaining this track is quite an achievement. Trains are often able to run when the nearby interstate highway stays blocked.

Soda Springs (40/85)
Lake Van Norden and the Soda Springs ski resort are on the left. On the other side of the valley to the right is Castle Peak, shaped like a fortress. Beside it is Black Butte Mountain (8,030ft).

Emigrant Gap (65/60)
Lake Spalding is on the right amid Alpine scenery.

Blue Canyon (70/55)
Once this was a hectic gold rush town.

American River Canyon (90/35)
Great views to your left as the Zephyr inches along cliffs 2,000ft above the

North Fork of the American River. Remains of gold mine workings can be seen opposite, and this valley stretches to Sacramento.

Alta (100/25)
Look for a red fire station on the right. Flumes built by gold miners are used to carry water to farms below the Sierras.

Gold Run (105/20)
The old post office is on your left. Until it became illegal in 1884, hydraulic gold mining washed away enormous areas of hillside. The Zephyr's tracks run along the original mine site.

COLFAX (125/60)
During the gold rush goods were brought to Colfax by mule for transfer to the mountains. Bartlett pears, Tokay grapes and Hungarian prunes now grow here. You continue down the western side of the Sierra Nevada (snowy mountains).

Auburn (25/35)
After they discovered gold at Coloma just to the south of here, Auburn supplied the camps and administered claims. Among several preserved buildings is an 1893 fire-house on the right, which had the first volunteer fire department west of Boston. Outlaws were publicly hanged in the grounds of the gold-domed Placer County court-house to your right.

Going east the train takes a different route through Auburn, letting you see more of the historic town. This includes a second (1891) firehouse topped by a red and white bell-tower.

As you leave, the town cemetery is seen on a hill to the right before you descend through less mountainous landscape to enter the fields, ranches and orchards of the Sacramento Valley.

ROSEVILLE (60/25)
The Zephyr picks its way through the complexities of Southern Pacific's rail yards.

McClellan Air Force Base (10/15)
On the right.

Approaching Sacramento, both sides of the track are engulfed by the Blue Diamond Almond Company. California produces two million tons of almonds a year and most of them get processed here.

SACRAMENTO (25/20)
For Sacramento and the rest of the California Zephyr's route to San Francisco, see *The Coast Starlight*. The Zephyr makes a stop at Suisun-Fairfield.

3 The Desert Wind

Chicago—Los Angeles

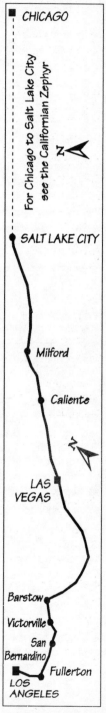

After following the California Zephyr route between Chicago and Salt Lake City, taking in Denver and the Rockies, the Desert Wind heads southwest on a further 800-mile journey to Los Angeles. As its name implies, this train travels partly through desert: your chance to sample this strange and wonderful country in comfort, along with the strange and wonderful Las Vegas.

Frequency: Daily. The westbound service leaves Chicago mid-afternoon to arrive in Omaha late evening and Denver early next morning. You reach Salt Lake City late on the second day, Las Vegas the following morning and Los Angeles by mid-afternoon.

Travelling east, trains leave Los Angeles at midday to arrive in Las Vegas early evening. You reach Salt Lake City early next morning, Denver mid-evening and Omaha early on the third day, arriving in Chicago late afternoon.

Reservations: All reserved.

Equipment: Superliner coaches.

Sleeping: Superliner economy, de luxe, family, special bedrooms.

Food: Complete meals, snacks, sandwiches, drinks.

Lounge Car: Video movies, games, hospitality hour.

Baggage: Check-in service at major cities.

CHICAGO
For Chicago and the route to Salt Lake City, see *The California Zephyr*.

SALT LAKE CITY
Having parted company with the Zephyr, the Desert Wind leaves Salt Lake City and travels past the Great Salt Lake. Every year 100,000 tons of salt are extracted from what was a pre-historic sea.

You continue into the night through Delta, a modest agricultural town on the edge of the Escalante Desert. Alfalfa seed is the local speciality.

MILFORD (180/120)
A railroad town for over a century, and a stop which gives access to six national parks, plus the resorts of Glen Canyon and Lake Powell. Indians discovered snowflake obsidian here for use as arrowheads.

Utah/Nevada State Line (90/30)
En route to Caliente you pass from Mountain to Pacific Time, so watches go back an hour (forward when travelling east).

CALIENTE (120/150)
As its Spanish name suggests, this town has hot springs and therapeutic mud baths. It plans to use geothermal energy to generate electricity and heat homes. Amtrak is at 100 Depot Ave, with its waiting room open 24 hours. Cathedral Gorge State Park is a few miles north.

You enter Rainbow Canyon for 26 miles along the Meadow Valley Wash, flowing into Lake Mead. Look for more rock formations and eight tunnels. The Wash is fed by streams which once provided water for steam trains.

Moapa (75/75)
One of the region's few towns, which produces tomatoes, melons and the famous alfalfa. On the left is a coal-burning Nevada Power station. The Sheep Range to the right is a sanctuary for mountain sheep.

After crossing the Muddy River you start to approach Las Vegas. The Spring Mountains are on the right, with Charlotte Peak (11,918ft) still covered in snow until mid-summer. Travelling north on the Desert Wind you get exceptional views of the neon light show of Las Vegas.

LAS VEGAS (150/190)
The 'entertainment capital of the world' was a Mormon settlement which failed. Today it's a 24-hour city where you can lose all your money or leave as a millionaire. You might take an even bigger gamble and get married, day or night, at one of the chapels.

In 1931 work on Hoover Dam started and gambling was legalised in Nevada. The boom began in Las Vegas, being closest to Los Angeles, accelerating when the big hotels and casinos arrived after the war. Half a million people now dedicate themselves to giving you a good time while parting you from your cash.

Summer temperatures reach over 120°F and annual rainfall is only four inches. Spring and autumn are the most comfortable times to visit.

Transport: Amtrak's station is at 1 Main inside the Union Plaza Hotel, built by the Union Pacific on the site of its original depot. You step virtually straight from the train into an inferno of slot machines. Ticket office and waiting room open 0600-2030. Information: 386-6896. Lockers, vending machines, luggage trolleys, restaurants, shops, taxi stand.

The only bus service you are likely to use (No 6) runs between downtown and the Strip (384-3540). It's inexpensive, frequent and spectacular at night. *Taxis:* Checker (873-2227) and Western (382-7100).
Greyhound: Next to the Union Plaza downtown and the Stardust Hotel on the Strip (382-2640).

McCarran Airport is near the southern end of the Strip.

Tours: For Las Vegas, Hoover Dam, Death Valley and the Grand Canyon contact Gray Line (384-1234) or Las Vegas Airlines (647-3056).

Visitors Bureau: 3150 Paradise Rd (733-2471). Open weekdays.

Telephone Code: 702.

Accommodation: Las Vegas has over 50,000 rooms but it pays to book ahead. Prices tend to be half those elsewhere in the US (especially just before Christmas) with drinks, hotels and food even better value downtown. Look for package deals at the big casinos.
AYH Hostel: 1236 Las Vegas Blvd (382-8119). Members $9, non-members $11.
Independent Hostel: 1208 Las Vegas Blvd (385-9955). AYH members $8, non-members $10.

Hotels downtown include the Four Queens at 202 E Fremont (385-4011); Fremont, 200 E Fremont (385-3232); Showboat, 2800 E Fremont (385-9123); El Cortez, E Fremont (385-5200) — singles and doubles $22.

Places on the Strip include the Dunes at 3650 Las Vegas Blvd (737-4110); Holiday Inn, 3475 Las Vegas Blvd (369-5000); Imperial Inn, 3265 Las Vegas Blvd (735-5102); Stardust, 3000 Las Vegas Blvd (732-6441) — Sun-Thurs $25, Fri-Sat $38.

Entertainment: Big names appear at the downtown Golden Nugget and at major hotels on the Strip. Particularly lavish shows take place at Caesar's, the Hilton and Bally's, and acts perform free all day at Circus Circus. You must be aged over 21 to gamble. The odds are said to be better downtown but the Strip is more exciting. You should set a limit to the amount you are prepared to lose and stick to it. Beware of free alcoholic drinks. Worth a visit is the Liberace Museum at 1775 E Tropicana Ave (798-5595). A glitter of costumes, cars and pianos. Open daily, donation.

Hoover Dam: 30 miles east (293-1081). Formerly known as Boulder Dam, this 726ft-high structure (the highest concrete dam in the US) created Lake Mead out of the Colorado River. A guided tour includes the internal mechanics. Open daily, admission.

Death Valley: Located 145 miles northwest is one of the hottest places in

America (786-2331). Temperatures of 120°F can be a killer, so it's best to go on an organised tour in air-conditioned transport. LTR Stage Lines (384-1230) operates September-May.

Valley of Fire: An hour's drive 55 miles northeast through the desert, this open air museum has Indian rock carvings 50,000 years old (397-2088). Open daily, free.

The Strip's array of hotels and casinos can be seen on your left as the train leaves Las Vegas and heads southwest towards the Mojave desert. Look for purple sage and spiny yucca plants.

Jean (30/160)
Wind yachts use the dry lake between here and Nipton as a racetrack. During storms the lake may flood to a depth of one foot.

Nevada/California State Line (40/150)
Cross near the small town of Nipton with the New York Mountains on the left and the Ivanpah Range, where gold and silver mines have reopened, on the right. As the Desert Wind gains altitude watch for giant Joshua trees, some over 30ft tall, and creosote or greasewood bushes. Rattlesnakes such as the deadly Mojave green are known to live here.

Cima Hill (60/130)
Part of the Providence Mountains and reaching 4,400ft. The eerily drifting Devil's Playground sand dunes stretch for five miles on your right.

Kelso (80/110)
Founded during the 19th Century to cater for wagon trains using trails crossing hills to your right. The cemetery on your left is for the descendants of Indians. Before dining cars came in, the Kelso hotel and restaurant were rest stops for rail passengers. Over the next few miles look for trees planted alongside the track to keep back encroaching sand. Cattle are successfully ranched here despite the meagre vegetation and water shortages.

Baker (110/80)
Across dry Soda Lake to your right is the start of Death Valley, where the altitude is below sea level and temperatures can top 130°F.

Afton Canyon (145/45)
Colourful rocks run for seven miles along the route of the underground Mojave River.

Yermo (160/30)
The train enters Union Pacific yards before changing to the Atchison, Topeka & Santa Fe line beyond Daggett.

Calico (172/18)
This ghost town is in hills to the right. Now restored, the site of California's biggest silver strike at the turn of the century gives a taste of the old West. An archaeological site has remains more than 2,000 years old. Avoid Calico in March unless you are looking for the world tobacco spitting championship.

Solar ONE (175/15)
The solar energy plant on your left appeared in the film *Bagdad Cafe*. Hundreds of mirrors direct the sun's rays on to a water tower 3,000ft high, producing steam to generate electricity.

Daggett (180/10)
Another pioneer plant on the left makes electricity by coal gasification. The Stone Hotel to your right is a hundred years old and beside it is Scotts Market, where miners traded gold and silver nuggets for dollars. After a 1908 fire the market was rebuilt from flameproof materials.

Marine Corps Logistics Base (185/5)
This is one of America's biggest military installations. Approaching Barstow, note the railroad cars converted into shops and restaurants on the left.

BARSTOW (190/35)
Capital of the Mojave. Barstow began as a station on the Santa Fe Trail and later became a railroad town. On the right is one of the few surviving Harvey House buildings, Casa del Desierto (house of the desert). Fred Harvey built a chain of restaurants and hotels in the 19th Century to service the new railway, and Judy Garland made their waitresses immortal in *The Harvey Girls*. Barstow is a tourist centre, with military bases and NASA's Goldstone satellite station nearby. Amtrak Thruway buses link with Mojave and Bakersfield.

Leaving North Street station, the Desert Wind travels through a complex of Santa Fe yards before setting out for the San Bernardino Mountains.

Edwards Air Force Base (15/20)
Beyond the Kramer Mountains to your right is a landing site for the NASA space shuttle.

Oro Grande (25/10)
Rightwood Mountain and several cement processing plants are on the left.

VICTORVILLE (35/65)
Cross the Mojave River, which runs 20ft below ground causing quicksand. Another cement plant is off to the right.

You start a long climb among impressive rocks and Joshua trees to Cajon Pass (Spanish for 'box canyon'), which the Union Pacific and Southern Pacific railroads also use to get to Los Angeles from the east. At their highest the tracks reach more than 3,800ft, travelling a border created by the San Andreas fault between the San Bernardino and San Gabriel Mountains. The fault is visible as a blue line on the hills. Stunning rock forms appear on both sides as the train begins a twisting 2,743ft descent towards San Bernardino, where desert scenes give way to palm trees.

SAN BERNARDINO (65/70)
The handsome grounds and station on the right at 1170 W 3rd are in Spanish mission style. Ticket office open 0500-2230. Other Spanish buildings blend with modern architecture and the heritage of Mormon settlers who came from Salt Lake City a hundred years ago. The McDonald brothers opened their first hamburger stand here in the 1930s, on their way to a fast food empire. The citrus fruit industry dates from the first navel orange crop grown in 1873. On your left is south California's highest peak, Mount San Gorgonio (11,502ft).

Riverside (20/50)
Home of March air force base. The town is part of an inexorable Los Angeles expansion.

Santa Ana Mountains (45/25)
You travel through a canyon formed by the Santa Ana River on your left. Prado Dam at the head of the canyon controls flooding.

Yorba Linda (50/20)
Birthplace of Richard Nixon, where the modest house built by his Quaker father stands next to a $21 million library. Despite Watergate, Orange County celebrates Richard Nixon Day.

FULLERTON (70/35)
The restored Santa Fe station's pink stucco and red tiles are seen on the right at 120 E Santa Fe Ave (open 0615-2300). Close by is the grand Union Pacific depot, moved to this site and now a restaurant. A Donald Duck citrus juice plant features on the right. Fullerton is a suburban stop as well as the station for Disneyland, the Movieland Wax Museum and Knott's Berry Farm. For details of these attractions, see *The San Diegans*.

From here to Los Angeles you pass through residential and industrial suburbs of Los Angeles County.

Santa Fe Springs (10/25)
Oil wells, tanks and derricks feature on both sides.

Redondo Junction (25/10)
In the yards and roundhouse on your left Amtrak superliners are set up for the Coast Starlight, Sunset Limited, Southwest Chief and Desert Wind.

Los Angeles River (30/5)
You accompany the concrete channel on your right. Designed for flood control and normally dry, it's been the scene of a hundred movie chases.

As the Desert Wind nears Los Angeles, City Hall's white tower dominates the skyline to your right.

LOS ANGELES
For Los Angeles, see *The Coast Starlight*.

4 The Pioneer

Chicago—Seattle

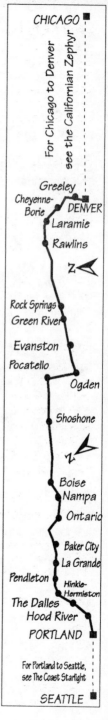

CHICAGO ■

For Chicago to Denver
see the Californian Zephyr

Greeley
Cheyenne-
Borie
Laramie
DENVER
Rawlins

Z

Rock Springs
Green River
Evanston
Pocatello
Ogden

Shoshone

Z

Boise
Nampa
Ontario

Baker City
La Grande
Pendleton
Hinkle-
Hermiston
The Dalles
Hood River
PORTLAND ■

For Portland to Seattle,
see The Coast Starlight

SEATTLE ■

After accompanying the California Zephyr and Desert Wind from Chicago to Denver, the Pioneer heads northwest via Wyoming and the continental divide. It takes in snow-covered mountains, the Columbia River gorge, and the cities of Portland and Seattle.

The Pioneer travels on part of the Overland Route, named after the trail and stage-coach line which preceded the railroad across country. The first premier passenger train on this line was the Pioneer Limited.

Frequency: The westbound service leaves Chicago mid-afternoon to arrive in Omaha late evening, Denver early next morning and Ogden mid-evening. You reach Boise during the night, Portland early afternoon and Seattle early evening.

Travelling east, trains leave Seattle early morning to arrive in Portland at midday and Boise towards midnight. You reach Ogden early next morning, Denver mid-evening and Omaha early on the third day, arriving in Chicago late afternoon.

Reservations: All reserved.

Equipment: Superliner coaches.

Sleeping: Superliner economy, de luxe, family, special bedrooms.

Food: Complete meals, snacks, sandwiches, drinks.

Lounge Car: Video movies, games.

Baggage: Check-in service at major cities.

CHICAGO
For Chicago and the route to Denver, see *The California Zephyr*.

DENVER
Your train parts company here with the California Zephyr and Desert Wind, which continue to Salt Lake City. The Pioneer leaves via freight yards and goes north towards Wyoming. You travel through industrial scenes at Pullman, Commerce City and Rolla, then accompany US 85 as far as Eaton.

  Approaching Lupton look for sugar processing plants, a steel mill and large greenhouses.

Lupton (22/33)
The Wattenberg oil and gas field is nearby.

Fort Vasquez (30/25)
Named after the first European to visit the site of Denver. Look for a reproduction of the frontier trading post on your left.

La Salle (43/12)
Fort St Vrain nuclear power plant is visible to the south, along with the Front Range of the Rockies. You continue through a region famous for sugar, potatoes and livestock.

Evans (50/5)
Named after Colorado governor John Evans, who was head of the Denver Pacific Railway. The DP joined forces with the Kansas Pacific (of Buffalo Bill fame) and both later merged into the Union Pacific.

GREELEY (55/40)
Publisher and abolitionist Horace Greeley followed his own advice to 'Go west young man!' by sponsoring this town in 1870. Situated on the Cache la Poudre River, Greeley is home to Northern Colorado University.

  Just past town is Greeley Junction, where a Union Pacific branch line heads east to Mathews.

Eaton (8/32)
Named after another governor of the state.

  The Pioneer continues along Lone Tree Creek valley, crossing the creek twice on the way to Borie. After Speer you travel west along the Borie Cutoff.

BORIE-CHEYENNE (40/55)
Amtrak's Cheyenne station is in Borie, with Thruway bus connections to Wyoming's capital and largest city. When the Union Pacific reached here a town was dismantled and brought by train from Julesburg, Nebraska. For a few months it filled with construction workers, saloons, gambling and prostitutes before the action moved on to Laramie. In 1868 the Denver Pacific arrived from Denver. Cheyenne's Romanesque station, designed by Henry Richardson in 1886, celebrates the days when this was a shipping point for eastbound beef. Cheyenne visitors bureau: 301 W 16th (778-1401).

Two Union Pacific steam locos operate main line excursions from a base in Cheyenne's roundhouse. Other steam locos can be seen at the roundhouse, and Holliday Park has an example of the world's largest, a Union Pacific *Big Boy*. Built in 1941 for the Cheyenne to Ogden run, it's 132ft long and had completed half a million miles before being retired in 1958.

Gold finds in the Black Hills to the north made Cheyenne merchants rich, and this wealth attracted outlaws such as 'Big Nose' George Parrott, Sam Bass and the James brothers. July's Frontier Days carnival relives wild west exploits.

The Pioneer continues along the Harriman Cutoff via Emkay. Trains travelling east use an older line which goes through Granite and Buford before rejoining the newer one at Dale Junction.

You pass through Hermosa Tunnel (1,800ft), the first bore of which was made in 1901, followed by another in 1918.

Tracks again separate to tackle the gradients of Sherman Hill, rejoining just before Laramie.

Sherman Hill (40/15)
This is the highest point on the line (8,015ft) but the original track, now abandoned, reached 8,242ft.

Approaching Laramie look for a Union Pacific welding plant on your left, producing quarter-mile sections of continuous rail. This has largely removed the 'clickety-clack' sound from American main lines.

LARAMIE (55/110)
The state's third largest city was named after a French fur trapper, Jacques LaRamie, and is located between the Laramie Mountains to the east and the Medicine Bow Range to the west. Greville Hodge, chief engineer on the Union Pacific, laid out the city in 1868 when a railway maintenance facility was established.

From Laramie's foundation until 1939 armies of 'tie-hacks' cut railroad ties (sleepers) in the surrounding mountains. Machinery replaced the hacks but ties and lumber are still produced. Laramie's 1872 prison, which once held Butch Cassidy, is part of a recreated end-of-the-tracks town.

Leave and accompany the Laramie River to your left, crossing near Bosler. Rock Creek oil field is to the south. You continue through a region mainly dedicated to livestock.

Wilcox (40/70)
The Hole in the Wall Gang robbed the Union Pacific's Overland Limited here on June 2 1899, an event retold in the film *Butch Cassidy and the Sundance Kid*. The gang dynamited $30,000 from a safe and made for the hills.

Ridge (50/60)
On your right is Como Bluff dinosaur graveyard, a rich source of fossils. The museum was built from dinosaur bones.

Medicine Bow (60/50)
A setting for Owen Wister's classic Western novel *The Virginian*.

Como (70/40)
The Pioneer crosses a small lake fed by warm springs.

Hanna (82/28)
This is the centre of a coal mining area. To the left is Elk Mountain (11,162ft), the most northern peak of the Medicine Bow Range. St Mary's Peak is on the right.

Continue via Percy and Walcott, where a branch line ran south to the former copper mines of Encampment.

Fort Steele (99/11)
The fort's remains are on your left near the Platte River crossing. The Rattlesnake Hills are to your right.

Sinclair (102/8)
This has been an oil company town since 1923. To the north is the Hole in the Wall canyon used by Butch Cassidy's gang. Also in the north distance are the Seminoe and Ferris Mountains.

RAWLINS (110/100)
Named after John Rawlins, who was General Grant's chief of staff during the Civil War. Like Cheyenne and Laramie, Rawlins was founded to build the Union Pacific. It's still an important transport centre, with a UP fuelling station connected by pipeline to Sinclair's refinery. The granite and brick depot replaced an original wooden building in 1901, when the notorious Wyoming State Penitentiary was also completed. During the Old Pen's 80 years as a prison 22 men were killed, riots were frequent and unruly inmates suffered in 'the hole'.

Soon after Rawlins you cross the continental divide at Creston (7,107ft), shown by a marker on the left. This is the second highest point on the Pioneer's route.

As you descend look right for the Red Desert, one of the world's largest areas of sand, where antelope live among the dunes.

Point of Rocks (75/25)
This oddly shaped sandstone formation is on your left, with the abandoned Seymore Mine and a ghost town to your right.

Continue through sparsely populated desert a mile above sea level, where wild animals such as antelope, deer and moose outnumber humans.

ROCK SPRINGS (100/14)
An Overland Stage stop for six years before the railroad came in 1868. Wyoming's fourth largest city was named after saline springs which ran dry when mining began to provide coal for steam trains. Low sulphur coal remains an important industry.

Nearing Green River look right for Sunset Rock, which receives the last reflection of sunset. On your left are Pulpit Rock (shaped like a giant lectern) and Kissing Rocks (two kissing faces).

GREEN RIVER (14/90)

'Trona capital of the world', where a quarter of the world's soda salt is produced. Many buildings date from the 1870s and some are made from adobe. The attractive station was completed in 1910. Man's Face Rock is beyond the depot to the left, with Castle Rock on the right. More rocks feature on both sides as you leave and cross the Green River.

Continue via Fish Cut to Peru, where helper locomotives assisted steam trains, then on to Burning Rocks Cut. Gilbert Peak (13,422ft) dominates the Uintah Mountains to the right.

Granger (40/50)

Where the Black's Fork and Ham's Fork Rivers meet. Granger was a stop for stage-coaches and the pony express before the railroad came. In 1881 the Oregon Short Line opened north from here to Boise, Portland and Seattle.

Your train crosses the Black's Fork River soon after leaving town, then Muddy Creek five times before Carter.

You travel through Aspen and Altamont tunnels, emerging from the Great Divide Basin's western rim to descend along the Bear River valley. Aspen tunnel was the Union Pacific's longest (5,941ft) until the Altamont tunnel (6,706ft) opened in 1949.

Approaching Evanston you pass Wyoming State Mental Hospital on a hill to your left.

EVANSTON (90/100)

The Overthrust Belt, rich in oil and minerals, is directly beneath the city. Oil storage facilities adjoin the track.

The Pioneer climbs 10 miles to crest the Wasatch Mountains at a height of 6,800ft, and between here and Ogden the descent is 2,500ft in 65 miles.

You travel through the Curvo tunnels into Echo Canyon, a stretch of track with spectacular formations such as Cathedral Rock and Steamboat Rock. Canyon walls rise a thousand feet as the line parallels Echo Creek.

Cross the Weber River in a region producing red fire clay, wool and livestock. Devil's Slide Rock is on the right. Strawberry Observation Peak (9,765ft) can be seen to the north as you proceed along the Weber Canyon, going through Round Valley and Sheep Rock tunnels. Electrified fencing beside the track is linked to signals to warn of rock slides.

The train leaves Weber Canyon and the Wasatch Range just before Uintah to enter the Great Basin — a vast depression which was once the inland sea of Lake Bonneville.

OGDEN (100/80)

A Mormon town laid out by Brigham Young in the 19th Century, Ogden grew as a Union Pacific junction. On May 10 1869 the Union Pacific and Central Pacific connected at nearby Promontory Point, creating the first transcontinental rail route. The Golden Spike Historic Site replicates the ceremony with life-size working models of the original locomotives. Open all year, free.

Ogden's Mediterranean-style Union Station was built in 1924 after fire destroyed its predecessor. Restored in 1978, it has museums and galleries with cars, firearms, art and railroad memorabilia. Amtrak buses connect to Salt Lake City.

POCATELLO (80/90)
Named after an Indian chief, Pocatello is the home of Idaho State University.

SHOSHONE (90/125)
A trading centre in one of the driest parts of the state, with not far away the Shoshone Ice and Mammoth Caves and the winter resort of Sun Valley (former home of Ernest Hemingway). Twin Falls is 20 miles south.

BOISE (125/40)
The capital of Idaho is situated on the Boise River, where prospectors found gold in 1861. A fort protected the Oregon Trail from Indians before the railway came, the city having been bypassed until 1887 because of a dispute with the Oregon Short Line Railroad. On your right is the beautifully preserved Spanish mission-style station at 1701 Eastover Terrace. Open 0600-1400 and 2130-2245 (Thu-Sun) and 0600-2300 (Mon-Wed).

Also on the right, down Capitol Blvd, is the Capitol building. The State Historical Museum is at 610 Julia Davis Drive. For tourist information call 334-2470.

After Boise your train proceeds carefully towards Nampa and the main Union Pacific line.

NAMPA (40/35)
Founded as a railroad town in 1885, it was named after Shoshone Chief Nampuh (Big Foot). In 1903 a fire broke out on the day wooden water mains were being replaced, destroying most of Nampa's business district. The town is surrounded by desert but wells and irrigation permit the growing of fruit and potatoes.

As you leave, note the irrigated fields to your right and distant mountains.

Idaho/Oregon State Line (30/5)
Cross the Snake River, rolling north towards Hells Canyon.

ONTARIO (35/110)
A trading and shipment centre for eastern Oregon's cattle ranchers and fruit growers.

The Pioneer again crosses the winding Snake River, briefly re-entering Idaho before returning to Oregon.

Payette River (6/104)
As you cross watch out for the many birds along its shores. The Snake River continues to your left as you travel on through rugged country.

Farewell Bend (20/90)
Mountains on each side reach a thousand feet as you enter a canyon of the Snake. Fences prevent encroachment of the track by sand dunes on the right.

Snake River (30/80)
Cross again, taking you from Idaho into Oregon. Changing from Mountain to Pacific Time, watches go back an hour (forward when travelling east).

Huntington (35/75)
The yard here was important during the age of steam trains, and the Pioneer pauses briefly to change crews.

Enter Burnt River valley and continue northeast after going through a long tunnel. A cement plant crowds both sides of the track.

Encina Pass (85/20)
The summit is 4,000ft above sea level, and as you descend into the Power River valley via a sequence of curves the whole train comes into view. Mount Dooley (5,392ft) is on the left.

BAKER CITY (110/60)
Ghost towns in the surrounding hills evoke the boom which followed a gold find in 1861. Hotel Antler, dating from 1912, is the white building in the middle of town on your right. Baker caters for cattle, wheat and lumber producers and is the focus of a recreation area. The Oregon Trail Regional Museum features fluorescent rocks.

The Pioneer now crosses a region of outstanding natural beauty, with Elkhorn Ridge and the Wallowa Forest on your left. The Wallowa Mountains and Eagle Cap Wilderness are to your right.

Haines (15/45)
Green-roofed buildings on the right shelter a hot artesian spring.

North Powder (25/35)
Cross Wolf Creek with the Wallowa Mountains still to your right. The Blue Mountains can be seen on the left as you pass the Powder River.

Union (45/15)
Look for geothermal springs on the right and Hot Lake resort to the left. Catherine Creek glides through the valley and Mount Prominence (6,725ft) is away on the right.

LA GRANDE (60/130)
Established in 1862, the town moved two miles to be next to the Oregon Railroad & Navigation Line, which arrived in 1884. This is the main shipping point for produce of the Grande Ronde River valley, a region of farms and ranches extending 25 miles. French-Canadian fur traders named this 'the great circle' in the 1820s and its lush landscape made a refreshing stop for pioneers on the Oregon Trail.

Amtrak's station is at Depot and Jefferson. Some older houses are preserved and City Hall is visible on the left. The airport is to the right. Visitors bureau: 1502 N Pine (963-8588).

After La Grande the Pioneer climbs laboriously into the Blue Mountains.

Kamela (45/85)

A watershed point which is 4,205ft above sea level. After cresting the summit the train begins its steepest descent on this part of the line. These hills and forested valleys are home to bears, rattlesnakes, deer and mountain lions. Watch also for herds of elk.

Meacham (55/75)

The original pioneer route came over the ridge on your left. The train pursues the Oregon Trail down to Pendleton, crossing the Umatilla River and Indian Reservation.

Gibbon (95/35)

Named after General John Gibbon, who was commander of the Union army's Iron Brigade.

PENDLETON (130/35)

The Pendleton Mills wool factory is to the right. As well as serving the lumber industry, the city processes wheat, fruit and vegetables. The McKennon Station Flour Mills and Grain Growers plant appears on the right. Amtrak is at S Main and Frazier. Round-Up week in September features bronco riding and stage-coach races at the rodeo grounds seen on your right.

You leave Pendleton and follow the Umatilla River.

HINKLE (35/85)

A modest station serves the neighbouring towns of Stanfield and Hermiston. The factory on your left makes vast quantities of potato products.

Progress through more farm and ranch country.

Umatilla (20/65)

The underground ammunition bunkers on the right are part of an army ordnance depot.

Heppner Junction (21/64)

Look right for your first glimpse of the Columbia River, which the Pioneer accompanies for 130 miles to Portland. All told, the river runs 1,200 miles from British Columbia to the Pacific. On the opposite shore is the state of Washington, and until 1812 this was the US/Canadian border.

John Day Dam (60/25)

Named after a Western scout, it's one of many dams on the Columbia, which generates a third of the country's hydroelectricity. A lock system can be seen across the river.

Stonehenge (62/23)

Also on the other side, to the right of a highway bridge, is a concrete replica of England's Stonehenge. It was erected as a memorial to First World War dead by Sam Hill, son-in-law of the rail tycoon Jim Hill.

Maryhill Museum (65/20)

On the far side, to the left of the bridge and half way up a mountain, is an art museum dedicated in the 1920s by the Queen of Romania. Sam Hill built the mansion on what had been a Quaker settlement.

Cross the Deschutes River. Volcanic Mount Hood (11,235ft) is on the right.

Dalles Dam (84/1)

To the right is one of the world's largest hydroelectric generators, constructed by army engineers. A train from Seufert Park in The Dalles will take you on a free tour of the plant.

THE DALLES (85/30)

A memorial marks where the Oregon Trail ended. This is a shipping centre, so look for wheat and lumber barges on the river. To your left is St Peter's Church with its red steeple, tigerwood organ and stained glass windows. Amtrak's station is at Liberty and Second.

Rowena Crest (5/25)

This impressive viewpoint is on the mountain to your right. Cherry orchards and curious rock formations appear as the train nears Mosier.

Memaloose Island (15/15)

An Indian burial ground on the island to the right has the grave of a trader who befriended local tribes.

Snow-capped Mount Adams (12,276ft) is in the distance as you cross the Hood River.

HOOD RIVER (30/90)

Where the Columbia, Hood and White Salmon Rivers meet. Amtrak's Empire Builder tracks are seen on the far side of the Columbia. The town of Hood River provides access to Multnomah National Forest in the south and Gifford Pinchot Forest to the north.

You continue through the Columbia Gorge's most striking section, as rain forest replaces the farmland of west Oregon.

Wyeth (20/70)

The windiest place in the state, where fruits and berries are grown to be packed in Hood River for shipment. The Cascade Mountains on your right are said to resemble an Indian resting on his back.

Cascade Locks (30/60)

These locks on the right bypassed the Cascade Falls in 1896. Walking trails such as the Pacific Crest start from here.

Bridge of the Gods (31/59)

A modern bridge to your right crosses the river on the site of a natural stone bridge, which Indians say was destroyed by volcanic eruptions.

Travellers' Tales
The Pioneer
William H Hughes

The trip from Seattle to Chicago took the better part of two days. Once out of the big city area and into the country the elevated seating area affords excellent sightseeing perspectives. Having lived in the West for years, I am still awed by the huge expanses and contrasts of the landscape.

Even in summer the air-conditioning is cool in the evenings. Blankets with the AMTRAK logo are available for purchase on the train, but they are quite small, so if an old blanket is lying around the house it's worth taking. Also, when choosing a seat immediately after boarding, checking the leg rest and seat reclining features can save a lot of heartache.

I soon noticed that most families came prepared for a long picnic. Many had coolers with soda, candy, chips and sandwiches. With kids that have to munch the entire trip it could become a bankrupting experience if purchases had to be made in the club car. However, everyone should take bottled water — not for sanitation but for taste. The water on the train is wretched.

Aside from the beautiful landscape, people watchers can especially enjoy this mode of travel. One couple in their thirties brought two portable Tvs, quickly changed into their matching jogging attire and settled down to an adventure of watching TV for the greater part of the journey.

After the first 12 hours of the journey, the chief attendant requested over the loud speaker that no one put any more paper towels in the toilets, as he had more to do than spend the entire trip unstopping toilets. This announcement was made almost every two to three hours — during the day. Evening seemed to bring rest to the toilets. Nevertheless, these requests were to continue all the way to Chicago, and each announcement brought a little more ire in the chief's voice. Although there are four or five toilets in the lower levels of each car, it seemed that two were constantly out of use.

I didn't try the dining car, so I can't comment on the service. However, I did frequent the club car which was like a fast food outlet. What they had to offer was fresh, hot and not too expensive. The top side of the club car was the observation car/lounge. In the evenings a movie was shown on the VCR, about 24 persons could be seated; however, a lot of neck stretching was necessary as the seats are directly behind each other.

The most humorous part of this leg occurred while crossing Minnesota. The club car ran out of sandwiches, and the chief attendant announced over the loudspeaker that while making the next stop he would pick up 250 Big Macs. He had called ahead and placed the order. The jubilation roared throughout the train. The last I saw of the Big Mac salesman was when he walked through the cars trying to sell the last five sandwiches.

Bonneville (35/55)

Bonneville Dam, built in 1938 at a cost of $88 million, is one of the Columbia's biggest. Note the locks for shipping and a fish ladder. Nearby Tanner Creek is Oregon's shortest river, flowing out of then back into the Columbia.

Beacon Rock (40/50)

On the right. At 800ft high it's the largest of its kind in America.

Horsetail Falls (41/49)
Seen to your left just before the small town of Larch Mountain.

Starvation Creek (42/48)
A canyon on the left extends 10 miles and is so narrow that sunlight never touches its floor.

Multnomah Falls (44/46)
On the left is the fourth highest falls in the country (620ft).

Bridal Veil (47/43)
Waterfalls resemble a white veil on the mountain to your left.

Rooster Rock (57/33)
This tall, thin spire of black volcanic rock is on your right.

Troutdale (60/30)
Look for filbert trees on the right and a bridge across the river.

   The train twists through east Portland, crossing the Willamette River on a steel bridge. The arches of Fremont Bridge are to the right and ocean-going ships can be seen on the water.

PORTLAND (90/30)
For Portland and the rest of the Pioneer's route to Seattle, see *The Coast Starlight*.

5 The San Joaquins

San Francisco/Oakland— Bakersfield

Fig trees, vineyards, date palms, orchards and oil wells — the San Joaquin valley is definitive California, with a heady mix of warmth and almond blossom.

Trains travel 300 miles between Oakland and Bakersfield, giving access to several national parks and some of the richest country in America.

Frequency: Three trains operate daily in both directions. Departure times are early morning, late morning and mid-afternoon, for a trip lasting six hours. Connecting buses link Oakland with San Francisco (25 minutes) and Bakersfield with Los Angeles (2½ hours).

An extensive Amtrak Thruway system operates in the Bay Area, the Sacramento valley and to Los Angeles. Trains and buses are funded by Amtrak and Caltrans — the California Department of Transportation — and are a good way to explore less visited parts of the state. Schedules are available from Amtrak agents or by post from Timetable, Caltrans, Division of Rail, PO Box 942874, Sacramento, CA 94274-0001.

Reservations: Unreserved.

Equipment: Horizon coaches.

Food: Tray meals, snacks, sandwiches, drinks.

Baggage: No check-in facilities.

Martinez
Antioch-Pittsburg
Berkeley
Stockton
River-bank
OAKLAND
SAN FRANCISCO
Turlock-Denair

N

Merced

Madera

Fresno

Hanford

Corcoran

Wasco

BAKERSFIELD

SAN FRANCISCO
For San Francisco, Oakland and the San Joaquin route to Martinez, see *The Coast Starlight*. San Joaquin trains stop at Berkeley.

MARTINEZ
As you leave you part company with California Zephyr and Coast Starlight tracks, which continue over a bridge to the left. Storage tanks and a Shell refinery appear on the right.

Mothball Fleet (12/10)
Across the bay on the left lies a fleet of merchant ships kept in 'mothballs'. Some date from the Second World War and many saw action in Vietnam. Between here and Antioch-Pittsburg, San Joaquin trains change from Southern Pacific tracks to those of the Santa Fe.

ANTIOCH-PITTSBURG (22/35)
Buses connect with Chico, Marysville, Sacramento and Stockton.
  You begin to escape the Bay Area. The Sacramento and San Joaquin Rivers converge on your left and you glimpse the deep-water channel uniting Stockton with San Francisco.

STOCKTON (35/25)
A setting for John Huston's *Fat City*, this inland port is a shipping and distribution centre 80 miles from the sea. Amtrak at 735 S San Joaquin opens 0830-2030. Thruway buses go north via Sacramento to Redding, gateway to Mount Shasta.
  Stockton's Magnolia District has many 19th Century houses and the Haggin Museum features paintings by Gaugin and Renoir. Visitors bureau: 46 W Fremont (800-841-4441).
  You leave and embark on typical wine country, where hundreds of vineyards supply local wineries.
  The train crosses the Stanislaus River.

RIVERBANK (25/15)
Used by river ferries during the 1880s gold rush, further development came with the Santa Fe Railroad. The attractive green and white station at 3243 Talbot Rd also serves neighbouring Modesto. Ticket office open 0800-2100.

Hetch Hetchy Aqueduct (3/12)
You cross the concrete-lined aqueduct which provides the Bay Area with water from the Sierra Nevada. You then cross the Tuolumne River.

TURLOCK-DENAIR (15/22)
The station is at Santa Fe Ave in Denair, though adjacent Turlock is considerably bigger. The Diablo Mountains appear distantly to your right.
  As you cross the Merced River look for almond trees on both sides — exceptional during late winter.

Atwater (15/7)

Note the preserved Second World War planes at an air base on the left.
 As you approach Merced the town's 1875 court-house is on your right.

MERCED (22/30)

The Court-house Museum dominates the main square. Built in renaissance style and now restored, it has a figure of Justice perched on the cupola. Amtrak's station at 324 W 24th opens 0700-2145.
 Buses take you east to one of America's great experiences, Yosemite National Park. Despite the occasional fire this remains a favoured destination, with attractions such as El Capitan (a granite dome twice as high as Gibraltar) and Yosemite Falls (2,425ft). The visitors centre (209-372-4461) opens daily, or you can write to the Information Office, Box 577, Yosemite NP, CA 95389. Late spring and early summer are best if you want to miss the crowds.
 Leave Merced with a Goodyear factory to your right.

Planada (5/25)

Ragged kadota fig trees grow on the left.
 The San Joaquin continues through some of America's most highly productive land, where specialities include figs, pistachio nuts and grapes. Back on your left you see the Sierra Nevada's Cathedral Mountains (13,000ft) before the train crosses the Fresno River.

MADERA (30/25)

This is an important farming town.

San Joaquin River (10/15)

You cross with a golf course to the right.

Fresno State College (20/5)

Look right for the college campus. As you enter Fresno you see a chubby water-tower on your right, near the Santa Fe Railroad offices.

FRESNO (25/30)

The 'raisin capital of the world', where Sunmaid has a huge packing facility. Grapes grown to the south mostly turn into raisins, while those grown further north become wine. The Meux Mansion at Tulare and R (near the station) is an ornate Victorian house built for a doctor.
 Fresno's station at 2650 Tulare (open 0700-2130) is Amtrak's nearest stop for Sequoia and King's Canyon National Parks in south Nevada. These have mountains, caves, and sequoia trees — the largest living things in the world — and are not so crowded as Yosemite. For information write to Sequoia and King's Canyon NP, Three Rivers, CA 93271, or the National Park Service, Fort Mason, Building 201, San Francisco, CA 94123 (415-556-0560).
 You leave with the water tower of Sunmaid's old plant on the right and continue among vineyards, then cross the Kings River.

HANFORD (30/20)

Named after James Hanford, a Southern Pacific paymaster who sometimes paid employees in gold. It's an important stop on the route between San Francisco and Los Angeles. Hundreds of Chinese came here to work on the railroad, leaving behind a Taoist temple on China Alley. You can visit the neo-classical court-house and the Court-house Square jail, now a restaurant, resembles the Paris Bastille. Amtrak's station at 432 W 7th opens 0645-1830 and 2000-2145. Buses connect to Visalia, the central valley's first settlement.

San Joaquin trains continue through a flat land of orchards and vineyards.

CORCORAN (20/25)

Look for a cotton gin facility to the right. Amtrak's station is at Whitley and Otis Ave.

Allensworth Park (10/15)

Seen on the right, this is the centre of the Tulare Lake region.

WASCO (25/22)

Another major farming town.

Shafter (2/20)

Look out for grapes and almond trees.

From here on you pass through Kern County oil field, with pumps operating on both sides of the track. The biggest refinery is to your left as you near Bakersfield, and a few minutes from this final destination you cross a canal before entering the Santa Fe rail yards. An old roundhouse is on your right.

BAKERSFIELD

Home of country music's Merle Haggard and Glen Campbell, the town's economy grew rapidly when oil was discovered at the turn of the century. Kern County Museum and Pioneer Village has more than 50 authentic buildings. The station at 1501 F opens 0530-2230. Amtrak buses link with various points in the Los Angeles area, as well as with trains from Los Angeles to San Diego.

6 **The San Diegans**

Los Angeles—San Diego

LOS ANGELES

For Los Angeles to Fullerton see The Desert Wind

Fullerton

Anaheim

Santa Ana

San Juan Capistrano

Oceanside

Del Mar

SAN DIEGO

This is one of Amtrak's busiest routes. The San Diegans run between two expanding cities, serving a burgeoning population along the way, and for part of this journey they hug the Pacific shoreline. Other pleasures include Disneyland, San Juan Capistrano and the Tijuana Trolley.

Frequency: Departures about every two hours in both directions from early morning until late evening (eight daily round-trips, two trains continuing to Santa Barbara). The journey takes under three hours. Amtrak Thruway buses and some trains connect Los Angeles with Santa Barbara via the San Fernando valley.

Reservations: Unreserved.

Equipment: Amfleet coaches. Custom class available. Railfone.

Food: Snacks, sandwiches, drinks.

Baggage: Check-in service on some trains.

LOS ANGELES
For Los Angeles, see *The Coast Starlight*. For the route from Los Angeles to Fullerton, see *The Desert Wind*.

FULLERTON (32/9)
This is Amtrak's stop for three of California's main tourist venues.

Disneyland: 1313 Harbor Blvd, Anaheim (714-999-4565). Opened in 1955, it's been added to ever since. California's greatest tourist attraction includes Fantasyland, Frontierland (recreating the Wild West), and Splash Mountain (the world's longest flume ride).

Knott's Berry Farm: 8039 Beach Blvd, Buena Park (714-220-5200). This recreated ghost town has become a complex of shops, restaurants and a hundred rides. Highlights include Montezooma's Revenge (0-55mph in five seconds) and the Corkscrew (first upside-down roller coaster). Steam locos and equipment formerly belonging to the Denver & Rio Grande Western and Rio Grande Southern operate over a 36in-gauge track. Open daily. Train rides are included in the price of admission.

Movieland Wax Museum: 7711 Buena Park Blvd, just north of Knott's Berry Farm. It boasts over 200 images of such disparate stars as Clint Eastwood and George Burns. The Black Box allows you to participate in scenes from *Halloween* and *Alien*.
When leaving Fullerton you can just see Disneyland's replica Matterhorn to the right. As you approach Anaheim, the city's enormous stadium appears beyond the station on the right.

ANAHEIM (9/9)
One of the country's fastest-growing residential areas, Anaheim was founded by German settlers and former gold miners from San Francisco. Its name combines the nearby Santa Ana River with *heim*, German for home. The Rams (football) and California Angels (baseball) play home games at the stadium. An ultra-modern railway station at 2150 E Katella Ave opens 0630-2230.
Leave for another brief run to Santa Ana via Orange County, famous for Valencia oranges.

Orange (4/5)
Seen away to the right, with an old station featuring on the left.

SANTA ANA (9/20)
Both the restored downtown and new developments reflect traditional Spanish architecture. Amtrak's station at 1000 E Santa Ana Blvd opens 0630-2230.
As you leave look right for two hangars which accommodated air balloons during the Second World War. They now house US Marine helicopters. The Santa Ana Mountains can be seen to your left.

US Marine Corps (8/12)
The air base is on the left.

Irvine (10/10)
Irvine is a scheduled stop for some trains.

   You continue through a land of orange groves interrupted by occasional small towns.

SAN JUAN CAPISTRANO (20/30)
Amtrak's depot at 26701 Verdugo features a restaurant and jazz venue. The 1776 mission where Juanero Indians converted to Christianity was damaged by an earthquake, but part of the adobe building stands in neatly kept grounds to your left. The famous swallows leave in October, returning (fairly) punctually on March 19.

   Soon after San Juan Capistrano you join the Pacific Ocean to the right, staying alongside until Del Mar. Enviable houses cling to cliffs on the left.

San Clemente (10/20)
Served by some trains in both directions. Richard Nixon lived at Casa Pacifica when he was president, and the beach here is one of the California's most beautiful.

San Onofre Nuclear Plant (16/14)
This eerie presence is next to the beach on your right. The extra-warm water attracts heedless surfers.

Camp Pendleton (25/5)
One of many naval facilities to be found in this part of the state. Watch for yachts and pleasure boats in a marina on the right.

OCEANSIDE (30/17)
The transit centre at 235 S Tremont is shared by Amtrak and Greyhound. Ticket office open 0545-2315 (Mon-Fri) and 0630-2315 (weekends). Mission San Luis Rey is on nearby Mission Ave.

Carlsbad (5/12)
A military boys' school can be seen on the right. You continue past a massive power plant, also to the right.

Del Mar Racetrack (15/2)
Immediately on the left.

DEL MAR (17/30)
This conservative town has exclusive beach apartments. A hundred annual events take place at the fairgrounds, and the Thoroughbred Club meeting is a regular venue for Hollywood stars past and present.

   Your train moves away from the Pacific and travels through rugged country towards San Diego. Look for the celebrated Torrey Pines as you descend via Soledad and Rose Canyons.

University of San Diego (20/8)
The campus is on the left.

Lindbergh Airport (25/5)
Runways are to the right.

SAN DIEGO
California's oldest and third largest city has smog-free sunshine, Spanish architecture and an easy-going atmosphere. The Portuguese explorer Juan Cabrillo discovered this bay in 1542 but settlement began later with a garrison and California's first Spanish mission. San Diego became part of the USA in 1847. The Santa Fe Railroad later brought expansion and the city continues to grow.

Transport: The station at 1050 Kettner Blvd is a beautiful, spacious Spanish-style building in the older part of downtown, not far from the waterfront. It was constructed for passengers coming to the 1915 Panama-California Exposition. Information: 239-9021. Ticket office open 0445-2100 (Mon-Fri) and 0530-2100 (weekends). Waiting room 0445-2330. Luggage store, Red Caps, taxi stand.
  The city is easy to negotiate on foot or bicycle, and San Diego Transit buses operate a comprehensive service (233-3004). Day Tripper passes can be used on all SDT routes, the San Diego Trolley (running from the station to San Ysidro on the Mexican border) and the Bay Ferry from Broadway Pier to Coronado.
Greyhound: Broadway and First Ave (239-9171).
Taxis: Yellow (234-6161) and Checker (234-4477).
Car Rental: Aztec, 2401 Pacific Hwy (232-6117).
  Lindbergh Airport is three miles north of downtown by taxi and SDT bus No 2.

Tours: Harbour cruises are available from Invader (234-8687) and trips to Santa Catalina Island from California Cruising (235-8600).

Visitors Bureau: 2688 East Mission Bay Dr (276-8200) and 11 Horton Plaza (236-1212). Open daily. For the latest events call 234-2787.

Telephone Code: 619.

Accommodation: For apartments contact International Travellers Accommodation, 2309 Fifth Ave (233-0287).
Armed Services YMCA: 500 W Broadway (232-1133). Dormitory and other rooms, not just for the military. Singles $20, doubles $30.
YWCA: 1012 C (239-0355). Women only. Singles $18, doubles $30.
Elliott AYH Hostel: 3790 Udall, Point Loma (223-4778). Members $10, non-members $14.
Imperial Beach AYH Hostel: 170 Palm Ave (423-8039). Five miles from Mexico. Members $8, non-members $11.
  The nearest campsite is Campland On The Bay, 2211 Pacific Beach Dr (274-6260). Take bus No 30.

Hotels include the Travelodge Downtown at 840 Ash (800-255-3050); Churchill, 827 C (234-5186); Pickwick, 132 W Broadway (234-0144); Budget, 1835 Columbus Dr (800-544-0164); Golden West, 720 Fourth Ave (233-7596); Clarke's Flamingo Lodge, 1765 Union (234-6787) — singles $33, doubles $43.

Balboa Park: A thousand acres of gardens, trees and parkland with the world's biggest pipe organ. In 1935 the California-Pacific Exposition here followed the Panama-California. Spanish-style buildings house art galleries, museums and theatres, and the information centre can provide a pass giving access to any four museums (239-0512). Most are free on the first Tues in the month.

Model Railroad Museum: 1649 El Prado (696-0199). It claims to be the largest of its kind in the world. Open daily, admission.

San Diego Zoo: At Balboa Park, north of the museums (231-1515). Koala bears and Chinese pheasants are among 3,400 creatures. Children's zoo, tours and an aerial tramway. Open daily, admission.

Old Town: On Old Town Ave (298-9167). Restored buildings, galleries and restaurants occupy the site of the first (1769) Spanish settlement. Write for information to 2783 San Diego Ave, San Diego, CA 92110. Free walking tours leave from the Machado y Silvas Adobe (237-6770). Highlights include the Casa de Estudillo built by the presidio commander in 1827.

La Jolla: This affluent northern suburb has beaches, scuba-diving and chic residents. Raymond Chandler used it as the setting for his last novel *Playback* and his former home is at 6005 Camino de la Costa. The Museum of Contemporary Art stands next to the ocean at 700 Prospect (454-3541).

San Diego Railroad Museum: In Campo, 50 miles east (697-7762). Locos of the Southern Pacific and California Western railroads, plus train rides on weekends from a restored depot at La Mesa. Admission.

Tijuana: Not classic Mexico, and less wild than it used to be, but an easy trip from San Diego. The trolley and bus No 932 both go to the border, though beggars and the concrete walkway make crossing on foot a bleak experience. Tijuana has low-price drinks, accommodation, food, shopping and bullfights. Go for blankets, leather goods, jewellery and tequila (US dollars are welcome). A valid visa is required for return to the United States, even after a one-day visit. For youth hostel rooms call 842523 or 832680.

7 The Empire Builder

Chicago—Seattle

This train travels more than 2,200 miles among wheat and cattle ranges, mountains, glacial lakes, forests and the Mississippi. America's northern plains were mostly wilderness until James J Hill built the Great Northern Railway between St Paul and Seattle. The Empire Builder takes its name from a train which ran on this route in the heyday of passenger travel.

Frequency: Daily. The westbound service leaves Chicago mid-afternoon to arrive in Milwaukee late afternoon and St Paul/Minneapolis around midnight. You reach Havre on the second afternoon, West Glacier by late evening and Spokane in the middle of the night, arriving in Seattle or Portland mid-morning.

Travelling east, trains leave Seattle or Portland late afternoon to reach Spokane by midnight and West Glacier early next morning. You reach Havre at midday and St Paul/Minneapolis early the following morning, arriving in Milwaukee early afternoon and Chicago mid-afternoon.

Reservations: All reserved.

Equipment: Superliner coaches.

Sleeping: Superliner economy, de luxe, family, special bedrooms.

Food: Complete meals, snacks, sandwiches, drinks.

Lounge Car: Video movies, games, hospitality hour.

Baggage: Check-in service at most stations.

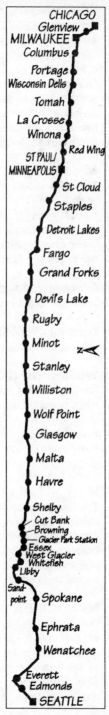

CHICAGO
Glenview
MILWAUKEE
Columbus
Portage
Wisconsin Dells
Tomah
La Crosse
Winona
ST PAUL
MINNEAPOLIS
Red Wing
St Cloud
Staples
Detroit Lakes
Fargo
Grand Forks
Devil's Lake
Rugby
Minot
Stanley
Williston
Wolf Point
Glasgow
Malta
Havre
Shelby
Cut Bank
Browning
Glacier Park Station
Essex
West Glacier
Whitefish
Libby
Sandpoint
Spokane
Ephrata
Wenatchee
Everett
Edmonds
SEATTLE

CHICAGO
For Chicago, see *The California Zephyr*. The Empire Builder departs on tracks of the Chicago, Milwaukee, St Paul & Pacific Railroad (known as the Milwaukee Road), which follows what was a plank road in the days of horse-drawn wagons.

On the right is the Chicago River, with the Merchandise Mart building and the cylindrical towers of Marina City. Also to the right are the Rock-Ola Jukebox factory and the tapered Hancock Building. Sears Tower is on the left. You continue among older buildings and the occasional spired churches of Chicago's northside.

Niles (4/20)
The Niles version of Pisa's leaning tower can be seen on your left.

GLENVIEW (24/60)
An important suburban station.

You travel north through residential areas, farms and industrial complexes owned by the likes of Fiat and AC.

Glenview Naval Air Station (2/58)
The base is on your immediate left.

Gurnee (15/45)
Marriott's Great American Amusement Park appears on the right.

Wadsworth (20/40)
The Des Plaines River is to the left, and you cross the Illinois/Wisconsin state line a few minutes later into 'America's dairyland'.

Franksville (40/20)
Named after the Frank Pure Food Company on the left, keeping old country traditions alive.

Mitchell Field (50/10)
The international airport is on the right.

As the Empire Builder nears Milwaukee look left for two of the city's finest churches. St Josaphat's, with its distinctive dome, was North America's first Polish basilica, built by immigrants using material salvaged from the Federal Building in Chicago. Next to it are the gold-domed spires of St Stanislaus Cathedral. Also on the left is the Allen Bradley clock, a Milwaukee landmark.

MILWAUKEE (60/70)
Wisconsin's biggest community and business centre (famous for its beer) is situated on a Lake Michigan bay which Potawatomi Indians called 'the gathering place by the waters'. Milwaukee grew fast during the 19th Century as immigrants arrived from Italy, Ireland, Poland, Scandinavia and Germany. One of them was the future Israeli premier, Golda Meir. Different ethnic groups continue to provide a lively cultural environment.

Transport: Union Station is at 433 W St Paul Ave. Ticket office and waiting room open 0600-2100 (Mon-Fri) and 0730-2100 (weekends). Lockers, newspapers, Red Caps, restaurant, taxi stand.

Many attractions are within walking distance of the Milwaukee River, and a skywalk system means you can get around without even going outdoors. MCT at 1942 N 17th (344-6711) operates a 24-hour bus service.

Taxis: Yellow (824-444) and Veteran (643-5522).

Car Rental: Suburban, 4939 S Howell (482-0300).

Greyhound: 606 N 7th (272-8900).

Mitchell Airport is six miles from downtown by bus and taxi.

Tours: MCT has summer excursions to the lake shore and historic sights. Boat trips are available from Iroquois Harbor Cruises (332-4194) and Emerald Isle (786-6886).

Visitors Bureau: 756 N Milwaukee (273-3950). Open Mon-Fri. Call 799-1177 for current events.

Telephone Code: 414.

Accommodation: Contact Bed & Breakfast of Milwaukee, 320 E Buffalo Street, Milwaukee, WI 53202 (271-2337).

Halter Home (AYH) Hostel: 2956 N 77th (258-7692). Members only, $8. Take No 57 bus.

Hotels include the Wyndham at 139 E Kilbourn Ave (276-8686); Astor, 924 E Juneau Ave (271-4220); Ramada Inn Downtown, 633 W Michigan Ave (272-8410); Sheraton Mayfair, 2303 N Mayfair Rd (257-3400); Wisconsin, 720 N 3rd (271-4900) — singles $44, doubles $48; Leilani, 18615 W Bluemand Rd (786-7100); Dillon Inn, 11111 W North Ave (778-0333).

Mitchell Park Conservatory: 524 S Layton Blvd (649-9800). Glass domes, each 85ft high and 140ft wide, house three collections of plants in dry, tropical and temperate environments. Open daily, admission.

Pabst Mansion: 2000 W Wisconsin Ave (931-0808). Built by beer baron Frederick Pabst in 1893, the mansion has 37 rooms and 12 baths as well as stained glass, carved woodwork and ornamental iron. Guided tours. Open daily, admission.

The Spirit of Milwaukee Theater: 275 W Wisconsin Ave (271-7122). Featuring an audio-visual review of the city's history and life today. Open daily, admission.

Milwaukee County Zoo: 10001 W Bluemound Rd (771-3040). Trumpeter swans and black rhino are among the endangered species. Children's zoo, guided tours and a miniature train. Open daily, admission. Take No 10 bus.

As you leave Milwaukee watch for the Mitchell Park Conservatory domes. The

County Stadium is on your left and the Miller Brewery (which made Milwaukee famous) to your right.

After crossing the Menomonee River your train passes through suburbs for 20 minutes towards a heartland of lakes and farms.

Pewaukee Lake (30/40)
The shoreline and town are on the left.

You cross the Rock River three times.

Watertown (50/20)
The steeple of St Bernard's Church appears above trees to the right, just before the campus of Marantha College. Cross the Crawfish River.

COLUMBUS (70/30)
Zion Evangelical Lutheran Church is to the left of Ludington Street station. The church's steeple bell, a gift from Germany's emperor, was cast from pieces of French cannon acquired during the Franco-Prussian War. Next to the church is City Hall, completed in 1892.

Wyocena (25/5)
Santa's Rocket stays grounded in a salvage yard on the right.

PORTAGE (30/20)
The town was founded to cater for traders and settlers needing a stopover between the Fox and Wisconsin Rivers. People had to portage (carry) goods across this strip of land when going from Lake Michigan to the Mississippi. Amtrak's station is at 400 W Oneida. Madison is 25 miles to the south.

Wisconsin River (15/5)
Joining on the left, cutting through miles of rock. A Baptist Indian church and cemetery are visible high up on the right.

WISCONSIN DELLS (20/45)
Situated in a canyon created by the Wisconsin River. Natural beauty combines with an amusement park to make this one of the state's big attractions, with rafting, boating and tours along the river. Amtrak's station is at Lacrosse Street. Park Lane Model Railroad Museum in nearby Reedsburg has 2,000 models of all ages and size.

As you leave you cross the Wisconsin.

Mauston (20/25)
Spired St Patrick's Church is to the right. Lake Decorah on the left was created by a dam across the Lemonweir River.

Camp Douglas (30/15)
The flow of the Wisconsin produced the red sandstone formations seen in Mill Bluff State Park to your left.

The Empire Builder

by Kenneth Westcott Jones

When the Victorian entrepreneur James J Hill built his Northern Pacific Railway across the plains of the Dakotas and through the Rockies to Puget Sound, he opened up vast new territories to settlement. They called him the 'Empire Builder' and it was not long before the crack train on his 2000 mile long line from St Paul to the Pacific North West carried this title.

Every afternoon at 3.15pm the great train rolls westward out of Chicago's Union Station, its double-decked Superliners consisting of reclining seat coaches, a massive dining car with splendid views from the tables 17 feet above the tracks, a glass-roofed vista-lounge with swivel armchairs, and an assortment of sleepers ranging from bedroom suites equipped with private showers to economy double bunk compartments. On the lower levels of the train there are such things as buffet lounges, recreation rooms, baggage areas, kitchens, and wide bedroom space for families and disabled travellers.

High sustained speed is not the object and the *Empire Builder* makes every stop on the line, all 39 of them. It has to, for it is the only passenger train over the former Northern Pacific (now part of the Burlington Northern system). But it still manages to average about 55 miles an hour, and it is, after all, a rolling hotel on wheels, sometimes rolling a bit much through the yards of such cities as Milwaukee, Minneapolis, and Spokane.

Nor is the train cheap to ride. Passengers in the five bedroom suites in each Superliner sleeper pay a good deal more than a first class flight over the same route. But they get to see things, wonderful things, and good meals are included in the fare. Porters even bring light breakfasts in bed.

Riding across the northern United States at scenic level, passengers enjoy views of the Mississippi River which is followed almost all the way to St Paul, 400 miles northwest of Chicago.

If any passengers wake up during the night, they may catch a glimpse of the stop at Fargo, North Dakota. This is where Wells-Fargo was founded, and it marks the start of the Western Plains. Much of the morning and afternoon is spent thundering across the Northern Prairies, but visual excitement comes after Browning, Montana, around seven in the evening. A sharp climb into the Rockies takes the train through the Marais Pass (at 5,400ft the lowest rail crossing of the Rocky Mountains) and on through the wonders of the Glacier National Park.

There are still 600 miles of mountains to come as the train leaves the 'Big Sky' country and approaches Idaho and Washington State, where the giant Cascade Range has to be threaded. High Rise Seattle and a glimpse of salt water completes the journey at half past ten the next morning, or a bit before since the *Empire Builder* has the habit of running a little ahead of its time card.

TOMAH (45/40)

The chamber of commerce occupies a Milwaukee Road Pullman car on the left, its sign supported by characters from *Gasoline Alley*. The comic strip's founder, Frank King, grew up here. Tomah's Wisconsin Dairyland tractor pull engages competitors from the whole Midwest.

Tomah Lake appears on the left as you suddenly enter a landscape of steep hills.

Tunnel City (5/35)

The Empire Builder runs on a single track through the 1,350ft tunnel.

Sparta (15/25)

The airport is on the right.

You join the La Crosse River on your right and follow it for 25 miles to the Mississippi.

Bangor (25/15)

Look for an imposing village hall on the right before you cross the La Crosse River.

LA CROSSE (40/40)

At the junction of the Mississippi, Black and La Crosse Rivers, and called after the name French trappers gave to a game played by Indians. Amtrak's station at 601 St Andrew opens 0830-1130 and 1830-2100.

Leaving town the train crosses the Mississippi River for the first time, going from Wisconsin into Minnesota. Islands divide the waterway into three channels.

Once across you enter one of this route's most attractive stretches, accompanying the river into Richard J Dover hardwood forest before travelling 40 miles through farmland and riverboat towns.

Number 7 Dam (5/35)

The dam and lock system to your right is one of several taming the river.

Number 6 Dam (20/20)

Also on the right.

WINONA (40/60)

The name is Indian for 'first-born daughter'. Sugar Loaf Mountain, rising 500ft on the left, was a ceremonial meeting place for the Sioux. Legend says that Chief Wa-Pa-Sha's outline could be seen before quarrying changed the mountain's shape. Winona has grown from its sawmill days into a shipping and manufacturing centre. Amtrak at 65 E Mark opens 0800-1100 and 1900-2130.

Grain elevators feature on the right as you leave.

Number 5 Dam (10/50)
Another in the federally-financed series.

Weaver (15/45)
'White bass capital of the world', with many fishing camps in the vicinity.
  Your train crosses the Zumbro River.

Wabasha (30/30)
At the 1856 Anderson House — the oldest hotel in the state — services include free shoe shines, hot bricks for warming the bed and pet cats to keep you company.

Lake Pepin (35/25)
Where the Chippewa River joins the Mississippi. This home of eagles is said to be where water-skiing was invented. Watch for the riverboat steamer.

Frontenac (50/10)
The small town dates back to a French fort built in 1723. Mount Frontenac ski resort is on the left.
  Nearing Red Wing note the Minnesota State Training School to your left. Opened in 1891, it resembles a German castle.

RED WING (60/65)
The city got its name from a Dakota chief whose emblem was a swan's wing dyed scarlet. The Milwaukee Road built the station in 1905 and Red Wing acquired it from the Milwaukee's successor, the Soo Line. Amtrak leases the waiting room area, restored to its original condition. The St James Hotel is on the left. Red Wing is famous for making shoes and pottery.

Cannon River (5/60)
Prairie Island nuclear power station is visible on your right before you cross the Vermilion River.

Hastings (20/45)
A domed 1871 court-house is on the left, with another lock and dam system to the right.
  The Empire Builder crosses the Mississippi.

St Paul Airport (45/20)
Across the river on the left, with the city skyline seen on palisades to the right.

Harriet Island (50/15)
On the right. During summer picturesque riverboats will take you to Fort Snelling.
  Nearing St Paul look right for the cathedral. The castle-like Schmidt brewery is to your left.

ST PAUL/MINNEAPOLIS (65/80)
The twin cities began as frontier towns on the banks of the Mississippi,

settled by immigrants from Scandinavia, Germany and Britain. Two million people now live here. Minneapolis, haunt of rock star Prince, is brasher and noisier than the state capital St Paul.

It's claimed that more art galleries and theatres exist here than anywhere outside New York. Around 900 lakes and parks provide year-round sports activity.

Transport: Amtrak's modern Midway Station at 730 Transfer Rd, St Paul, serves both cities. Ticket office and waiting room open 0500-0100. Lockers, vending machines, luggage trolleys, taxi stand. Thruway buses connect to Duluth, birthplace of Robert Zimmerman.

Minneapolis and St Paul have skyways that make it easy to get around on foot even during winter. Mile-long Nicollet Mall in Minneapolis is the country's largest pedestrianised area.

MTC bus maps and timetables are available from IDS Crystal Court, 7th and Nicollet Mall (827-7733).

Taxis (St Paul): City Wide (292-1616) and Yellow (222-4433).

Taxis (Minneapolis): Town (331-8294) and Yellow (824-4444).

Car Rental: Ugly Duckling, 6405 Cedar Ave S (861-7545).

Greyhound (St Paul): 7th and St Peter (222-0509).

Greyhound (Minneapolis): 29 N 9th (371-3311).

The airport is eight miles from downtown by Airport Express (726-6400), MTC bus No 35 and taxis.

Tours: Twin Cities, 3920 Nicollet Ave (827-7777) and Gray Line (591-0999). Mississippi sternwheel riverboats leave from Harriet Island (227-1100).

Visitors Bureau: 1219 Marquette Ave, Minneapolis (348-4313) and 445 Minnesota, St Paul (297-6985). Open weekdays. The Capitol and IDS Center have information booths.

Telephone Code: 612.

Accommodation: For bed & breakfast contact the visitors bureau or write to Room at the Inn (Minnesota), 1426 Sheldon Ave, MN 55108. The University of Minnesota housing office often has cheap rooms (624-2994).

Minneapolis hotels include the Whitney at 150 Portland Ave (339-9300); Northstar, 618 2nd Ave S (338-2288); Luxeford, 1101 La Salle Ave (332-6800). St Paul hotels include the St Paul at 350 Market (292-9292); Radisson, 11 E Kellog Blvd (292-1900); Excel Inn, 1739 Old Hudson Rd (771-5566).

Minneapolis Institute of Arts: 2400 3rd Ave S (870-3131). Among 70,000 exhibits are Rembrandts, Chinese jade, Roman sculptures and a 2,000-year-old mummy. Tours, films and lectures. Closed Mon, free Thurs.

American Swedish Institute: 2600 Park Ave, Minneapolis (871-4907). This turn-of-the-century mansion has wood panels and carvings, Swedish art, glassware, furniture and a library. Closed Mon, admission. The Svenskarnas Dag festival takes place each May in Minnehaha Park.

Landmark Center: 75 W 5th (292-3272). St Paul's 1902 Federal Court building has been restored to its Romanesque splendour, with guided tours of the chambers and courtrooms. Open daily, free. It also houses the Minnesota Museum of Art (closed Mon).

James Hill House: 240 Summit Ave, St Paul (297-2555). James J Hill made his fortune as founder of the Great Northern Railroad (later to become the Burlington Northern). He spared no expense when building this mansion in 1891. Open Wed, Thurs and Sat, admission. It's one of many fine houses on Summit Ave, where F Scott Fitzgerald lived.

Twin City Model Railroad Club: 1021 Bandana Blvd E, St Paul (633-1303). Three thousand square feet of O-Scale railroad are located in the former Northern Pacific maintenance shops. Open daily, donation.

Leaving St Paul you see Minneapolis in the left distance, dominated by the 57-storey IDS Tower.

ST CLOUD (80/60)
On the shores of the Mississippi, and shipping granite from local mines.
  The Empire Builder continues through the night.

STAPLES (60/60)
This former railroad town became run down but has started to attract new industries.

DETROIT LAKES (60/55)
The 400 lakes have fishing and other pursuits. Amtrak is at 116 Pioneer.

Red River (53/2)
Cross the river and go from Minnesota into North Dakota.

FARGO (55/60)
Named after William Fargo of the Wells Fargo Express Company, North Dakota's biggest city is at the heart of the Red River valley. The station at 420 4th Street W also serves Moorhead in Minnesota. Bonanzaville USA in West Fargo relives pioneer days with a village reconstructed from original buildings.

GRAND FORKS (60/80)
Where the Red Lake River meets the Red River. Grand Forks is the home of North Dakota University. Buses connect downtown with Amtrak's station at 5555 DeMers Ave, and Thruway buses travel north to Winnipeg, Canada.

DEVIL'S LAKE (80/60)
Catchily called 'the goose and duck hunting capital of America', the town is situated along North Dakota's largest lake. Sioux and Chippewa Indians named it the Evil Spirit Lake, telling of water monsters, thunderbirds and overturned canoes.

RUGBY (60/65)

The geographical centre of North America, with a stone monument and museum to prove it. The Canadian border is less than 50 miles away.

MINOT (65/50)

Located on the Mouse River, this service stop for the Empire Builder was called the Magic City after it apparently grew overnight when the Great Northern arrived. It still prospers thanks to oil and the military, and the July state fair takes place here. Amtrak's station at 400 First Ave NW opens 0800-1145 and 1830-2015.

STANLEY (50/65)

The modest town's economy is based on grain and livestock. Mountrail County court-house can be seen to the right of the station.

WILLISTON (65/80)

At the western edge of Lake Sakakawea, where oil finds during the 1950s brought boomtown conditions. Many wells appear along the route. Garrison Dam on the Missouri has increased farming activity.

   You join the Missouri on your left, following it for most of the next 60 miles.

Fort Buford (15/65)

Where Chief Sitting Bull surrendered (1881) after the battle of the Little Bighorn (1876). The officers' quarters, a cemetery and other relics can be seen at the fort.

Fort Union (20/60)

This was one of last century's liveliest fur trading posts, and Wild West excitement returns each June with the Fort Union Rendezvous.

North Dakota/Montana State Line (22/58)

Enter big sky country and change from Central to Mountain Time. Watches go back an hour (forward when travelling east).

   For 700 miles the Empire Builder crosses the plains of northern Montana, where cattle are more common than people and sheep more common than cattle. Watch also for herds of antelope.

Culbertson (50/30)

Just west of town you cross Big Muddy Creek into Fort Peck Indian Reservation. Sitting Bull lived here after surrendering.

   Cross the Poplar River.

WOLF POINT (80/45)

A sculpture on the left recalls frontier days when this town was a wolf trappers' trading post. Each July Wolf Point hosts the Wild Horse Stampede — 'granddaddy of Montana rodeos'.

Fort Peck Dam (30/15)

Built in 1940, this earth-filled dam is 250ft tall and forms a 383 square mile

lake.
   As you approach Glasgow look for a large letter 'G' on the left hillside.

GLASGOW (45/55)
Many of the fossils and dinosaur bones found here are displayed at Fort
Peck Museum. You accompany the Milk River from here to Havre.

Tampico (15/40)
This small community is on the right.

Saco Hot Springs (35/20)
A large bell hangs on the Methodist church to your right.
   Cross part of Lake Bowdoin, where the wildlife refuge on the left is mainly
for water birds. If both trains are on time you should pass the eastbound
Empire Builder at this point.

MALTA (55/70)
Local cattle empires inspired the Western artist Charles Russell, and ranching
is still big business.

Wagner (10/60)
Where in 1901 Butch Cassidy and the Sundance Kid (Harry Longabaugh)
robbed the Great Northern's Oriental Limited of $68,000.
   Continue beside the northern edge of Fort Belknap Indian Reservation, with
the Bear Paw Mountains ahead to your left. In 1877 Chief Joseph of the Nez
Perce Indians surrendered to the US army after a 1,700-mile retreat with the
words 'From where the sun now stands I will fight no more forever'.

HAVRE (70/95)
Look left for a preserved Great Northern S-2 steam loco as you approach the
station at 235 Main. Ticket office open 0900-1630. Havre's business centre
has expanded since the discovery of natural gas. Indians formerly hunted
buffalo by driving them over the town's cliffs, and a museum at the site
shows skeleton remains.

Milk River (5/90)
The river departs to the north, entering Canada before finding its source in
Montana's Glacier National Park.

SHELBY (95/30)
The unlikely venue for a heavyweight boxing championship between Jack
Dempsey and Tom Gibbons held in 1923. Chaos ensued when the match
was cancelled then reconvened before 7,000 fans and 17,000 gatecrashers.
Dempsey won but received no prize money after his manager disappeared
with $300,000. Several banks failed and Shelby wisely never held another
championship. Thruway buses connect with Great Falls and Butte.

CUT BANK (30/32)
Mid-winter temperatures here are among the country's coldest.

You leave on tracks supported by a trestle across Cut Bank Creek, getting your first view ahead of the Rocky Mountains. This horizon becomes ever more impressive as the train nears Glacier National Park.

Lewis and Clark Monument (20/12)
An obelisk on the left commemorates Meriwether Lewis's search for a pass through the mountains.

BROWNING (32/20)
This is the heart of the Blackfeet Indian Reservation and a good place to shop for native American goods. The Museum of the Plains Indians features art from 11 tribes.

The Empire Builder approaches Glacier Park Station on a high trestle over Two Medicine River.

GLACIER PARK STATION (20/60)
Open during summer to provide a gateway into one of America's most beautiful national parks, with 200 lakes, 10,000ft high mountains and 50 living glaciers. Timber was brought from Oregon and Washington by the Great Northern to build Glacier Park Lodge on your right, next to the 1913 station. For information on boating, hiking and skiing call 406-888-5441.

When Glacier station closes out of season, access to the park may still be possible via Browning or Essex.

Having enjoyed relatively easy conditions so far your train now has to tackle the jagged barrier ahead.

Marias Pass (15/45)
The continental divide here is at a lower elevation (5,216ft) than at any other point between Canada and New Mexico. Indians may have crossed Mystery Pass, but Lewis and Clark were unable to chart an accurate route. John Stevens, working for the Great Northern, finally discovered a path in 1889. Operating in temperatures of minus 40°F, he earned the statue dedicated to him on the right. A monument on the left recalls President Theodore Roosevelt, after whom the adjacent highway was named.

As you descend the western side of the pass the scene becomes still more breathtaking, with waterfalls and gorges among the mountains.

Flathead River (45/15)
Joining from the left and crossed on another trestle.

ESSEX (60/25)
A flag stop for the Empire Builder. The Izaak Walton Inn on your right was called after the English writer and angler.

WEST GLACIER (25/35)
Gateway to the western part of Glacier National Park, where the yearly snowfall averages 100-200 inches. You cross the Flathead River again.

Columbia Falls (20/15)

A preserved steam engine can be seen on the left and an Anaconda aluminium plant to the right.

WHITEFISH (35/110)

The German-style station on your left at N Central Ave complements the Alpine scenery. Open 0500-1245 and 1530-2330. Whitefish is located in a valley of the Flathead National Forest, close to resorts such as Whitefish Lake and Big Mountain. Flathead Lake — the largest west of the Mississippi River — is 25 miles away.

LIBBY (110/55)

Located in the middle of Kootenai National Forest, popular with hunters and fishermen. The town's sawmills and log processing plants are sometimes open to visitors.

Between Libby and Sandpoint you leave Montana for Idaho, changing from Mountain to Pacific Time. Watches go back an hour (forward when travelling east).

SANDPOINT (55/80)

Situated next to Lake Pend Oreille and close to the Schweitzer ski area.

Travelling through the night the Empire Builder departs Idaho for Washington.

SPOKANE (80/120)

The 'monarch of the inland empire' is situated next to the Spokane River and surrounded by farmland. It's an important railroad junction where the Great Northern route meets the Spokane, Portland & Seattle. The old Great Northern clock tower is a downtown landmark. Amtrak's station at W 221 First Ave opens 1100-0330 (Mon-Fri) and 1915-0330 (weekends). Visitors bureau: W 926 Sprague Ave (747-3230).

Bing Crosby attended Gonzaga University, where the library has photographs, memorabilia and a bronze statue. The Museum of Native American Cultures is at E 200 Cataldo. You can sample Spokane's grander days at the Grace Campbell House, W 2316 First Ave (next to the Cheney Cowles Museum). Empire Lines (624-4116) runs a bus service to the Grand Coulee Dam, 80 miles east. Sung about by Woody Guthrie, the dam was begun in 1933 as part of Roosevelt's New Deal.

The Empire Builder divides into two trains at Spokane and what follows is the continuation to Seattle. For the route to Portland, see the next section.

EPHRATA (120/65)

Set among fertile land which is fed by water from the Columbia River project.

Rock Island Dam (35/30)

On the left, the dam holds back the Columbia. You cross the river five minutes later.

WENATCHEE (65/175)

One of the 'apple capitals of the world'. These orchards in the Cascades foothills have perfect conditions for producing one seventh of the country's crop. North Central Washington Museum gives spirited demonstrations of apple sorting.

Leave past warehouses and lumber yards with the Wenatchee River on your left. To enjoy the best scenery for the next hour you should sit on the left side of the train.

Cashmere (15/160)

Look for more apple warehouses. The local specialities are Turkish delight-type sweets called aplets (made from apples) and cotlets (from apricots).

You cross the river several times as you near the Cascades to your left.

Leavenworth (25/150)

Watch for Bavarian-style buildings among the orchards.

The Empire Builder starts a long climb, entering the first of many tunnels before crossing the river.

Merritt (60/115)

The train slows further as it gains height among rivers, mountains and marshes.

Icicle Canyon (65/110)

The best views are now to your right. Keep a look out for elk, deer and beaver.

Cascade Tunnel (75/100)

Completed in 1929, this is one of the longest (7.79 miles) in the western hemisphere. It helped replace 43 miles of stiff grades with an easier 34-mile route. Stevens Pass is 500ft higher at 4,061ft.

It takes 15 minutes for your train to leave the tunnel and begin the 65-mile descent to Everett, providing terrific views of the Cascades and Puget Sound.

Cross the Skyomish River, which you accompany to Everett. A waterfall features on the left but the best scenery remains to the right. Rocks, streams, ravines and mountains, along with pine and fir forests, make this a complete Washington experience.

You cross the Skyomish on another dramatic high trestle, with Mount Baker-Snoqualmie National Forest ranger station to the right.

Skyomish (100/75)

This logging town has an interesting Burlington Northern station.

Sunset Falls (115/60)

Seen on the left before you cross the river again.

Grotto (117/58)

A small village with mountains rising high on your right.

The Empire Builder crosses the river twice as it leaves the Cascades for less demanding terrain.

Monroe (150/25)
An old station stands on your right away from the tracks.

EVERETT (175/25)
This was a focal point for the lumber industry even before the railroad came, thanks to its natural inland port. Boeing's 747/767 assembly plant is housed here in what may be the world's biggest building. Trailways Northwest buses connect to Vancouver, British Columbia.

South of the city you join Puget Sound on the right for 15 miles, with the Olympic Mountains in the distance. Islands in the Sound include Bainbridge and Whidbey, linked to the mainland by ferry.

EDMONDS (25/30)
The 'gem of the Puget Sound' is a residential town, its Old Milltown shopping arcade created inside a turn-of-the-century Ford garage. The train stops at 211 Railroad Ave. Ticket office open 0830-1715. Nearby is the dock where ferries leave for Kingston and the Olympic Peninsula.

Shilshole Bay Marina (15/15)
Countless boats are moored on your right and Bainbridge Island is across the Sound.

The Empire Builder crosses Salmon Bay inlet to proceed briefly inland. Chittenden Locks on the left are part of a waterway system linking the bay with Lake Washington. On the right is a statue of the Norwegian explorer Leif Ericson.

You return to the shoreline by way of a US naval reservation and travel along Seattle's waterfront. Pier 70 on your right is America's largest restored wooden building. The former warehouse has 40 shops and restaurants, connected to downtown by a trolley running on tracks beside the train. Seattle's Space Needle is to your left before you pass through a mile-long tunnel and complete your journey at King Street Station.

SEATTLE
For Seattle, see *The Coast Starlight*.

7A The Empire Builder

Spokane—Portland

SPOKANE (80/150)
For Spokane and the route from Chicago, see the previous section. Through coaches for Portland continue to Pasco via Flathead Tunnel (seven miles long).

PASCO (150/115)
Where the Columbia and Snake Rivers meet. This rail and shipping point is the furthest seagoing vessels can voyage up the Columbia, and its name derives from a shortening of Pacific Steamship Company. Once claimed by the British, this territory joined the USA in 1846. Pasco's station at Clark and Tacoma also serves Kennewick and Richland.

Columbia River (75/40)
Oregon is on the far side.

Roosevelt (80/35)
Barges shipping grain are a common sight between here and Vancouver.

John Day Dam (100/15)
Around 5,900ft long and completed in 1968 at a cost of $487 million, it produces enough electricity to serve Portland three times over. Locks carry eight million tons of shipping a year and boast one of the highest (113ft) single lifts in the world.

Maryhill (105/10)
An unlikely setting for the Maryhill Castle Art Museum, dedicated by the Queen of Romania in the 1920s. On a hill to the north is a concrete replica of Stonehenge built by Sam Hill to honour First World War troops.

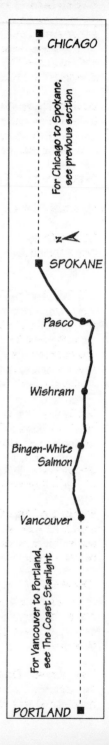

CHICAGO

For Chicago to Spokane, see previous section

SPOKANE

Pasco

Wishram

Bingen-White Salmon

Vancouver

For Vancouver to Portland, see The Coast Starlight

PORTLAND

WISHRAM (115/30)

Named after an Indian settlement and known to Lewis and Clark, this was the site of a legendary rail workers' beanery.

On the other side of the Columbia River the Pioneer travels between Seattle and Salt Lake City on Union Pacific tracks. A rail bridge ahead takes the Burlington Northern line south to Klamath Falls.

Dalles Dam (10/20)

Dalles is French for 'trough' and describes the narrow channel made by the river. An 8,700ft zig-zag shaped dam provides irrigation and power, as well as creating Horsethief Lake. The town of Dalles is on the opposite shore.

Mount Hood (15/15)

Look left for the pyramid of Oregon's tallest mountain, 11,235ft high and permanently snow-capped.

Lyle (25/5)

Cross the Klickitat River, with the Indian burial ground of Memaloose Island on the left.

BINGEN-WHITE SALMON (30/80)

Named after the White Salmon River and the German town of Bingen, it's set among orchards. The city of Hood River is on the far shore.

For the next 55 miles your train travels through the Columbia Gorge, cut into ancient rock by the river, and the land changes from near desert to rain forest. Lewis and Clark were the first white people to venture this far, and settlers on the Oregon Trail sometimes preferred not to risk crossing the river.

Cooks (15/65)

Wind Mountain (2,500ft) is immediately to the right. One of the few remaining log flumes transports lumber to a sawmill beside the river.

Stevenson (30/50)

Amtrak's Pioneer stops at Cascade Locks across the water.

Bridge of the Gods (33/47)

Ahead to your left, replacing a stone bridge Indian legend says their god destroyed when angered by his sons arguing over a maiden. The two sons became Mount Hood and Mount Adams, and the maiden Mount St Helens.

Sheridan's Point (35/45)

Philip Sheridan, later a Civil War general, defended settlers from Indian marauders here in 1855. Nearby the final spike was driven in 1908 to complete the Spokane, Portland & Seattle route between Pasco and Vancouver.

Bonneville Dam (36/44)

The Columbia's first great dam was worked on by Woody Guthrie, and this engineering feat half a mile wide created Lake Bonneville. A fish ladder lets salmon swim upstream to spawn.

Beacon Rock (40/40)
The 840ft rock on the right is second only to Gibraltar. It was named by Lewis and Clark as an unmistakeable guide for travellers.

Multnomah Falls (42/38)
Second highest in the country, the falls cascade 620ft on the Oregon side of the river.

Cape Horn (48/32)
You leave the Columbia Gorge by way of a 2,369ft tunnel through the western Cascades.

VANCOUVER (80/22)
For Vancouver and the rest of the Empire Builder route to Portland, see *The Coast Starlight*.

8 The Southwest Chief

Chicago—Los Angeles

Amtrak's fastest trip from Chicago to the Pacific is along the Santa Fe Trail. The route was first used by Indians and Spanish conquistadors, then by mule caravans, wagon trains, stage-coaches and gold prospectors. You travel 2,246 miles through eight states past wheat fields, ranches, missions, pueblos, mountains and deserts. Close to this route are Santa Fe, Taos and the Grand Canyon.

The Southwest Chief follows a line built by the Santa Fe Railway, which the Super Chief took in 1937 to cut 15 hours from the time of its predecessor, the Chief. The latter succeeded two other luxury trains, the California Limited and the Santa Fe De Luxe.

Frequency: Daily. The westbound service leaves Chicago late afternoon to reach Kansas City soon after midnight and Lamar early next morning. You reach Albuquerque late afternoon and Flagstaff (for the Grand Canyon) late evening, arriving in Los Angeles early on the third day.

Travelling east, trains leave Los Angeles mid-evening to reach Flagstaff early next morning, Albuquerque early afternoon and Lamar late evening. You arrive in Kansas City early on the third day and Chicago mid-afternoon.

Reservations: All reserved.

Equipment: Superliner coaches.

Sleeping: Superliner economy, deluxe, family, special bedrooms.

Food: Complete meals, snacks, sandwiches, drinks.

Lounge Car: Video movies, travelogues, hospitality hour, bingo, Indian Country guide.

Baggage: Check-in service at most stations.

CHICAGO
Joliet
Streator
Chillicothe
Galesburg
Fort Madison
La Plata
Marceline
KANSAS CITY
Lawrence
Topeka
Emporia
Newton
Hutchinson
Dodge City
Garden City
Lamar
La Junta
Trinidad
Raton
Las Vegas
Lamy
ALBUQUERQUE
Gallup
Winslow
Flagstaff
Kingman
Needles
Barstow
San Bernardino
Pomona
Pasadena
LOS ANGELES

Travellers' Tales
Grand Central Station Chicago
William H Hughes

Arriving at Grand Central Station in Chicago was painless. There are showers and change rooms in the basement of the station. Lockers are available too, for your clothes and valuables while showering, but I hadn't brought a lock (a small padlock would have been sufficient). However, I tipped the attendant to watch my unlocked locker and he gladly consented. After two days on the train the shower was welcome. A six hour layover allowed me to go up to the Sears Building observation level. The view of Chicago downtown and Lake areas from that height is usually only possible from a plane.

CHICAGO
For Chicago, see *The California Zephyr*. The Southwest Chief leaves Chicago and travels south on Santa Fe tracks, with the city skyline back to the right. Your train runs among railyards, refineries, power plants and factories.

McCook (36/14)
On your right is the Illinois & Michigan Canal connecting the Great Lakes with the Mississippi. Also to your right is a big limestone quarry.

Illinois State Prison (48/2)
A daunting presence on the left.

JOLIET (50/45)
Early buildings in Stone City were made from limestone, and quarries still operate. Named after the explorer Louis Joliet, this manufacturing centre with important rail and water connections, is called the 'city of spires' because of its many historic churches. Amtrak's station at 50 E Jefferson opens 0830-2100.

Lorenzo (12/32)
Cross the Kankakee River, a tributary of the Illinois. To your right, Reston Pond cools water for an atomic generator.

STREATOR (45/40)
This coal mining town also specialises in glass containers.
   The Southwest Chief leaves Streator and crosses the Vermilion River, entering flat Illinois farmlands.

Illinois River (38/2)
Cross the 420-mile long waterway.

CHILLICOTHE (40/42)
Next to the river, this is the nearest stop to Peoria, 24 miles south.
   Continue through prolific farm country producing wheat, corn, soya beans and alfalfa. In the haymaking season you can expect to see giant rolled bales

in the fields. The open-topped barns are where hay was stored before baling became more common.

GALESBURG (42/45)
Settled by Presbyterians from Oneida, New York, this was the scene of an 1858 Lincoln-Douglas debate. The Southwest Chief uses the station at 184 N Broad. Galesburg was the home town of Olmstead Ferris, who developed popcorn. One of his relations invented the Ferris wheel.

Mississippi River (35/10)
North America's greatest river joins on the right. A few minutes later you cross from Illinois into Iowa on the longest (3,347ft) double-track, double-decked bridge in the world. The structure pivots so that bigger boats can pass.

Approaching Fort Madison note the Santa Fe steam engine on your left. The old Santa Fe station is now a museum.

FORT MADISON (45/65)
The Southwest Chief's only stop on its brief passage through Iowa is this industrial city on the site of Fort Madison. In 1813 US soldiers burned the fort to divert attacking Indians while settlers escaped through a tunnel to the river. One Chimney Monument on your right commemorates the fort. This is Amtrak's nearest stop to Keokuk, five miles south along the Mississippi.

After Fort Madison you go from Iowa into Missouri across the Des Moines River.

LA PLATA (65/35)
This small farming town is in a region popular for hunting deer, pheasant and turkey. La Plata Lake is to the left and Kirksville, home of Northeast Missouri University, 10 miles north.

MARCELINE (35/95)
Childhood home of Walt Disney, who is said to have created Mickey Mouse while travelling on the Southwest Chief. Walt Disney Park to your right has a steam loco from the Santa Fe Railway.

Mendon (10/85)
Waterfowl migrate to Canada each year from Swan Lake game reserve on the right. Hunters account for several hundred thousand.

Bosworth (15/80)
Cross the Grand River, bordered by pecan trees.

Missouri River (65/25)
Cross on a 135ft high bridge. To the right are the remains of Fort Osage, built in 1808.

Sugar Creek (85/10)
Frequented by outlaw Jesse James, who died at nearby St Joseph (1882).

KANSAS CITY (95/50)

'The heart of America' is located in Missouri rather than Kansas. It was named after Kanza Indians who traded with the city's founder, John Calvin McCoy. This settlement on a bend in the Missouri became the place where wagon trains were equipped for the Santa Fe, California and Oregon Trails.

After the Civil War, with the coming of railroads, Kansas City turned to agriculture and transport. The stockyard district reflects Cowtown history, and the Royal Livestock and Horseshow has been going since 1899. Around the turn of the century, the architect George Kessler set out to create 'one of the loveliest cities on earth'. Today's Kansas City claims to rival Paris for boulevards and Rome for fountains.

Transport: Union Station at 2200 Main supersedes the adjacent Old Union Station, a stone building notorious for the 1933 'Pretty Boy Floyd' massacre. The new station (third biggest in the country) also serves Kansas City, Kansas, on the other side of the river. Information: 421-3622. Ticket office and waiting room open 24 hours. Lockers, newspapers, Red Caps, shops, taxi stand.

Kansas City covers 300 square miles so most people get around by car. Metro buses (221-0660) and the Kansas City Trolley (221-3399) operate downtown. In Kansas City, Kansas, buses are run by the Transportation Department (371-6402).

Taxis: Yellow (471-5000) and Economy (621-3436).
Car Rental: Thrifty, 2001 Baltimore (842-8550).
Greyhound: 1101 N Troost (698-0080).

The airport is 20 miles northwest by taxi and KCI Express bus (243-5950).

Tours: Self-guided walking tours are available from the Historic Kansas City Foundation, 20 W 9th (471-3391) and Plaza Merchants Association, 4625 Wornall (753-0100). For Missouri *River Queen* excursions (May-November) call 842-0027.

Visitors Bureau: 1100 Main (221-5242). For the latest events call 474-9600.

Telephone Code: 816 in Missouri, 913 in Kansas.

Accommodation: For bed & breakfast try the Washington Inn, 4545 Washington (561-7232). Downtown hotel rates can be expensive, but look for weekend deals.

Hotels include the Raphael at 325 Ward Pkwy (756-3800); Westin Crown Center, 1 Pershing Rd (474-4400); Best Western Stadium Inn, 7901 E 40 Hwy (861-9400); Travelodge, 921 Cherry (471-1266) — singles $35, doubles $38; Belton Inn, 155 S 71 Hwy (331-6300); Drury Inn-KC Stadium, 3830 Blue Ridge Cut-off (923-3000).

The Parks: Among the city's 300 parks is America's third largest, Swope Park. Others include Loose Park at 51st and Wornall (famous for roses) and Shawnee Mission Park.

Crown Center: 2450 Grand Ave, opposite the station (274-8444). A complex of shops, offices and hotels which incorporates an indoor waterfall and the headquarters of Hallmark Cards. Free concerts in summer.

Country Club Plaza: Two miles south of Crown Center is America's first (1922) shopping precinct, with Spanish-style buildings, fountains and sculpture.

Kansas City Museum: 3218 Gladstone Blvd (483-8300). Housed in the mansion of lumber king R A Long, the museum includes a replica trading post. Closed Mon, donation.

1859 Jail-Museum: 217 N Main, Independence (252-1892). Frank James was a resident during Wild West days. The museum also features a schoolhouse and marshal's office. Open Tues-Sat, admission.

———————————————

You depart Kansas City, Missouri, and cross the state line into Kansas City, Kansas.

LAWRENCE (50/32)
This was a station on the Underground Railroad founded by abolitionists. During the 1863 Quantrill's Raid a band of pro-Confederate guerillas attacked the peaceful town, killing 150 residents. Kansas University began here in 1866. The 1906 Santa Fe depot at Baldwin, 12 miles south, has vintage rail equipment and memorabilia (913-594-6982). Diesel-powered trips take place on the Midland Railway.

TOPEKA (32/65)
Capital of Kansas. The Menninger Foundation — a world leader in the treatment of mental illness — has a collection of Freud's papers.

EMPORIA (65/65)
Home of Emporia State University and the *Emporia Gazette*. The newspaper's editor, William White, gave the city Peter Pan Park.

NEWTON (65/35)
One of America's largest Mennonite settlements, Newton was founded in 1872 by Russian immigrants. Seed they brought for winter wheat helped Kansas become the world's breadbasket. Wichita is 10 miles south.

HUTCHINSON (35/95)
This is the biggest wheat market anywhere, with 50 grain elevators. Nearby is one of the world's largest salt mines.
   From here to Dodge City you pass through oil country, so nodding pumps feature on both sides of the track.

Kinsley (65/30)
A sign on the right says Kinsley is exactly 1,561 miles from both San

Francisco and New York.

DODGE CITY (95/42)
A trading post then an army fort, the city prospered when the Santa Fe Railway came in 1872. It became 'the cowboy capital of the world', shipping longhorn steers brought on cattle drives from Texas and the south. Lawlessness then took hold as Dodge turned into 'the wickedest little city in America'. Bat Masterson, Wyatt Earp, Doc Holliday and Colonel George Custer restored order. Many of the gunfighters who died were buried on Boot Hill, seen to your left, and the hangman's tree survives. Front Street on your right looks much as it always did, though things are calmer now.

Visitors bureau: 4th and W spruce (227-3119). Amtrak's station is at Central and Wyatt Earp, where two sundials on the right signify a change of time zone — which in fact takes place further west. The rail yards still ship cattle and wheat.

Cimarron (15/27)
Where the Santa Fe Trail crossed the Arkansas River to your left.

GARDEN CITY (42/75)
Supposedly named by a hobo when he saw the garden of the founder's wife. Garden City boasts the world's biggest public swimming pool and largest grain elevator. Nearby are the world's biggest buffalo herd and a huge natural gas field.

Holcomb (5/70)
Where the murders described in Truman Capote's *In Cold Blood* really happened.

In this part of the Sunflower State look for fields of these plants, grown for oil and as cattle feed.

Coolidge (50/25)
Leave Kansas and enter Colorado, changing from Central to Mountain time. Watches go back an hour (forward when travelling east).

Cross the Arkansas River, which you follow to La Junta.

LAMAR (75/45)
'Goose hunting capital of America'. As you near the station look left for a Madonna of the Trails statue erected by the Daughters of the Revolution.

John Martin Dam (10/35)
The dam forms a reservoir frequented by herons and cranes.

Las Animas (25/20)
Named after the Rio de las Animas Pendidas (river of lost souls), this is where a wagon train of settlers camped and disappeared overnight, apparently having been attacked by Indians.

Bent's Old Fort (35/10)

Seen among trees to the right, it was built to protect fur traders and serve wagons on the Santa Fe Trail. Kit Carson worked at the fort, which has now been restored.

LA JUNTA (45/75)

Where the Santa Fe Trail meets the Cimarron Cut-off. This is the home of the Santa Fe Railroad's divisional headquarters, and the surrounding Arkansas River valley is famous for cantaloup melons. Outlaws such as Belle Star inscribed their names on nearby rocks. On a clear day you can see Pike's Peak a hundred miles to the north.

After La Junta your train leaves the valley and swings south across the Commanche National Grassland.

Sunflower Valley (50/25)

Farms here produce wheat, corn and sugar beet.

Nearing Trinidad look right for the snow-covered Sangre de Cristo Range and the twin Spanish Peaks of the Colorado Rockies. Indians called these mountains 'the breasts of mother earth'.

TRINIDAD (75/65)

The name (meaning 'trinity') appears to your left on a hill, known as Simpson's Rest after the pioneer buried there. Fisher's Peak (10,000ft) is also on your left. Trinidad is best known for the battle fought between Spanish and US settlers on Christmas Day 1867. The Pioneer Museum and Old Baca House show early settlement life. Amtrak's station is on Pine Street.

Purgatoire River (5/60)

You cross and begin the steep climb to Raton Pass.

Morley (20/45)

An old coal mine and the ruins of a Spanish mission feature on a hill to the right.

Wootton Ranch (35/30)

On the right is the ranch owned by Dick Wootton, paid for by a toll road which became obsolete when the railway arrived. The original Santa Fe Trail can be seen on the right and Interstate 25, which you accompany most of the way to Albuquerque, to the left.

Raton Pass (40/25)

This is the highest point (7,588ft) on the Southwest Chief's journey.

Entering a long tunnel you go from Colorado into New Mexico.

RATON (65/105)

This railroad and mining town in the foothills of the Sangre de Cristo Mountains is the nearest stop to the Philmont Ranch, a 137,441-acre estate owned by the Boy Scouts.

Clifton House Ruins (5/100)
A resting place to your left on the Santa Fe Trail.

Maxwell (20/85)
The 1¾ million-acres Maxwell Wildlife Refuge formerly belonged to Lucien Maxwell — hunter, trapper and a friend of Kit Carson.

Springer (35/70)
Cross the Cimarron River with Baldy Peak (12,441ft) on the far right.

Wagon Mound (60/45)
The butte on the left, shaped like a wagon and horses, was a distinctive landmark on the Santa Fe Trail.

Shoemaker Canyon (80/25)
Pines and cottonwoods flourish in what was a trade route for plains and Texas Indians.

Watrous (85/20)
On the left are the ruins of Fort Union, founded in 1851 and one of the largest in the Southwest. Ahead to the right are the higher Sangre de Cristo Mountains — called 'the blood of Christ' by Spanish settlers because of hardships suffered crossing them.

LAS VEGAS (105/100)
The other Las Vegas. Immediately before the station note La Castenada Hotel on your right (once a Harvey House). The first of Fred Harvey's dining rooms opened at Topeka, Kansas, in the spring of 1876 on the Atchison, Topeka & Santa Fe line. Orders taken on the train were ready to be served on arrival. Theodore Roosevelt joined his Rough Riders for a reunion at La Castenada in 1899.

Indians knew this region for thousands of years before Coronado discovered it in 1541. White settlers arrived in the 1830s and the town grew rapidly when the railroad came in 1879. Prosperity also attracted the likes of Billy the Kid.

You leave Las Vegas, with its roundhouse seen on the right. A letter 'H' on the hill to the left signifies New Mexico Highlands University.

Bernal (20/80)
The ruins of a Las Vegas-Santa Fe stage-coach relay station are on the right. Martinez Canyon is to the left.

Starvation Peak (30/70)
Legend claims 30 settlers climbed the small, flat-topped mesa ahead on the left to defend themselves from Navajo Indians by throwing rocks. They were later starved to death.

S-Curve (35/65)
As you descend a sequence of curves, both ends of the train come into view.

Pecos River (45/55)
The 1775 Mission of San Miguel is on the left.

Rowe (65/35)
Pecos Indians lived here in New Mexico's largest pueblo. After conversion to Christianity by the Spanish in 1617, they built the adobe mission seen in ruins across the valley to your right. Known as the Pecos National Monument, it rests on land donated by Greer Garson. The entrance to the actress's Forked Lightning ranch is marked by pink pillars on the right.

Continue past Glorieta Mesa on the left and Santa Fe National Forest to the right.

Glorieta (80/20)
The site of one of the Civil War's most western battles. A Baptist retreat centre can be seen on the right.

Between here and Lamy the Southwest Chief descends Glorieta Pass (a thousand feet in 10 miles). The route twists through dry, red-rock canyons and hills thick with juniper, tamarisk, scrub oak and ponderosa pine.

Apache Canyon (95/5)
This narrow granite gorge cuts through one of the oldest parts of the Rockies.

LAMY (100/65)
Called after Jean Baptiste Lamy, a 19th Century missionary. The ruins of his school are on your left as you enter town. Amtrak's adobe-style station at County Road 41 opens 0900-1700. Construction difficulties prevented Santa Fe Railway tracks reaching Santa Fe, 15 miles to the north. Lamy Shuttle buses connect with The Southwest Chief and you can book through tickets. Call 505-982-8829 for departures from Santa Fe.

Founded in 1610, Santa Fe is the Southwest's oldest city and the highest (7,000ft) state capital in the US. Formerly known as La Villa Real de Santa Fe de San Francisco de Asis, it's famous for Spanish architecture, opera, galleries, Indian crafts and restaurants. You can visit San Miguel Mission and the oldest house in the United States. Visitors bureau: 201 W Marcy (800-777-CITY).

Taos, 75 miles further north, has a pueblo culture going back 900 years. For information call 800-732-8267.

As you leave Lamy you lose sight of the Sangre de Cristo Mountains back on your right.

Los Cerrillos (15/50)
Rich in minerals, including gold and turquoise. The Ortiz Mountains appear in the left distance. This was the site of the earliest (1830s) US gold mine, and of Amtrak scenes for the first *Superman* film.

Santo Domingo (30/35)
On the right, dating from 1598. Look for beehive-shaped hornos — ovens used for baking bread.

San Felipe (35/30)
The pueblo was established 500 years ago. A Catholic church and Kiva (religious council chamber) feature on the right.

Sandia Crest (55/10)
Seen over to your left in the Cibola National Forest, the mountain reaches 10,678ft. These 'watermelon mountains' go bright red at sunset, when trees on their slopes resemble seeds.

Nearing Albuquerque look for the tower and gold globe of the Federal Office building to your right.

ALBUQUERQUE (65/140)
A centre for business, government and the military, located 5,312ft above sea level. It was named after the Duke of Albuquerque and founded next to the Rio Grande (big river), being ruled by Spain and Mexico before it was won for the United States in 1846. The railroad came in 1880 and today's population of 400,000 represents a quarter of that of the state. Much sought after for its dry, invigorating climate.

Transport: Amtrak's attractive station was built in local style at 314 First SW, five blocks from downtown. Tiwa Indians sell silver and turquoise jewellery on the platform. Ticket office and waiting room open 0930-1800. Information: 242-7816. Free baggage store, vending machines, luggage trolleys, taxi stand.

Sun-Tran buses (843-9200) take you to most places (Mon-Sat).
Taxis: Yellow (247-8888) and Albuquerque (883-4888).
Car Rental: In a city 20 miles long by 25 miles wide a car can be useful. Rent-a-Wreck is at 500 Yale Blvd (256-9693).
Greyhound: 300 Second SW (243-4435).
The airport is five miles from downtown by bus No 50 or taxi.

Tours: American West (255-5710) and Okupin (867-3817). The Albuquerque Trolley (242-1407) has a commentary guide. Walking tours of the Old Town start from the Albuquerque Museum (Wed-Sun from April to October, free).

Visitors Bureau: 625 Silver SW (243-3696). Open weekdays.

Telephone Code: 505.

Accommodation: Write to New Mexico Bed & Breakfast Association, Box 2925, Santa Fe, NM 87504. In Albuquerque try the Mauger Estate, 701 Roma (242-8755) and Casita Chamisa, 850 Chamisal Rd (897-4644).

KOA's nearest campsite is at 5739 Ouray Rd NW (831-1911). Take bus No 15.
International Hostel (IYHF): 1012 W Central Ave (243-6101). Members $8, non-members $10.

Hotels include the Sheraton Old Town Inn at 800 Rio Grande (843-6300); La Posada, 125 2nd (242-9090); Rio Grand Inn, 1015 Rio Grande Blvd (843-9500); Holiday Inn Midtown, 2020 Menaul (884-2511); American Family

Lodge, 2108 Menaul (884-2480); Gaslight Inn, 601 Central Ave NE (247-0416) — singles $16, doubles $22.

Old Town: Off Central Ave and Rio Grande Blvd (243-3215). Colourful activity around the plaza with artists, craft shops, good food and adobe buildings. The 1706 San Felipe de Neri Church is impressive.

Albuquerque Museum: 2000 Mountain Rd, in Old Town (242-4600). Over 400 years of New Mexican art and history, exploring the culture of the Rio Grande valley. Closed Mon, admission.

Indian Pueblo Cultural Center: 2401 12th NW (843-7270). Traditional food, crafts and dancing. Open daily, admission. Take bus No 36.

Sandia Peak: East of Albuquerque off Interstate 25. See mountains and desert, plus the lights of night-time Albuquerque and Santa Fe. The Sandia Peak Tram takes you up on the longest tramway in the world, gaining 4,000ft in 15 minutes (298-8518). Sandia Crest (10,680ft) is 300ft higher and can be reached by road from the east side.

National Atomic Museum: 20358 Wyoming Blvd, Kirkland Air Base (845-6670). Documentary film and exhibitions show how atomic bombs were developed for use at Hiroshima and Nagasaki. Open daily, free.

You leave Albuquerque past the University of New Mexico's sports stadium on the left. Rio Grande Park and Zoo are to the right. The Southwest Chief begins to depart the Rio Grande valley and enter New Mexico's desert country. A guide from the Inter-Tribal Indian Ceremonial Association joins the train between here and Gallup to describe highlights en route.

The Ladron Mountains can be seen to your right and the Manzano Range on the far left horizon. As you cross the Rio Grande on its way to the Gulf of Mexico, look for lavender-coloured tamarisk trees (salt cedars).

Isleta Indian Reservation (15/125)
St Augustine Church on the left was built in 1613 and is still in use. Away to the right is Mount Taylor, an extinct volcano (11,301ft).

Your train crosses the River Puerco, a tributary of the Rio Grande, and starts climbing 3,000ft to the continental divide.

Kneeling Nuns (48/92)
The rock formation on the right resembles two nuns at an altar.

Route 66 (50/90)
This famed highway crosses the track on a wooden bridge.

Mesita Pueblo (55/85)
To the left. Gypsum cliffs on the right reveal uranium workings. You join the San Jose River on the left before crossing it several times ahead.

Laguna Pueblo (60/80)
The youngest and largest of the pueblos you pass on this route.

Paraje Pueblo (63/77)
A mission building can be seen on the left.

McCarty's Pueblo (68/72)
Part of the Acoma Indian Reservation to your left, where a 200-year-old church dominates the bluff.

Anzac (75/65)
Mount Taylor produced the black lava beds seen on your left, favoured by warmth-loving rattlesnakes.

From now until Gallup the Southwest Chief travels among the Red Cliffs, some of which are 7,000ft high. Legend says the hills became red after a wounded stag shed blood escaping. The desert sun produces spectacular changes of colour.

Grants (90/50)
An Anaconda uranium smelter is on the right.

Continental Divide (110/25)
Cross at Campbell's Pass.

Pyramid Rock (130/10)
Behind this landmark to your right is the spire of Church Rock, where Indians claim a jilted maiden leaped to her death.

Red Rock State Park (132/8)
Each August, 50 tribes gather on the right for ceremonial dancing, games and culture.

GALLUP (140/90)
'Indian capital of the world'. Half the population are native Americans, including Acoma, Zuni, Hopi, Navajo and Apache. It's a good place to buy silver jewellery, baskets, pottery, rugs and blankets. Amtrak's station is at 210 E Highway 66.

Gallup gives access to the Four Corners region comprising the Painted Desert, the Petrified Forest, Mesa Verde National Park and the South Colorado Mountains.

New Mexico/Arizona State Line (10/80)
Arizona does not observe Daylight Savings Time, so watches go back an hour (forward when travelling east) only from November to April.

You continue through desert country of mystical beauty, where the wide plains are interrupted by mesas and buttes. Winds have carved the red and yellow sandstone into spires and caves.

Holbrook (70/20)
A trading place for Hopi, Navajo and Apache. On your right is the Blevins House where Marshal Owens shot five outlaws.
The train joins the Little Colorado River for the next few minutes.

WINSLOW (90/60)
About 20,000 years ago a meteor hit the earth 23 miles west of here, causing a crater 600ft deep and 4,000ft wide. 'Meteor City' is another trading post for Hopi and Navajo. The station at E 2nd Street is a good example of Spanish-style architecture.

Canyon Diablo (25/30)
Cross on a 544ft high bridge, with a trading post and store ruins to the right. You continue through more canyons and high desert country. Near Flagstaff look right for Mount Agassiz (12,340ft) and Humphrey's Peak (12,670ft).

FLAGSTAFF (60/160)
Almost 7,000ft above sea level, the town was so named after settlers celebrated the country's hundredth birthday by making a flagstaff out of a pine tree stripped of branches. Amtrak's station at 1 E Santa Fe Ave opens 0645-2330. Thruway buses connect with Sedona and Phoenix to the south. Tours operate between the station and the Grand Canyon, Monument Valley, Oak Creek Canyon, the Painted Desert and the Petrified Forest.
   Buses leave for the southern rim of the Grand Canyon early in the morning, and you can book through tickets via Amtrak. The Colorado River created this canyon 190 miles long and 10 miles wide, revealing two billion years of history. The best way to appreciate it is to walk one of the trails — that on the south rim being easiest. Muleback rides must be booked a year in advance.
   For tours and lodge accommodation contact the Reservations Department, Box 699, Grand Canyon, AZ 86023 (638-2401). Flights are available from Grand Canyon Airlines (638-2407). Temperatures reach 100°F during summer but fall below freezing in winter, so take sensible precautions.
   The Southwest Chief leaves Flagstaff and travels among the Coconino Forest's ponderosa pines. Lowell Observatory, from where the planet Pluto was discovered, is on a hill to your right.

Seligman (80/80)
This mining and cattle-trading town was founded by the railroad in 1882 at the junction of the Santa Fe line and a route south to Prescott.

KINGMAN (160/64)
Another railroad town, where buses connect with Las Vegas, Nevada.

Arizona/California State Line (50/14)
You change from Mountain to Pacific Time. Since Arizona does not observe Daylight Savings Time, watches go back an hour (forward when travelling east) only from November to April.

NEEDLES (64/160)

California's most eastern city was named after neighbouring rock pinnacles. This is the Mojave Desert, often registering America's hottest temperatures.

BARSTOW (160/100)

For Barstow, and the route to San Bernardino, see *The Desert Wind*.

After San Bernardino you enter the sprawling congestion of southern California.

Fontana (15/15)

A disused Kaiser steel plant can be seen on the left.

Cucamonga (20/10)

Watch for the picturesque station building.

POMONA (30/32)

Though named after the Roman goddess of fruits, residential development has overtaken orchards and vineyards. September's Los Angeles County Fair here attracts more people than any other in the USA. The Atchison, Topeka & Santa Fe station located in the fairgrounds features rolling stock and locomotives, including the largest steam and diesel engines ever made. The Southwest Chief stops at N Garey Ave (open 0600-2115).

Leave Pomona with the San Gabriel Mountains on your right.

Glendora (10/22)

Houses nestle among hills on both sides.

Azusa (15/17)

The Monrovia Nursery to the right is one of the biggest in the world. You cross a frequently dry San Gabriel River.

Monrovia (20/12)

Another Spanish-stye depot is seen on the right. Your train joins the Colorado Freeway (Interstate 210) and outpaces commuting traffic for several minutes.

You cross Colorado Blvd, site of Pasadena's Tournament of the Roses parade, then leave the freeway and enter a brief tunnel before emerging in downtown Pasadena. Red-domed City Hall is on your left and the Green Hotel's towers and balconies to your right.

PASADENA (32/25)

The name is a Chippewa word for 'crown of the valley'. Pasadena has celebrated the Roses Tournament since 1890, and a million visitors arrive each New Year's Day for the Rose Bowl football game. The 1908 Gamble House features traditional southern California architecture. Information bureau: 171 S Los Robles Ave (818-795-9311). Amtrak's station at 222 S Raymond Ave opens 0630-2100.

Cross the Arroyo Seco on a steel trestle before approaching downtown Los Angeles, with Dodger Stadium on a hill to the right.

Los Angeles River (20/5)

As you join this usually dry concrete channel, the Los Angeles skyline comes into view ahead. Prominent on your right are the Post Office building's twin domes and the tower of City Hall. The county jail is seen to your left just before the station.

LOS ANGELES

For Los Angeles, see *The Coast Starlight*.

9 The Sunset Limited

New Orleans—Los Angeles

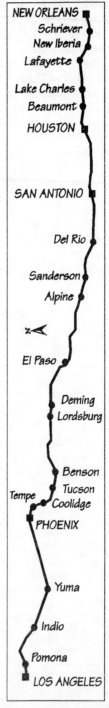

Travelling west, you head into two sunsets via the swamps of bayou country, flirt with Mexico's border and cross the Texas range. You see mountains, deserts and California's orange groves. The original Sunset Limited began in 1895 as an all Pullman service (complete with silver finger-bowls) between San Francisco and New Orleans. Passengers continued to New York by ship.

Frequency: Three trains a week operate in each direction. The westbound service leaves New Orleans mid-afternoon on Mon, Wed and Sat to arrive in Houston late evening and San Antonio during the night. You reach El Paso by the second afternoon, Tucson mid-evening and Phoenix two hours later, arriving in Los Angeles early on Wed, Fri or Mon morning.
  Travelling east, the Sunset Limited leaves Los Angeles late Sun, Tues and Fri evening, reaching Phoenix early morning, Tucson mid-morning and El Paso late afternoon. You reach San Antonio early the following morning and Houston towards midday, arriving in New Orleans mid-evening on Tues, Thurs or Sun.

Reservations: All reserved.

Equipment: Superliner coaches.

Sleeping: Superliner economy, de luxe, family, special bedrooms.

Food: Complete meals, snacks, sandwiches, drinks.

Lounge Car: Movies, games, hospitality hour.

Baggage: Check-in service at main stations.

NEW ORLEANS

The Big Easy has jazz, Mardi Gras, voodoo and Creole cooking. It also has more bars and churches per person than anywhere else in the country. Immortalised by Tennessee Williams and William Faulkner, this unique city was founded by the French, taken over by the Spanish, then bought by the US in 1803. Settlers from France, Spain, England, Germany and the Caribbean have made it America's most cosmopolitan city.

Relaxed charm and ragged beauty make New Orleans the ideal place for letting the good times roll. Louis Armstrong and Fats Domino were born here and blues, soul and Cajun bands are easy to find. Jazz venues include Mahogany Hall, 309 Bourbon (525-5595) and Preservation Hall, 726 St Peter (523-8939).

New Orleans gets humid during long hot summers and sees the occasional hurricane.

Transport: Amtrak shares with Greyhound the modern Union Passenger Terminal at 1001 Loyola Ave. Information: 528-1610. Ticket office open 0545-2030. Waiting room 24 hours. Lockers, vending machines, luggage trolleys, restaurant, shop, taxi stand.

The RTA operates buses throughout the city and streetcars along the Riverfront and St Charles Ave (569-2700).
Taxis: Checker (943-2411) and Liberty Bell (822-5974).
Car Rental: Budget, 1317 Canal (467-2277).
Greyhound: 1001 Loyola Ave (525-9371).

Buses by Louisiana Transit (737-9611) and Airport Rhodes (469-7555) go to Moisant Airport at Kenner, 15 miles west of downtown.

Tours: City and plantation tours from Gray Line (587-0861) and New Orleans (487-1991). Steamboat Company river cruises (586-8777) take in the Audubon Zoo. Free walking tours go from the Jean Lafitte Historical Park, 916 N Peters (589-2636).

Visitors Bureau: 1520 Sugar Bowl Dr (566-5011) and 529 St Ann (566-5031). Open daily.

Telephone Code: 504.

Accommodation: A wide range is available, from ultra-modern to historic. Call the Tourist Commission (566-5011) or Housing Bureau (566-5021). Or contact New Orleans Bed & Breakfast, Box 8163, New Orleans, LA 70182 (822-5046).
YMCA: 936 St Charles Ave (568-9622). Singles $26, doubles $32.
Marquette House AYH Hostel: 2253 Carondelet (523-3014). Members $10, non-members $14.

Hotels include the Fairmont at 123 Baronne (529-7111); Bourbon Orleans, 717 Orleans (800-521-5338); Cornstalk, 915 Royal (523-1515); Landmark French Quarter, 920 N Rampart (800-535-7862); LaSalle, 1113 Canal (523-5831) — singles $27, doubles $30; Old World Inn, 1330 Prytania (566-1330) — singles $28, doubles $35.

French Quarter: The Vieux Carré centres on Jackson Square, where the first settlers built fine decorated houses. Soak up atmosphere at the French Market and along Bourbon Street.

Jackson Square: Originally the Place d'Armes, where armies marched and public executions took place. Later it became a park renamed after General Andrew Jackson, whose bronze statue stands opposite the cathedral. A good place to see artists and street musicians.

Pontalba Apartments: Constructed on two sides of Jackson Square over a hundred years ago for the Baroness Micaela Pontalba, these buildings have handsome balconies and cast ironwork. The 1850s House at 523 St Ann (568-6968) opens Wed-Sun, admission.

Mardi Gras: 'The greatest free show on earth' takes place during the week before Lent, with parades, bands and every kind of revelry. Book your accommodation in good time. The Germaine Wells Mardi Gras Museum at 813 Bienville (523-5433) shows flamboyant costumes (closed Sat, free).

Old US Mint: Decatur and Esplanade Ave (568-6968). This 1835 building has carnival exhibits as well as the New Orleans Jazz Collection. Look for Louis Armstrong's first trumpet. Open Wed-Sun, admission.

Louisiana Railroad Museum: At 4th and Huey P Long Ave, Gretna, just across the river (361-0479). Located in a restored Illinois Central caboose and a former Southern Pacific freight house near the Texas & Pacific station. The museum features 9in-gauge steam trains and photographs. Open Mon-Sat, admission.

You depart New Orleans with the Superdome sports complex (four times bigger than Houston's Astrodome) to the right. Buildings on the left belong to the Picayune States-Item Times and Xavier University.

Huey P Long Bridge (20/50)
Ahead on the left, the bridge was named after a right-wing senator and governor who ruled Louisiana in the 1930s. Before the 4.4-mile bridge was opened, trains crossed here on barges. The Sunset Limited inches over, giving views of the Avondale shipyard and industrial landscape to your right. New Orleans' skyline is beyond. The Mississippi curves away to your left, showing how the Crescent City acquired its nickname.

   Your train slowly descends from the bridge and enters a bayou country of swamps, forests, mansions and Spanish moss. 'Bayou' comes from the Choctaw word *bayuk*, meaning a sluggish stretch of water. The French-born pirate and smuggler Jean Lafitte frequented this area.

Harahan (30/40)
The cemetery on your right has graves above the ground to cope with the swamp conditions.

Mississippi River (40/30)
As you travel beside levees look for grain loading facilities on the river banks.

Highway 90 (45/25)
On your left is the highway which the Sunset Limited accompanies for 1,100 miles to El Paso. You pass an oil refinery on the right and lose sight of the Mississippi to the north.

Des Allemands (50/20)
Its name is French for 'of the Germans'. The bayou is on the right.

Note the first of many Louisiana sugar cane fields to the left. Land here is so wet that much of this line had to be built on pilings.

Bayou LaFourche (65/5)
Cross at the town of the same name.

Bayou Blue (67/3)
Cross just before Schriever.

SCHRIEVER (70/80)
This industrial town is closely involved with off-shore drilling.

You cross Chacahoula Swamp, its graceful cypress trees decorated with Spanish moss.

Bayou Boeuf (15/65)
To your left is more evidence of the oil industry, as the McDermott plant assembles giant rigs. Pontooned helicopters service platforms in the Gulf of Mexico.

Your train crosses Bayou Chene.

Morgan City (25/55)
Called after Charles Morgan, who built this section of the line when it belonged to the Louisiana & Texas Railroad. The Intercoastal Waterway on the left reaches from Brownsville, Texas, to New York, giving inland industries access to the Gulf.

Atchafalaya River (26/54)
Over 200ft deep, the river has busy embankments on both sides.

Garden City (40/40)
Look for a plantation estate to the right.

Jeanerette (65/15)
A church and another above-the-ground cemetery (or 'city of the dead') are to your right.

As you approach New Iberia, mansions and the towers of St Peter's Church appear on the right.

NEW IBERIA (80/22)

Commercial activity coexists here with French and Spanish heritage. Among the antebellum homes is Shadows on the Teche. Edward McIllhenny (founder of the Tabasco Sauce Company) created Avery Island as a 200-acre sanctuary for egrets, herons and ibises.

Between here and Lafayette the Sunset travels through typical southern Louisiana countryside. Watch for mansions and sugar plantations after you cross the Vermilion River.

LAFAYETTE (22/80)

'Capital of Acadiana'. Longfellow called these bayous, forests and flowers the Eden of Louisiana. French Acadians came from Nova Scotia when the British took over there in the 18th Century, and Cajuns are their descendants. Lafayette is home to oil companies as well as the University of Southwestern Louisiana. Amtrak's station is at 133 E Grant. Buses connect with Baton Rouge, 50 miles east.

Rayne (15/65)

'Frog capital of the world', with jumping contests at the annual frog festival.

Mermenteau River (40/40)

Cross the river connecting Lake Charles and the Intercoastal Waterway.

LAKE CHARLES (80/80)

Though barely 16ft above sea level, this deepwater port ships oil, chemicals and cement.

Calcasieu River (5/75)

As you cross look for a duelling-pistol design on the highway bridge to your left — a reminder of when pirates operated here.

Orange (40/40)

Cross the Sabine River and enter the Lone Star state of Texas. For a while the landscape remains Louisiana-like with cypresses, rice fields and an occasional alligator. Between here and El Paso you cover 941 miles in Texas.

BEAUMONT (80/100)

A town situated on the Neches River. In 1901 the Lucas Gusher began delivering 75,000 barrels of oil a day at nearby Spindletop Field. Beaumont produces more professional footballers than anywhere else in the country, and the athlete Babe Didrikson Zaharias once lived here. Port Arthur is five miles southeast.

Irrigated rice fields can be seen on the right half an hour after you leave Beaumont.

Trinity River (50/50)

Cross as you approach Liberty.

San Jacinto River (70/30)

You cross the river on its way to Galveston Bay. On your left in the far distance is the 570ft San Jacinto Monument.

Nearing Houston you pass Santa Fe railyards on the left, busy with long lines of freight wagons. As the city skyline comes into view look for the Allied Bank spires and the chisel-shaped towers of the Pennzoil building.

HOUSTON (100/250)

The biggest city in Texas covers 500 acres. A brash, bustling place where both banker and redneck can feel at home, it was founded in 1836 by New York property developers who called it 'Baghdad on the bayou'. Oil brought prosperity and tall buildings, and a 50-mile ship canal links port facilities to Galveston on the coast. The oil business has its ups and downs but Houston remains energetic and slightly undisciplined.

Houston is hot in more ways than one, sharing the same latitude as the Sahara. For most of the year the weather is subtropical, but luckily air-conditioning prevails.

Transport: Amtrak's station is at 902 Washington Ave, near downtown but not in a safe neighbourhood. Information: 224-1577. Ticket office open 0630-2400 (Mon, Tues, Fri, Sat), 0800-2400 (Wed, Thurs) and 0630-1600 (Sun). Lockers, vending machines, luggage trolleys, taxi stand.

Metro buses (635-4000) operate throughout the city and to outlying areas. Maps and schedules are available from 912 Dallas.
Taxis: Yellow (236-1111) and Liberty (695-4321).
Car Rental: Rent-A-Heap, 5722 Southwest Fwy (977-7771).
Greyhound: 2121 S Main (222-1161).

The Intercontinental Airport is 25 miles north by Airport Express (523-8888). Hobby Airport (for domestic flights) is nine miles southeast. Take bus No 50 from downtown.

Tours: Gray Line (223-8800) and Unlimited (694-1519).

Visitors Bureau: 3300 Main (523-5050). Open weekdays.

Telephone Code: 713.

Accommodation: Contact the Bed & Breakfast Society, 921 Heights Blvd (868-4654).
YMCA: 1600 Louisiana Ave (659-8501). For men and women, $15.
International AYH Hostel: 5302 Crawford (523-1009). Less than $10 per night.
Houston Youth Hostel: 5530 Hillman ((926-3444). Dormitory rooms for men and women, $7. Take bus No 36.

Hotels include the Westin Galleria at 5060 W Alabama (960-8100); Holiday Inn-Downtown, 801 Calhoun (659-2222); Luxeford, 1400 Old Spanish Trail (796-1000); Sheraton Town and Country, 910 West Belt (467-6411);

Brookhollow Hilton, 2404 North Loop West (688-7711); Grant, 8200 Main (668-8000) — singles $28, doubles $35.

Port of Houston: Watch non-stop activity in America's third largest, somewhat polluted, port from a platform on Kirby Drive (open daily). There are boat trips most days and free tours of the MV *Sam Houston*, for which you need reservations three months in advance. Contact the Port of Houston, PO Box 2562, Houston, TX 77252 (225-4044).

Sam Houston Park: Bagby and Lamar (655-1912). This green space in the middle of downtown contains historic buildings such as the 1847 Kellum-Noble House (oldest brick house in Houston). The Texas History Museum has items from the 16th Century to the present. Open daily, free.

Lyndon B Johnson Space Center: 20 miles south on I-45 (483-4321). Better known as NASA, headquarters of the manned space programme, it has rockets, lunar vehicles, moon samples and training simulators. Film shows and tours daily. Admission. Take the Park and Ride Shuttle No 246.

San Jacinto Battleground: 22 miles southeast on TX 225 (479-2421). Where Sam Houston defeated Santa Anna in 1836 to create an independent Texas. Great views can be had from the 570ft monument (elevator admission charge). Free museum open daily. Tours of the *USS Texas* (admission).

After Houston the Sunset Limited embarks on its longest run without a scheduled stop. The landscape changes radically as you leave the Gulf Coast's green humidity for drier conditions, where cacti replace the live oaks and Spanish moss.

Watch for fields of rice, soya beans and cotton. Many birds can be seen in this region, including delicate white egrets.

Sugarland (50/200)
A large Imperial Sugar processing plant appears to your right before you cross the Brazos River.

Richmond and Rosenberg (60/190)
These towns were famous in prohibition days for gambling and women. A brick court-house is on the right.

Soon after Richmond look right for rice elevators storing the local crop.

Colorado River(110/140)
Cross the Texas Colorado River — no relation to its bigger namesake.

Columbus (111/139)
The dome and clock of an old court-house can be seen to the left. Approaching the station look left also for an ancient live oak, formerly the town's hanging tree.

Weimar (125/125)
The depot on the left is now a library.

Randolph Air Force Base (220/30)
The runways are to the left and a mission-style tower on the right.

SAN ANTONIO (250/185)
A modern, relaxed city which great numbers of tourists (even other Texans) visit to unwind. Named by explorer Domingo Teran when he arrived on St Anthony's Day 1691, San Antonio has existed under six flags. These influences show in the Spanish missions, Mexican ambience, fiestas and stockyards. Not forgetting the Alamo.

April's Fiesta is a Mexican Mardi Gras featuring a river parade, rodeos and the Night in Old San Antonio.

Transport: Amtrak's station at 1174 E Commerce is an elegant Spanish-style building with stained glass and an imposing staircase. Information: 223-3226. Ticket office and waiting room open 24 hours. Lockers, vending machines, luggage trolleys.

See downtown on foot or by VIA's replica 1907 Trolley (438-3846). VIA buses (227-2020) serve the metropolitan area.
Taxis: Checker (222-2151) and Yellow (226-4242).
Car Rental: Rent-A-Clunker (922-9464).
Greyhound: 500 N St Mary's (270-5800).

The airport is eight miles north by taxi and Supervan shuttle (344-7433).

Tours: Alamo (735-5019) and San Antonio City (680-8724) visit the Alamo and missions, and the San Antonio Trolley does a 45-minute circuit of downtown. Riverboats leave from the Paseo del Rio dock on Commerce (222-1701).

Visitors Bureau: 210 S Alamo (299-8123) and 317 Alamo Pl (299-8155). Open daily.

Telephone Code: 512.

Accommodation: Contact King William Bed & Breakfast Registry, 201 E Rische (227-1190).
AYH Hostel: 621 Pierce (223-9426). Members $10, non-members $12. Take bus No 11.

Hotels include El Tropicano at 110 Lexington (223-9461); Menger, 204 Alamo Pl (223-4361); Travelodge on the River, 100 Villita (226-2271); Seven Oaks, 1400 Austin Hwy (824-5371); Town and Country, 6901 San Pedro (344-4511); Rodeway Inn Downtown, 900 N Main (223-2951); Traveler's, 220 N Broadway (226-4381) — singles $16, doubles $24.

Paseo Del Rio: This two-mile walk through parkland beside the meandering river has music, bars, restaurants, boat rides and a cosmopolitan parade of people (227-4262).

The Alamo: On Alamo Pl (255-1391). This is one of the city's oldest buildings and the most visited attraction in Texas. Scene of the battle (1836) for Texan independence in which 188 defenders, including Davy Crockett and Jim Bowie, died fighting Santa Anna's overwhelming forces. Museum and guided tours. Open daily, free.

King William District: These Victorian houses on the southern edge of downtown were built for German merchants. The Steves Homestead at 509 King William (225-5924) opens daily, admission.

The Missions: San Antonio is not called Mission City for nothing. Apart from the Alamo, four others are on the Mission Trail starting at S Alamo and Market. All open daily, free. For information call 229-5701.

Mission Concepcion: 807 Mission Rd (533-7109). The oldest unrestored mission (dating from 1731) has its original frescoes.

Mission San Jose: Roosevelt Ave and Mission (922-0543). Biggest and most impressive, with a church, granary and aqueduct. A mariachi mass takes place on Sundays.

Mission San Juan Capistrano: 9107 Graf (534-3161). Quiet, with a pretty bell tower.

Mission San Francisco de la Espada: 10040 Espada (627-2064). The aqueduct built in the 1730s between here and Mission San Jose is still in use.

The Sunset Limited, accompanied by through cars from the Texas Eagle, leaves San Antonio for prairie country. Cacti, sage and yuccas thrive in the arid conditions.

Laughlin Air Force Base (175/10)
Seen over to your left.

DEL RIO (185/160)
Queen city of the Rio Grande, otherwise known as 'the wool and mohair capital of the world'. Del Rio is famous for sheep and goats and is the home of the Val Verde winery (the oldest in Texas). Immediately to the south is the Mexican town of Ciudad Acuna, which you can see on bluffs across the river.
On the left is the Rio Grande, separating the US from Mexico.

Amistad Reservoir (15/145)
Amistad is Spanish for friendship, and the reservoir was a joint project of the US and Mexican governments. Around 30 miles long and 20 miles wide, it dams the Rio Grande near its junction with the Devil River.
Over the next 200 miles the Sunset Limited climbs 3,500ft. Watch for prickly pear cacti, yuccas and woolly grandpa's beard. Persimmons, mesquite and greasewood (creosote bush) also grow here.

Pecos River (50/110)
Cross a canyon on the state's highest railroad bridge (321ft).

Eagle Rock Canyon (70/90)
Nearby in 1883 the last spike was driven to complete the second transcontinental railway. As you approach Langtry you see strange rock formations jutting from the canyon wall.

Langtry (71/89)
Where 'Judge' Roy Bean ran the saloon and dispensed his version of law west of the Pecos. Reverence for Lily Langtry caused him to change the town's name from Vinegarone.

Dryden (140/20)
Look for parts of the wall which was built to keep out Pancho Villa's raiders.

SANDERSON (160/100)
Roy Bean owned another saloon here when the town enjoyed a wild reputation. Outlaws and rustlers mingled with cattle ranchers and sheepmen. Amtrak's halt at 201 Downey is a servicing stop for the Sunset Limited.

Leave with the ruined brick walls of the Sanderson Wool Commission to your right. Wool remains a significant industry in this region.

An Apache Indian cave and cooking mound feature on the right five minutes from Sanderson. Sheep and goat ranching are impractical west of here because of predators such as coyote, puma, bobcats and eagles.

Haymond (60/40)
The former cow camp is a now ghost town, with a cemetery and deserted buildings on the right.

Warwick Flat (65/35)
A crossing place on the Commanche War Trail, running a thousand miles from upper Texas to Chihuahua.

As you travel among the Glass and Del Norte Mountains watch for deer, pronghorn antelope, jackrabbits and javalina (wild pigs). Mount Ord (6,814ft) is on the left and Altvda Mountain (6,860ft) to the right.

Approaching Alpine you see the rodeo grounds on your right. The letters SR on a hill signify Sul Ross University.

ALPINE (100/220)
The seat of Texas's largest county, Brewster. Alpine's Spanish-style station at 101 W Holland is used by tourists bound for Big Bend National Park. Mitre Peak (6,100ft) is on your right.

Proceed through colourful canyonlands to Paisano Pass, the highest point (5,000ft) on this journey. Chinati Peak (7,730ft) is ahead on the left.

Marfa Ghost Lights (20/200)
For 50 years mysterious lights have appeared at intervals over the desert to your left.

Marfa (25/195)

The domed, stone building on the right is the 1886 Presidio County court-house. The adobe walls of a Second World War POW camp can be seen on the left.

Also on the left, 10 minutes west of Marfa, is the wooden windmill used as a film location for *Giant*.

Valentine (60/160)

Bear Mountain and Mount Livermore (8,332ft) are to the right.

As you descend from the high plains, fields begin to appear. Van Horn is ahead in the right distance.

Quitman Mountains (90/130)

Change from Central to Mountain Time, so watches go back an hour (forward when travelling east).

For the first time in 24 hours you part company with Highway 90, which continues north.

Hot Wells (100/120)

A ruined adobe school can be seen on your right, the Eagle Mountains to your left.

Sierra Blanca (120/100)

Home of the last adobe court-house still functioning in Texas. The Sierra Blanca Peak (6,970ft), seen among the mountains to the right, looks light because it contains soapstone.

Fort Hancock (150/70)

The fort's remains are on the right.

As you approach Fabens note the bright decorations on graves in a Mexican cemetery to your right.

Fabens (180/40)

A mission-style church is on the left, next to a cotton ginning plant.

Ysleta (190/30)

Home of the longest-surviving ethnic group in Texas, the Tigua Indians. Ysleta also has the second oldest church in the country (1682).

Near El Paso you travel through industrial scenes with oil and copper refineries. On your left is a large shell surrounding the civic auditorium.

EL PASO (220/85)

Encircled by the mile-high Franklin Mountains, this laid-back city was named after a pass (El Paso del Rio del Norte) created by the Rio Grande. Nearby are Carlsbad Canyon National Park, Las Cruces and Cloudcroft ski resort.

Amtrak's renovated station at 700 San Francisco dates from 1904-5 and was designed by Daniel Burnham, who created Union Station in Washington. Ticket office open 1100-1900. Visitors Bureau: 5 Civic Center Pl (534-0686). The Gardner AYH Hostel is at 311 E Franklin (532-3661) — members $10.

El Paso maintains close links with Ciudad Juarez in Chihuahua, Mexico, seen above palisades to your left as you leave. On your right are the campus and stadium of the University of Texas.

On top of the Sierra de Cristo Rey ahead to your left is a 33ft statue of the crucifixion known as the Christ of the Rockies. Pilgrims climb four miles to the 4,576ft summit to celebrate the Feast of Cristo Rey. This point is the meeting place of Texas, Mexico and New Mexico.

Rio Grande (5/80)

A Southwestern Portland Cement plant appears on the right and a mineral refinery to the left. You cross the river and enter New Mexico.

Sunland Park Race Track (7/78)

Seen on the right.

US/Mexico Border (10/75)

The dividing line is signalled by a white post 30ft to the left of the tracks.

The mountains seen on both sides are the Portillos. The Lincoln County cattle wars to the north of here resulted in the shooting of Billy the Kid by Pat Garrett at Mesilla in 1881. In 1916 this barren land also witnessed Pancho Villa's marauders on their way to attack the town of Columbus.

Florida Mountains (75/10)

Florida Peak is prominent close on your left. A hole in the ridge at about 7,300ft is known as the Window Peak. To your right, the Cooke's Peak Range rises to 8,408ft.

Cross the Mimbres River near Deming, with the Luna County court-house clock tower on the left.

DEMING (85/50)

Deming is the scene each August of the world's only duck races.

This area has 70,000 irrigated acres producing wine, peanuts, pecans, beans, cotton and grain sorghums. A mild climate among the Cooke's and Florida Mountains makes it popular for retirement. Other resorts can be found to the north near Silver City, where Billy the Kid grew up. Amtrak is at 301 E Railroad Ave. Nearby Rock Hound State Park is a Mecca for mineralogists.

Continental Divide (25/25)

The lowest elevation (4,587ft) for any rail crossing of America's divide. Water falling to the west of here flows into the Pacific and to the east into the Atlantic.

LORDSBURG (50/110)

Located in a hollow between the Burro and Pyramid Mountains, Lordsburg began as a railroad town. The government bought the land from Mexico in 1854 so that a line could be built to California.

On the right soon after Lordsburg you pass a dry lake where mirages transform the sand into sheets of water.

Steins (20/90)
The site of the final battle between Apache chief Cochise and the US cavalry.

New Mexico/Arizona State Line (25/85)
Arizona does not observe Daylight Savings Time so watches go back an hour (forward when travelling east) only between April and October.

Cochise's Face (35/75)
On a ridge of the Chiricahua Mountains rising 9,795ft on your left is the commanding outline of Cochise gazing at the sky. The Peloncillo Mountains away to your right are rich in gold, silver and copper.

Dos Cabezas (60/50)
In the Sulphur Hills on the left look for this 'two heads' rock formation named after Cochise and the Indian agent Thomas Jeffords.

Wilcox (65/45)
From an altitude of 4,167ft here the Sunset Limited will descend 3,000ft to Phoenix.

Wilcox Playa (70/40)
A dry lake creates convincing mirages, even reflecting mountains on the left.

Dragoon (95/15)
During wars with the cavalry between 1861 and 1872, Cochise and the Chiricahuas occupied the Dragoon Mountains to your left.
You cross the San Pedro River.

BENSON (110/55)
This was formerly a stop for the Butterfield stage-coach from St Louis to San Francisco, a 2,800-mile journey which took 55 days. When the railway came along in 1880 Benson developed into a shipping point for the mines around Tombstone, 25 miles south.

You leave with the Rincon Mountains on your right and travel to Tucson through a series of canyons along the Pantano Wash. Look for the spiked leaves of yucca plants from which Indians made shoes and baskets.

The buildings seen away to the right 15 minutes from Benson were a film set for *Little House on the Prairie.*

East and westbound trains proceed on different lines part of the way between Benson and Tucson, allowing the eastbound Sunset an easier climb. Sometimes the tracks are half a mile apart.

Durant Castle (25/30)
This large house is high up on your right.

Vail (27/28)
You travel on the higher of two overlapping bridges — eastbound trains use the one below — and continue down through Texas Canyon, catching sight of the train ahead.

Santa Rita Shrine (37/18)
A pink Catholic church stands circled by desert on the right.

Davis Monthan Air Force Base (47/8)
Around 5,000 planes are mothballed in an aircraft 'boneyard' on the right, preserved in dry desert air. Next to the tracks is the Pima Air Museum featuring Second World War bombers.

Approaching Tucson you enter the railyards of the Santa Fe Pacific (once the Southern Pacific).

University of Arizona (50/5)
The stadium and campus are on the right. Low down on the south horizon is the Santa Rita Range.

TUCSON (55/60)
The state's second largest city began in 1776 as a supply station for the Mission San Xavier del Bac. It became capital of Arizona from 1867 to 1877, and Spanish, Mexican and Confederate flags have flown here. Half a million people now live on the banks of the Santa Cruz River.

Tucson is a centre for farming, government and high-tech industry only 60 miles north of the Mexican border. It's bounded by mountains — Santa Ritas to the south, Santa Catalinas to the north, Rincons in the east and Tucsons to the west. The city is a thousand feet higher than Phoenix, so temperatures are slightly cooler.

Transport: The mission-style station is at 400 E Toole. Information: 623-4442. Ticket office and waiting room open 0815-2145 (Sun, Mon, Thurs), 0815-1545 (Fri, Sat) and 1415-2145 (Tues, Wed). Lockers, vending machines, newspapers, taxi stand.

Sun Tran (792-9222) operates buses and the 4th Ave trolley.
Taxis: Checker (623-1133) and Arizona Stagecoach (889-9681).
Car Rental: Care Free (790-2655).
Greyhound: 2 S 4th Ave (792-0972).
The airport is six miles south by bus No 16.

Tours: Gray Line (622-881). Pleasure Bent (884-0777) visits nearby ghost towns.

Visitors Bureau: 130 S Scott Ave (624-1889). Open daily.

Telephone Code: 602.

Accommodation: Contact Old Pueblo Bed & Breakfast, PO Box 13603, Tucson, AZ 85732 (790-2399).
Old Pueblo Youth Hostel: 411 E 9th.
Hotels include the Santa Rita at 88 E Broadway (791-7581); Continental Inn, 750 W 22nd (624-4455); El Rancho, 225 W Drachman (622-7411); Motel 6, 1031 E Benson Hwy (628-1264); Franciscan Inn, 1165 N Stone Ave (622-7763); Congress, 311 E Congress (622-8848) — singles $25, doubles $30.

Historic Tucson: Many places are within walking distance of the station. The Pima County court-house features a mosaic-tiled dome and a courtyard fountain. Tucson became a walled city (or presidio) when the Spanish built a barrier against Indians, and the court-house preserves a small part of the wall. El Tiradito (the wishing shrine) at Simpson and Granada is where dreams come true for believers who light a candle.

Arizona Heritage Centre: 949 E 2nd. Featuring Spanish and Indian exhibits, a replica copper mine, vintage cars and a stage-coach. Open daily, free.

Saguaro National Monument: In two sections, east and west of the city (296-8576). The eastern part has older and bigger stands of giant saguaro cactus, which live for 200 years but only grow in two states. Saguaro blossom — Arizona's state flower — appears in May and June.

Mission San Xavier del Bac: Nine miles southwest, the most elaborate and beautiful of America's missions. Father Kino came in 1692 and built a church two miles to the north, the mission being completed a hundred years later.

Tombstone: 65 miles southeast on Route 80. The town too tough to die began as a mining settlement in 1877. Tombstone was the scene of the OK Corral shootout between Wyatt Earp, Doc Holliday and the Clantons. It looks little different today with its saloon, church and Epitaph building. Information from the Tourist Association, 9 S 5th (457-2211).

You depart Tucson with the Santa Catalina Mountains on your right. Mount Lemmon (9,157ft) is famous for skiing.

Pima Air Park (30/30)
The base on the left refurbishes jets for sale around the world. The Little Owl Head Mountains can be seen to the right.
   In the fertile country ahead look for cotton, pecans, cabbage and broccoli.

Picacho Pass (40/20)
Picacho Peak (3,382ft) is on the left, the Picacho Range to the right.
   Saguaro cacti appear on both sides for the next few miles. A saguaro can grow to 40ft and store 2,000 gallons of water. Look also for barrel cactus, tree-like chollas and the spindly ocotillo shrub, which got its name (Spanish for little torch) because it produces bright red flowers after winter rain.

Randolph (55/5)
The town on your left has streets named after civil rights activists such as Martin Luther King and Eldridge Cleaver.

COOLIDGE (60/45)
Cross the Gila River. On the reservation to your left is the Casa Grande National Monument. Remains of a four-storey building date back 600 years to a Hohokam Indian village.

Arizona Boy's Ranch (20/25)
Seen on the left.

Williams Air Force Base (30/15)
Military aircraft and buildings are on the right.

Superstition Mountains (35/10)
The Lost Dutchman silver mine, somewhere in the mountains to your right, was never found again after its German prospector's death.

As you approach Tempe look right for the campus of Arizona University — the biggest and oldest in the state. Frank Lloyd Wright designed its red-roofed music hall.

TEMPE (45/15)
Effectively this is a part of Phoenix.

You cross the Salt River, bringing water from the White and Sierra Anchor Mountains to central Arizona.

Phoenix Airport (5/10)
Sky Harbor International is immediately to the left.

PHOENIX (15/180)
The capital of Arizona, sprawling over 393 square miles and surrounded by mountains. It's situated on the ruined villages of Indians who lived here until the 15th Century, using irrigation to tame the desert. Settlers in the 19th Century gave the place its name by prophesying a city would rise again like the legendary bird. In 1911 the Roosevelt Dam, 75 miles to the north, harnessed the Salt River and fulfilled their prophecy.

Phoenix has over 300 days of sun a year and only seven inches of rain, so summer can be extremely hot.

Transport: Amtrak's station is a renovated building downtown at 401 W Harrison. It isn't a safe area at night. Information: 253-0121. Ticket office and waiting room open 0645-1415 and 1645-2400 (Sun, Mon, Thurs), 0645-1415 (Fri, Sat) and 1645-2400 (Tues, Wed). Lockers, taxi stand.

Phoenix Transit buses (253-5000) operate Mon-Sat.
Taxis: Yellow (252-5252) and Ace (254-1999).
Car Rental: Associated, 14 S 22nd (275-6992).
Greyhound: 5th and Washington (248-4040).

The airport is 4 miles southeast by bus No 13 and the Super Shuttle (244-9000). Free limousines operate to many hotels.

Tours: Gray Line (254-4550). The Capitol walking tour includes the Capitol Museum and Confederate Monument (255-3618). Desert excursions are available from Arizona Awareness (947-7852).

Visitors Bureau: 505 N 2nd (254-6500). Open weekdays. For the latest events call 252-5588.

Telephone Code: 602.

Accommodation: Contact Bed & Breakfast in Arizona, PO Box 8628, Scottsdale, AZ 85252 (995-2831). Many hotels have low rate specials during summer, if you can take the heat.
AYH Youth Hostel: 1026 N 9th (262-9439). Dormitory rooms $8, non-members $12.
YMCA: 350 N 1st Ave (253-6181). Singles $17, weekly $60.
   Hotels include the Executive Park at 1100 N Central Ave (252-2100); Heritage, 401 N 1st (258-3411); Crescent, 2620 Dunlop Ave (943-8200); Days Inn, 2735 W Sweetwater Ave (993-7200); Arizona Ranch House Inn, 5600 N Central Ave (279-3221); Kon Tiki, 2364 E Van Buren (244-9361).

Heritage Square: 6th and Monroe (262-5071). Restored 19th Century houses give a taste of old Phoenix. The 1895 Rosson House opens Wed-Sat, admission.

Arizona Historical Society Museum: 1242 N Central Ave (255-4470). Pioneer days revisited. Try your hand at the telegraph or wielding a branding iron. Open Tues-Sat, free.

Desert Botanical Garden: 1201 E Galvin Pkwy (941-1225). In Papago Park, five miles east of downtown, there are more than 1,800 types of cacti. Open daily, admission. Take bus No 3.

Phoenix Zoo: Near the Botanical Garden (273-7771). The zoo has a thousand species of wildlife, including Arabian oryx. Open daily, admission.

Encanto Park: An oasis in the middle of the city at 15th Ave and Encanto, with a lake, nature trails and a swimming pool. Open daily.

Arizona Railway Museum: At Erie and Delaware in Chandler, 20 miles southeast (821-1108). Housed in a building resembling a train depot are items relating mainly to railways of the Southwest. Open weekends, donation.

The Sunset Limited leaves Phoenix and continues west into the night.

Hassayampa River (40/140)
Cross the river. Legend says that those who drink from this river never tell the truth again.
   You accompany the Gila River across the Sonoran Desert.

YUMA (180/110)
A resort set in farmland irrigated from the Colorado River. Yuma Prison is now a state park open to the public.

Colorado River (20/90)
When crossing you pass from Arizona into California. Since Arizona does not

observe Daylight Savings Time, watches go back an hour (forward when travelling east) only from November to April.

INDIO (110/110)
The 'date capital of the world' hosts a date festival each February. This is Amtrak's nearest stop to Palm Springs and the Salton Sea (California's largest lake).

Colton (90/20)
Cross the Santa Ana River with the San Gabriel Mountains on the right.

Ontario (100/10)
The international airport to your left is a likely future stop for the Sunset.

POMONA (110/45)
Amtrak operates out of two stations, the Sunset Limited using the Southern Pacific one at 156 W Commercial. Pomona was called after the Roman goddess of fruits, though residential development has overtaken orchards and vineyards. September's Los Angeles County Fair here attracts more people than any other.

Leave with St Joseph's Church to the left and St Paul's mission-style church next to the California Polytechnic on the right.

San Gabriel River (15/30)
You cross the usually dry river bed.

El Monte Airport (17/28)
Seen on the right, it was named after nearby Mount Wilson (5,700ft).

Cross the concrete-lined Rio Hondo and enter a short tunnel to Temple City, where the train emerges in the centre strip of the San Bernadino Freeway.

California State University (33/12)
The Los Angeles campus is to your right before you part company with the freeway.

LA County Hospital (37/8)
These tall buildings are on the right, and to the left is the concrete channel of the Los Angeles River. Dodger Stadium is ahead on a hill.

You cross the river, with the Post Office building's twin domes and the tower of City Hall prominent on the right. The county jail can be seen to your left just before the station.

LOS ANGELES
For Los Angeles, see *The Coast Starlight*.

10 The Texas Eagle

Chicago—San Antonio

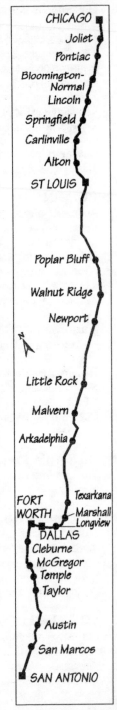

CHICAGO
Joliet
Pontiac
Bloomington-
Normal
Lincoln
Springfield
Carlinville
Alton
ST LOUIS

Poplar Bluff

Walnut Ridge

Newport

Little Rock

Malvern

Arkadelphia

FORT   Texarkana
WORTH   Marshall
              Longview
DALLAS
Cleburne
McGregor
Temple
Taylor

Austin

San Marcos

SAN ANTONIO

From Chicago to San Antonio the Eagle makes a 1,308-mile journey down the middle of America, travelling through Lincoln land then crossing the Mississippi River before continuing via the Ozarks to Arkansas and Texas. Pine forest and lakes north of Dallas give way to cattle country as the train makes for San Antonio, where (on three days a week) through coaches to Los Angeles join the Sunset Limited. An alternative through service of the Eagle goes from Dallas to Houston via Corsicana.

Frequency: Daily to San Antonio and Houston. Southbound trains leave Chicago late afternoon to reach St Louis by midnight and Little Rock early next morning. You arrive in Dallas mid-afternoon and San Antonio late evening (or Houston mid-evening).

Travelling north, trains leave San Antonio early in the morning (or Houston mid-morning) to reach Dallas mid-afternoon and Little Rock by midnight. You arrive in St Louis early next morning and Chicago early afternoon.

Reservations: All reserved.

Equipment: Superliner coaches.

Sleeping: Superliner economy, de luxe, family, special bedrooms.

Food: Complete meals, snacks, sandwiches, drinks.

Lounge Car: Movies, games, hospitality hour.

Baggage: Check-in service at main cities.

CHICAGO

For Chicago, see *The California Zephyr*. On the first stretch of its journey as far as St Louis, the Eagle uses tracks of the Illinois Central Gulf Railroad (ICG), travelling through Chicago's industrial suburbs.

You get views of the city as you look back while crossing the Chicago River, which gave French explorers a passage from Lake Michigan almost to the Mississippi. A few minutes out of Union Station you cross the Chicago Sanitary Ship Canal. This reverses the river's flow and is part of an inland waterway between the Great Lakes and the Mississippi, running 30 miles from Chicago to Lockport.

Bridgeport (15/30)
Settled by Irish immigrants working on the Illinois & Michigan (I & M) Canal, Bridgeport was the home town of Chicago's former mayor Richard Daley.

Willow Springs (30/15)
The wooded enclave on your left has a population of deer.

Lambert (32/13)
Cross the Calumet Sag Channel linking Lake Michigan with the Sanitary Ship Canal. You continue to Joliet through urban parkland of the I & M Canal National Corridor.

Lockport (38/7)
As you accompany the towpath look for restored buildings on your right.

Illinois State Prison (41/4)
Joliet's correctional centre is to the right.

JOLIET (45/52)
For Joliet, see page 108.

You leave with the Des Plaines River and conservation area to your right, next to the I & M Canal. On your left a limestone quarry is followed by a US army arsenal with munitions stored underground.

Kankakee River (15/37)
Cross this tributary of the Illinois.

Braidwood (20/32)
The tall towers on the left belong to a Con Edison nuclear power plant.

Dwight (35/17)
In 1860 the then Prince of Wales attended Dwight's small white pioneer Gothic church. The station on the right dates from 1892, and just beyond it is a single-storey brick building with a clock. This is the only one of three banks designed by Frank Lloyd Wright still in existence. On the left is an impressive old windmill.

The train crosses the Vermilion River.

PONTIAC (52/30)
Named after an Indian chief. The Eagle misses this stop when travelling north.

Normal (25/5)
Illinois Normal School was a teacher's college which grew to become the State University. Its dormitories and other campus buildings are on the right.

BLOOMINGTON-NORMAL (30/33)
The birthplace of Adlai Stevenson, and where Abraham Lincoln delivered his last speech before becoming president. George Pullman also lived here. His luxury *Pioneer* was too wide for some railroads until Mrs Lincoln used one after her husband's assassination. Alterations were made so it could pass, and from then on the name Pullman became synonymous with sleeping cars.

Funk's Grove (8/25)
The state's only tract of virgin timber, mostly maple, was given by Eugene Funk of Funk Seeds.
  Just before Lincoln you cross Kickapoo Creek.

LINCOLN (33/30)
The only town to be named after Lincoln before he became president. He christened it in 1853 using water-melon juice, and you can see a 'slice of water-melon' statue to the left of the Broadway and Chicago Street station. Also on the left is the domed Logan County court-house where Lincoln practised law.
  Cross the Sangamon River as you approach Springfield, with the Illinois Fairgrounds on your right.

SPRINGFIELD (30/40)
The state capital and centre of Lincoln land. A chance to visit the house he owned, the place he was married and the grave where he and his family are buried. He made his farewell address in 1861 at the depot a short distance from the present station. The Old State Capitol was the scene of his 'house divided' speech.
  Springfield's present Capitol and Supreme Court can be seen on the right. Amtrak's station at Washington and 3rd opens 0600-2130, with buses connecting to Galesburg and Peoria.

Lake Springfield (10/30)
You cross the lake's western tip.

CARLINVILLE (40/30)
The spired Macoupin County court-house on the left dates from when Carlinville aspired to being the state capital. When Standard Oil operated coal mines here the workers lived in Sears, Roebuck & Co houses that arrived in sections. The mines closed but some of the houses remain. A new passenger shelter has opened next to Amtrak's former facility at 128 Alton, but the Eagle misses out this stop when travelling north.

Macoupin Creek (5/25)
Crossed at Beaver Dam State Park.

ALTON (30/40)
In 1838 this Mississippi River port's newspaper editor, Elijah Lovejoy, was lynched by a mob opposing his anti-slavery views. Alton later became a supply point for the Union army.

Cross the Wood River. Unseen to your right is Lewis and Clark State Park, where the Missouri and Mississippi Rivers meet. Lewis and Clark's expedition wintered here before setting out west.

Cahokia Diversion Canal (10/30)
Levees on both sides prevent flooding when the Mississippi rises.

Lenox (11/29)
Your train runs next to tracks once used by the Wabash Cannonball between St Louis and Detroit.

Granite City (14/26)
Steel and other heavy industries become a feature as you near St Louis. The Eagle leaves the ICG and takes to tracks of the Terminal Railroad Association (TRRA).

Mississippi River (22/18)
Cross high above on the Merchants Railroad bridge as you leave Illinois for Missouri. Look for barges on the river and the St Louis skyline to your left.

Eads Bridge (30/10)
Pass beneath the city's oldest bridge, which had the longest steel spans anywhere when it was completed in 1874.

Gateway Arch (35/5)
On your right is the country's tallest (630ft) monument, at the base of which is the Old Cathedral. Old riverboats are moored on the left.

Busch Memorial Stadium (38/2)
On the right is the home of the Cardinals baseball team.

ST LOUIS (40/240)
The Gateway to the West was founded by Pierre Laclede in 1764 and named after France's King Louis IX. Acquired by President Jefferson as part of the 1803 Louisiana Purchase, St Louis stands on high ground next to where the Mississippi River joins the Missouri. The original fur trading post became a base for Lewis and Clark, and wagon trains gathered here before going west. The massive Saarinen Arch is a symbol of those early days.

Transport: Amtrak's modern station at 550 S 16th replaces the old Union Station. Information: 331-3300. Ticket office and waiting room open 0600-2330 and 0330-0430. Lockers, vending machines, taxi stand.

Bi-State Transit (231-2345) operates buses, with free travel on the Levee Line between Union Station and the river.
Taxis: Yellow (991-1200).
Car Rental: Cut-Rate, 10232 Natural Bridge (426-2323).
Greyhound: 801 N Broadway (231-7800).
The airport is 14 miles northwest by taxi, Greyhound and bus No 104.

Tours: Gray Line (241-1224). During summer you can take the downtown St Louis Tram tour, with open-air cars stopping at major attractions. A pass allows unlimited stop-offs. The *Tom Sawyer* and *Huck Finn* provide river cruises (621-4040).

Visitors Bureau: 10 S Broadway (421-1023). Open daily. Also at 445 N Memorial Dr (241-1764) and Kiener Plaza. Call 421-2100 for the latest events.

Telephone Code: 314.

Accommodation: Contact Bed & Breakfast in St Louis, 4418 W Pine Blvd, St Louis, MO 63108 (533-9299).
Huckleberry Finn AYH Hostel: 1904 S 12th (241-0076). Members $9, non-members $14. Take bus No 73.
Hotels include Days Inn at the Park, 4630 Lindell Blvd (367-7500); Marriott Pavilion, 1 Broadway (421-1776); Best Western St Louisian, 1133 Washington Ave (421-4727); Comfort Inn, 3730 S Lindbergh Blvd (800-228-5150); Quality Inn, 7350 Hanley Rd (800-228-5151).

National Museum of Transport: 3015 Barrett Station Road (965-7998). This is America's greatest collection of railroad engines and equipment. The outdoor exhibition covers 40 acres and has more than 70 locomotives, plus streetcars, buses and aircraft. Open daily, admission.

Museum of Westward Expansion: Next to Gateway Arch, 702 N 1st (425-4465). The museum shows wagon trains and pioneer life. A ride up to the Arch's observation deck gives you unbeatable views of the city and beyond. Open daily. Museum free, admission to observation deck.

Cupples House: 3673 W Pine (658-3025). A hundred years old, the house has lately been restored. It features wooden floors and carvings, plus an art gallery. Closed Sat, admission.

Anheuser-Busch Brewery: 1127 Pestalozzi (577-2626). You can tour the plant, see the Clydesdale horses and sample a free beer. Open Mon-Sat, free. Take bus No 40.

Texas Eagle trains depart St Louis on the Missouri Pacific section of the Union Pacific Railroad for a run of four hours to Poplar Bluff.

Mississippi River (30/210)
Mark Twain country, where the shipyard on your left builds boats for use on the river.

Jefferson Barracks (35/205)
Chief Blackhawk of the Sac Indians was imprisoned at this 18th Century military post.

Pevely (70/170)
Where the Texas Eagle parts company with the Mississippi.

Big River (120/120)
Cross to the north of Ironton. This area boasts some of the world's largest lead mines, and formerly produced iron ore.

POPLAR BLUFF (240/50)
Winner of the 'all American city' award. Poplar Bluff is a manufacturing centre, located in southern Missouri farmland near the Ozark Mountains and Wappapello Lake. Amtrak is at 400 S Main.

Missouri/Arkansas State Line (20/30)
You cross into the smallest state west of the Mississippi.

WALNUT RIDGE (50/26)
Close by are Lake Charles State Park and one of Arkansas' first settlements, Old Davidsonville. Walnut Ridge is Amtrak's nearest stop to Jonesboro.

NEWPORT (26/80)
The town grew after the Cairo & Fulton Railroad arrived. At neighbouring Jacksonport, beside the White River, Confederate troops massed during the Civil War.

Arkansas River (79/1)
Cross the river dividing North Little Rock from Little Rock. The Capitol dome and city skyline can be seen to your left.

LITTLE ROCK (80/45)
French explorers called it La Petite Roche, and Arkansas' biggest city has been the state capital since 1821. Its Capitol building is a smaller version of that in Washington, DC. A previous Greek-style state house at 300 W Markham now shows Arkansas history. The Museum of Science occupies Little Rock Arsenal.

Highlights of the year include May's Riverfest and the autumn State Fair. Visitors bureau: Markham and Main (376-4781). Amtrak is at Union Station Square, Markham and Victory. Ticket office open 0500-1600 (Mon-Sat) and 1500-2430 (Sun).

The Texas Eagle leaves with the Capitol again on the left. Your train eases through suburbs before entering hillier country covered in forests of pine and hardwood.

Benton (30/15)

Most of America's aluminium comes from bauxite mined here.
   Cross the Saline River just after Benton.

MALVERN (45/21)

The original town of Rockport, situated on the Ouachita River, transferred here
and called itself Malvern Station. Amtrak's stop at 200 E 1st serves Hot
Springs National Park, established in 1832. The Hot Springs visitors centre is
at Central and Reserve (501-624-3383).

Ouachita River (20/1)

Crossed with Arkadelphia away to your right.

ARKADELPHIA (21/80)

This former steamboat landing stage is now better known for colleges and
aluminium plants.
   You cross the Little Missouri River 20 minutes later.

Prescott (25/55)

Prescott's red-roofed station is on the right. To the west is the Trail of Tears
travelled by Indians forced to move to Oklahoma reservations.

Hope (40/40)

The 'watermelon capital of the world' claims the all-time record (265 pounds).
This area also produces chickens and cattle, and is famous for deer hunting.
A kiln chimney on the right shows where bricks were made.
   Between Hope and the Red River watch for boisdarc trees, with their
enormous green seed pods and wood which was used for horse-drawn farm
implements.

Red River Valley (55/25)

Cross the river on its way south, eventually to join the Mississippi. The
valley's red earth washes into the water to give the river its name. Soya beans
and grain grow on land which once raised cotton.

Homan (65/15)

Pecan trees prove this really is the South.

Texarkana Airport (70/10)

Seen immediately to your left.

TEXARKANA (80/75)

When the train stops, its front end is in Texas while the rear hasn't left
Arkansas. Texarkana's unique position calls for two mayors and two police
departments. The post office is America's only federal building to straddle a
state line. Amtrak's station at 100 E Front opens 0630-1330 (Mon-Sat), 1500-
2200 (Tues, Fri, Sun) and 0630-1110 (Wed).
   Your train leaves on Texas & Pacific tracks associated with the Missouri
Pacific, proceeding south along the Texas border.

Sulphur River (20/55)
A paper mill features on the left as you cross.

Atlanta (30/45)
Prehistoric Indian settlements have been discovered here.

Jefferson (50/25)
This was one of the state's earliest ports and an old cemetery can be seen on the right.

MARSHALL (75/25)
The birthplace of Ladybird Johnson. When Texas seceded from the Union in 1861 this became one of its biggest cities, making ammunition and saddles for the Confederate army. After the fall of Vicksburg, Marshall was the Missouri governor's capital. Shreveport, Louisiana, is 25 miles west.

LONGVIEW (25/160)
Home of the Schlitz brewery, which produces four million barrels of beer a year.

Gladwater (20/140)
In the middle of east Texas oil country, where the industry has expanded since a major discovery in 1931. Production fields feature on both sides of the track, with a Texaco refinery to the left.

Your route follows the Sabine River for the next 50 miles through country famous for beef cattle and quarter-horses.

Big Sandy (40/120)
Garner Ted Armstrong's Ambassador College is on the right, bounded by white-fenced fields.

Grand Saline (85/75)
The town is named after a 700ft deep salt mine on the left.

Mesquite (110/50)
Thorny mesquite scrub trees are common throughout the Southwest. Mesquite Rodeo is housed in the large building on your left.

The Dallas skyline appears to the right, with a Texas Fairgrounds Ferris wheel in the distance.

DALLAS (160/65)
Your train stops directly opposite the Hyatt Hotel, mesmerised by its reflection in the glass facade familiar from TV's *Dallas*. 'The city that should never have been' possessed few natural resources and no transport links until the railway arrived. Founded as a log cabin trading post in 1841, it became a utopian colony of artists and scientists. It's now America's seventh largest city, specialising in banking, oil and transport, with Santa Fe and Union Pacific freight trains much in evidence.

Fashionable Dallas has more shops, Cadillacs and divorces than any other

US city. It's the home of J R Ewing, the stetson and the world's biggest computer centre. Neighbouring Fort Worth tends to be more relaxed.

Transport: Union Station at 400 S Houston is a splendid renovated white marble building. Information: 653-1101. Ticket office open 1000-1730. Lockers, vending machines, newspapers, luggage trolleys, restaurant, shops, information centre, taxi stand. A walkway leads to the Hyatt Regency Hotel and Reunion Tower.

Dallas is designed for cars but DART buses (979-1111) operate downtown and to the suburbs.

Taxis: Yellow (426-6262) and Terminal (350-4445).

Car Rental: All-State, 3206 Live Oak (741-3118).

Greyhound: S Lamar and Commerce (655-7000).

Dallas/Fort Worth Airport — larger than Manhattan — is 16 miles west, with bus and taxi connections to both downtown areas. Take the Super Shuttle from 729 E Dallas Rd (817-329-2001).

Tours: Kaleidoscope (522-5930). Gray Line (824-2424) has tours around Dallas, Fort Worth and to the Southfork Ranch.

Visitors Bureau: 1201 Elm (746-6677). Open weekdays.

Telephone Code: 214.

Accommodation: Contact Bed & Breakfast Texas, 4224 W Red Bird Lane, Dallas, TX 75237 (298-5433).

AYH Hostel: 1451 E Northgate, in the suburb of Irving (438-6061). Members $9, non-members $12.

Hotels include the Hyatt Regency at 300 Reunion Blvd (651-1234); Stoneleigh, 2827 Maple Ave (871-7111); Colony Parke, 6060 N Central Expressway. (750-6060); Holiday Inn-Downtown, 1015 Elm (748-9951); Holiday Inn, 10650 N Park Pl (373-6000); Park Cities Inn, 6101 Hillcrest Ave (521-0330).

Reunion Tower: Next to Union Station (741-3663). The best views of Dallas are to be had from the top of this 50-storey building. Open daily, admission.

Old City Park: 1717 Gano (421-5141). Historic buildings relocated from the surrounding area include a blacksmith's shop, general store, railway depot, church and antebellum mansion. Closed Mon, admission.

State Fair Park: Two miles east on 2nd Ave (670-8400). The art deco Texas Centennial buildings date from 1936. The park has symphony concerts, opera, roller coaster rides and an October State Fair. The following museums are located here.

Age of Steam Railroad Museum: Featuring locomotives, passenger cars, freight cars and Dallas's oldest train station (428-0101). Open daily during the

State Fair, otherwise Thurs-Sun. Admission.

Museum of Natural History: Authentic environments are recreated with a chance to handle some of the exhibits (670-8457). Open daily, free.

Through cars to Houston travel southeast via Corsicana and College Station-Bryan, home of Texas A & M University. The remaining coaches leave Dallas with Dealey Plaza and the Texas School Book Depository on the right. President John F Kennedy was killed here on November 22 1963 and the scene familiar from newsreels still sends a shiver. A museum at the depository commemorates Kennedy's life.

Cross the Trinity River, with the Texas Stadium a massive white structure on your right.

Grand Prairie (25/40)
Dallas naval air station and the Ling-Tempco-Vought aircraft factory are on the left.

Arlington (35/30)
Part of the University of Texas can be seen to the right. Six Flags Over Texas amusement park is in the distance.

Handley (45/20)
Man-made Arlington Lake is on your left. Lee Harvey Oswald (President Kennedy's assassin) was buried in Rose Hill Cemetery to your right.

FORT WORTH (65/40)
The sister city of Dallas became a shipping point for cattle when citizens financed a 26-mile link to the Texas & Pacific Railroad. After the line opened in 1876 cattle no longer had to be driven north to Kansas. Fort Worth now has other industries but the old Cowtown flavour persists. Visitors bureau: 100 E 15th (817-336-8791). Amtrak's station at 1501 Jones opens 0915-1630.

You leave on the Santa Fe line and continue towards Texas hill country.

CLEBURNE (40/60)
Named after the Confederate General Pat Cleburne in 1867, having formerly been known as Camp Henderson. The city deals in crops and livestock, especially longhorn cattle.

Balcones Fault (15/45)
Limestone hills suddenly rise out of the prairie as the train follows this fault line to San Antonio.

Brazos River (17/43)
After crossing the Noland River you cross the Brazos. This runs left into Lake Whitney — 15,000 acres of water created by a dam.

Meridian (28/32)

Watch for angora goats raised for their mohair. Look also for fields of cotton still common in the South.

Bosque River (30/30)

Cross, then accompany the river for the next 30 miles.

Clifton (40/20)

Founded by Swedish and Norwegian settlers. On your right is one of this region's many limestone quarries.

Middle Bosque River (55/5)

You cross shortly before Crawford.

MCGREGOR (60/32)

This is Amtrak's stop for McGregor's bigger neighbour Waco, 20 miles east.

Moody (10/22)

A small town possessing a large TV antenna (2,200ft).

TEMPLE (32/55)

This key rail junction was named after a Santa Fe surveyor in 1880. The Gulf, Colorado & Santa Fe Railroad connects here with the Missouri, Kansas & Texas. Temple's Santa Fe depot has vintage furniture and equipment, including a working telegraph. Amtrak's station at 315 W Ave B opens 1000-1800. Nearby are Fort Hood and Killeen.

Your train continues on the M-K-T line among ranchland and tree-covered hills.

Little River (25/30)

Crossed near the town of the same name.

San Gabriel River (40/15)

As you cross look right for pecan trees growing on its banks.

TAYLOR (55/42)

The Eagle changes from M-K-T back to Union Pacific tracks at this rail centre, which ships much of the prairie's ranch and farm produce.

Round Rock (22/20)

A residential town for commuters to Austin.

Camp Mabry (35/7)

The US army establishment is on the right.

AUSTIN (42/40)

Capital of Texas and former capital of the Texas Republic, Austin was founded in 1839 on hills beside the Colorado River. It's the home of Texas University at Austin (50,000 students) and the Lyndon Johnson Library. The

Capitol is seven feet taller than that in Washington, DC.

Tourist centres are located in the Capitol and at 412 E 6th (478-0098). The AYH Hostel, 2200 S Lakeshore Blvd (444-2294), and Taos Hall (AYH) at 2612 Guadalupe (474-6905) have beds from $7. Amtrak's station at 250 N Lamar Blvd opens 0800-2030 (Mon, Wed), 0800-1530 (Tue, Thurs, Fri, Sun) and 1300-2030 (Sat).

Colorado River (2/38)
Look back to your left as you cross for Austin's skyline, a striking feature of which is the Capitol's ornate pink dome.

Aquarina Springs (37/3)
Clear springs on the right are the source of the San Marcos River, which you cross as you enter San Marcos.

SAN MARCOS (40/85)
Home of Southwest Texas State University — the alma mater of President Johnson. San Marcos hosts an annual cooking contest for chilli afficionados.

Cross the Guadalupe River.

New Braunfels (20/65)
The town was founded in 1845 by the German Prince Carl von Solms-Braunfels.

San Antonio International (50/35)
The airport is on your right.

Olmos Park (52/33)
You travel through the middle of a golf course with Trinity University away to your left.

San Antonio comes into view on the left, with the green-roofed Tower Life building the city's oldest skyscraper. Look also for the InterFirst building and the 750ft Tower of the Americas.

King William District (75/10)
Victorian houses can be seen to your left beyond the Pioneer flour mill.

Lone Star Brewery (78/7)
The brewery museum appears on your right just before you cross the San Antonio River.

SAN ANTONIO
For San Antonio and through travel on Tues, Thurs and Sun to Los Angeles, see *The Sunset Limited*.

11 The City of New Orleans

Chicago—New Orleans

City of New Orleans trains cut the US neatly in two, covering more than 900 miles from the Great Lakes to the Gulf of Mexico. Between Chicago and laid-back New Orleans are prairies, farms, coal mines and plantations. Plus the birthplace of blues and rock and roll, and the Mississippi River basin where Civil War history was made.

Frequency: Daily. The southbound service leaves Chicago early in the evening to reach Memphis early next morning and New Orleans by early afternoon.

Travelling north, trains leave New Orleans mid-afternoon to reach Memphis before midnight. You arrive in Chicago mid-morning.

Reservations: All reserved.

Equipment: Heritage coaches. Dome car.

Sleeping: Heritage bedrooms, roomettes.

Food: Tray meals, snacks, sandwiches, drinks.

Baggage: Check-in service at most stations.

CHICAGO
Homewood
Kankakee
Rantoul
Champaign-Urbana
Mattoon
Effingham
Centralia
Du Quoin
Carbondale
N
Fulton
Dyersburg
MEMPHIS
Batesville
Grenada
Winona
Durant
Canton
Jackson
Hazlehurst
Brookhaven
McComb
Hammond
NEW ORLEANS

CHICAGO
For Chicago, see *The California Zephyr*.

HOMEWOOD (45/30)
A leafy suburb of the Windy City.

KANKAKEE (30/45)
Located next to the Kankakee River.

Gilman (20/25)
This agriculture and railroad centre is a scheduled stop for City of New Orleans trains travelling north.

RANTOUL (45/20)
The US Air Force training base at nearby Chanute Field has an aviation museum.

CHAMPAIGN-URBANA (20/35)
Champaign is a manufacturing centre as well as the inspiration for a Bob Dylan song. Less industrial Urbana is home to the University of Illinois. Amtrak's station at 116 N Chestnut opens 0630-2200.

MATTOON (35/22)
Another manufacturing town set among Illinois farm country, with Lincoln Log Cabin State Park close by. Eastern Illinois University is 12 miles east at Charleston.

EFFINGHAM (22/45)
Industrial scenes continue to predominate.

Little Wabash River (8/37)
You cross the river on its way to join the Ohio.

CENTRALIA (45/50)
Amtrak's train from Kansas City, the River Cities, meets the City of New Orleans here for the journey south. The station at 100 E Broadway opens 1545-2345 and Centralia's rail yards are this region's most impressive.

CARBONDALE (50/105)
Home of Southern Illinois University, Carbondale got its name as the centre of a coal mining area. Nearby Crab Orchard wildlife refuge has many wintering birds.

Cairo (60/45)
'Little Egypt' is located where the Mississippi and Ohio Rivers meet at the borders of three states — Illinois, Missouri and Kentucky. General Grant occupied this commanding position during the Civil War.

Illinois/Kentucky State Line (62/43)
You cross the border southeast of Cairo.

FULTON (105/50)
South and Central American banana cargoes were formerly distributed from here.

Kentucky/Tennessee State Line (2/48)
Crossed just south of Fulton.

DYERSBURG (50/90)
Named after William Dyer, a colonel in the war of 1812, the town processes cotton and other farm produce.

After travelling most of the way from Chicago in darkness, the City of New Orleans arrives at Memphis around dawn.

MEMPHIS (90/65)
Situated on bluffs overlooking the Mississippi, Memphis was named after the capital of ancient Egypt by Andrew Jackson in 1819. It became a major port and is now the largest city in Tennessee. Hardwoods, soya beans and other agricultural products have lately replaced cotton as the main cargo. Amtrak's station at 545 S Main opens 0800-1700 (Mon-Sat) and 2100-0600 (daily). Visitors bureau: 207 Beale (526-4880). AYH Hostels: 1084 Poplar and 217 N Waldran (527-7174). Members $10, non-members $14.

Blues and dixieland jazz feature in the Beale Street area of W C Handy's home town. Graceland, where the King of Rock died in August 1977, is 10 miles south at 3794 Elvis Presley Blvd. You can tour the mansion — with its costumes, trophies and pool room — and place flowers on Elvis's grave. The almost equally legendary Peabody Hotel is at 149 Union. The lobby boasts ornate ceilings, a marble fountain and live ducks. At the Lorraine Motel the room and balcony where Dr Martin Luther King was assassinated in 1968 are kept as a memorial.

You cross the Tennessee/Mississippi State Line 10 miles south of Memphis. Between here and New Orleans your train largely accompanies the route of Interstate Highway 55.

Coldwater River (30/35)
Crossed halfway between Memphis and Batesville.

BATESVILLE (65/45)
An attractive town close to the Sardis Lake recreational area. The former home of the South's greatest novelist, William Faulkner, is 20 miles east at Rowan Oak, Oxford.

Travellers' Tales
The City of New Orleans
by John Ainsworth

The "City of New Orleans" from Chicago to New Orleans does not include the cheaper variety of sleeping cars, so we went coach class. The seats were surprisingly roomy — lots of leg room, reclining chairs and a pillow provided — but we could have done with taking a rug. We found ourselves in the dome car, just at the bottom of the stairs to the "rooftop conservatory" which is available to all passengers; so there was quite a lot of "passing traffic".

It was fascinating watching the lights of Chicago as we did an early evening tour of the city to get from Union station to the Illinois Central line south. (Following the rationalisation of passenger services with Amtrak, the process of getting from one company's tracks to the station which was historically that of another company means a slow shunting back and forth around loop lines — not at all like the high speed exits and entries to European cities.)

All went well till Carbondale, a small town in southern Illinois where some carriages from Kansas City joined us. It was about 12.30am and we had been lulled into a sort of sleep by the purring of the air-conditioning. When it went off as the locomotive was detached we realised that we were sharing the car with the American champion snorer. With that and the baby crying at the other end of the car, the wait of some 45 minutes seemed interminable. Eventually there were some bumps and shouts from outside, the air-conditioning came back on to drown the noises off and we headed south. I dozed more than slept, saw Memphis in the night — but there was no mystical statue of Elvis illuminating the night sky, only lots of railway yards — and woke in the Deep South.

Dawn produced mist rising from little rivers; a muffin and coffee from the cafe car was consumed in the dome car as we wound our way through swamps, woodland and cotton fields and stopped at half a dozen wayside Mississippi stations — bang in the middle of neat small town squares, just like the movies. About lunchtime we reached Big Easy.

So followed three days in the hot October sun, with jazz, the *Natchez* steam paddleboat, streetcars and a stay at a lovely old guest house in the Garden District, which we found on the hotel list at the railway station, complete with swimming pool surrounded by banana trees (St Charles Guest House, $48 a night double).

Yalobusha River (44/1)
Cross just north of Grenada.

GRENADA (45/18)
A centre for Mississippi's cotton industry. Amtrak's stop serves neighbouring Grenada Lake to the east.

Look for cotton fields, mansions and processing plants as the train progresses deeper into the South. This region of farms and forests is where the early Delta blues singers played and made their first recordings.

WINONA (18/25)
Manufacturing and farming were encouraged when a direct rail line between Lake Michigan and the Gulf of Mexico was completed south of Winona in

1860. The building to the left of Front Street station is the Wisteria Hotel.
You continue amid cotton country and Indian reservations.

DURANT (25/30)
The Spaniard Hernando de Soto discovered this region in the 16th Century.

Pickens (12/18)
The modest town is surrounded by acres of cotton.

Vaughan (18/12)
Scene of the Casey Jones train wreck in April 1900 when the Cannonball
Express, speeding to make up time between Memphis and Canton, crashed
into another train. Engineer Jones died on board No 638 but his skill saved
all the passengers' lives. Vaughan's depot has a museum in his honour.

Big Black River (20/10)
Cross 20 miles east of Yazoo City.

CANTON (30/34)
The domed building on your left is the Madison County court-house.
The train continues south among cotton plantations, pine forests, pecan
trees and fruit orchards. Ross Barnett Reservoir is to the east.

Memorial Stadium (25/9)
The ground is used by both Jackson and Mississippi State Universities. On
the Jackson skyline ahead to your left is a Capitol similar to that in
Washington, DC.

JACKSON (34/28)
Mississippi's largest city, located beside the Pearl River, has long been the
state capital. It began as a trading settlement and survived being burned
down during the Civil War. You can tour the Capitol and the 1842 Governor's
Mansion. The Old Capitol is now a history museum. Visitors bureau: 921 N
President (960-1891). Amtrak's station at 300 W Capitol opens 0730-1030 and
1700-1930.
As the train departs, the Mississippi Arts Centre and Davis Planetarium can
be seen to the left.

Crystal Springs (24/4)
The 'tomato capital of the world' is famous for its bumper crops.

HAZLEHURST (28/19)
Another agricultural town.

Wesson (13/6)
The preserved Old Wesson Hotel on your left once boasted a casino where
passengers could while away time and money between trains.

BROOKHAVEN (19/22)

A recruiting town during the Civil War, Brookhaven now deals in oil, timber and farm produce. This station graced with magnolias is Amtrak's nearest stop for Natchez, 50 miles west. Many of the 500 antebellum homes there are furnished in original style and are open to visitors during the Natchez Pilgrimage (four weeks in March and April, three weeks in October).

You leave Brookhaven among old residential suburbs.

Bogue Chitto River (2/20)

Seen on the left.

MCCOMB (22/50)

Named after Colonel McComb, who was in charge of railroad rebuilding after the Civil War. The town's famous azalea trees are especially fine in spring.

Magnolia (10/40)

Look for mansions on the right.

Tangipahoa River (12/38)

Cross the river which continues to your left.

Mississippi/Louisiana State Line (20/30)

You cross just south of Osyka.

Kentwood (27/23)

On the left soon after town is Camp Moore Cemetery and Museum. This was a training ground for Confederate troops during the Civil War.

Amite (36/14)

New Orleans-type ironwork can be seen on many of the houses.

Independence (45/5)

An above-the-ground cemetery (or 'city of the dead') is to your right. Look for plantations of strawberries on both sides of the track.

HAMMOND (50/60)

'The strawberry capital of the world'. Amtrak's station at NW Railroad Ave opens 0900-1730. The Railroad Museum has a preserved depot, steam engines and coaches.

Ponchatoula (6/54)

A Louisiana Express locomotive features on the left.

The train enters Cajun country, an eerily beautiful land of forests and swamps where egrets fly among the live-oaks and ghostly Spanish moss drapes cypress trees.

Interstate 55 (7/53)

The highway on the right was built on concrete pilings to overcome this wet wilderness.

Pass-Manchac (10/50)

Cross the waterway linking Lake Pontchartrain with Lake Maurepas, on the right.

Lake Pontchartrain (15/45)

You skirt the shores of the state's biggest lake to your left.

Moisant Field (33/27)

New Orleans's international airport appears on the left.

Xavier University (51/9)

The campus buildings are seen on the right. As you approach New Orleans the city's skyline ahead to the left features the massive Superdome.

NEW ORLEANS

For New Orleans, see *The Sunset Limited*.

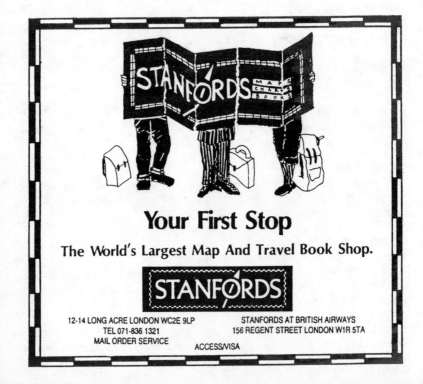

12 **The River Cities**

Kansas City—New Orleans

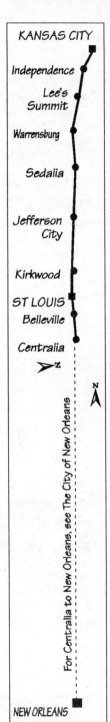

River Cities trains travel across the whole of Missouri from Kansas City to St Louis, then continue to Centralia before going south with the City of New Orleans. It's a thousand-mile journey through some of the country's best farmland, from the centre of America to the Gulf of Mexico.

Frequency: Daily. The southbound service leaves Kansas City mid-afternoon to reach St Louis mid-evening and Memphis early next morning, arriving in New Orleans early afternoon.

Travelling north, trains leave New Orleans mid-afternoon to reach Memphis before midnight, arriving in St Louis early next morning and Kansas City early afternoon.

Reservations: All reserved.

Equipment: Amfleet coaches. Heritage coach (Kansas City-New Orleans). Dome car from Carbondale to New Orleans.

Food: Tray meals, snacks, sandwiches, drinks.

Baggage: No check-in service.

KANSAS CITY
For Kansas City, see *The Southwest Chief*. The River Cities trains leave Kansas City, Missouri, through eastern suburbs then pass beneath Interstate 70 (on its way from Utah to Maryland).

INDEPENDENCE (18/15)
Some of the West's most famous trails — the California, Oregon and Santa Fe — came through here and established the town's prominence. It's now a Kansas City suburb and a headquarters for the Mormons. You can visit President Harry S Truman's former home, and the Truman Museum has a replica of his White House office.

LEE'S SUMMIT (15/36)
This became a shipping point after the Missouri Pacific railroad arrived in the 1840s.

WARRENSBURG (36/30)
Carrie Nation, of Temperance League fame, attended college here. The stone-built depot at 100 S Holden dates from 1890.

SEDALIA (30/62)
Starting as a railroad town in the 19th Century, this became a supply post during the Civil War. Scott Joplin wrote *Maple Leaf Rag* in the town saloon. Sedalia hosts the annual summer State Fair.

Missouri River (60/2)
On your left is the river, and to your right is the dome of Jefferson City's white limestone Capitol.

JEFFERSON CITY (62/110)
Named after the third president of the US, Jefferson City became the Missouri capital in 1821. The University of Missouri is to the north at Columbia. Winston Churchill first spoke of the iron curtain in a 1946 radio speech at nearby Fulton's Westminster College.

From Jefferson City the River Cities route accompanies the Missouri River for more than 70 miles towards St Louis.

Hermann (50/60)
The town celebrates its German inheritance during spring's Maifest, when you can tour Bavarian-style houses.

Washington (80/30)
Your train loses touch with the Missouri before beginning a climb to St Louis.

KIRKWOOD (110/22)
A prominent suburb of St Louis.

ST LOUIS (22/30)
For St Louis, see *The Texas Eagle*.

Leave with the giant Busch Stadium and the even harder to miss Gateway Arch on your left.

Mississippi River (4/26)
Crossing takes you from Missouri into Illinois.

BELLEVILLE (30/45)
Your train continues through this industrial and mining suburb then heads due east across Illinois to Centralia.

CENTRALIA (45/55)
For Centralia and the rest of the River Cities route to New Orleans, see *The City of New Orleans*.

13 The Northeast Corridor

Boston—Washington

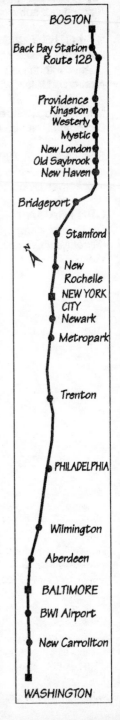

BOSTON
Back Bay Station
Route 128

Providence
Kingston
Westerly
Mystic
New London
Old Saybrook
New Haven

Bridgeport

Stamford

New
Rochelle
NEW YORK
CITY
Newark

Metropark

Trenton

PHILADELPHIA

Wilmington

Aberdeen

BALTIMORE

BWI Airport

New Carrollton

WASHINGTON

This is Amtrak's busiest route and the only one where the corporation owns both track and stations. Since 1986 Amtrak has been the dominant carrier between New York and Washington, holding 35% of the air-rail market. Trains are frequent and fast, especially on the electrified section between Washington and New Haven, and en route you experience cities, rural scenery and seascapes. Some trains (such as the Patriot) operate all the way from Boston to Washington. Others (including Metroliners) run over only part of the line. All services may not stop at every station indicated, so check when buying your ticket.

Frequency: Daily. Trains run almost 24 hours a day out of New York. Metroliner services operate between New York and Washington.

Reservations: About half the trains are reserved, including Metroliners, the New England Express and Executive Sleepers.

Equipment: Amfleet coaches. Through trains from Boston to Washington have club cars. Railfone is available in all dinette cars.

Sleeping: Roomettes and bedrooms on the Executive Sleeper, unreserved sleeping accommodation on the Night Owl.

Food: All trains except Clockers have snacks, sandwiches and drinks. Club cars offer complimentary meals and the sleeper includes free breakfast.

Baggage: Check-in service on the Night Owl and Executive Sleeper only.

BOSTON

Boston is New England's biggest city and 'the hub of the solar system', where the Lowells spoke only to Cabots and the Cabots spoke only to God. English Puritans came in the 17th Century and the Revolution began in 1770 when British troops fired on a group of colonists.

One of America's most sophisticated and beautiful cities, Boston's modern buildings mix with the old to create a winning blend.

Transport: Amtrak's restored South Station at Atlantic Ave and Summer was Boston's first beaux arts building. Information: 482-3660. Ticket office open 0530-2230. Waiting room 24 hours. Lockers, newspapers, Red Caps, restaurants, shops, taxi stand. MBTA operates commuter trains from South Station to points south and west. It operates to points north and northwest from North Station, 126 Causeway (772-5000). The Boston & Maine Railroad also uses North Station (800-392-6099).

You can see the city best on foot, with help from an MBTA system (722-3200) which includes bus, trolley and subway (the 'T'). A T passport gives unlimited travel on buses and subway.
Taxis: Checker (536-7000) and Green (628-0600).
Car Rental: Brodie, 24 Eliot (491-7600).
Greyhound: 10 St James Ave (423-5810).

Logan Airport is in East Boston, accessible by subway, taxi and Airways Shuttle bus (267-2981).

Tours: Gray Line, 275 Tremont (426-8805). Harbour and island trips are available from Boston Harbor Cruises (227-4320).

Visitors Bureau: An information booth opens daily on Boston Common at Tremont and Park (800-858-0200). The Convention and Tourist Bureau is at Prudential Plaza West, PO Box 490, Boston, MA 02199 (536-4100) and the National Park Service at 15 State (242-5642).

Telephone Code: 617.

Accommodation: Contact Boston Bed & Breakfast, 16 Ballard Street, Newton (332-4199).
International AYH Hostel: 12 Hemenway (536-9455). Members $12, non-members $16.
YMCA: 316 Huntington Ave (536-7800). For men and women. Singles $28, doubles $42.
Berkeley Residence Club (YWCA): 40 Berkeley (482-8850). Women only. Singles $34, doubles $45.

The Massachusetts Hotel Association at 148 State has a brochure listing accommodation. Hotels include the Park Plaza in Park Sq (426-2000); Lenox, 710 Boylston (536-5300); Eliot, 370 Commonwealth Ave (267-1607); Copley Square, 47 Huntington Ave (536-9000); Susse Chalet, 800 Morrissey Blvd (287-9100); Quality Inn, 275 Tremont (426-1400).

John Hancock Building: 200 Clarendon (572-6427). Outstanding views can be had from the 60th floor of New England's tallest building (740ft). Open daily, admission.

Museum of Fine Arts: 465 Huntington Ave (267-9300). Featuring art from ancient Egypt, Asia and Europe, along with portraits of Americans such as George Washington. Closed Mon, admission.

John F Kennedy Historic Site: 83 Beals, Brookline (566-7937). This was the birthplace on May 29 1917 of the future president.

Freedom Trail: Most of Boston's historic buildings can be explored by following the Freedom Trail marked in red on the sidewalk. Information and a free map are available from the booth on Boston Common. Highlights include the Old State House, the Old South Meeting House, Paul Revere's House, the *USS Constitution* and Bunker Hill Monument. The latter is a 221ft granite memorial to the battle fought nearby. Its staircase leads to views of the city and harbour. Most places on the Trail are open daily, free.

The Capitol, seen high above the city as you leave, has a marble dome with a statue of 'the independent man'. For the best coastal views you should take a seat on the left when travelling south.

BACK BAY STATION (5/10)
Trains pause to receive passengers (or discharge passengers if travelling north). Back Bay's subterranean station serves Copley Square and the downtown hotels. It's a major stop for commuter trains.
   You leave and continue for several minutes below ground, occasionally surfacing amid concrete car parks with glimpses of the Boston skyline back to your right.

ROUTE 128 (10/28)
A suburban halt before you enter the flat landscape of eastern Massachusetts. You leave with freight and warehouse facilities to the right and continue via suburbs interspersed with woodland.

Attleboro (20/8)
The Branson Museum exhibits prehistoric items found locally. Look for an imposing white church and steeple on the left as you leave town.
   Approaching Providence you cross the border into Rhode Island. The city centre skyscrapers and Capitol appear ahead, with freight yards on the right.

PROVIDENCE (28/22)
The capital of America's smallest state has buildings from the 18th and 19th Centuries. The 1786 John Brown House at Benefit and Power is furnished in authentic style. The Roger Williams Memorial is on the site of the initial 1636 settlement.
   Other highlights include a green-domed Capitol and the Athaeneum Library, where Edgar Allan Poe courted Sarah Whitman, his inspiration for *Annabel*

Lee. Visitors bureau: 30 Exchange Terrace (274-1636). The YMCA at 160 Broad (456-0100) is for men and women, $30 a day, $70 a week. Amtrak trains stop at 100 Gaspee, a new building next to the Capitol and 10 minutes walk from downtown. Ticket office open 0500-2315.

Note the post-modern apartment block on the left as you leave.

East Greenwich (12/10)
An old seaport where the 1773 General Varnum House and garden are preserved in their original condition.

Narragansett Bay and its colourful yachts appear on the left before your train departs temporarily inland through wooded countryside.

KINGSTON (22/10)
A quiet town with a picturesque, grey station flanked by evergreens. Some 18th Century buildings date from when this was a trading centre for plantation owners, and the George Fayerweather House was built by the blacksmith son of a slave. The University of Rhode Island is nearby. Amtrak is at Railroad Ave, West Kingston. Open 0600-2400 (Mon-Fri), 0600-1500 (Sat) and 1500-2400 (Sun). Note the lumber company mural on the right.

This is Amtrak's nearest station to Newport, the former colonial seaport famous for its naval base, mansions and jazz festival. Sights include the Friends Meeting House (1699) and the Old Colony House (1739).

You continue through wooded country with streams and marshes.

WESTERLY (10/10)
An 18th Century town on the border between Rhode Island and Connecticut, where old industrial buildings feature across the track from the solid brick and red tile station.

Between here and New Haven the train accompanies an attractive shoreline on the left.

Stonington (5/5)
This well-preserved coastal town had Connecticut's first lighthouse (now a museum). You can tour vineyards in summer and take boat trips to the Isle au Haut.

As you leave past a marina and dry dock look right for a Christmas tree plantation. Watch also for railroad cars converted into homes.

MYSTIC (10/10)
Completed in 1905, the wooden station on the right has been restored to its pink and yellow glory. The town owes its existence to the sea and shipbuilding, being situated on the Mystic River. Among the vessels constructed here were America's first ironclad (the *Galena*) and the clipper *Andrew Jackson*, which voyaged to San Francisco round Cape Horn in a record 89 days. Mystic Seaport Museum has one of the biggest outdoor displays in the country and a 19th Century whaling ship is moored in the recreated New England village.

Your train leaves past another marina before continuing along an embankment where water and pleasure craft can be seen on both sides. The shoreline ahead features inlets, trees and herons.

NEW LONDON (10/20)

On the River Thames (pronounced thames) which trains cross on a steel bridge just before entering the large Romanesque station designed by H H Richardson. Ticket office open 0400-0030. New London was one of the earliest settlements, quickly growing rich on whaling. The Lyman Allyn Museum on Mohegan Ave is dedicated to a whaling captain and features early American furniture.

Seagoing tradition still continues at the US Coastguard Academy. Its training vessel *Eagle* can be seen moored on the left or in full sail on the river. Nearby shipyards launched the world's first nuclear submarine, *Nautilus*.

From here to Old Saybrook trains run mostly alongside the beach, with the waters of Niantic Bay a few feet from the tracks. Look for sunbathers, fishing boats and enviable houses.

Connecticut River (14/6)

You cross on a drawbridge and continue via marshes.

OLD SAYBROOK (20/30)

The blue and white station dates from 1873.

Long Island Sound and many small islands appear on your left as the train speeds along this coastal stretch. Approaching New Haven you see a power plant and docks to the left before your train crawls through rail yards into the station.

NEW HAVEN (30/25)

Where the first sulphur matches and Colt revolvers were made. Founded in 1638 as Quinnipiac and renamed two years later, New Haven became one of the strictest Puritan towns. It's now the state's third busiest port. Visitors bureau: 900 Chapel (787-8822).

Amtrak's restored Union Station at 50 Union Ave opens 0555-2215 (Mon-Fri), 0640-2215 (Sat) and 0740-2215 (Sun). Trains pause here as electric locomotives replace diesel for the journey to Washington. Look right for Amtrak trains from Springfield and Hartford joining the main Northeast Corridor. Metro-North trains can be seen on the left.

New Haven surrounds the Green where three historic churches survive. Also worth a visit are Fort Nathan Hale and the Pardee-Morris House. You can take a cruise on Long Island Sound from Long Wharf Dock.

Nearby Yale University was named after an early benefactor, Elihu Yale. Free guided tours include the 1752 Connecticut Hall (oldest on campus) and the Harkness Tower (rising 221ft). A Gutenburg Bible is one of 400,000 books in the Beinecke Library.

You leave New Haven via rail yards, houses and industry.

Milford (5/20)

The scene of an annual oyster festival.

Cross the Housatonic and Pequonnock Rivers.

BRIDGEPORT (25/24)

Connecticut's largest city has 1,300 acres of parkland and the state's biggest zoo. City Hall was named after the socialist mayor Jasper McLevy, in office 1933-57. Amtrak at 525 Water opens 0610-2230. Visitors bureau: 10 Middle (576-8494).

Showman P T Barnum (also a Bridgeport mayor) was buried in Mountain Grove Cemetery, where Tom Thumb's grave is marked by a life-size 2ft statue. On your right as you leave is the Barnum Museum containing an Egyptian mummy and the clothes worn by Tom Thumb.

Ocean-going ships dock in the harbour on the left.

Westport (10/14)

A handful of New Yorkers commute further into Connecticut but this is as far as most will travel. Houses here and along the coast to Stamford are among the most expensive and fashionable. Nearby Sherwood Island is the place for swimming in Long Island Sound.

As you near Stamford look for the most modern part of the city ahead to your right.

STAMFORD (24/18)

Research City claims to have more international corporations than anywhere outside New York or Chicago. Smart new office blocks and malls have transformed the skyline. Visitors bureau: 2 Landmark Sq (359-3305). Amtrak shares the glass and concrete Transportation Center on Washington Blvd with Metro-North trains (seen on the left). A walkway links the platforms. Ticket office open 0525-2200.

Greenwich (6/12)

First settled by the Dutch, this is now probably the richest town in Connecticut, being the home of many film and TV stars. Places of interest include the Bush-Holley House (a colonial saltbox) and the US Tobacco Museum.

From here on you lose touch with Long Island Sound and travel through an increasingly urban landscape towards New York City.

NEW ROCHELLE (18/30)

You part company with Metro services operating out of New York's Grand Central.

Pelham Bay (4/26)

Massive Coop City apartment blocks appear on the right as you cross the bridge. Calvary Hospital is to the left.

Trains cross the Hutchinson River and progress through the deprived South Bronx, entering Hell Gate Viaduct. In 1917 the Hell Gate Route (or New York Connecting Railroad) linked the New York, New Haven & Hartford line with the Pennsylvania Railroad.

Manhattan State Hospital (10/20)

A sombre 1930s building on your right.

Continue looking right for views of Manhattan as the train travels over Randalls and Wards Islands then through Astoria. Rail yards extend on both sides before you enter a tunnel on Long Island, taking you beneath the East River and Manhattan to Penn Station.

NEW YORK CITY (30/15)

Manhattan, Wall Street, 42nd Street, West Side Story and *Breakfast at Tiffany's* — everyone visits New York in the movies. A world leader in fashion, finance and advertising, the city has inspired businessmen and bankers as much as artists and writers.

Niew Amsterdam began in 1625, and the following year Peter Minuit bought Manhattan from the Indians for $24. Today's population is three million, plus 11 million commuters. Nowhere else has so much energy and excitement, though crime and urban decay seem as much part of the fabric as Fifth Avenue and the St Patrick's Day parade. Unique, funny and alarming, not everybody loves New York but no one forgets it.

Transport: Amtrak uses Pennsylvania Station at 7th Ave and W 31st, beneath Madison Square Garden. Sadly this is not a patch on the station (demolished in 1963) which Thomas Wolfe described as 'vast enough to hold the sound of time'. Metroliner information: 736-3967. Ticket office open 0530-2330. Waiting room 24 hours. A Metropolitan lounge for first class passengers opens 0530-2130 (weekdays) and 0700-2200 (weekends). Baggage room, newspapers, restaurants, snack bars, shops, taxi stand, subway. Other Amtrak ticket offices are at 1 E 59th, the World Trade Center and Rockefeller Plaza. The Long Island Railroad (718-454-5477) also operates from Penn Station.

Grand Central Terminal at 89 E 42nd and Park Ave remains endearingly atmospheric. The beaux arts building, completed in 1913 by Cornelius Vanderbilt, replaced a smaller (1898) station unable to cope with increased traffic. The Vanderbilt family's oakleaves emblem is incorporated into the vaulted ceiling of the main concourse. Grand Central's 'city within a city' cost $65 million and originally had 48 tracks on two levels, plus tennis courts, an art gallery and a hospital. The Municipal Arts Society organises free tours each Wednesday.

More than 500 Metro-North (532-4900) commuter trains operate daily from Grand Central to the suburbs and Connecticut, so rush hours can be frantic. Amtrak stopped using Grand Central in April 1991.

Manhattan's logical grid of streets and avenues makes it easy to find your way around. Driving — or trying to park — isn't recommended. The visitors bureau has maps and schedules for public transport, and more details are available from the NYC Transit Authority, 370 Jay Street, Brooklyn, NY 11201. Call 24 hours a day for bus and subway information (718-330-1234).

Taxis: Look for a yellow cab with a lighted sign and hail it by raising your arm. For complaints or lost property contact the Taxi Commission (869-4513). For Skyline radio cabs call 718-482-8686.

Travellers' Tales
Lost and Found in Penn Station
by John Ainsworth

In the dark recesses of the underworld that is Penn Station, Amtrak's only NYC terminal as Grand Central is sadly now only a commuter terminus, is a little room, more like a cage, inhabited by a solitary New Yorker whose only contact with the human race seems to be when they have lost something on Amtrak. Penn station itself is a scruffy, chaotic underground conglomeration of offices, shops, fast food outlets, and people. There is none of the upmarket feel of Washington's Union station or the spaciousness of Grand Central or Philadelphia's main halls. Somehow, the "Lost and Found" here would not fit in one of those places.

On the last leg of our travels I had lost a small headset radio on the train from New Orleans to New York, probably when transferring from coach class to sleeper at Atlanta. I thought it worth a chance it was found — or at least I could register a claim for insurance.

We found the office tucked in a corner near the checked baggage counter and walked in. "I think I lost a radio on the Amtrak train from New Orleans," I said half apologetically to the little man behind the cluttered desk opposite. "Why did you do that?" he snapped back with no hint of humour or anger.

I tried to explain the circumstances but what our friend (I didn't discover his name but will call him Al) wanted was an audience. "Americans are stupid; look what they leave on trains." He took great delight in opening his cupboard and showing us ghetto blasters (how can you mislay these?), umbrellas, bags — and then he rummaged in the back of the cupboard and pulled out a brown envelope and showed us a diamond dress ring. "Tell me you've lost in and it's yours," he said. Later my partner regretted she didn't take him up on the offer.

It took Al a good few minutes more to find the appropriate form at the back of his cupboard, give us a number and direct us to the Police Office to make a report. I guess he wanted to prolong his contact with the world outside his closet.

The Police Office was another little room far from the world outside — the officer behind his grille asked us to wait. Eventually another young cop came in, led us out and down more stairs to another little office and took the details, gave us a copy of the statement and sent us out to the rain of New York with a warning not to trust anybody in this city.

We got the money back from the insurance and we never saw any violence in New York. But the experience of the "Lost and Found" in the bowels of Penn Station was an attraction not too many tourists find.

Amtrak's official line on Lost and Found is that "Carry-on articles lost or left on trains or in stations should be reported to a station baggage agent as soon as possible. Every effort will be made to recover the item promptly. Amtrak cannot accept responsibility for lost articles."

No doubt items found should be reported in the same way. It makes sense also to report anything lost or found to the car attendant or conductor, especially when travelling long distance.Written confirmation of any loss is advisable in case an insurance claim needs to be made.

John Pitt

Car Rental: Discount, 240 E 92nd (410-2211).

Greyhound: Port Authority Terminal, 8th Ave (730-7460).

New York is served by three airports, the largest being John F Kennedy (located in Queens). Access is by taxi, bus and limousine. The JFK Express (718-330-1234) is a subway and bus service connecting with Brooklyn and Manhattan. Carey Express buses (718-632-0500) operate a direct service between JFK and the Port Authority Terminal via Grand Central.

La Guardia Airport, also in Queens, is similarly served by Carey buses. Water Shuttle boats (212-687-2600) can take you to Pier 11 on the East River.

Newark Airport is 14 miles southwest, with New Jersey Transit buses (201-460-8444) connecting to the Port Authority Terminal. Olympia Trails buses (201-964-6233) run from Newark to Grand Central and the World Trade Center.

Tours: Gray Line (397-2600) and Crossroads (581-2828). Boat tours are available from Circle Line (563-3200) and flights from Island Helicopter (683-4575). The Staten Island Ferry (806-6940) provides a trip round the harbour and the Statue of Liberty for just 25 cents.

Visitors Bureau: 2 Columbus Circle (397-8222) and 42nd Street in Times Square. For free daily events call 360-1333.

Telephone Code: 212 for Manhattan and the Bronx. 718 for Queens, Brooklyn and Staten Island.

Accommodation: Contact New World Bed & Breakfast at 150 5th Ave, Suite 711, New York, NY 10011 (675-5600).

AYH Hostel: 891 Amsterdam Ave (932-2300). Maximum stay seven days. Members $19, non-members $23.

YMCA Vanderbilt: 224 E 47th (755-2410). Singles $36, doubles $48.

YMCA West Side: 5 W 63rd (787-4400). Singles $32, doubles $46.

YWCA Brooklyn: 30 Third Ave (718-875-1190). For women only. Singles from $68 a week.

Hotel prices tend to be high apart from some weekend rates. Hotels include the Waldorf-Astoria at 301 Park Ave (355-3000); Algonquin, 59 W 44th (840-6800); Salisbury, 123 W 57th (246-1300); Chelsea, 222 W 23rd (243-3700); Gorham, 136 W 55th (245-1800); Tudor, 304 E 42nd (986-8800); Pickwick Arms, 230 E 51st (355-0300) — singles $45, doubles $80.

Statue of Liberty: Reached by Circle Line ferry from Battery Park (269-5755). Liberty enlightening the world, lately refurbished, was designed by Frederic Bartholdi and paid for by the French. See Manhattan from the observation deck or climb 162 steps for views from The Lady's crown. Also on the island is the Immigration Museum (open daily, admission).

World Trade Center: West of Church Street in the financial district. These twin towers are the tallest buildings in the city and you can see up to 100 miles from the observation decks (466-7397). Open daily, admission.

Empire State Building: 350 5th Ave (736-3100). The people's favourite skyscraper was the world's tallest building when completed in 1931. The 87th and 102nd floor observation decks have terrific views, especially at night. Go early to miss the crowd. Open daily, admission.

St Patrick's Cathedral: 5th Ave and 50th. The Gothic towers of New York's Roman Catholic cathedral contrast with the adjacent Rockefeller Center's more modern lines.

Central Park: Bounded by 59th and 110th Streets, and by 5th Ave and Central Park West. Here you can watch New York at play, listen to concerts and see free Shakespeare. The park also has America's oldest carousel, a zoo and Strawberry Fields (dedicated to John Lennon). Open daily. Also visitors centre: 64th Street (397-3156).

United Nations: 405 E 42nd, overlooking the East River (963-7713). Take a guided tour of the Secretariat Building, General Assembly Hall and Hammarskjöld Library. Free tickets can be obtained to watch meetings. Open daily, admission for tours.

Stock Exchange: 20 Broad (656-5168). Formed in 1792 when a group of brokers met at the junction of Wall and William Streets. Free film and tours. Open weekdays.

You depart Penn Station by means of a 2½-mile tunnel under the Hudson River, surfacing three minutes later in New Jersey. The Hudson tunnels were the first structural links across the river to New York City, and train services started when Pennsylvania Station opened in 1910.

The city's outline on the far left features the Empire State Building and the World Trade Center. Beyond the New Jersey Turnpike bridge to your right is the Giants Stadium.

Hackensack River (10/5)
Crossed as you lose sight of New York.

Trains follow and then cross the Passaic River before pulling into Newark's echoing art deco Pennsylvania Station.

NEWARK (15/14)
New Jersey's largest city is one of the country's biggest manufacturing centres. It was the birthplace of the novelist Stephen Crane. Amtrak's station at Raymond Plaza W opens 0550-2145 (Mon-Sat) and 0645-2145 (Sun). The Thomas Edison Historic Site in the suburb of West Orange preserves the inventor's laboratory. Look for his original gramophone and the first movie camera.

You leave past brick-built factories and other more modern plants.

Elizabeth (6/8)
This former New Jersey capital, now bound to Newark by continuous

suburbs, was an important town during the Revolution. Watch for a General Motors factory to your right.

Rahway (10/4)
Old brownstone buildings appear on both sides.

METROPARK (14/26)
Amtrak's station at 100 Middlesex-Essex Tpk opens 0530-2230 (Mon-Fri) and 0630-2230 (weekends).
   Continue among industrial plants owned by some of the country's biggest corporations, with the scene occasionally brightened by a stretch of farmland. You cross the Rariton River.

New Brunswick (8/18)
A scheduled stop for a few trains, New Brunswick is where Rutgers University (seen on the right) began in 1776. Look right also for the headquarters of Johnson & Johnson.
   The train continues among semi-rural scenes until factories, chemical plants and warehouses take over again towards Trenton.

Princeton (18/8)
The University's ivy-clad campus on the right features Albert Einstein's house. Other famous Princeton residents have included Woodrow Wilson, Aaron Burr and J P Morgan. The Art Museum has pictures by Cezanne, Van Gogh and Picasso, and panels in University Chapel are carved in wood from Sherwood Forest. Information: 609-452-3000. New Jersey Transit trains run to Princeton from Penn Station, New York.

TRENTON (26/32)
This is the home of the 1792 Capitol and New Jersey's State Museum. Amtrak's lived-in station at 72 S Clinton Ave opens 0530-2130.
   You leave past older parts of the city, crossing the Delaware River near where Washington crossed in 1776 to attack the Hessian Garrison. The Capitol's gold dome is on your right. Crossing the river takes you from New Jersey into Pennsylvania.

Holmesburg Junction (20/12)
Holmesburg Prison is on your right. The Tacony-Palmyra bridge crosses the Delaware to your left.

Schuylkill River (30/2)
Cross the river and enter Philadelphia via Fairmount Park, with the zoo on your left. An old signal box mural proclaims 'the city of brotherly love' as Philadelphia's skyline appears in the left distance. As you get closer to the station watch for Boathouse Row and the Parthenon-style Museum of Art.

PHILADELPHIA (32/22)
'On the whole I'd rather be in Philadelphia' was W C Fields' epitaph to malign his birthplace. William Penn founded the city in 1682 on a peninsula between

the Schuylkill and Delaware Rivers. It became America's capital from Independence until 1800, by when it was the world's second largest English-speaking community.

Apart from its historic buildings and museums, Philadelphia is famous for cheesesteaks, pretzels and an alarming crime rate. The city has been home at various times to Benjamin Franklin, Sammy Davis Jr, Dizzy Gillespie, Chubby Checker, Rocky, Live Aid and TV's *thirtysomething*.

Transport: Stately 30th Street Station at 30th and Market is one of Amtrak's busiest. Recently restored at a cost of $100 million, it has a first class passenger lounge and electronic train information. Information: 895-7123. Metroliner information: 824-4224. Ticket office open 0510-2245 (Mon-Fri) and 0610-2245 (weekends). Waiting room 24 hours. SEPTA commuter trains operate to Trenton. Newspapers, Red Caps, restaurants, shops, taxi stand.

Penn Center Station is at 1617 John F Kennedy Blvd. Ticket office open 0910-1400 and 1500-1730 (Mon-Fri). Closed weekends and holidays. Amtrak ticket-holders travel free by commuter train from 30th Street to this downtown station.

The historic district is best explored on foot, using maps from the visitors bureau. SEPTA operates buses, trolleys and the subway (574-7800).
Taxis: Yellow (922-8400) and Quaker City (728-8000).
Car Rental: Thrifty (365-3900).
Greyhound: 10th and Filbert (931-4000).

The airport is eight miles southwest by taxi, Delux bus (463-8787) and Airport Express trains (call SEPTA for times).

Tours: Gray Line (569-3666) and Philadelphia (271-2999). The Fairmont Park Trolley takes in most sights and allows unlimited stop-offs (879-4044). Water cruises are available on the *Spirit of Philadelphia* (923-1419) and the riverboat *Liberty Belle* (238-0887).

Visitors Bureau: 16th and JFK Blvd (636-1666). The National Park Visitor Center is at 3rd and Chestnut (597-8974). Open daily. Call 627-1776 for recorded information.

Telephone Code: 215.

Accommodation: Contact Philadelphia Bed & Breakfast, PO Box 4755, Philadelphia, PA 19134 (634-4444).
AYH Hostel: Chamounix Mansion, a historic building in Fairmount Park (878-3676). Members $9, non-members $14. Some family rooms. Closed December.
YWCA: 2027 Chestnut (564-3430). Women over 18 only. Singles $25. Take bus No 42.

Hotels include the Four Seasons at 1 Logan Sq (963-1500); Holiday Inn Midtown, 1305 Walnut (735-9300); Quality Inn Center City, 501 N 22nd (568-8300); Quality Inn Chinatown Suites, 1010 Race (800-228-5151); Chestnut Hill, 8229 Germantown Ave (242-5905); Apollo, 1918 Arch (567-8925).

Museum of Art: 26th and Benjamin Franklin Pkwy (763-8100). The half a million works include Van Gogh, Picasso, Renoir and Rubens. Plus American crafts, a Japanese teahouse and an Indian temple. Guided tours. Closed Mon, free Sun morning.

Fairmount Park: Covering 4,500 acres from downtown to the city's northwest boundary, the park has forests, waterways, sports fields and museums. Highlights include Boathouse Row (19th Century buildings used by rowing clubs), Strawberry Mansion (the largest in the park) and Memorial Hall (dating from the 1876 Centennial).

City Hall: Broad and Market (686-1776). Completed in 1900 and topped by a 37ft bronze statue of William Penn, this 548ft tower is the tallest masonry structure in the world. Open weekdays, free tours and observation deck.

Independence Park: A historic square mile which draws five million tourists each year. Most buildings are open daily, free. The following are among the highlights.

Independence Hall: On Chestnut Street. Opened in 1732, this is where the Declaration of Independence (1776) and Constitution (1787) were adopted. You can tour the Assembly Room and Old City Hall, where the Supreme Court held sessions from 1791 to 1800.

Liberty Bell Pavilion: On Market. Originally cast in England in 1751, the State House Bell hung in Independence Hall for over 200 years before moving to this new glass-walled home.

You depart Philadelphia with the university's Franklin Field on your right next to the Convention Hall. The train continues amid smokestack industry and residential suburbs.

Commodore Barry Bridge (11/11)
This imposing steel structure on the left spans the Delaware River between Chester, PA, and New Jersey. Look for ships being loaded.

Pennsylvania/Delaware State Line(15/7)
The Delaware River is on your left as you enter the Small Wonder State — the first to ratify the Constitution. A Phoenix Steel complex appears to your right and Sun Oil refineries can be seen on both sides.

Brandywine Creek (18/4)
Cross the creek, flowing into the Christina River on the left. The Christina eventually joins the Delaware.
   From here to Wilmington you progress through Fort Christina Park, site of the first Swedish settlement in 1638. The Holy Trinity (Old Swede's) Church and graveyard on the right date from 1698, and the church is still in use.
   Near Wilmington look for the station's decorative clock tower on your right.

WILMINGTON (22/25)
The 'chemical capital of the world', where in 1802 Eleuthere Irenee du Pont founded a gunpowder mill. The site is now occupied by the Hagley Museum of industrial history. Wilmington's 1871 Opera House has a splendid cast-iron facade. Amtrak's refurbished station at Martin Luther King Blvd and French opens 0530-2200. Look left for the cutter *Mohawk*, kept as a memorial to the Second World War Battle of the Atlantic.

You leave via further industrial scenes with a twin-spired church on the right.

Newark (8/17)
A scheduled stop for some trains, but not to be confused with Newark, New Jersey. On the left as you depart is a Chrysler plant which originally made tanks.

Delaware/Maryland State Line (14/11)
Cross into exotically shaped Maryland, sculpted by Chesapeake Bay and the Potomac River. At Hancock the state is only five miles wide. Stone markers (one white, one black) in a field on your right signify the state boundary.

Elkton (15/10)
Where wedding chapels saw thousands of quickie marriages during the 1930s. A quarry can be seen off to the right.

You continue through a colonial countryside of streams, woods and traditional buildings.

Northeast River (16/9)
The tree-lined river on your left flows towards Chesapeake Bay.

Perryville (20/5)
Located on the Susquehanna River, with a brick-built station to the left.

Cross the Susquehanna with Chesapeake Bay on the left and three bridges spanning the river upstream to your right.

Havre de Grace (23/2)
This neat town on the south shore of the bay was burned by the British during the war of 1812.

ABERDEEN (25/22)
Home of the Aberdeen Proving Grounds and US Army Ordnance Museum.

Cross the mile-wide Bush River, with the Susquehanna Wildlife Refuge on your left.

Edgewood (9/13)
William Paca, a signatory to the Declaration of Independence, was born near this prosperous small town.

Cross the Gunpowder River, also a mile wide, and pass the Maryland National Guard headquarters on the left. Industrial scenes return as you near Baltimore and pass beneath Interstate 40. An old brownstone district features on your right, with the downtown skyline ahead to the left.

BALTIMORE (22/12)

Birthplace of the American railroad and one of the country's busiest ports, Baltimore has been the home of Billie Holliday, Scott Fitzgerald and Babe Ruth. During the 1830s Edgar Allan Poe lived in poverty at 203 N Amity and was buried in the grounds of Westminster Church in 1849.

Commercial life has recently revived, and you can get panoramic views from the World Trade Center. Visitors bureau: 1 E Pratt (659-7300). Amtrak's station at 1515 N Charles opens 0530-2130. The AYH Hostel is near the station at 17 W Mulberry (576-8880).

The B & O Railroad Museum at 901 Pratt (237-2387) occupies an 1884 roundhouse. Locomotives, rolling stock and replicas are featured, plus the country's first passenger and freight station. Open Wed-Sat, admission.

As you leave you travel through a tunnel to another district of traditional brownstones, with the Calvert Whiskey distillery on the right.

B/W INTERNATIONAL (12/10)

One of the airports serving Washington. This is not a stop for all trains.

NEW CARROLLTON (10/10)

A key transport junction in the capital's northern suburbs, where the station and yards of Washington's Metro Rail can be seen next to Amtrak's stop.

After New Carrollton you enter the District of Columbia by crossing the Anacostia River. Look right for the 555ft Washington Monument. Also on the right, beyond Amtrak's maintenance facility, are the dome and tower of the Shrine of the Immaculate Conception.

WASHINGTON

'Southern efficiency and Northern charm' was the way President Kennedy described Washington. This elegant city of neo-classical public buildings was designed by Pierre Charles L'Enfant on what had been a swamp. The architecture, boulevards and green spaces are a suitable setting for Washington's main business — government.

Events to watch for include the cherry blossom festival in April and the Independence Day parade. Summer here can be oppressively humid.

The tourist areas are clean and good-looking but Washington also has its darker side. Drugs and other crime make parts of the city unsafe, so stay on the beaten track.

Transport: Amtrak's 1907 Union Station at 50 Massachusetts Ave is as impressive as the city's other major buildings, with ancient Rome's Baths of Diocletian inspiring Daniel Burnham's design for the waiting room. Renovation has turned it into one of the network's showpieces. Metroliner information: 484-5580. Ticket office open 0530-2230. Waiting room 24 hours. A hundred shops and restaurants, nine movie theatres, lockers, vending machines, newspapers, luggage trolleys, Red Caps, taxi stand, subway. Other Amtrak travel centres are at 1721 K and 400 Seventh, and tickets are sold in Room S-101 of the Capitol (weekdays 1000-1730).

Washington is best appreciated on foot, most places being within easy distance of the station. Metrobus (637-7000) operates throughout the city as well as into Maryland and northern Virginia. The Metro Center at 11th and G is the focal point for an expanding Metrorail subway, which has a stop at Union Station.

Taxis: Diamond (387-6200) and Yellow (544-1212).

Car Rental: Thrifty, 1001 12th NW (986-0922).

Greyhound: 1005 1st NE (565-2662).

Dulles Airport, 25 miles west, is the main international flight centre, accessible by bus or taxi. Washington National is in Arlington, Virginia, four miles from downtown by subway. Baltimore/Washington International (BWI) is 30 miles northeast by bus, rail and taxi. Call 703-685-1400 for Washington Flyer buses to all airports.

Tours: The visitors bureau has advice on dozens of tour companies. Landmark Service Tourmobiles (554-7950) visit the main attractions, including Arlington Cemetery and Mount Vernon. Unlimited stop-offs can be made en route.

Visitors Bureau: 1455 Pennsylvania Ave (789-7000). Open Mon-Sat. For recorded information call 737-8866. Another information centre is at Union Station (open Mon-Sat) and the International Visitors Information Service (IVIS) opens weekdays at 733 15th NW (783-6540).

Telephone Code: 202.

Accommodation: Call the Bed & Breakfast League (363-7767) or Bed & Breakfast Ltd (328-3510).

International AYH Hostel: 1009 11th NW (737-2333). Members only, $14.

Contact the Hotel Association for special rates and package deals among 40,000 rooms (833-3350). Hotels include the Grand Hyatt at 1000 H (800-228-9000); Hampshire, 1310 New Hampshire Ave (296-7600); Gramercy, 1616 Rhode Island Ave (800-368-5957); Harrington, 11th and E (800-424-8532); Rock Creek, 1925 Belmont Rd (462-6007); Allen Lee, 2224 F (331-1224) — singles $33, doubles $42.

The Capitol: At the east end of the Mall (224-3121). America's most important building was completed in 1800, when the Senate and House of Representatives met in joint session on November 22. The familiar white dome is an addition to the original design. Open daily, free tours.

Supreme Court: 1st and E Capitol (479-3000). Housed in a white marble building, the court sits for two weeks every month from October to June (you are invited to watch). At other times members of staff give free lectures. Open weekdays.

White House: 1600 Pennsylvania Ave (456-7041). Occupied by every president since George Washington, and a million people visit each year (open Tues-Sat mornings, free). You get tickets from a booth on the Ellipse at Constitution Ave.

Washington Monument: On the Mall at 15th (426-6839). The highest structure in the city has a line in the marble one third of the way up, where construction stopped for 26 years when the money ran out. Finally completed in 1888, the monument has stunning views from its observation deck. Expect a long wait for the elevator. Open daily, free.

Lincoln Memorial: West end of the Mall (426-6895). This classical Greek temple overlooks a reflecting pool. The walls surrounding Abraham Lincoln's 19ft statue are inscribed with his speeches. Open daily.

National Archives: Between 7th and 9th on Constitution Ave (501-5205). Another classical-style building, containing such documents as the Declaration of Independence, Constitution and Bill of Rights. Open daily, free.

Smithsonian Institution: A complex of museums mostly located between 6th and 14th (357-2700). All are open daily, free. Highlights include the following.

Air and Space Museum: Independence Ave and 6th. Featuring the Wright brothers' *Kitty Hawk*, Lindbergh's *Spirit of St Louis*, the Apollo 11 command module and a walk-through model of Skylab. Film shows, planetarium and tours.

Museum of American History: 14th and Constitution Ave. Look for the gold crescent moon on the cylinder of a 1926 green and gold Pacific type loco from the Southern Railway's Crescent Limited. The museum also has Edison's phonograph, George Washington's false teeth and the flag which inspired the national anthem.

Museum of Natural History: 10th and Constitution Ave. The 45½-carat Hope Diamond (biggest blue diamond in the world) and the Fenkovi African elephant (largest ever recorded) are among 60 million exhibits.

13A The Northeast Corridor

New Haven— Springfield—Boston

Some Northeast Corridor trains branch left at New Haven and travel inland through one of Connecticut's most appealing landscapes.

NEW HAVEN
For New Haven, see the preceding section.

WALLINGFORD (17/7)
A spired church can be seen on your right.

MERIDEN (7/10)
Situated between Mount Beseck and the Hanging Hills, the Heritage House Museum here recreates life in the 1700s. Views can be had of Long Island Sound from the tower of Castle Craig, accessible via Hubbard Park. Amtrak's station at 60 State opens 0600-2200 (weekdays).

Beaver Pond (4/6)
Seen on your left, with Silver Lake to your right.

BERLIN (10/10)
Famous in the 18th Century for making tinware. Berlin is the nearest station to New Britain.

HARTFORD (10/8)
Founded in 1633 and capital of Connecticut since 1875, Hartford is the state's biggest city after Bridgeport. It was originally a landing post called Sucking, and when Puritan colonists displaced the Dutch the latter named the English *jankes* (thieves). Hence the word Yankee was invented. Tourist Information: 165 Capitol Ave (566-2304). Amtrak's station at Union Place opens 0600-2330.

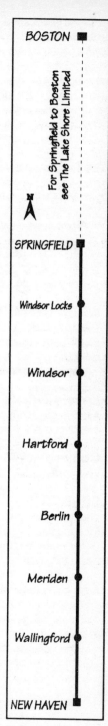

BOSTON

For Springfield to Boston see The Lake Shore Limited

N

SPRINGFIELD

Windsor Locks

Windsor

Hartford

Berlin

Meriden

Wallingford

NEW HAVEN

The white-domed Old State House designed by Charles Bulfinch in 1792 is now a museum. Watch for the new Capitol's gold-plated dome high on your right as the train arrives. The State Library and Supreme Court opposite the Capitol has the table at which Lincoln signed the emancipation document.

A host of companies make Hartford a leading insurance centre of the US. The Travellers Insurance building on the site of the Charter Oak is one of the country's tallest (527ft). Wadsworth Athaeneum, opened in 1842 as America's first art museum, features guns, porcelain and French paintings.

Mark Twain (*Tom Sawyer*) and Harriet Beecher Stowe (*Uncle Tom's Cabin*) have their homes preserved at Nook Farm. Noah Webster, of dictionary fame, lived in a saltbox farmhouse at 22 S Main.

Connecticut River (5/3)
Seen on the right. Between here and Old Saybrook the river runs through one of America's prettiest valleys.

WINDSOR (8/5)
The town was first settled in 1663 amid colonial tobacco farms.
Your train crosses the Farmington River.

WINDSOR LOCKS (5/20)
The 19th Century canal on your right supplies water to Dexter and Sons, a paper products maker. Bradley Air Museum features more than 50 aircraft, including a 1909 Bleriot.
Cross the Connecticut River.

Enfield (10/10)
A future president of New Jersey College, Jonathan Edwards, is said to have preached here in colonial times.

Connecticut/Massachusetts State Line (28/7)
You leave the Constitution State for the Bay State.

SPRINGFIELD
This 17th Century trading post on the banks of the Quinnitukqut River (Indian for 'long tidal') has become an industrial city which hosts the Eastern States Exposition. The Springfield Armory has a massive military collection and the Basketball Hall of Fame honours the sport's inventor, James Naismith. Free museums downtown include the Museum of Natural History (one of America's oldest) and the Connecticut Valley Historical Museum.

Visitors Bureau: 34 Boland Way (787-1548). Amtrak at 66 Lyman opens 0530-0030. Buses connect with Montpelier and Burlington, Vermont (see *The Montrealer*).

Some trains continue from Springfield to Boston. For this part of the route, see *The Lake Shore Limited*.

14 The Crescent

New York—New Orleans

The original Crescent began in 1891 as the Washington and Southwestern Vestibule Limited, an overnight train between Washington and Atlanta. It was operated by the Richmond & Danville Railroad, predecessor to the Norfolk Southern (whose line the present train uses south of Washington). The Vestibule featured luxurious staterooms, a library and an observation car. It became a solid train from New York to New Orleans in 1906 and was later renamed the Crescent City Limited. The Southern Railway continued to operate it until Amtrak took over in 1979.

Today's train makes a 1,380-mile journey from New York to the relaxed charm of New Orleans. Southern hospitality permeates the train from the start as staff and passengers strike up a rapport. Amtrak's friendliest train travels the Northeast Corridor before heading southwest across Civil War country to Atlanta, Birmingham and the South.

Amtrak's Gulf Breeze coaches separate at Birmingham and continue south to Mobile via Montgomery.

Frequency: Daily. The southbound service leaves New York mid-afternoon, reaching Washington early evening and Greensboro just after midnight. You arrive in Atlanta early next morning, Birmingham late morning and New Orleans early evening.

Travelling north, trains leave New Orleans early in the morning to reach Birmingham early afternoon, Atlanta mid-evening and Greensboro during the night. You arrive in Washington early on the second day and New York by early afternoon.

Reservations: All reserved.

Equipment: Heritage coaches.

Sleeping: Heritage bedrooms, roomettes, slumbercoach.

Food: Complete meals, snacks, sandwiches, drinks.

Baggage: Check-in service at most stations.

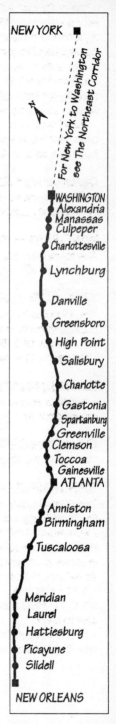

NEW YORK

For New York to Washington
see The Northeast Corridor

WASHINGTON
Alexandria
Manassas
Culpeper
Charlottesville

Lynchburg

Danville
Greensboro
High Point
Salisbury
Charlotte
Gastonia
Spartanburg
Greenville
Clemson
Toccoa
Gainesville
ATLANTA

Anniston
Birmingham

Tuscaloosa

Meridian
Laurel
Hattiesburg
Picayune
Slidell

NEW ORLEANS

NEW YORK
For New York and the route to Washington, see *The Northeast Corridor*.

WASHINGTON
The Crescent leaves through a tunnel beneath the Capitol before emerging with the Capitol building on the right. Also on the right are the Bureau of Engraving, the Washington Monument and Jefferson Memorial. You cross the Potomac River with the 14th Street road bridge to the right.

The Pentagon (5/10)
The nerve centre of the US military network (23,000 personnel and 29 acres). Nearby Arlington Cemetery was the last resting place for General Pershing, Admiral Byrd, President Taft, Joe Louis and Robert Kennedy. President John F Kennedy's grave is marked by an eternal flame.

Pass the airport to your left, then the enormous Crystal City hotel and office development on the right. As you approach Alexandria look left for Metro trains.

ALEXANDRIA (15/30)
The 'cradle of history' began in the 1740s as a port on the Potomac and now attracts a million visitors each year. Amtrak's station is at 110 Callahan Dr. Ticket office open 0515-2130. The grey stone building on your right is the George Washington Memorial Masonic Temple.

Tours of Old Town Alexandria start at the Ramsay House, 221 King (703-549-0205). The city has hundreds of restored buildings, a cobblestone waterfront and the nation's second oldest apothecary shop. Gadsby's Tavern and Museum in Market Square was the focus for business and social gatherings. You can travel along the Potomac on the *Spirit of Mount Vernon* to visit George Washington's mansion and gardens.

MANASSAS (30/30)
Fiercely fought over during the Civil War, when two battles around a strategic rail junction cost 24,000 lives. The present station on the right at 9500 West dates from 1915. Bristow Air Park is to the left.

You leave past a cemetery and grain elevators on the right then travel among forests and farms.

Remington (20/10)
Look for the farmers' market on the right before you cross the Rappahannock River and approach Culpeper. Factories and warehouses gather on the right.

CULPEPER (30/60)
The Union army had headquarters here during the Civil War, and the Cavalry Museum features weapons and equipment. Culpeper's red-brick station is on the right, with the city beyond.

The train continues, accompanying the Blue Ridge Mountains and Shenandoah National Park to the west.

Rapidan River (15/45)

Civil War battles were fought at nearby Cedar Mountain, Port Republic and the Wilderness.

Continue through farmland with dogwoods and apple trees.

Orange (30/30)

The James Madison Law Office can be seen on the left just before town. Look left also for Montpelier Station and President Madison's estate.

CHARLOTTESVILLE (60/65)

Named after King George III's wife Charlotte, this is where Thomas Jefferson founded the University of Virginia. He created his unique home, Monticello, on a nearby hill. Meriwether Lewis, William Faulkner and President James Monroe were also Charlottesville residents, and you can visit Monroe's Ash Lawn estate. Visitors bureau: 415 E Market (295-3141). Amtrak's Union Station at 810 W Main opens 0530-2100, and buses link with the state capital, Richmond.

On your right as you leave is the University of Virginia Medical Center, then other academic buildings and the Rotunda.

Monroe (55/10)

Sweet Briar College is across the highway to your right. You continue among rolling green fields with hedgerows, cattle, barns and streams.

Cross the James River on a high trestle and enter the Rivermont Tunnel.

LYNCHBURG (65/65)

Named after John Lynch, who founded a ferry service here after the town grew rich on tobacco. It's now one of Virginia's main industrial and education centres, with many Victorian houses. Amtrak at Kemper and Park Ave opens 2030-0530. Appomattox Court House, where Lee surrendered to Grant, is 21 miles east.

You travel through mellow Piedmont countryside and the forested Blue Ridge Mountains, which range from Pennsylvania down to northern Georgia and are part of the Appalachians.

DANVILLE (65/60)

The 'world's best tobacco market' is situated on the Dan River and was briefly a Confederate capital (in 1865). Danville was the birthplace of Lady Astor and boasts the world's largest textile mill. A marker on Riverside Drive commemorates the 'wreck of the old 97' train crash in 1903.

Virginia/North Carolina State Line (5/55)

Crossed as your train continues into the night.

GREENSBORO (60/25)

Famous for its golf tournament. In 1871 England's General Cornwallis defeated General Greene here at the Guilford court-house.

HIGH POINT (25/40)
So named because it's the highest point on the route between Charlotte and Goldsboro.

SALISBURY (40/50)
Daniel Boone grew up in this colonial town set among hills and lakes. Amtrak's station is at Depot and Liberty.

A short distance to the north at Spencer is the North Carolina Transport Museum (704-636-2889). On the site of the Southern Railway's biggest repair plant, the museum has locomotives, equipment and memorabilia from Indian times to the present. Open daily, donation. Steam and diesel rides take place April-December.

CHARLOTTE (50/25)
Also named after George III's wife, this was the first place in America where gold was discovered. It's the biggest city in the Carolinas and the country's leading producer of cotton cloth. Each May the World 600 Auto Races take place at the Motor Speedway. Amtrak at 1914 N Tryon opens 2000-0400 (daily) and 0900-1800 (Wed, Thurs, Fri).

Charlotte was the birthplace (in a log cabin) of President James Polk. You can take a self-guided tour of the Old City from the visitors bureau at 229 N Church. Highlights include a settlers cemetery and the blushing pink splendour of Overcarsh House. Latta Plantation Park at Huntersville has costumed guides and a 19th Century merchant's house.

GASTONIA (25/55)
Your train makes a slight detour west to take in this industrial community. A Revolutionary battle was fought at nearby Kings Mountain.

North Carolina/South Carolina State Line (5/50)
Cross between the Carolinas.

SPARTANBURG (55/40)
A manufacturing town set among countryside famous for peaches, Spartanburg was named after the Spartan regiment of the South Carolina militia.

GREENVILLE (40/35)
The birthplace of Joanne Woodward and Jesse Jackson. Bob Jones University has been here since 1827. The textile industry dominates Greenville and inexpensive clothes can be bought at many factory outlets.

CLEMSON (35/35)
Another university town, which until 1943 was called Calhoun (after politician John Calhoun).

South Carolina/Georgia State Line (20/15)
The Crescent journeys deeper into the South through wooded country. Watch for fast-growing kudzu vines spreading over the ground and smothering all

in their path. They were imported from Japan to combat soil erosion and
have become a menace throughout the South.

TOCCOA (35/40)

Home of Toccoa Falls (186ft) and a college of the same name. The traditional
station building features to your right and a spired church on your left.

You leave past warehouses and freight trains into more tree-covered hills,
lumber yards, orchards and occasional fields. Nearing Gainesville, factories
and freight trains gather on both sides.

GAINESVILLE (40/55)

On the eastern edge of Lake Sidney Lanier (Georgia's largest), where the
Lake Lanier Islands offer beaches, camp-sites, fishing and boating. Amtrak's
station at 116 Industrial Blvd also serves Athens, home of the University of
Georgia (America's oldest state college). Ticket office open 0600-0800 and
1700-2140. The train stops across a barriered road junction.

Leave via factories, lumber yards and freight cars, then pass beneath a
highway bridge. A flea market can be seen to the right. As the day becomes
lighter you travel through less mountainous scenery where cattle, horses and
ploughed fields become more common.

Norcross (35/20)

Industry returns, with MARTA commuter trains apparent on both sides. An old
green Pullman car is sidelined to your left.

Oglethorpe University (40/15)

The campus buildings are on the right.

As you approach Atlanta the city's spired skyscrapers appear ahead to the
left.

ATLANTA (55/130)

Atlanta is a big place for banking, trade and shopping, but magnolias still
bloom along the older streets. Spring fills the parks with flowering azaleas and
dogwoods. The city became a focal point during the 1960s civil rights
movement.

Atlanta began in 1837 as a railroad town called Terminus and it remains a
transport hub. General Sherman's destruction in 1864 couldn't stop growth
for long, and today most of the big corporations (including Coca-Cola and
CNN) are resident. The glass building on the left of the station belongs to
AT & T.

Transport: Amtrak's Brookwood (Peachtree) stop is at 1688 Peachtree,
three miles north of downtown (take bus No 23). Information: 872-9815. Ticket
office and waiting room open 0630-2130. Lockers, vending machines,
luggage trolleys.

MARTA operates the buses and subway trains (848-4711).
Taxis: London (688-5658) and Checker (351-1111).
Car Rental: Atlanta, 3185 Camp Creek Pkwy (763-1160).
Greyhound: 81 International Blvd (522-6300).

Hartsfield Airport is 10 miles south by taxi, MARTA train, shuttle van (525-2177) and Airport Express bus (455-1600).

Tours: Gray Line (767-0594) and Burton's (525-3415). Walking tours are available from the Preservation Centre, 401 Flatiron Building (522-4345).

Visitors Bureau: 233 Peachtree (659-4270). There are information centres at 3393 Peachtree Rd (266-1398) and the airport (767-3231).

Telephone Code: 404.

Accommodation: Contact Bed & Breakfast Atlanta, 1801 Piedmont Ave NE, Atlanta, GA 30324 (875-0525).
YMCA: 22 Butler (659-8085). Men only. Singles $16.
  Hotels include the Ritz Carlton at 181 Peachtree (659-0400); Ibis, 101 International Blvd (800-535-0707); Terrace Garden Inn, 3405 Lenox Rd (800-241-8260); Barclay, 89 Luckie (424-7991); Rodeway Inn, 330 W Peachtree (577-6970); Travelodge, 1641 Peachtree (873-5731) — singles $40, doubles $44.

State Capitol: 206 Washington (656-2844). Topped by a dome of gold leaf mined in north Georgia, the building houses state offices, the Georgia History Museum and several Confederate flags. Open daily, free.

New Georgia Railroad: 10 Central Ave (656-0769). On three Saturdays each month a steam engine takes vintage passenger cars for an 18-mile tour of the city. On the other Saturday trains go to Stone Mountain Park and Village, site of the world's largest granite outcrop, to see carved figures of Jefferson Davis, Robert E Lee and Stonewall Jackson. Trains leave from Milepost Station, close to the 1869 Georgia Railroad freight depot (Atlanta's oldest building).

Atlanta Historical Society: 3101 Andrew Dr (261-1837). Incorporating the Swan House (a 1928 Italian-style villa), the 1840s Tullie Smith House and an exhibition hall. Open daily. Admission except for exhibition hall. Take bus No 40.

Martin Luther King Historic District: See Dr King's birthplace at 501 Auburn Ave. The Ebenezer Baptist Church is where he preached. Open daily, free. The Center for Nonviolent Social Change at 449 Auburn Ave (524-1956) has a library, films and a museum. Open daily, admission.

Big Shanty Museum: At Kennesaw, 25 miles north of Atlanta (427-2117). The museum has the *General* steam locomotive which Northern soldiers stole in 1862, along with two cars of a Western & Atlantic passenger train. It was captured half way to Chattanooga, later inspiring Buster Keaton's classic film. Open daily, admission.

You depart Atlanta via the city's western industrial suburbs, with extensive freight yards on the right and the Chattahoochee Brick Company to the left. You cross I-75 and the Chattahoochee River before re-entering a landscape of tree-covered hills and ridges.

Douglasville (35/95)
One of many quiet towns encountered on this part of the route. An imposing Commercial Bank and the Young Refining Corporation are to your right.

Villa Rica (50/80)
Look for the Golden Hosiery Mills on your right among the pine trees and dogwoods.

Bremen (65/65)
The Hubbard Slacks Company building is seen on the right. The train moves slowly out of Bremen past a church and graveyard on the left, then starts to climb a series of S-shaped curves into the hills.

Tallapoosa (75/55)
One of Georgia's finest golf courses is on your left as you near town. The American Thread Company is to your right.

The Crescent picks up speed, crossing the attractive Tall River before climbing further into forest. Look for logs being loaded on railroad wagons to your left. Cross the Tallapoosa River.

Georgia/Alabama State Line (90/40)
You pass from Eastern to Central Time, so watches go back an hour (forward when travelling east).

The land becomes more densely wooded as you enter Talladega National Forest at the southern end of the Appalachian Mountains.

Heflin (105/25)
This was once a gold rush town. In the left distance you can see the state's tallest mountain, Mount Cheaha (2,407ft).

ANNISTON (130/90)
One of the Alabama's main manufacturing centres, with an old brick station on the right.

Anniston Depot (10/80)
Look for Second World War Sherman tanks guarding silos at the US army's largest military depot, stretching some distance on your right.

Lincoln (15/75)
The town's modest blue railroad building is on the right.

Pell City (30/60)
A Chrysler plant features on the right before you continue via Chula Vista Mountain Tunnel.

Travellers' Tales
The Crescent

by John Ainsworth

It felt like the end of the holidays as we got a taxi before dawn from our guest house in St Charles through the darkened streets, past an early and eerie streetcar to be at Union Station for 7.00 to head back to New York and Britain on Amtrak's "Crescent". The night before we had been dancing to the Original Crescent City Jazz Band on the paddle-steamer *Natchez*. A long 30 hour train journey was not really to be savoured.

Still, the day had its own quiet pleasures. We left on time and wended our way past the cemeteries with their tombs set above the earth and out towards Lake Pontchartain. It was a calm sunny, southern morning; there were little piers with fishing cottages at their outer ends; outboard motor boats heading out to fish — and then out across the long low viaduct to Slidell.

Then a gentle run all morning long to Birmingham, Alabama, first through the swamps and wilderness of Mississippi, then through the backwoods, with never a sight of the Interstate, only a few humble cottages and here and there a neat township, where we briefly saw the "front rooms" — a black congregation emerging from church in their Sunday best, neat town squares, and where they were still open, neat stations with luggage trollies lined up — but little luggage. It felt like this was how America should be.

Birmingham was an industrial interlude but the station was surrounded more by reminders of the past — disused warehouses, a derelict town centre hotel and even a private railroad car in the adjacent platform. From there to Atlanta it was rolling hills, the track curving up and around, with only one stop, at Anniston, where we spent miles passing a vast Army Stores Depot, neatly laid out.

Atlanta station may not have been impressive — a single narrow platform on a bridge above a freeway and the passengers were queuing up along the street outside to board the train. But passengers aplenty there were too — a party of some 100 senior citizens who filled two sleeping cars. In the city all eyes and ears were on a vital baseball game which the Braves needed to win to reach the World Series. (And they did.)

And so to bed after a day reading, looking at the view, playing cards and drinking coffee. We woke nearly in the north and at breakfast time, the man on the P.A. pointed out the sights as we entered Washington — we had good views of the Lincoln Memorial, Washington Monument and the Capitol — reminding us of an enjoyable three days earlier in the holiday but to some passengers an excitement in the midst of a Trans-American journey.

We spent 45 minutes refuelling — time to look around the recently re-designed Union Station with its 100 shops and 25 food outlets — liked the Great Train Store with its videos of trains playing, model trains and railwayana — and then on to the last and familiar leg along the busiest main line, on to New York.

Gahaba River (65/25)

Crossed by means of two high bridges. The river continues on your left.

Undulating, forest-covered hills begin to give way to industrial scenes as the Crescent nears Birmingham.

Irondale (70/20)
Freight wagons assemble on the right. Look right also for the Sloss Furnace (dating from 1890). On the left is the Dr Pepper Company.

Red Mountain (85/5)
A 55ft statue on the mountain to your left represents Vulcan, the Roman god of fire and forge. It was originally made for the 1904 St Louis World's Fair and is the largest cast-iron statue ever made. A stairway inside leads to the top for views from the observation deck.

BIRMINGHAM (90/60)
The home town of Willie Mays, Nat King Cole and Hank Williams Jr, Alabama's largest city has long been an industrial one. Amtrak's stop at 1819 Morris Ave stands opposite manufacturing plants and brick chimneys. Ticket office open 0900-1700. On the left is the University of Alabama Medical School.

Birmingham relieves the industrial gloom by filling its parks and gardens with roses and dogwood trees. The zoo has Siberian tigers and golden spider monkeys. Visitors bureau: 2027 First Ave N (323-5461).

Coaches of the Gulf Breeze, having accompanied the Crescent this far, travel south to Mobile via the state capital, Montgomery.

The Crescent leaves among rail yards with Vulcan still dominating the skyline to your left.

Bessemer (22/38)
On the right are the Royster Guano Company and a former Pullman-Standard factory. You should soon be passing the northbound Crescent, assuming both trains are on time.

TUSCALOOSA (60/90)
The University of Alabama, home of the Crimson Tide football team, is to your right as you approach the station. Named after a Choctaw Indian chief, Tuscaloosa was once Alabama's capital.

Your train skirts a golf course on the left then travels through swamp country. Sleepy towns, sunburned houses and characteristic general stores can be seen among the forest plantations and logging sites.

Mound State Monument (15/75)
The prehistoric mounds on the right were used by Indians for ceremonial purposes, though a temple on the highest mound is more recent.

Black Warrior River (35/55)
The Crescent slows to clank across a steel drawbridge into more swamp country. Another track runs along a raised bed to the left.

Tombigbee River (45/45)
Note the white cliffs as you cross. This is part of the Tenn-Tom project linking the Tennessee, Ohio and upper Mississippi Rivers with the Gulf of Mexico.

Livingston (70/20)
Named after Robert Livingston, who negotiated the Louisiana Territory sale in 1803.

York (75/15)
Look for picturesque stores on the right and a sawmill to the left.

Alabama/Mississippi State Line (80/10)
You enter the land of cotton and magnolias.

MERIDIAN (90/60)
Birthplace of Jimmie Rodgers, whose memory lives on at the annual country music festival. Meridian is a major rail junction where the tracks radiate in six directions. Amtrak's station at 1901 Front opens 0830-1700.

As you leave look for a faded Gulf Mobile Sohio Railroad building falling apart on the left.

Key Field (8/52)
Light aircraft are kept in hangars to your right. Some of the other planes belong to the Mississippi National Guard. You cross Chunky Creek and pass a natural gas facility on the left.

LAUREL (60/30)
A trading centre for farmers, with a fire station on the left and disused tracks running into the trees.

Cross the Leaf River just before Hattiesburg station, where an old baggage car is displayed between two steam locos.

HATTIESBURG (30/60)
The home of Southern Mississippi University and the Magnolia Classic golf tournament. The city was founded on the railroad and lumber industries, and Amtrak's red-tiled station is at 308 Newman. Ticket office open 0900-1000 and 1500-1600 (Mon-Sat). Closed Sun. To the right is a futuristic coal-fired electricity generating plant. You pass a square-towered church on the left as you leave.

Poplarville (40/20)
Birthplace of Theodore Bilbo, who was a US senator and segregationist governor of Mississippi.

PICAYUNE (60/15)
Your last stop in this state.

Pearl River (5/10)
Crossing takes you into the flat, subtropical landscape of southern Louisiana.

SLIDELL (15/55)
A residential town for commuters to New Orleans. Main Street is seen on the left beyond a battered station.

Lake Pontchartrain (10/45)

It's worth taking the Crescent just for this six-mile crossing of the lake's eastern tip. Your train runs along a causeway immediately above the surface, giving sensational views across 630 square miles of water. Especially wonderful at sunset (or sunrise if travelling east). Look for fishing shanties on stilts and a road bridge to your left.

Soon after Lake Pontchartrain you glimpse the New Orleans skyline on your left. Look for Tulane University, then the Greenwood Cemetery with 'above the ground' graves. On arrival in New Orleans the Crescent stops for a moment before reversing into the station.

NEW ORLEANS

For New Orleans, see *The Sunset Limited*.

15 The Silver Star

New York—Miami

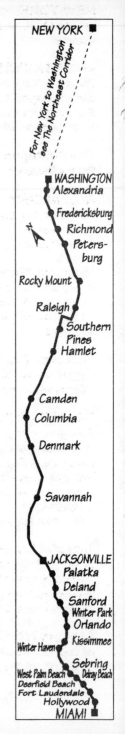

Another train with a party atmosphere, the Silver Star travels from the northeastern cities down to Florida's subtropical resorts. On the way you encounter the nation's capital, historic Virginia, North Carolina's pine forests, Old Savannah and Lake Okeechobee, plus the beach communities leading to Miami.

A separate section continues from Kissimmee to Florida's west coast at Tampa.

Frequency: Daily. The southbound service leaves New York early in the morning to reach Washington just after midday, Richmond mid-afternoon and Columbia late evening. You arrive in Savannah and Jacksonville during the night, then Miami soon after midday.

Travelling north, trains leave Miami mid-afternoon to reach Jacksonville late evening, then Savannah and Columbia during the night. You reach Richmond late morning, Washington early afternoon and New York early evening.

Reservations: All reserved.

Equipment: Amfleet coaches.

Sleeping: Heritage bedrooms, roomettes, slumbercoach.

Food: Buffet-style dining car. Tray meals, snacks, sandwiches, drinks.

Baggage: Check-in service at most stations.

NEW YORK

For New York and the Silver Star route to Washington, see *The Northeast Corridor.*

WASHINGTON

The Silver Star leaves through a tunnel beneath the Capitol before emerging with the Capitol building on the right. Also on the right are the Bureau of Engraving, the Washington Monument and Jefferson Memorial. You cross the Potomac River with the 14th Street road bridge to your right.

The Pentagon (5/10)

For the Pentagon, see page 182.

ALEXANDRIA (15/50)

For Alexandria, see page 182.

Soon after Alexandria the Silver Star crosses the first of many inlets leading to the Potomac.

Quantico Marine Base (30/20)

A stop for Palmetto and Carolinian trains, with the airfield and assault course on your left. A museum features Second World War aircraft and tanks.

You leave with the Potomac away to the left and continue among forests and rivers.

Falmouth (46/4)

A small residential and manufacturing town.

Cross the muddy Rappahannock River with a highway bridge to the right.

FREDERICKSBURG (50/50)

George Washington lived here as a boy and Mary Washington's garden at 1200 Charles still has the box hedges she planted. George's brother Charles owned the Rising Sun Tavern. Visitors bureau: 706 Caroline (373-1776).

Nearby Fredericksburg and Spotsylvania Military Park has exhibitions relating to four Civil War battlefields. Amtrak's station is at Caroline and Lafayette Blvd.

Your train leaves with the city's airport and runways to the left.

Jackson Shrine (15/35)

Stonewall Jackson died in the modest white house on the left.

You cross the Mattaponi and Pamunkey Rivers as the Silver Star travels through appealing countryside with logging operations and occasional marshes near the track.

Ashland (40/10)

As your train runs through the main streets look for Randolph-Macon College on the left, dating from 1830.

RICHMOND (50/30)

State capital since 1779 and a Confederate capital during the Civil War, Richmond is Virginia's largest city after Norfolk. The old tobacco town has recently revived after a period of decline. The Cultural Link Trolley which runs from the Science Museum at 2500 W Broad takes in 35 historic landmarks. The Confederate Museum features General Lee's sword. Visitors bureaux: 1700 Robin Hood Rd (358-5511) and 6th Street Marketplace (788-6829).

The impressive modern station on the right at 7519 Staples Mill Road is some way from downtown. Open 24 hours. You can take a free tour of the Capitol, which Jefferson helped design, and of the Philip Morris plant (the biggest cigarette factory on earth).

As the Silver Star leaves it curves right through busy goods yards.

James River (14/16)

Cross with the Interstate 95 bridge to your right.

As you near Petersburg, the houses start to take over from trees.

PETERSBURG (30/80)

Trains stop at South Street Station, Ettrick, serving passengers for Petersburg. Ticket office open 0945-1715 and 2100-0500. Petersburg is another city with tobacco and Civil War connections. The conflict ended 75 miles west of here when General Grant accepted Robert E Lee's surrender at Appomattox.

Virginia University is high to your left as you depart on Seaboard Coast Line tracks crossing another muddy river, the Appomattox, into Petersburg proper.

Meherrin River (30/50)

Crossed near Emporia.

Virginia/North Carolina State Line (35/45)

You enter the Tar Heel State, so named after Jefferson Davis promised to tar the heels of soldiers to make them stand their ground.

Roanoake River (45/35)

Cross the river on its way from the Blue Ridge Mountains to the Atlantic.

Approaching Rocky Mount you cross the Tar River.

ROCKY MOUNT (80/80)

North Carolina grows the biggest tobacco crop in America and much of it comes here to be traded, along with cotton and other produce. Amtrak at 101 Hammond opens 1030-1900 and 2100-0500.

Wilson (20/60)

A yearly tobacco auction brings people from all over the country, and warehouses and curing facilities can be seen on both sides of the track. This is a scheduled stop for Palmetto and Carolinian trains.

Selma (45/35)

The modest town serves adjacent farm communities. It's another stop for the Palmetto and Carolinian.

RALEIGH (80/65)

The city of oaks was named after its founder Sir Walter Raleigh, whose statue stands in Capitol Square. It was subsequently proclaimed North Carolina's 'unalterable seat of government'. The Capitol, completed in 1840, was restored for the US bicentennial. For information on the Victorian neighbourhoods contact the visitor centre at 301 N Blunt (733-3456).

Amtrak at 320 W Cabarrus opens 0830-2100 (Mon-Fri), 0830-1130 and 1830-2130 (weekends). The North Carolina Museum shows life from the first settlements through Revolutionary days to the Civil War. Raleigh's education establishments — including the state's three main universities — have attracted high-tech industries.

North Carolina Central Prison (5/60)

The prison's forbidding walls are to the left.

North Carolina State University (7/58)

Also seen to the left before you continue among lakes, streams and hills thick with pine forest.

Near Southern Pines look left for corrals where racehorses are prepared.

SOUTHERN PINES (65/30)

The train holds up traffic at a road crossing amid manicured bushes.

HAMLET (30/70)

A rail town with a sign which proclaims it 'the all-American city'. Log trains are set up in the yard to the right. Also on the right is the canopied Main Street station, which houses a museum and is a registered historic building.

Industry again gives way to trees, fields and white-spired churches as you continue south.

Carolinas State Line (7/63)

Cross from North to South Carolina, entering the Palmetto State.

CAMDEN (70/30)

Home of the Colonial Cup steeplechase, this is one of South Carolina's oldest cities. It was fought over frequently during the Revolution.

COLUMBIA (30/55)

On the banks of the Congaree River, Columbia has been the state capital since government moved here from Charleston in 1786. The Hampton-Preston Mansion shows how statesman Wade Hampton lived in the 19th Century. Visitors bureau: 301 Gervais (254-0497). Amtrak's station at 850 Pulaski opens 0830-1600 (Mon-Sat) and 2230-0630 (daily).

The South Carolina Railroad Museum is 25 miles north at Rockton (704-393-0335). The line between Rockton and Rion, where some of the last steam trains ran, is currently being renovated. Locomotives and rolling stock in the collection include a Seaboard office car and a hospital/command car. Open on the third weekend each month (April-October).

DENMARK (55/80)
A railroad town located in the midst of swampland.

South Carolina/Georgia State Line (55/25)
You enter what was once Britain's 13th colony.

SAVANNAH (80/130)
America's first planned city was laid out in leafy squares with azaleas and dogwood trees. English colonists founded Savannah in 1773 on a bluff next to the river, and tobacco and cotton wealth led to great warehouses, merchants' mansions and the cotton exchange. After the Civil War the cotton market and Savannah went downhill, but a thousand buildings in the downtown area have been restored.

The Savannah visitors centre is in the former Central of Georgia railway station at 301 W Broad (944-0456). Amtrak's present stop is four miles from downtown at 2611 Seaboard Coastline Dr. Open 24 hours. Bus tours are available from the Historic Savannah Foundation (233-7703).

The Great Exposition at 303 W Broad (next to the visitors centre) occupies a railway shed on the site of the 1779 Siege of Savannah. It has presentations of the siege alongside historic train engines and dining cars.

You leave via freight yards and continue through swampland, trees, farms and villages. Watch for egrets and anglers along the streams.

Hunter Airfield (5/125)
This US army establishment is on your left just before you cross the Ogeechee River.

Richmond Hill (10/120)
Home of the Richmond Hill Plantation, created by car magnate Henry Ford.

Altamaha River (45/85)
Cross yet another river flowing towards the Atlantic, away to the left.

Jesup (50/80)
This is a stop for Silver Meteor trains. The town was named after Morris Jessup, who financed the line which is now part of the Seaboard Coast railroad. Look out for the Jesup Shrimp Inc building on your right and a very old freight wagon to your left.

After Jesup you travel inland through eastern Georgia, seeing many more logging operations.

Big Satilla Creek (70/60)
You cross the creek and, a few minutes later, the Satilla River.

Folkston (85/45)
To the west and south is Okefenokee Swamp, incorporating a wildlife refuge. You can see the swamp's beguiling scenery and animal life from a canoe or by walking canal trails. Camp sites here are raised on platforms to outwit the alligators.

Georgia/Florida State Line (95/35)
Cross high above the St Mary's River into the Sunshine State.

JACKSONVILLE (130/60)
This industrial centre is the second largest US city in area, reaching from the St John's River to the Atlantic. Jacksonville has inexpensive accommodation but is not a tourist resort. The most attractive part is along the river, with its boardwalk and park. Visitors bureau: 6 E Bay (353-9736).

The Cummer Art Gallery is in what used to be a lumber baron's mansion at 829 Riverside Ave. Jessie Ball du Pont Park features the Treaty Oak, an 800-year-old tree under which settlers and Indians concluded a truce.

Jacksonville's station at 3570 Clifford Lane opens 24 hours, and Greyhound buses connect with Tallahassee, 160 miles west.

You leave amid rail yards, warehouses and loading facilities, with the St John's River on the left. Continue south through a constantly changing countryside of hardwood forests, lakes and rivers until palm trees start to appear among the rolling hills.

Ortega River (16/44)
Cross with the St John's River on your left and a marina to your right. Beyond is the sprawl of Jacksonville.

US Naval Air Station (20/40)
Seen across the highway to your left, alongside the Armed Forces Reserve Center.

St John's River (35/25)
Visible among trees on the left as you continue through a land of woods, Spanish moss and small lakes.

Just before Palatka you cross on the right a tributary of the St John's River.

PALATKA (60/25)
Indian for 'cows crossing', Palatka has exotic palm trees gracing its station on the left. The Silver Star has to stop twice to accommodate the train's length.

Look for azalea bushes as you leave past traffic held up at a road crossing — something which happens often on this section of the route.

As you cross the St John's River, dairy farms and orchards appear.

Park Crescent (10/15)
Crescent Lake is to the right.

DELAND (25/20)
Founded by Henry Deland in 1876, this is the home of Stetson University. A ferry operates from 2309 Riverride Rd to Hontoon Island, famous for Timucuan Indian settlements. Amtrak's station at 2491 Old New York Ave opens 1330-2300. The Daytona Beach 500 auto races, held January-February, draw fans to the International Speedway 25 miles east.

St John's River (12/8)
Crossed on a steel bridge.

SANFORD (20/20)
When the South Florida Railroad arrived in 1884, joining Sanford to Jacksonville, this became a shipping point for the produce of central Florida, as well
as a landing place for steamboats. Amtrak's station at 800 Persimmon Ave
opens 0645-1500. The Auto Train terminates at 600 Persimmon Ave (open
0800-1630). Sidings for dealing with Auto Train cars can be seen to your left.
   You leave via factories and housing estates, with a cement plant on the left,
and urban scenes continue most of the way to Winter Park.

WINTER PARK (20/15)
Your train trundles through the streets of one of this area's more fashionable
towns. The park itself is on your left. Rollins College — the oldest in the state
— has a Spanish-style campus featuring the Cornell Fine Arts Centre.
   The Silver Star continues through suburbs to Orlando.

Florida Hospital (5/10)
This imposing structure on both sides of the track is connected by an
overhead walkway.

Church Street Station (11/4)
The old train station on the left has become part of an entertainment complex,
complete with 19th Century steam loco. Other delights include Rosie
O'Grady's Bar and the Cheyenne Saloon. The high-rise buildings of Orlando
can be seen ahead.

ORLANDO (15/20)
Tourism has turned a modest agricultural town into this city of ¾ million,
boosted by visitors all year round. Attractions include Disney World, the
Epcot Center and Sea World.
   Situated among lakes and citrus groves, Orlando's daytime temperatures
from June to September are often over 90°F. Even the coldest months rarely
get below 50°F. Humidity, as elsewhere in Florida, can be high.

Transport: Amtrak's station is at 1400 Sligh Blvd. Information: 843-7611.
Ticket office open 0700-2200. Waiting room 0700-2230. Baggage store,
vending machines, newspapers, luggage trolleys, Red Caps, taxi stand.
   Most hotels are some distance from downtown, and the big attractions
further away still, but there is plenty of scheduled transport. The main
companies include Beeline Tours (841-1397) and Gray Line (422-0744). Tri-
County buses operate in Orlando and to the airport (841-8240).
Taxis: Town and Country (828-3035) and Yellow (422-4455).
Car Rental: Alamo, 8200 McCoy Rd (857-8200).
Greyhound: 300 W Amelia (843-7720). Serves all major attractions.
   The airport is a few miles southeast of downtown by bus and Airport
Limousine (859-4667).

Tours: Disney World orientation tours are a useful introduction (827-8233).

Visitors Bureau: 8445 International Dr (351-0412). Open daily. Take bus No 8 from downtown.

Telephone Code: 407.

Accommodation: Orlando doesn't lack hotels, especially around International Drive, and rooms are available on Disney property. The latter are more expensive but discounts can be had off-season (September-December). Book well in advance at the Central Reservations Office, Box 10100, Lake Buena Vista, FL 32830 (824-8000).
Travelodge (AYH): 409 Magnolia (423-1671). Members only.
Plantation Manor International Hostel: 227 N Eola Dr (843-8888). Beds $12, rooms $26.
Young Women's Community Club (AYH): 107 E Hillcrest (425-2502). Women only, $10.
   Hotels in Orlando include the Peabody, 9801 International Dr (352-4000); Stouffer, 6677 Sea Harbour Dr (351-5555); Park Suite, 8978 International Dr (352-1400); Radisson Inn, 8444 International Dr (345-0505); Heritage Inn, 9861 International Dr (352-0008).

Sea World: 7007 Sea World Dr, 20 miles southwest of Orlando (351-3600). With dolphins, whales, sea lions, penguins and sharks. Open daily, admission. Take Greyhound or Tri-County bus No 8.

Spaceport USA: At Kennedy Space Center, an hour's drive east (452-2121). Bus tours take in the museum, rocket garden, shuttle launch site and Cape Canaveral. IMAX film show. Open daily, admission.

Disney World: This 27,400-acre hotel and amusement complex is the main attraction. Over 750 million passengers have used the world's biggest monorail system. Disney World opens throughout the year, with admission by one-day ticket or 'passport'. For information, advance tickets and a free guide contact Box 10000, Lake Buena Vista, FL 32830 (824-4321). Highlights include the Magic Kingdom (roller coasters and Mickey Mouse), the Epcot Center and the MGM Studio (animation techniques and classic films).

After suburban Orlando your train heads west among orange groves, lakes, trees and rivers.

KISSIMMEE (20/40)
Amtrak's closest station to Disney World is at 416 Pleasant. Visitors bureau: 1925 E Spacecoast Hwy (800-432-9199). A livestock market (the oldest cattle auction in Florida) takes place each Wednesday.
   Leave with the Monument of the States visible among the downtown buildings on your left. This 70ft high feature is said to have rocks from every state in the Union.

Auburndale (25/15)

Crossing point for tracks of the Silver Star and Silver Meteor, where through coaches to Tampa separate from the rear of the train.

WINTER HAVEN (40/35)

An alternative stop to Orlando for visiting Disney World and Cypress Gardens. Winter Park is the off-season home of Boston's Red Sox baseball team. The picturesque station at 1800 7th SW opens 0700-2145.

Leave across a canal linking on the right with Lake Ship, one of Florida's 30,000 lakes. Oranges and other citrus fruits grow in profusion on both sides of the track. Look also for herds of beef cattle.

Bok Tower (8/27)

Next to a disused station on the left is a carillion with 50 bells. It was named after the founder of the *Ladies' Home Journal*.

As you near Sebring, Lake Jackson comes into view on the right.

SEBRING (35/85)

Sebring is a farming, packing and distribution centre, established early this century.

Lake Istokpoga (20/65)

Seen on the right, with Sebring racetrack away to the left.

Cross the Kissimmee River, on course between Lake Kissimmee and Lake Okeechobee. The latter is the biggest lake in the southern United States and fourth biggest in the country. Catfish are a speciality. On the far side is the swamp wilderness of Everglades National Park.

Okeechobee (40/45)

Indian for 'plenty big water'. This is a scheduled stop for the Silver Meteor.

You travel the next 59 miles at up to 79mph down the longest straight stretch of track east of the Mississippi.

Indiantown (65/20)

The town was named after Seminole Indians.

You rattle across the Okeechobee Canal, connecting Lake Okeechobee with the Atlantic.

WEST PALM BEACH (85/20)

Look for millionaire mansions, expensive shops and polo fields. West Palm Beach is linked to the island community of Palm Beach by three bridges. Clear Lake can be seen to the right. Amtrak's Spanish-style station is on the left at 201 S Tamarind Ave (open 0800-1930).

The Henry Flagler museum on Cocoanut Row in Palm Beach honours Henry Morrison Flagler, builder of the Florida East Coast Railway that brought development from Jacksonville to Key West. Flagler's home is now a museum, and his private passenger car stands in the grounds.

Leave West Palm Beach past the airport to your right and travel among houses and waterways until industrial scenes interrupt.

DELRAY BEACH (20/10)
This attractive, low-key resort began as a settlement for artists. It's the home of the Morikami museum of Japanese culture.

Boca Raton Airport (4/6)
Seen immediately on the left. Boca Raton has Spanish buildings and an authentic 1920s atmosphere. This is one of the few parts of the coast where the beaches and dunes remain in their natural state.

DEERFIELD BEACH (10/15)
Palm trees line both sides as you near the station.

Pompano Beach Racetrack (5/10)
On your right, next to where the Goodyear blimp *Enterprise* is based.

FORT LAUDERDALE (15/12)
This is one of Florida's biggest resorts and a major port for cruise ships. It's also the seat of Broward County, named after Napoleon Broward, the governor who brought about early Everglades drainage schemes. Visitors bureau: 208 SE 3rd Ave (527-8755). Amtrak is at 200 SW 21st Ter, open to the street beyond. This is a busy stop during high season. Ticket office open 0700-1845. Take bus No 9 to downtown.

Fort Lauderdale boasts eight miles of beach and an intricate system of waterways to make yachting the regular mode of transport. Downtown has a historic district and Ocean World features sea lions, sharks and otters.

Departing Fort Lauderdale you pass the airport on your left before continuing through 'America's Venice'.

HOLLYWOOD (12/20)
First developed in the 1920s. Watch for the Hollywood Boulevard sign to your left.

Nearing Miami you can see the high-rise hotels of Miami Beach away to the left, past a junked car depot. Freight yards spread out on the right.

MIAMI
'America's Casablanca', Miami was originally founded for growing citrus fruits when Henry Flagler brought his Central Florida railroad here in the late 19th Century. Tourist development came in the 1920s, and the ostentatious hotels of Miami Beach (10 miles long and 300ft wide) now bring millions of sunlovers each year. It's also one of the world's largest cruise ports.

Greater Miami incorporates Key Biscayne (home of President Nixon's winter White House), Coral Gables, Hialeah and the elegant Coconut Grove. Half of the city's two million population is of Spanish descent. Crime and drug-running do exist, but you are unlikely to encounter *Miami Vice* or Don Johnson among the swaying palms.

Even in winter the temperatures here reach the 70s. This is peak season, avoiding summer's humidity and showers. Spring and late autumn are probably best.

Transport: Amtrak's station at 8303 NW 37th Ave in Hialeah has bus links to downtown (7 miles south) and Miami Beach. Information: 835-1221. Ticket office and waiting room open 0630-1900. Lockers, vending machines, newspapers, luggage trolleys, Red Caps, taxi stand. Take bus L for Miami Beach.

Metro-Dade runs buses throughout the metropolis (638-6700). Free maps and information are available at 111 NW 1st. Metrorail trains operate every day, with transfers to Metrobus. Northside station is close to Amtrak's depot. The South Florida Trolley Company (948-8823) also uses Metrobus stops.
Taxis: Metro (888-8888) and Yellow (444-4444).
Car Rental: Value, 1620 Collins Ave (532-8257).
Greyhound: 99 NE 4th (374-7222).

The airport is eight miles west of downtown by taxi, Metrobus No 20 and Supershuttle vans (871-8488). Many hotels provide free taxis.

Tours: American Sightseeing (688-7700). Boat cruises on the *Island Queen* start from Miamarina, 5th and Biscayne Bay (379-5119).

Visitors Bureau: 4770 Biscayne Blvd (539-3000). Closed Sun. More information can be had from the Chambers of Commerce at Key Biscayne (361-5207), Coconut Grove (444-7270) and Miami Beach (672-1270).

Telephone Code: 305.

Accommodation: Miami has an abundance of rooms, from economical to ultra-luxurious. The peak rates and biggest crowds are in winter, when prices can double. Contact the Miami Beach Hotel Association, 407 Lincoln Rd (531-3553).
Miami Beach AYH Hostel: 1438 Washington Ave, in the historic district (534-2988). Members $9, non-members $11. Singles $18, doubles $26. Take bus C from downtown.

Downtown hotels include the Pavilion at Chopin Pl (577-1000); Howard Johnson's, 1100 Biscayne Blvd (358-3080); Dupont Plaza, 300 Biscayne Blvd Way (358-2541).

Miami Beach hotels include the Alexander at 5335 Collins Ave (865-6500); Seville Beach, 2901 Collins Ave (532-2511); Thunderbird, 18401 Collins Ave (931-7700); Waves, 1060 Ocean Ave (531-5835) — singles and doubles $40.

Gold Coast Railroad Museum: 12450 Coral Reef Dr (253-0063). Among several Pullman cars is the *Ferdinand Magellan* used by presidents from Roosevelt to Reagan. The steam locomotives here once belonged to the Florida East Coast Railway. Half hour train rides take place at weekends. Open daily, admission.

Little Havana: Around Calle Ocho (SW 8th Street), where many settled after leaving Castro's island. Walking tours can be had from the Development Authority, 970 SW 1st (324-8127). The Cuban Museum is at 1300 SW 12th Ave (858-8006). Open daily, donation.

Art Deco District: From 6th to 23rd Streets, Miami Beach. Over 800 structures from the two decades after 1930 make this the largest collection of art deco buildings anywhere. Tours start from 1236 Ocean Drive. For more details contact the Miami Design Preservation League, 1201 Washington Ave (672-1836).

Seaquarium: On Key Biscayne (361-5703). This ocean aquarium features dolphins, sharks, manatees and killer whales. Nearby Planet Ocean provides a quieter look at underwater life. Both open daily, admission.

Key West: The Key West extension of the Florida East Coast Railway was completed in 1912, running 114 miles (with 17 miles of bridging). A 1936 hurricane destroyed the line but the right of way now forms the base for a spectacular highway. Greyhound buses travel down from Miami to Ernest Hemingway's old haunt.

15A The Silver Star

Kissimmee-Tampa

The southbound service follows the Silver Star schedule to Kissimmee then continues to Tampa by mid-morning. Travelling north, trains leave Tampa early evening to connect at Kissimmee mid-evening with the Silver Star from Miami.

KISSIMMEE
For Kissimmee and the Silver Star route from New York, see the previous section. You leave Kissimmee and continue travelling southwest across central Florida to the Gulf Coast.

LAKELAND (60/22)
The home of Florida Southern College, Lakeland is at the centre of a vast citrus fruit region. It has the state's main trading exchange and juice extraction plants. Close by is the world's largest phosphate mine.

Plant City (5/17)
Your train trundles slowly through the town.

TAMPA
The name is Indian for 'sticks of fire'. Settlement didn't begin here until Fort Brooke was established in 1824, and most of Florida's early tourist development concentrated on the east coast. Henry Plant brought his railroad late in the 19th Century, then built the 'world's most elegant' Tampa Bay Hotel. During the Spanish-American War this became a headquarters for Theodore Roosevelt.

Many of Tampa's first residents were Cuban refugees who brought with them their cigar-making skills. Tampa is now a tourism and retirement centre, where the

NEW YORK ■

For New York to Kissimmee, see The Silver Star

Kissimmee ●

Lakeland ●

■
TAMPA

Florida State Fair takes place in February.
St Petersburg, adjacent to the south, is quieter and more residential.

Transport: Amtrak's station at 601 Nebraska Ave and Twiggs is an Italian-style building in the process of restoration. Information: 229-2473. Ticket office and waiting room open 0830-2015. Lockers, vending machines, luggage trolleys, taxi stand. Thruway buses link to Amtrak's base at 3601 31st N, St Petersburg (522-9475). Open 0915-1915. Other buses connect with Clearwater Beach and Sarasota.

HART buses run in the Tampa region (254-4278). The Municipal Transit System (530-9911) operates in St Petersburg.
Taxis: Yellow (253-0121) and United (253-2424).
Car Rental: Budget (800-527-0700).
Greyhound: 610 E Polk (229-2112).

Tampa Airport is six miles from downtown by taxi, limousine and HART bus No 30. Contact The Limo (822-3333) for transport to St Petersburg's Clearwater Airport.

Tours: Five Star (331-8232) and Gray Line (822-3577). Boat trips can be had with Spirit of Tampa (273-9485).

Visitors Bureau: 100 S Ashley Dr, Tampa (223-1111) and 401 3rd Ave S, St Petersburg (821-4069). Open weekdays.

Telephone Code: 813.

Accommodation: Contact Florida Suncoast Bed & Breakfast, PO Box 12, Palm Harbor, FL 33563 (748-5118).
YMCA: 116 5th S (822-3911). Men only, $16.
AYH Youth Hostel: 326 First Ave, St Petersburg (898-7100).

Tampa hotels include the Hilton at 200 Ashley Dr (223-2222); Bay Harbor Inn, 7700 Courtney Campbell Pkwy (885-2541); Ramada Hotel North, 820 E Busch Blvd (933-4011); Safari Resort, 4139 E Busch Blvd (988-9191); Holiday Inn Busch Gardens, 2701 E Fowler Ave (971-4710); Red Roof Inn, 5001 US 301 (623-5245).

Busch Gardens: 3000 Busch Blvd (971-8282). Take bus No 5 to Florida's biggest attraction after Disney World. There are more than 3,000 birds and animals, and a monorail takes you among the lions and rhinos. Open daily, admission.

Ybor City: Tampa's Cuban city within a city centres on Ybor Square, with its Spanish-style buildings, restaurants and shops. You can see cigars being hand rolled at the Cigar Factory, 1901 13th (open daily, free). The Ybor City Museum is at 1818 9th Ave (247-6323). Open Tues-Sat, admission. For more information contact the Chamber of Commerce, 1513 8th Ave (248-3712).

Railroad Historical Museum: 341 Main, at nearby Dunedin (733-4151). Located in an 1889 station of the Orange Belt Railroad, with artifacts belonging to early Scottish settlers. Open Tues, Thurs, Sat mornings. Closed June-October.

Salvador Dali Museum: 1000 3rd S, St Petersburg (823-3767). For admirers of the eccentric Spanish surrealist. Closed Mon, admission.

16 The Silver Meteor

New York—Miami

The Silver Meteor train travels the eastern part of the USA between New York and Florida. Like the Silver Star it takes in the nation's capital, the Carolinas and Old Savannah. The Silver Meteor also serves Charleston.

A separate section of the train goes from Auburndale to Tampa, on Florida's west coast.

Frequency: Daily. The southbound service leaves New York late afternoon to arrive in Washington mid-evening and Charleston early next morning. You reach Jacksonville mid-morning, Orlando early afternoon and Tampa mid-afternoon. The Miami section arrives at its final destination early evening.

Travelling north, trains leave Tampa midday (or Miami mid-morning) to reach Orlando early afternoon and Jacksonville late afternoon. You arrive in Charleston mid-evening, Washington early next morning and New York late morning.

Reservations: All reserved.

Equipment: Amfleet coaches.

Sleeping: Heritage bedrooms, roomettes, slumbercoach.

Food: Buffet-style dining car. Tray meals, snacks, sandwiches, drinks.

Baggage: Check-in service at most stations.

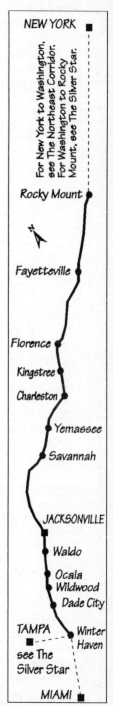

NEW YORK

For New York to Washington, see The Northeast Corridor. For Washington to Rocky Mount, see The Silver Star.

Rocky Mount

Fayetteville

Florence

Kingstree

Charleston

Yemassee

Savannah

JACKSONVILLE

Waldo

Ocala
Wildwood
Dade City

TAMPA
see The
Silver Star

Winter
Haven

MIAMI

NEW YORK
For New York and the route to Washington, see *The Northeast Corridor*. For Washington to Rocky Mount, see *The Silver Star*.

ROCKY MOUNT (80/80)
North Carolina grows America's biggest tobacco crop and much of it comes here to be traded, along with cotton and other produce. Amtrak at 101 Hammond opens 1030-1900 and 2100-0500.

Wilson (20/60)
A yearly tobacco auction brings people from all over the country, and warehouses and curing facilities can be seen on both sides. This is a scheduled stop for Palmetto and Carolinian trains.

Selma (45/35)
The modest town serves adjacent farm communities. It's another stop for the Palmetto and Carolinian.

The Silver Meteor continues on the Seaboard Line through tobacco, cotton and soya bean country.

FAYETTEVILLE (80/80)
This farming centre founded by Scottish immigrants in the 18th Century is the home of Fort Bragg.

Carolinas State Line (35/45)
Cross from North into South Carolina.

Dillon (45/35)
This is a stop for the Palmetto. You cross the Pee Dee River 20 minutes later.

FLORENCE (80/30)
As 'the denture capital of the world', Florence claims to make a thousand sets of false teeth every week. The town was founded with the coming of the railroad and it maintains extensive Seaboard Coast Line yards. Look for a steam locomotive on your right soon after the station. Buses connect with the nearby resort of Myrtle Beach.

Cross the Lynches River 10 minutes from Florence as the Meteor travels among farms of the coastal plain. Look for the distinctive barns used for storing tobacco.

KINGSTREE (30/45)
Cross the Black River soon after leaving town.

Santee River (10/35)
You cross the river then travel alongside Francis Marion Forest on your left. The swamps, oak trees, pines and lakes cover 250,000 acres. Francis Marion acquired his nickname 'the swamp fox' after raiding from these marshlands during the Revolution. As a master of the surprise attack he never camped in the same place for more than two nights.

Lake Moultrie (20/25)
Seen behind a levee on your left. Further inland is Lake Marion.
Cross the Cooper River on its way from Lake Moultrie to Charleston.

CHARLESTON (45/45)
Founded in 1670, Charleston was named after King Charles II. Its brightly coloured mansions and cobblestone streets have largely recovered from the devastating hurricane which hit the city in 1988.

Charleston is located where the Cooper and Ashley Rivers meet on the Atlantic coast, and this position made it one of the most prosperous early American ports. More growth came in 1830 with the country's first steam train service. Local people called it 'the best friend of Charleston'.

More than 700 merchants' houses survive, and you can visit many of them during the spring festival. Contact the Historic Charleston Foundation, 51 Meeting (722-3405). Down on the waterfront you can watch gulls glide over Battery Park as striking sunsets paint the ocean.

Transport: Amtrak's station is at 4565 Gaynor Ave in North Charleston, seven miles from downtown (take the Durant Ave bus). Information: 744-8264. Open 0430-2200.
SCE & G buses (747-0922) operate downtown Mon-Sat.
Taxis: Yellow (577-6565).
Car Rental: Thrifty (552-7531).
Greyhound: 3610 Dorchester Rd (744-4247).

Tours: Gray Line (722-1112) and Adventure (762-0088). Carriage rides are available from Charleston Carriage (577-0042).

Visitors Bureau: 85 Calhoun (722-8338). Open daily. Film shows.

Telephone Code: 803

Accommodation: Contact Charleston Bed & Breakfast, 1031 Tall Pine Rd, Mount Pleasant (884-8208).
Rutledge-Museum Guest House: 114 Rutledge Ave (722-7551). Beds $15, single rooms $35.
Hotels are very expensive downtown, but reasonably priced motels can be found across the Ashley River on US 17 South.

Charleston Museum: 360 Meeting (722-2996). The museum started in 1773 and now has half a million items, including snuff boxes and silver. Open daily, admission. Tickets also give admission to the Joseph Manigault House (an Adam-style mansion) and the 1772 Hayward-Washington House.

St Michael's Church: At Broad and Meeting. The oldest of Charleston's 181 churches resembles St Martin's-in-the-Field, London. City Hall, the Federal Court, the Post Office and the County Court House occupy the other 'four corners of law'.

Charles Towne Landing Park: 1500 Old Towne Rd, on the site of the first settlement. The park has trails, a reconstructed village and a sailing ship. The animal enclosure features wolves and bears.

Fort Sumter: A short boat ride from the municipal marina (722-1691). The Civil War's first engagement took place here in 1861 when the garrison surrendered to Confederate General Pierre Beauregard after two days of bombardment. Free tours of the restored buildings.

You depart Charleston via substantial rail yards and cross the Ashley River before travelling along the coastal plain. Here you cross in succession the Edisto, Ashepoo and Combahee Rivers.

YEMASSEE (45/45)
The town was named after Yemassee Indians.

Interstate 95 (5/40)
The train passes under a highway that stretches down the coast from Maine to Miami.

Savannah River (30/15)
Look for a concrete highway bridge on your right as you cross the river into Georgia.

SAVANNAH
For Savannah and routes to Jacksonville and Tampa, see *The Silver Star*.

JACKSONVILLE (80/60)
Silver Meteor through coaches to Miami continue via Waldo.

WALDO (60/40)
This is Amtrak's stop for the nearby college town of Gainesville. Waldo was a major rail junction until the workshops moved away in 1929. Watch for an old Seaboard caboose parked permanently on the right just past the station.

Lochloosa (20/20)
Lake Lochloosa is on the right.

OCALA (40/25)
Ocala is one of Florida's main centres for the training and breeding of thoroughbred horses. Amtrak at 531 NE 1st opens 2145-0645. The Appleton Museum features Napoleon's sword and silver thrones from India.

   A mile to the east is the state's oldest tourist attraction, Silver Springs. You can take glass-bottom boat rides, see wild animals and visit the car museum. The 366,000-acre Ocala Forest wilderness is also close by.

WILDWOOD (25/30)
A centre for farming and distribution.

Center Hill (20/10)
Note the Spanish-style station buildings.
  You continue beside the protected Withlacoochee Forest. Florida was among the first states to designate parks as a sanctuary for native plants and animals.

DADE CITY (30/40)
Amtrak's stop for Zephyrhills.

WINTER HAVEN (40/35)
For Winter Haven and the rest of the Silver Meteor route to Miami, see *The Silver Star*.

17 **The Colonial**

Boston—Newport News

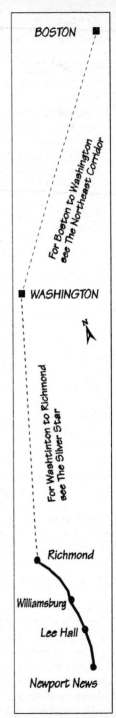

BOSTON ■

*For Boston to Washington
see The Northeast Corridor*

■ *WASHINGTON*

N

*For Washinton to Richmond
see The Silver Star*

● Richmond

Williamsburg ●

Lee Hall ●

Newport News

On a journey through time, the Colonial travels from Boston along the Northeast Corridor to Washington, then through Virginia to the state capital, Richmond. Here you turn east towards Newport News on the Atlantic coast, taking in historic Williamsburg and the Tidewater region.

Frequency: Daily. The southbound service leaves Boston early in the morning to reach New York just after midday and Washington mid-afternoon, arriving in Richmond early evening and Newport News mid-evening.

Travelling north, trains leave Newport News early in the morning to reach Richmond mid-morning and Washington by noon. You arrive in New York mid-afternoon and Boston mid-evening. Sunday trains start from Richmond.

On Sundays only, the northbound Colonial is augmented by the Tidewater. This leaves Newport News mid-afternoon to arrive in Richmond late afternoon and Washington mid-evening. New York (the Tidewater's final destination) is reached late evening.

Reservations: All reserved.

Equipment: Amfleet coaches.

Food: Tray meals, snacks, sandwiches, drinks.

Baggage: No check-in service.

BOSTON
For Boston and the route to Washington, see *The Northeast Corridor*. For Washington to Richmond, see *The Silver Star*.

RICHMOND
The Colonial continues south from Richmond on the Seaboard Coast Line.

Virginia Science Museum (10/55)
The dome can be seen on your right. Housed in the Seaboard Line's former Broad Street Station, the museum features a planetarium and space theatre.

Still in Richmond the train progresses through a sequence of rail yards, transferring to the Chesapeake & Ohio before heading southeast alongside the James River.

Main Street Station (15/50)
The station on the right is now disused.

James River (17/48)
Glimpsed to your right before you cross a canal and proceed through more Chessie yards at Fulton.

Byrd Airport (25/40)
Aircraft and runways are on the left.

The landscape gets flatter as you move into Virginia's Tidewater region, where plantation mansions appear along the river.

New Kent (45/20)
The forestry establishment on your right produces fledgling pine trees.

Chickanominy River (50/15)
Seen on the right, the Chickanominy flows towards the James River.

WILLIAMSBURG (65/10)
America's largest restored town was named after King William, and it became the state capital in 1699. You can recapture colonial days in this reconstruction of public buildings, taverns, gardens and houses. Costumed townspeople drive carriages, work in the shops and generally add atmosphere.

In summer it can get very hot, humid and crowded, so visit during spring or autumn if possible.

Transport: Amtrak uses the Transportation Center, 468 N Boundary. Information: 229-8750. Ticket office and waiting room open 0730-2100 (Mon, Tues, Fri) and 0730-1500 (Wed, Thurs, Sat). Open 1330-2100 on Sundays. Lockers, vending machines, luggage trolleys, taxi stand.

Buses from the visitors centre go to most parts of the historic area, which is best seen by strolling among the buildings.
Greyhound: Alongside Amtrak's station (229-1460).

The airport is 16 miles away by bus and taxi from the station.

Tours: Tickets are available at the Courthouse of 1770 for carriage rides and guided tours. Williamsburg Limousine (877-0279) visits Jamestown, Yorktown and the Carter's Grove Plantation.

Visitors Bureau: 201 Penniman Rd (229-6511). Passes give admission to up to 12 buildings. Open weekdays.

Telephone Code: 804.

Accommodation: Rooms are expensive and hard to find during summer. For up-to-date information, including guest houses, pick up a free guide from the visitors centre.
Sangraal-by-the-Sea (AYH) Hostel: 30 miles away on Rte 626. Members $9, non-members $12. Contact PO Box 187, Urbanna, VA 23175 (776-6500).
   Plenty of hotel rooms exist but those in Colonial Williamsburg must be booked well ahead. Contact the Williamsburg Foundation, Box B, Williamsburg, VA 23187 (229-1000).
   Hotels include the Williamsburg Inn at S Francis (229-1000); Fort Magruder Inn, 6945 Pocahontas Trail (220-2250); Quality Inn-Colony, 309 Page (229-1855); Holiday Inn, 804 Capitol Landing Rd (229-0200); Governor's Inn, 506 N Henry (229-6605); King William Inn, 824 Capitol Landing Rd (229-4933).
   Among the less expensive motels on Rte 60 is Motel 6 (565-3433) — singles $30, doubles $38.

College of William and Mary: At the end of Duke of Gloucester Street. This is the country's second oldest college (1693), where Jefferson studied and the Phi Beta Kappa Society began. It includes the Wren Building (1695) and the President's House (1734).

The Capitol: At the other end of Duke of Gloucester Street. This is where Patrick Henry denounced King George III's stamp tax.
   Other buildings include the Raleigh Tavern, the Governor's Palace, the Magazine (where arms are demonstrated), Bruton Parish Church and the James Anderson House.

US Army Transportation Museum: At Fort Eustis, 20 miles south (878-1115). The collection features a railroad ambulance car, a hospital kitchen car and an industrial crane, plus aircraft and a marine park. Open daily, free.

Jamestown: This is part of the historic triangle, along with Yorktown and Williamsburg. English settlers established the New World's first legislature here in 1619, though the Old Church Tower is all that remains standing from those days. Also featured are the Tercentenary Monument, a Confederate fort and the foundations of the first Statehouse. Open daily, admission. The visitors centre has films and free guides (229-1733). Tours are given by national park rangers.

Yorktown: Settled in 1630, Yorktown was a port and trading centre for the tobacco industry. The Revolution ended in 1781 when Lord Cornwallis was defeated here, and the battlefield is much visited. Many colonial buildings survive or have been reconstructed. The Victory Center (887-1776) has displays and films (admission). The visitor centre shows Revolutionary war exhibits (898-3400). Open daily.

You leave Williamsburg with its historic district to your right.

Busch Gardens (5/5)

This Old Country theme park (complete with steam train) can be seen on the right.

LEE HALL (10/10)

The Colonial stops at the restored station only on request. Soon after Lee Hall the train crosses a section of the city reservoir.

NEWPORT NEWS

The city was founded in 1619 on a harbour shared with Norfolk, Hampton and Portsmouth. The port of Hampton Roads (14 miles long and 40ft deep) is where the James, York, Elizabeth and Nansemond Rivers flow into Chesapeake Bay.

Newport News claims to have the world's biggest shipbuilding yard and largest naval base. The Mariners Museum features a splendid nautical collection. The War Museum has weapons, uniforms and vehicles from the American Revolution to Vietnam. In Newport News Park you can go boating, fishing and camping. For information throughout the peninsula call 838-4184. Amtrak's station is at 9304 Warwick Blvd. Ticket office open 0700-2130 (Mon, Tues, Fri) and 1400-2130 (Sun). Open 0700-1030 and 1800-2030 on Wed, Thurs, Sat.

18 The Cardinal

New York—Chicago

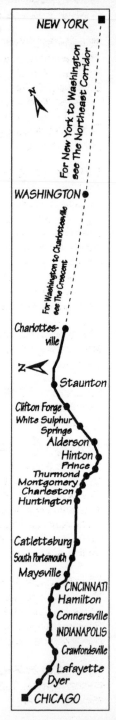

This 1,154-mile journey takes you through some of America's best scenery. After travelling from New York to Washington, the Cardinal sets out across Virginia to Charlottesville, the Blue Ridge Mountains and the Shenandoah valley. You continue west via the Appalachians, the Ohio River valley and Cincinnati, crossing central Indiana's cornfields to Chicago.

Frequency: Three trains a week in each direction. The westbound service leaves New York mid-morning on Sun, Wed and Fri to reach Washington early afternoon, Charlottesville late afternoon and Charleston late evening. You arrive in Indianapolis early next morning and Chicago late morning on Mon, Thurs or Sat.

Travelling east, trains leave Chicago early evening on Tues, Thurs and Sat to reach Indianapolis around midnight and Charleston next morning. You arrive Charlottesville mid-afternoon, Washington mid-evening and New York late evening on Wed, Fri or Sun.

Reservations: All reserved.

Equipment: Amfleet coaches.

Sleeping: Heritage bedrooms, roomettes, slumbercoach.

Food: Complete meals, snacks, sandwiches, drinks.

Baggage: Check-in service at main stations.

NEW YORK
For New York and the route to Washington, see *The Northeast Corridor*.

WASHINGTON
The Cardinal leaves through a tunnel beneath the Capitol before exiting with the Capitol building on the right. Also on the right are the Bureau of Engraving, the Washington Monument and Jefferson Memorial. You cross the Potomac River with the 14th Street road bridge to your right.

The Pentagon (5/10)
For the route from here to Charlottesville, see *The Crescent*.

CHARLOTTESVILLE (120/55)
For Charlottesville, see page 183. As you leave via residential and commercial suburbs, a colonnaded soccer ground features on your right.

The Cardinal heads west through farms, orchards and forests, and begins climbing the Blue Ridge Mountains. The idyllic Shenandoah valley to your right is the home of bear, bobcat, fox and 200 species of birds. Skyline Drive covers more than a hundred miles of mountain ridge, where there are spectacular colour changes in autumn.

You travel through a long tunnel — the first of many on this route — and descend towards Staunton.

Waynesboro (35/20)
After passing this small town next to the river you continue among cattle and sheep farms, with mountains on the right.

Interstate 81 (52/3)
As you pass beneath two highway bridges look for the neo-classical building on your right.

STAUNTON (55/70)
This was the birthplace of Woodrow Wilson. Look right when the train stops at 1 Middlebrook Ave (next to a large passenger building) to see colourful Chessie System rail cars used as station architecture. Staunton's Museum of American Frontier Culture shows farm life in the 18th and 19th Centuries.

You leave amid houses perched on hills, with Victorian buildings seen away to the left. As you climb, the tops of the trees on your left scarcely reach the tracks. Watch for horses, cattle, sheep and eagles.

Elliott Knob (15/55)
This dark purple mountain is to your right (4,458ft).

Nearing Clifton Forge the Cardinal passes through busy yards of the Chesapeake & Ohio, with freight trains on the left and a picturesque railroad building on the right.

CLIFTON FORGE (70/50)
Nearby Douthat State Park has 5,000 acres of lake fishing, swimming and mountain hiking.

Thruway buses link Amtrak's station with Roanoke, the home of Virginia's Museum of Transportation (703-342-5670). Located in a 1917 Norfolk & Western freight depot, this features steam, diesel and electric locos as well as passenger and freight cars. The collection also includes vintage automobiles, trucks and trolleys. Steam train rides take place during October. Open daily, admission.

Leave Clifton Forge with a hospital and factories to your right.

Covington (12/38)
Below the small town on your right is Highway 64.

You continue into the mountains via more tunnels and cross the Virginia/West Virginia border just before White Sulphur Springs. Note the golf course and immaculate grounds of Greenbrier Spa on the right.

WHITE SULPHUR SPRINGS (50/30)
The station is at 315 Main. People have come to bathe in Greenbrier's mineral waters since 1778, and the 2,600-acre resort has everything from golf to ice-skating.

Look for waterfalls among the wooded mountains on both sides as you continue.

ALDERSON (30/30)
Trains stop here only on request. The building high on the left is a women's prison.

Greenbrier River (18/12)
The river on the right has been reduced to a stream.

New River (28/2)
For 120 miles you follow the New River as it cuts a tree-lined gorge through the Appalachians (the oldest mountains in America). On the left are Bluestone Lake and dam.

HINTON (30/30)
Elegant houses can be seen on the hill. Hinton's railroad past is shown by the brick station to your right, next to a space where the yards used to be.

Bass Lake (5/25)
Ethnic cabins appear on the right.

PRINCE (30/15)
This mountain village has another large depot, from which access to nearby Beckley is by Yellow Cab.

THURMOND (15/45)
Trains curve right into Thurmond, stopping only on request.

New River Gorge Bridge (20/25)
The world's longest (1,700ft) steel arch bridge carries highway traffic across

the valley. At 876ft, it's America's second highest.

You carry on through dramatic, rugged scenery with waterfalls, mountains and a sheer drop to the boulder-strewn river.

Approaching Montgomery the Cardinal's tracks diverge from the river. The mayor's office is among houses to your left.

MONTGOMERY (45/30)
West Virginia's Institute of Technology building is on the left.

Kanawha River (8/22)
You join the river on your right, pursuing it most of the way to Charleston. Barges load coal from a mine on the far side.

Continue through semi-rural scenes, with wooded mountains on the far side and industrial plants below. As you near Charleston, its gold-domed Capitol is visible on the right.

CHARLESTON (30/55)
Situated on the Kanawha River and surrounded by mountains, Charleston is famous for white-water rafting. The most impressive buildings apart from the Capitol are the Cultural Centre and the Governor's Mansion. Amtrak's stone and brick station at 350 McCorkle opens 0730-2400 (Fri, Sun); 0730-1900 (Sat); 0730-1530 (Wed, Thurs); 1100-1900 (Mon); 1530-2400 (Tues).

Some of Charleston's chemical production facilities appear on both sides as you cross the river, with rail yards to the right.

Institute (10/45)
This is where Union Carbide produce methyl isocyanate. A leak at a similar plant in Bhopal, India, killed 3,000 people.

HUNTINGTON (55/20)
Downtown is seen to the right. Huntington ships great quantities of coal and the Heritage Village (located in former Baltimore & Ohio yards) shows this inland port's rail history. Amtrak's small brick station is on the left at 8th Ave and 10th.

Big Sandy River (15/5)
Most of the train comes into view as you cross the river and make a long right curve. A concrete highway bridge is on the right. Crossing takes you from West Virginia into Kentucky.

CATLETTSBURG (20/60)
Tri-State Station at Winchester Ave and 10th also serves Ashland, Kentucky, and Kenova, West Virginia.

The Cardinal's route to Cincinnati is along the southern shore of the Ohio River, forming the Kentucky/Ohio border on your right. The best viewing is on this side of the train. When travelling east you should have daylight to observe the houses, barges, locks, bridges, power stations and factories. Ohio's bluffs are on the far side.

Ashland (6/54)
The historic industrial city to your left is noted for oil and steel. A big Armco plant can be seen on the right.

Greenup Dam (45/15)
The lock on this side of the river was built in the 1950s.

SOUTH PORTSMOUTH (60/50)
The modest Main Street station also serves Portsmouth, Ohio. A white Baptist church features on the right as you leave and pass beneath a suspension bridge. A highway bridge crosses the river, busy with barges.

Falls City (25/25)
You make slow progress through this small town then lose touch with the Ohio for a while, travelling among fields and tree-covered hills. The river and industry return near Maysville, where a lawned cemetery can be seen on the left.

MAYSVILLE (50/85)
This atmospheric river city on the edge of blue grass country has tobacco auctions and New Orleans-style architecture. Amtrak's brick and tile station is at W Front.

Augusta (20/65)
White houses and an imposing grammar school appear to the left, but the best viewing remains on the right.

Zimmer Power Station (30/55)
The cooling tower and chimneys of this nuclear generating plant dominate the Ohio shore.

Interstate 275 (50/35)
You travel under the highway crossing the river to your right.
  Cross the Licking River as Cincinnati comes into view.

Covington (70/15)
You cross the Ohio River, scene of a September festival. Other bridges span the river on both sides and Riverfront Stadium is to the right.

CINCINNATI (85/50)
The 'Queen City of the West' was formerly known as Porkopolis after its pork-packing industry. The local speciality — Cincinnati chilli — contains not only beans and meat but also a choice of cheese, onions, spaghetti or hot dog.
  In 1988 many new parks, plazas and buildings were built to celebrate Cincinnati's bicentennial.

Transport: Amtrak uses the old Union Terminal at 1031 Vine. It's a superb example of art deco, with the highest unsupported masonry dome in the world. Open 0930-1700 and 2300-0630. Lockers, vending machines, luggage trolleys, shops, cafes, museum, taxi stand.

Queen City Metro bus schedules and information are available from the downtown office at 122 W 5th (621-4455).

Taxis: Yellow (241-2100).

Greyhound: 1005 Gilbert Ave (352-6000).

The airport is 14 miles southwest across the river in Covington, Kentucky. It can be reached by taxi, limousine and the Jetport Express (283-3702).

Visitors Bureau: 300 W 6th (621-2142). Open weekdays. Call 421-4636 for the information line.

Telephone Code: 513.

Accommodation: Contact Ohio Valley Bed & Breakfast, 6876 Taylor Mills Rd, Independence, KY (356-7865).

Youth Hostel: 2200 Maplewood Ave (651-2329). Singles $8.

Hotels include the Holiday Inn-Downtown at 800 W 8th (241-8660); Hilton, 15 W 6th (381-4000); Red Roof Inn, 5300 Kennedy Ave (531-6589) — singles $40, doubles $50.

Fountain Square: E 5th and Vine. The square has interesting architecture, a fountain, gardens, shops and free concerts. Information from the Downtown Council, 120 W 5th (479-3191).

Contemporary Arts Center: Near Fountain Square at 115 E 5th (721-0390). Featuring music events, films and multi-media shows. Closed Sun, free Mon.

Cincinnati Zoo: 3400 Vine (281-4700). The zoo breeds gorillas and white tigers. Open daily, admission.

Departing Cincinnati the Cardinal travels north through heavy manufacturing scenes.

HAMILTON (50/50)
Near enough to Cincinnati still to be industrial.

Ohio/Indiana State Line (30/20)
You cross into the Hoosier State in darkness.

CONNERSVILLE (50/80)
The seat of Fayette County on the Whitewater River was founded in 1813. It now makes everything from auto parts to dishwashers.

INDIANAPOLIS (80/65)
Indiana's capital since 1820 is at the geographical centre of the state. It's famous for industry and the Indianapolis 500 motor race, which takes place on the Sunday of Memorial Day. For tickets and information call 248-6700. This event is said to draw the world's largest single day crowd.

Transport: Amtrak operates from the Union Terminal. Information: 263-0550. Ticket office and waiting room open 0600-1630 (Mon, Wed), 0800-1630 (Tue, Thurs, Fri), 0600-1000 (Sat) and 0800-1200 (Sun).
  Metro buses run throughout the city (635-3344).
Taxis: Yellow (637-5421).
Car Rental: Rent-A-Bent, 2233 E Washington (632-4429).
Greyhound: 127 N Capitol Ave (635-4501).
  The airport is six miles southwest by taxi or bus No 9.

Visitors Bureau: 201 S Capitol (237-5200). Open Mon-Sat. Call 237-5210 for the latest events.

Telephone Code: 317.

Accommodation: Hotels include the Holiday Inn Union Station at 123 W Lousiana (631-2221); Canterbury, 123 S Illinois (634-3000); Atkinson, Illinois and Georgia (639-5611); Tower Inn, 1633 N Capitol Ave (925-9831); Inn Towner, 401 E Washington (637-6464) — singles $36, doubles $45; Ace, 7201 E Washington (356-7227) — singles $20, doubles $28.

Union Station: 39 Jackson Place (266-8740). This Romanesque building from the 1880s has been authentically restored to include hotels, shops and restaurants. Guests can sleep in real Pullman cars. Open daily.

Children's Museum: 3000 N Meridian (294-5437). Biggest of its kind in America, the museum has toy trains, carousel rides and a petting zoo. Open Tues-Sun, free. Also open Mon from May to September.

Motor Speedway: 4790 W 16th (241-2500). The 2½-mile track was built in 1909 and encompasses an entire golf course. Bus tours can be had except in May. The Indy Hall of Fame shows cars, films and memorabilia. Open daily, free if under 16.

City Market: 222 E Market (634-9266). One of the few original city markets left in the US, this 19th Century building has 15 ethnic sections. Closed Sun.

Indiana Transportation Museum: At Forest Park, Noblesville, 20 miles north (773-6000). The collection features cars from the Santa Fe, Burlington and Louisville & Nashville railroads, plus locomotives and Henry Flagler's Florida Coast Line business car. There are museum and main line train rides. Open Wed-Sun and some weekends from May to November, admission.

Depart Indianapolis with the massive Hoosier Dome on your right, then the downtown area.

Brownsburg (25/40)
Your train progresses through less urban landscapes as it heads for the corn and soya bean fields of central Indiana.

You pass several small towns and for a while accompany Interstate 74 on the right. Just before Crawfordsville the Cardinal transfers from Conrail tracks to those of the Seaboard System (formerly the Monon Railroad).

CRAWFORDSVILLE (65/30)
Home of Wabash College, one of many such establishments seen on this part of the journey. You cross Cherry Creek then pass beneath Interstate 74.

Linden (10/20)
Cross tracks of the Norfolk & Western line.

LAFAYETTE (30/90)
You accompany a pretty valley and get close-ups of this typical mid-American city when the train runs directly down main street. Lafayette is the home of Purdue University and was the birthplace of Sears, Roebuck founder Alvah Roebuck.

Wabash River (10/80)
Cross before travelling beneath Interstate 65 on its way to Chicago.

Tippecanoe Battlefield (15/75)
On the left is where General Harrison defeated the Shawnee Indians in 1811. You continue via the small communities of Brookston and Chalmers.

Reynolds (35/55)
Cross the former Toledo, Peoria & Western line.
You change from Eastern to Central Time, so watches go back an hour (forward when travelling east).

Rensselaer (50/40)
This is a stop for Amtrak's Hoosier State trains which run between Indianapolis and Chicago.
Cross the Kankakee River then proceed through Shelby, Lowell and Creston as you travel Indiana's plains.

Cedar Lake (80/10)
The lake is visible on the left just before you reach the town.

DYER (90/50)
You enter an industrial environment that will persist most of the way to Chicago. The Cardinal transfers back to Conrail here from the Seaboard track used since Crawfordsville.

Eggers Woods Forest (24/26)
A rare splash of green appears on the right.

Hammond-Whiting (25/25)
For Hammond-Whiting see pages 247 and 260.

Roby (35/15)
For Roby see page 247.

Comiskey Park (40/10)
For Comiskey Park, see page 248.

CHICAGO
For Chicago, see *The California Zephyr*.

19 **The Adirondack**

New York—Montreal

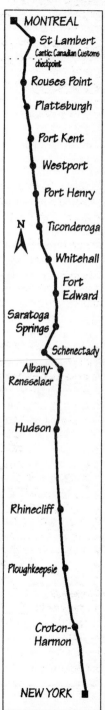

This train takes you from New York to the Gallic charm of Montreal via the Hudson valley, the Adirondacks, Lake Champlain, Vermont's Green Mountains and the St Lawrence River. A daytime journey that is particularly beautiful during autumn.

US citizens crossing into Canada do not need passports but should carry legal documents, such as a birth certificate or voter registration paper, showing proof of identity. A driving licence is not enough. Non-US citizens not resident in America require a valid passport or acceptable travel papers (in some cases a visa).

Frequency: Daily. The northbound service leaves New York mid-morning to reach Albany early afternoon, Plattsburgh early evening and Montreal mid-evening.

Travelling south, trains leave Montreal mid-morning, reaching Plattsburgh early afternoon, Albany late afternoon and New York mid-evening.

Reservations: Unreserved except for custom class.

Equipment: Turboliner coaches.

Food: Snacks, sandwiches, drinks.

Baggage: No check-in service.

NEW YORK

For New York, see *The Northeast Corridor*. You leave Pennsylvania Station on Empire Corridor tracks along a 10-mile route, opened in 1991 at a cost of $89 million. This used to be the New York Central's west side freight line, built by the Hudson River Railroad, and passenger services previously ran here until 1872.

You emerge from a tunnel with the Jacob Javits convention centre to your left (on the site of the old 30th Street rail yards) then continue via Riverside Tunnel. Harlem's Cotton Club is below on the right as you exit.

The Hudson River and Henry Hudson Parkway are to the left, then the North River Water Plant. This is the world's largest sewage treatment works. You pass beneath the Hudson Parkway, which continues on the right.

George Washington Bridge (8/32)

Spanning the river to your left, this was the longest suspension bridge in the world when completed in 1931. Just before the bridge look for the 'little red lighthouse' featured in a children's book and now preserved.

Fort Tryon Park appears on the right beyond the highway, then you pass Inwood Hill Park. Among the high-rises of New Jersey's palisades across the river is the cupola of St Michael Villa, run by the Sisters of St Joseph.

Spuyten Duyvil Bridge (15/25)

Cross the Harlem River Ship Canal on a 610ft-long swing bridge which was restored to accomodate this line. The Hudson Parkway bridge is to your right.

Metro-North trains join the line here on the right after travelling from Grand Central Station.

Yonkers (20/20)

Where Elisha Otis invented the safety elevator. Imposing houses in the hills prove the desirability of New York's fourth largest city. The Hudson River Museum occupies an 1876 mansion.

Hastings-on-Hudson (26/14)

Seen on the left, this was the home of Florenz Ziegfeld, whose wife Billie Burke appeared as the good witch in *The Wizard of Oz*.

Irvington (29/11)

The town is named after Washington Irving, creator of Rip Van Winkle. His *Sunnyside* home can be seen on the right just past the station.

Tappan Zee Bridge (30/10)

The bridge carries the NYS Thruway three miles across the Hudson ahead to your left. Also to your left is the Phillips Manor, one of many estates in this lush landscape which have belonged to the well-heeled and famous.

Ossining (35/5)

Look for the guard towers of Sing Sing Correctional Facility, where convicts were sent 'up the river' to do time. The main house is on your left, the annex to your right.

You continue through the most beautiful part of the Hudson valley.

CROTON-HARMON (40/35)
The 18th Century Van Cortlandt Manor here belonged to the state's first lieutenant-governor, and it was visited by Generals Washington and Lafayette. Across the river are the twin towers of Indian Point atomic power station and the town of Stony Point.

Peekskill (10/25)
Once a frontier trading post, this was an American army headquarters during the Revolution.

Across the river is Dunderberg Mountain, at the southern end of the Hudson Highlands. Bear Mountain Bridge carries the Appalachian Trail across the river.

Highland Falls (17/18)
The falls can be seen cascading 100ft down cliffs on the far side.

West Point (18/17)
This is the country's oldest (1802) military academy, where cadets have included Ulysses Grant, Robert E Lee, George Custer, Stonewall Jackson and Dwight Eisenhower. Washington positioned troops here during the Revolutionary war. The Gothic chapel has stained glass windows and the world's largest church organ.

After West Point the river narrows at the eastern end of Constitution Island. Nearby World's End is its deepest point (202ft).

You travel through Breakneck Tunnel and alongside Sugarloaf Mountain, with Storm King Mountain across the river.

Bannerman's Castle (24/11)
Located on Pollopel Island in mid-river, the 'castle' was built during the early 1900s as a private arsenal, complete with moat and drawbridge.

Beacon (26/9)
Signal fires on the mountain to your right warned a revolutionary army post of approaching British troops. A bridge links Beacon with Newburgh, across the river.

Danskammer (28/7)
On the other side of the Hudson are the Roseton and Danskammer Power Plants, as well as the red buildings of the Royal Kedem Winery.

As you approach Poughkeepsie, rock quarries can be seen on the near shore.

POUGHKEEPSIE (35/14)
Founded by the Dutch in 1683, this was once the state capital. It's now a manufacturing city famous for cough drops and ball bearings. Interesting buildings include Clinton House and Glebe House on the corner of Main and N White. The Vassar College Art Gallery has Rembrandt prints and Tiffany

glass. Amtrak's station at 41 Main opens 0600-2105.

As you leave, note the cantilever bridge across the river to your left. This was the largest rail bridge in the world when completed (1888) but it's been out of use since a fire in 1974.

Continue past Franklin Roosevelt's home on the right then the mansion of Frederick Vanderbilt. The town of Hyde Park is on the near shore, with Fallkill Creek waterfall to the right.

Look for an old lighthouse at the south end of Esopus Meadows in mid-stream. German-style houses on the other side of the water show why this valley has been called the Rhine of America. You travel through the village of Staatsburg.

RHINECLIFF (14/20)
The station at Hutton and Charles is Amtrak's nearest stop to Kingston and Rhinebeck. The latter has several historic buildings and America's oldest hotel, the Beekman Arms (1776). This was a favourite with Franklin Roosevelt.

Kingston Rhinecliff Bridge (4/16)
The bridge was completed in 1957. On both sides of the track is the marshland of Tivoli Bays — a haven for fish and birds.

Look across the river for the Hudson's oldest lighthouse, and the Saugerties Light at the mouth of the Esopus River. Watch also for the Carmelite Sisters Convent.

Germantown (10/10)
First settled by Germans, this is now the centre of a fruit-growing region. Cement plants and barges can be seen across the river.

Catskill (16/4)
Located on the west shore, Catskill was the home of Samuel Wilson (better known as Uncle Sam).

Houses take advantage of dramatic riverbank locations as you enter a land dominated on the left by the forests and gorges of the Catskills. This recreation area is bigger than Rhode Island and its mountains rise to 4,000ft.

Roeliff River (15/5)
Docks feature on the right as you cross the river and approach Hudson, with the 1872 Hudson-Athens Lighthouse to the left. This is one of 13 lights on the river still operated by the US Coast Guard.

HUDSON (20/15)
Dutch settlers called this Claverock Landing because of its luxuriant clover fields, but in 1785 it was renamed after the explorer Henry Hudson. Among the former whaling port's gardens and estates is the Persian-style Olana, a 37-room extravaganza designed by landscape artist Frederic Church. Hudson is also home to the American Museum of Fire Fighting. The railway station at 69 S Front is Amtrak's oldest on this line, opening 0615-2230 (Mon-Fri) and 0700-2230 (weekends).

Castleton-on-Hudson (11/4)
The Smith Memorial Bridge can be seen overhead, then the mile-long bridge connecting the New York State Thruway with the Massachusetts Turnpike.

As your train nears Albany the city skyline appears on the left, its most outstanding feature being the Empire State Plaza. Glenmont Power Station is across the river.

ALBANY-RENSSELAER (15/20)
The state capital's port facilities developed with the arrival in 1825 of the Erie Canal linking Lake Erie with the Atlantic. A railway came six years later when New York's first steam train, the *DeWitt Clinton*, ran on the Mohawk & Hudson.

Sleek buildings such as the 44-storey Corning Tower contrast with the Old State Capitol's Gothic lines. The Schuyler Mansion is an 18th Century Georgian house which was visited by George Washington and Benjamin Franklin.

Amtrak's East Street station is in adjacent Rensselaer and opens 0550-2230. Nearby is 17th Century Fort Crailo, America's oldest fortress, where tradition says a British surgeon wrote *Yankee Doodle Dandy*.

You cross the Hudson as you leave past freight yards. The romantic buildings on your left once belonged to the Delaware & Hudson Railroad and now house State University headquarters. Albany's city centre is on the left.

Approaching Schenectady through the environs of General Electric, look right for the gold dome of City Hall. The red-brick Van Curler Hotel to your left is now part of a community college.

SCHENECTADY (20/25)
The city that lights and hauls the world began in 1661 as a fur trading station, its name being Indian for 'through the open pines'. The Locomotive Works took care of haulage and Thomas Edison's Machine Works created the light. Edison's factory became General Electric — one of this region's main employers. Amtrak's station at 332 Erie Blvd opens 0615-2315.

Leave with the 17th Century stockade district to your right as the Adirondack changes from Empire Corridor tracks to those of the Delaware & Hudson. After shaking off Schenectady's factories and power lines, look for logging and timber-processing plants among the wooded hills.

SARATOGA SPRINGS (25/20)
Before the First World War the Vanderbilts and Whitneys came here to sample the waters, take curative baths and mix with their own kind. They enjoyed the best hotels, lavish casinos, gardens and America's oldest race track. Potato crisps were supposedly invented after Cornelius Vanderbilt asked for his chips to be sliced extra-thin.

No longer an exclusive resort of the rich, Saratoga Springs retains its bath-houses and you can still take the waters. The 1777 Battle of Saratoga, a turning point in the Revolutionary war, took place 12 miles to the east and the site is now a military park. Amtrak's modern station at West Ave opens 1030-1800.

As you leave through a cutting lined with evergreens look for a junkyard on the left, followed by a field with pheasants. You cross the Hudson River with a highway bridge to the left.

FORT EDWARD (20/22)
Wood-framed houses can be seen on both sides. The original fort was set up here during the French and Indian war. A sequence of locks later linked the Hudson to the Champlain Canal, creating a waterway through to the St Lawrence. East Street station also serves neighbouring Glen Falls. Lake George, a few miles north, has cruises and water skiing. In winter there are car races on the ice.

You continue through peaceful countryside into the heart of the Adirondacks, the home of eagles, bobcat and deer.

Champlain Canal (10/12)
The canal can be seen on your right behind a row of trees. This is the best side of the train from which to view the scenery ahead.

WHITEHALL (22/25)
A lock system connects the canal with Lake Champlain's South Bay. Rutland, Vermont, is five miles east. You leave via a short tunnel.

Lake Champlain (5/20)
Seen on the right as you cross South Bay and enter the six million acres Adirondack Forest Preserve.

A few minutes later you pass a channel on the right joining South Bay with Lake Champlain (named after its discoverer Samuel de Champlain). You follow this shoreline for most of the next 100 miles, with Vermont on the far side.

TICONDEROGA (25/25)
The name is Iroquois for 'between two waters'. Amtrak's station consists of a small white box and telephone on Route 9, some distance from both town and fort. The Adirondack stops here only on request. The fort, seen on bluffs ahead to your right, was set up by the French in 1755. This crucial position on the La Chute River between Lakes Champlain and George was constantly fought over during the Revolution, changing hands several times before being abandoned and destroyed. It has now been restored.

Leave the station with the fort on your right before you enter a brief tunnel and continue among the Adirondacks. Vermont's Green Mountains are visible across the lake.

PORT HENRY (25/20)
Trains stop only on request. A magnificently ornate town hall appears to the left of the station as you leave, and abandoned railroad beds on the right.

Continue among hay fields, forests and mountains, with Lake Champlain's rocky shore still on the right.

WESTPORT (20/42)
This is a small community famous for fishing. Lake Placid Sightseeing buses connect with the Adirondack.

Your train pursues a line between Lake Champlain on the right and mountains to the left as it crosses high above the pretty Bouquet River.

Willsboro (20/22)
Trout and salmon fishing are a big attraction on the lake and along the dammed Bouquet River.

For the next 25 miles the Adirondack travels a route hacked into cliffs high above the lake, giving terrific views as it negotiates hundreds of curves among birch trees, tunnels and houses.

PORT KENT (42/14)
Trains stop here during summer, when ferries cross to Burlington, Vermont.

Ausable River (3/11)
Watch for herons as you cross the tree-lined waterway which starts below the state's tallest mountain, Mount Marcy (5,344ft).

Valcour Island (7/7)
On the right. On October 11 in 1776, Benedict Arnold's ships were defeated here by the British as they competed for control of Lake Champlain.

At this point you leave Adirondack State Park — the biggest in the USA.

Plattsburgh Air Force Base (12/2)
The base is immediately to your left as you near Plattsburgh. Look for yachts moored on the right.

PLATTSBURGH (14/35)
On the left as you enter this military and industrial city you see a Delaware & Hudson Railroad turntable and the Thomas Macdonough Monument. The latter was erected following an 1814 victory over the British fleet from Canada. Amtrak's green-canopied station waiting room opens an hour before trains leave.

You part company with Lake Champlain and travel across corn fields and forests towards the Canadian border.

ROUSES POINT (35/45)
This is the Adirondack's last stop in the USA. An American Customs checkpoint for those travelling south is housed in the building on your right. Customs stickers can be seen adorning checked freight trains.

You cross the US/Canada border and pass through St Jean, where a cannon guards the military college on your right.

CANTIC (45/30)
This is the Canadian Customs checkpoint for those travelling north and is not a passenger stop. After inspection the train proceeds over the flat, nondescript landscape of southern Quebec.

ST LAMBERT (30/10)
You pause briefly at this station operated by VIA Rail. Timber yards and apartment blocks feature on the right.

Cross the St Lawrence on a long steel bridge to approach Montreal through industrial scenes and Canadian National freight yards. High-rises appear on the right.

MONTREAL
Built on an island where the St Lawrence, Ottawa and Richelieu Rivers meet, Montreal hosted the 1967 Worlds Fair and the 1976 Olympic Games. It's Canada's second biggest city and the second largest French-speaking community in the the world.

The French settled here in 1642 but explorers had arrived a hundred years earlier. The British took over in 1760, then (briefly) American revolutionaries. Montreal today is a major port and commercial centre.

Like the rest of Quebec Province, Montreal gets very cold in winter, with temperatures usually below zero well into March. Luckily, the city can deal with even the heaviest snowfall. July highs can reach the 80s.

Transport: The excellent Gare Centrale (Central Station) on Rene Levesque Blvd is used by Amtrak, commuter trains and Canada's VIA Rail (871-1331). Reservations and information: 800-426-8725. Ticket office open 0730-1930 (Amtrak) and 0630-2100 (VIA Rail). Waiting room 24 hours. Restaurants, shops, newspapers, Red Caps, taxi stand.

MUCTC runs an efficient bus and subway system throughout the city (288-6287). Le Metro operates 0530-0030.
Taxis: Champlain (273-2435) and Diamond (273-6331).
Car Rental: Hertz, Central Station (842-8537).
Greyhound: 505 Blvd de Maisonneuve. Terminal also used by Voyageur and Voyageur-Colonial (842-2281).

Dorval Airport is 12 miles from downtown by bus, limousine and taxi. For Aerocar buses call 397-9999. Limousines include Contact (631-5466) and Murray Hill (937-5311).

Mirabel Airport is 35 miles from downtown, with buses and taxis to Dorval and the city centre.

Tours: Gray Line (280-5327) and Murray Hill (937-5311). Walking tours can be had during summer from Les Montrealistes (744-3009) and boat trips May-October from Harbor Cruises (842-3871).

Visitors Bureau: 1001 rue du Square-Dorchester (871-2015) and 174 rue Notre-Dame. Open daily.

Telephone Code: 514.

Accommodation: Contact Montreal Bed & Breakfast, 4912 ave Victoria, Montreal, PQ H3W 2N1 (738-9410) or the Downtown B & B Network, 3458

ave Laval, Montreal, PQ H2X 3C8 (289-9749).
Auberge (IYHF) Hostel: 3541 Aylmer (843-3317). Members $10, non-members $12.
YMCA: 1450 rue Stanley (849-8393). For men and women. Singles $30, doubles $50.
YWCA: 1355 Rene Levesque Blvd (866-9941). Women only. Singles $42, doubles $50.

Hotels include La Citadelle at 410 Sherbrooke (844-8851); Delta, 450 Sherbrooke (286-1986); Maritime, 1155 rue Guy (932-1411); Chateau Versailles, 1659 Sherbrooke (933-3611); Lord Berri, 1199 Berri (845-9236); Chateau de l'Argoat, 524 Sherbrooke (842-2046); Manoir, 157 Sherbrooke (285-0894) — singles $30, doubles $35.

Mont-Royal: Walk, picnic or just enjoy the views in this natural park dominated by the mountain which gave the city its name (872-6211).

Museum of Fine Arts: 1379 Sherbrooke (285-1600). The museum has European and North American paintings, plus international exhibitions. Open daily, admission.

St Joseph's Oratory: 3800 rue Queen Mary (733-8211). The world's largest church, St Joseph's is dedicated to Canada's patron saint. Beneath its green copper dome is the original chapel founded by Brother Andre, said to be able to cure the sick. Open daily, donation.

Canadian Railway Museum: 120 St Pierre in Saint Constant, one mile south of Montreal (632-2410). The biggest rail museum in the country has 120 items of rolling stock, including Canada's oldest surviving steam and diesel-electric locos, plus the *Rocket* (first electric streetcar in Montreal). Train rides are available. Open May-October, admission.

20 The Montrealer

Washington—Montreal

Amtrak's alternative to the Adirondack travels between Washington and Montreal via New York City and New England. The Montrealer follows the usual Northeast Corridor route from Washington before heading north at New London.

Much of this journey takes place in darkness, so the Adirondack is a better bet for scenery. But the Montrealer has a lively atmosphere (thanks to Le Pub) and gives 'leaf peepers' easy access to Vermont.

US citizens crossing into Canada do not need passports but should carry legal documents, such as a birth certificate or voter registration papers, showing proof of identity. A driving licence is not enough. Non-US citizens not resident in America require a valid passport or acceptable travel papers (in some cases a visa).

Frequency: Daily. The northbound service leaves Washington mid-afternoon to arrive in Philadelphia early evening and New York mid-evening. You reach New London before midnight, Waterbury early next morning and Montreal mid-morning.

Travelling south, trains leave Montreal late afternoon, reaching Waterbury mid-evening and New York early next morning. You arrive in Philadelphia mid-morning and Washington just before midday.

Reservations: Reserved north of New York.

Equipment: Amfleet coaches.

Sleeping: Heritage roomettes, bedrooms.

Food: Complete meals, snacks, sandwiches and drinks.

Lounge Car: Le Pub has live entertainment and complimentary snacks.

Baggage: Check-in service at most stations.

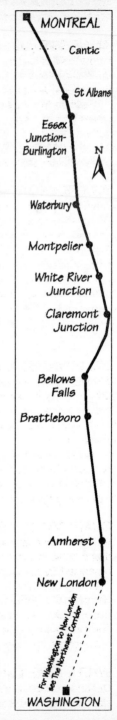

NEW LONDON (55/180)

For New London and the route from Washington, see *The Northeast Corridor*.

AMHERST (180/45)

Home town of the University of Massachusetts and Amherst College (founded in 1821 by Noah Webster). Emily Dickinson's house at 280 Main is owned by the college. Another former Amherst poet was Robert Frost.

This is the Montrealer's nearest stop to Northampton, eight miles southwest, where you can see the Cornet Joseph Parsons House (1658) and Wiggins Tavern (1786).

Your train continues through the night, crossing the Connecticut River and the Massachusetts/Vermont border.

BRATTLEBORO (45/30)

Named after its original proprietor, William Brattle, the town grew around Fort Dummer. This was established by the British in 1724 as Vermont's first permanent settlement. Fort Dummer State Park is two miles to the south. Brattleboro's Museum and Art Center is in the old train depot and Amtrak's present station is at Vernon Road. Tourist bureau: 180 Main (254-4565).

Bed & breakfast accommodation can easily be found in this area, but you should book early during the foliage season (peaking mid-October). Contact Vermont B & B, Box 139, Brown's Trace, Jericho, VT 05465 (800-442-1404); American B & B, Box 983, St Albans, VT 05478; B & B New England, Box 815, Brattleboro, VT 0531 (257-5252).

BELLOWS FALLS (30/22)

The first bridge across the Connecticut was built here in 1785, and one of the country's first canals went around the falls. A fish ladder lets Atlantic salmon spawn upstream.

The Green Mountain Railroad (802-463-3069) operates diesel trains from Union Station to Chester, as well as foliage specials to Ludlow. It uses the Green Mountain freight line and tracks of the former Rutland Railroad. Trains run June-September (to Chester) and September-October (to Ludlow).

Between here and White River Junction you briefly cross the border into New Hampshire before returning to Vermont.

CLAREMONT (22/30)

An old cotton and woollen mill city founded in 1762 on the Sugar River, which drops 300ft to provide water-power. Historic Mill District walking tours are organised by the Chamber of Commerce, Tremont Square (543-1296).

Among Claremont's other sights are a 19th Century opera house and New Hampshire's oldest Catholic church, St Mary's. Amtrak's station is at Plains Road. Nearby Andover's Historical Society Museum features an 1874 depot complete with station master's office.

You cross the Connecticut River again.

WHITE RIVER JUNCTION (30/80)

Quechee Gorge State Park has river fishing and walking trails. Amtrak's station at Railroad Row also serves Lebanon (another mill city) and Hanover (home of Dartmouth College). Open 2145-0830. Further east is the New Hampshire lakes region, including Lake Winnipesaukee.

You travel on amid the hills and forests of eastern Vermont towards the Green Mountains, with the Worcester Range on the right.

MONTPELIER (80/12)

The state capital is located on a pass through the mountains, along the wooded banks of the Winooski River. It was first settled in 1789 and named after a French city. The 18th Century Greek-style State House has a delicately beautiful gold dome. Tourist bureau: 134 State (828-3236).

Nearby Barre claims to be the granite centre of the world, and at Granitesville you can tour a quarry which has been worked for a hundred years.

Continue among green hills, pine trees, rivers and streams, with the orange and purple shaded Green Mountains seen ahead as the train climbs.

WATERBURY (12/27)

Amtrak's old red-brick station on the left opens 2015-0630 and also serves Stowe. Local ski resorts include Sugarbush and Jay Peak.

Bolton Valley (10/17)

Another ski area can be seen to your right as you leave the attractively scattered small town and continue via Green Mountains National Forest. On your right is the state's highest mountain, Mount Mansfield (4,393ft). A toll road from Stowe leads to the summit, from where you can see Lake Champlain.

ESSEX JUNCTION-BURLINGTON (27/30)

Amtrak's station at 29 Railroad Ave opens 0525-2300 and is the stop for Smugglers Notch ski resort. A white Vermont Federal Bank building features on your left and a graveyard to your right.

Vermont's largest city, Burlington, is seven miles west on the shore of Lake Champlain. This is a resort and industrial centre as well as home to the University of Vermont and Trinity College. In 1981 Burlington showed its maverick spirit by electing a socialist mayor. Except in winter, ferries operate across the lake to Port Kent in New York, served by Amtrak's Adirondack trains.

The Shelburne Railway Museum is seven miles south of Essex, and its buildings include the 1890 Shelburne depot (802-985-3346). Other highlights are a Central Vermont steam loco, an inspection car from the Woodstock Railroad and a Lake Champlain steamboat. Open May-October, admission.

The Montrealer leaves among wooden houses and travels 30 miles down part of the Champlain valley. Look for dairy farms, hayfields and logging operations. Warehouses and factories accumulate as you get closer to St Albans.

ST ALBANS (30/55)

The station at Washington and 3rd is the last stop in the USA, and this is the American customs checkpoint for those travelling south. St Albans is known for its railroad shops and granite mills.

During the Civil War a Confederate raiding party from Canada entered St Albans, killed several residents and robbed the banks of $200,000. They failed in their attempt to burn the town before fleeing back north of the border. Franklin County Museum at Taylor Park describes the raid and also has a collection of rail exhibits.

You leave via yards with freight trains gathered on your left before entering a land of fields, woods, marshes and lakes. Between here and Cantic you cross the US/Canada border.

CANTIC (55/40)
For Cantic, see page 231.

St Lambert (30/10)
For St Lambert, see page 232.

MONTREAL
For Montreal, see *The Adirondack*.

21 The Lake Shore Limited

Boston—Chicago

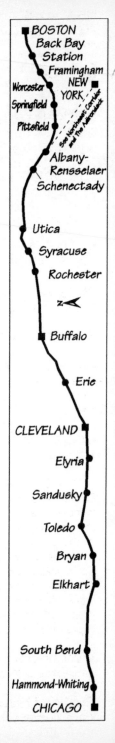

This train follows the 'water level route' once used by the Twentieth Century Limited. Boston trains travel through central Massachusetts before crossing the Berkshire Hills to Albany. New York trains reach Albany via the Hudson River valley. All trains then accompany the Mohawk River and Erie Canal along a famous Indian highway, and the Lake Shore Limited touches Lake Erie before hurrying across northern Indiana to Chicago.

Frequency: Daily. The westbound service leaves Boston late afternoon (or New York mid-evening) to reach Albany late evening. You arrive in Cleveland early the following morning and Chicago early afternoon.

Travelling east, trains leave Chicago early evening to reach Cleveland during the night. You arrive in Albany mid-morning and Boston mid-afternoon (or New York early afternoon).

Reservations: All reserved.

Equipment: Amfleet coaches.

Sleeping: Heritage roomettes, bedrooms. New York trains also have slumbercoaches.

Food: Tray meals, snacks, sandwiches, drinks. Complete meals on New York trains.

Baggage: Check-in service at most stations.

NEW YORK
For New York, see *The Northeast Corridor*. For the route to Albany, see *The Adirondack*.

BOSTON
For Boston, see *The Northeast Corridor*.

BACK BAY STATION (5/27)
Trains leave Boston's restored South Station and travel along the southern edge of the business district, pausing to pick up passengers at Back Bay. This area was formerly covered by the Charles River, so railway tracks had to be built on causeways.

You depart Back Bay and see the city skyline before you head into the wooded landscapes of central Massachusetts. Fenway Park, home of baseball's Red Sox, is on the left.

Newton (20/7)
Pass through the suburb of Riverside and cross the Charles River.

Wellesley (22/5)
Prestigious Wellesley College is on the right.

FRAMINGHAM (27/30)
The old train depot is now a fish restaurant. New England's Wildflower Association has 400 species of native plants at Framingham's Garden in the Woods.

You continue via the small towns of Ashland, Cordaville, Southville and Westboro.

Lake Quinsigamund (25/5)
The watersports area on the right is circled by houses.

WORCESTER (30/80)
Former residents have included Robert Benchley and Isaiah Thomas, who founded the Antiquarian Society and published one of America's first newspapers, the *Massachusetts Spy*. Blue and white Holy Cross College is on the hillside to your left.

Worcester's industrial development began in 1828 when the Blackstone Canal linked it to Providence. A railroad replaced the canal 20 years later. Worcester claims to have made the first calliope, carpet loom and liquid-fuel rocket. Amtrak's depot at 45 Shrewsbury opens 0700-2230. Old Sturbridge Village, 20 miles southwest, reconstructs early New England life. Note the impressive old station building decaying on the right as you leave.

West Warren (45/35)
A miniature golf course is on the left.

Quaboag River (50/30)
You accompany this river on your right for several miles.

Chicopee River (60/20)
Look for a waterfall to the right.

SPRINGFIELD (80/75)
Home of the Springfield rifle and Garand semi-automatic, the city started in
the 17th Century as a trading post on the banks of the Quinnitukqut River (the
longest river in New England). When a railroad opened in 1839 between here
and Worcester, Springfield became industrialised.

The Armory features one of the world's largest military collections, and the
Basketball Hall of Fame honours the game's inventor, James Naismith.
Visitors bureau: 34 Boland Way (787-1548). Amtrak's station at 66 Lyman
opens 0530-0030, with buses connecting to Montpelier and Burlington,
Vermont.

Connecticut River (5/70)
Crossed with the stone-arched Memorial Bridge to your left, alongside the
Eastern States Exposition fairgrounds.

Westfield River (7/68)
You follow the river through Oronoco, Russell, Huntington, Chester and
Middlefield. Watch for paper mills and sawmills.

The Lake Shore Limited continues via some of the state's finest scenery,
including the Berkshire Mountains and Chester Blanford State Forest, where
there are deer, bobcat and wild turkey. Nearing Pittsfield you cross the
Appalachian Trail.

PITTSFIELD (75/65)
The capital of Berkshire County, surrounded by mountains, forest and lakes,
is where Herman Melville wrote *Moby Dick* in 1851. Melville's home is now a
museum and the Public Library has a room dedicated to him. Visitors bureau:
Berkshire Common Pl (443-9186).

Hancock Shaker Village on the slopes of nearby Lebanon Mountain is a
museum dedicated to the country's oldest religious sect. The Berkshire
Scenic Railway at Lenox offers weekend rides along part of the Housatonic
valley. Its museum occupies the restored Lenox station (413-637-2210).

Richmond Pond (10/55)
The lake is on the left. During summer the Boston Symphony Orchestra plays
concerts at Tanglewood, the former home of Nathaniel West.

Massachusetts/New York State Line (20/45)
You enter the Empire State via the Taconic Mountains and State Line Tunnel,
with views ahead of the Catskills and the Hudson River valley.

Chatham (55/10)
The wooden station is on your right. A 'beefalo' farm to your left crosses
cows with buffalo.

The train continues through the upstate New York communities of Niverville,
Post Road Crossing, Van Hoesen, Brookview and East Greenbush.

ALBANY-RENSSELAER (65/24)
For Albany-Rensselaer, see page 229.

SCHENECTADY (24/75)
For Schenectady, see page 229.
 Cross the Mohawk on a steel bridge as you leave, accompanying this river on the left as far as Utica. The Mohawk Trail was the main colonial passage from the east to the Great Lakes. Mohawks fought the Mohicans at Kinquariones, on a rocky cliff overhanging the tracks.

Erie Canal (10/65)
You pursue the canal, seen to your left, much of the way between here and Rochester. Look for the first in a series of locks.

Amsterdam (25/50)
This is the home of Coleco, maker of cabbage patch dolls. Among the town's buildings are several associated with Sir William Johnson and his family, who allied themselves to Iroquois Indians during the French and Indian war. Sir William built the mansion to your left for his daughter. Fort Johnson on your right dates from 1749. Eight missionaries who were killed trying to convert Indians to Christianity are commemorated by a shrine.
 The Lake Shore Limited proceeds through a valley of woods, hills and dairy farms.

Nelliston (35/40)
The stone depot with green shutters on the left is now an Elks Lodge. A marker on the other side of the river indicates the site of the Revolutionary army base at Fort Plain.

Palatine Bridge (40/35)
The home of Lifesavers candies and Beech-Nut Products. Next to Caroga Creek on the right is the Old Palatine Church, completed in 1770.

Fonda (45/30)
Montgomery County court-house is opposite the station, with the Fonda fairgrounds on the right.

St Johnsville (48/27)
Famous for its leather tanning and dye factories, St Johnsville is the halfway point along the Mohawk valley.

Herkimer (60/15)
The town featured in Edmond's *Drums Along the Mohawk*.

Erie Canal (68/7)
You cross above a sequence of locks. Built between 1817 and 1825, the canal spans New York state from Albany on the Hudson to Buffalo on Lake Erie. It was enlarged and partly relocated in the 20th Century to incorporate Lake Oneida.

The approach to Utica is among factories and junk yards.

UTICA (75/45)
Situated on the Mohawk River and the New York State Barge Canal, Utica was called Old Fort Schuyler until renamed in 1798 after a city in north Africa. Rapid growth came with the Erie Canal, and General Electric has another big factory here. Union Station to your left opened in 1914. Extensive rail yards feature on the right.

Look right as you near Rome to see a sculpture above the Paul Revere brass factory.

Rome (15/30)
The Stars and Stripes first flew at the Battle of Oriskany in 1717, inspiring Francis Bellamy to compose the Pledge of Allegiance. Fort Stanwix battle site is now part of downtown. The Erie Canal began here on July 4 1817, and you catch another glimpse of it on the right as your train leaves for the northern highlands.

SYRACUSE (45/80)
Salt City, where for many years local mines produced most of the nation's salt. Extraction methods are shown at the Salt Museum. The Erie Canal Museum is in an old lock building at 318 Erie Blvd. Amtrak's station at Manlius Center Rd in East Syracuse is among rail yards more than 10 miles from downtown. Open 24 hours. You see long Conrail trains being set up on the right as you leave among factories, warehouses and refineries.

LeMoyne College (4/76)
Seen high on the left, the college was named after the French missionary Simon LeMoyne.

MacArthur Stadium (7/73)
The Chiefs' baseball ground is on the left.

Onondaga Lake (8/72)
On the right is the place where Father LeMoyne first discovered salt reserves.

New York State Fairgrounds (13/67)
The annual fair takes place from late August to early September. The race track is on the right.

Erie Canal (32/48)
You rediscover the canal to your right after Weedsport, then cross into more rural landscapes. For the next 40 minutes the Lake Shore Limited travels among orchards, farmhouses and fields of dark earth.

Clyde (38/42)
You can see this colonial town's cemetery on the left.

East Palmyra (58/22)

A picturesque church stands on the hill to your left.

Nearing Rochester, the dairy farms and greenery dwindle as factories and freight yards take over.

Sibley Clock Tower (78/2)

The clock was named after Hiram Sibley, founder of Western Union.

ROCHESTER (80/55)

Where Kodak (established 1880) is the biggest employer. The turreted Eastman Kodak building features to your right and the Genessee Brewery on your left. Rochester was 'the flour capital of the world' in the early 18th Century, when the town grew along the upper falls of the Genessee. It later became the Underground Railroad's northern terminal.

The New York Museum of Transportation on East River Rd (716-533-1113) has a Philadelphia snow-sweeper and a Genessee & Wyoming caboose, along with buses, vintage cars and trolleys.

The Rochester & Genessee Valley Museum is in a restored Erie Railroad station to the south of the city (716-533-1431). There are locos and cars from the New York Central, Baltimore & Ohio and Erie-Lackawanna Railroads.

Cross the Genessee River as you leave, with a futuristic Times-Square building dominating downtown to the left.

Erie Canal (5/50)

Crossed for the last time. A massive limestone mine can be seen on the right.

Bergen (20/35)

You pass the town on your right as rolling landscapes give way to flatter country towards the Great Lakes.

Lancaster (47/8)

Fences surround Alden Penitentiary on the left. Lancaster's airpark is to the right.

BUFFALO (55/90)

Situated next to Lake Erie and separated from Canada by the Niagara River. After the Civil War many railroads converged here, creating important markets and railway car industries. Buffalo remains a rail centre as well as an industrial city.

The Lake Shore Limited stops at Depew Station on Dick Road (open 24 hours). Note the art deco clock tower of the old depot, which used to handle 30,000 passengers a day. The Allentown area features Victorian buildings, shops and restaurants. Information from the Chamber of Commerce, 107 Delaware Ave (852-7100).

Between here and Toledo the train justifies its name by skirting the southern shoreline of Lake Erie — sometimes visible on the right. It's a flat land of fields and hedges.

New York/Pennsylvania State Line (60/30)

You briefly enter the Keystone State, founded by William Penn in 1682.

ERIE (90/90)

Gem City is Pennsylvania's third largest community and its only port on the lake. It was named after the Eriez Indians. During the war of 1812 Admiral Perry scored a local victory over the British, and the hull of his flagship *Niagara* can be seen moored at the end of State Street. Dickson's Tavern, his base before the battle, was another station on the Underground Railroad. Escaped slaves hid in the tavern's walls before continuing their journey. Amtrak is at 14th and Peach.

The Lake Shore Railway Museum is 15 miles away at North East (814-825-2724). The collection is housed in a New York Central passenger station built in 1899 for the Lake Shore & Michigan Southern Railway. On show are locomotives, sleepers, refrigerated freight cars and a wooden business car. Open Wed-Sun from July to August, free.

Pennsylvania/Ohio State Line (30/60)

The name Ohio comes from an Iroquois word for 'beautiful'.

You continue via the fishing village of Conneaut, then the towns of Ashtaboula and Mentor (birthplace of President Garfield).

CLEVELAND (90/28)

Founded in the 18th Century by General Moses Cleaveland and misspelt by his men on the official document. On the shores of Lake Erie, this is Ohio's largest city and a big industrial centre, though it has lately acquired a less sooty image.

Superman was created here by Jerry Siegal and Joe Schuster. Cultural institutions include a symphony orchestra and the Rock 'N Roll Hall of Fame.

Transport: Amtrak's Lakefront Station is at 200 Cleveland Memorial Shoreway, opposite the Municipal Stadium. Information: 696-5115. Ticket office and waiting room open 0400-1300, 1400-1730, and 0001-0300 (Mon-Sat), and 0400-0845 and 0001-0300 (Sun). Lockers, vending machines, luggage trolleys, taxi stand.

RTA buses run downtown and to outlying areas (621-9500).

Taxis: Yellow (623-1500) and Americab (881-1111).

Car Rental: Budget (433-1949).

Greyhound: 1465 Chester Ave (781-1400).

Hopkins Airport is 10 miles southwest by taxi, RTA train and bus No 66X.

Tours: North Coast (579-6160). Trolley Tours operate May-December (771-4484). Holiday Boat Charters cruise Lake Erie as well as the Cuyahoga and Rocky Rivers (771-2628).

Visitors Bureau: 3100 Tower City Center (621-7981). Free maps. Call 621-8860 for events.

Telephone Code: 216.

Accommodation: For rooms in local homes call Cleveland Private Lodgings (321-3213) in advance of your visit.
Stanford House (AYH) Hostel: 6093 Stanford Rd, Peninsula (467-8711). A historic house 20 miles south of Cleveland (take No 77F bus). Beds $8.
  Hotels include the Stouffer Tower City Plaza at 24 Public Square (696-5600); Bond Court, 777 St Clair Ave (771-7600); Clinic Center, 2065 E 96th (791-1900); Holiday Inn Lakeside, 1111 Lakeside Ave (241-5100).

Museum of Art: 11150 East Blvd (421-7340). The collection includes Picassos, French impressionists and Rodin's *Thinker.* Closed Mon, free.

Tower City Center: An ultra-modern extravaganza of shops, offices and mall located in the Terminal Tower (771-0033).

Museum of Medicine: 1100 Euclid Ave (368-3648). A hypochondriac's delight, where thousands of objects display all branches of medicine. Open daily, free.

Museum of Natural History: Wade Oval (231-4600). Featuring many rare prehistoric exhibits. Open daily, free Tues and Thurs.

Leave Cleveland with the Municipal Stadium on the right and a Goodyear plant on the left before you cross the Cuyahoga River.

Cleveland Hopkins Field (10/18)
The international airport is to your right.

ELYRIA (28/32)
A manufacturing city on the Black River, Elyria was founded in the 19th Century by Herman Ely. Oberlin College was the first in the country to enrol blacks and women on equal terms with white males.

Amherst (10/22)
New York Central's depot has been faithfully maintained, with old rail cars displayed on the left of the tracks. A large Pillsbury factory is to the right.

Vermilion River (15/17)
A river famous for its fishing fleet. Look for Lake Erie to your right after you cross, then travel on through Vermilion and Huron (birthplace of Thomas Edison).

Hudson (24/8)
Cross the Huron River.

SANDUSKY (32/45)
Once another stop on the Underground Railroad, this is now busy port shipping coal and local wine. Amtrak's modest station is on the left at N Depot and Hayes Ave. Cedar Point amusement park is nearby and you can

reach Lake Erie Islands by car ferry.

The Mad River & NKP Railroad Museum at 253 Southwest in Bellevue includes a Chicago, Burlington & Quincy dome car (the first in the country) as well as historic buildings (419-483-2222). Open Wed-Sun from May to September.

Leave Sandusky through its manufacturing district and cross Sandusky Bay before veering east towards Toledo. On your right is the top of one of Cedar Point's six roller coasters.

Lake Erie (12/33)
Visible for the last time away to the right.

Davis-Bessie Nuclear Plant (20/25)
Seen beneath a plume of steam in the right distance before you continue among vineyards, apple orchards and peach trees.

Clay Center (27/18)
The small town is surrounded by a limestone quarry.

Maumee River (40/5)
The scene becomes more industrial as you cross the river with Toledo's outline on the right and the train curves left among some of the world's biggest grain elevators. Conrail trains gather on both sides.

TOLEDO (45/50)
The birthplace of Theresa Brewer and Joe E Brown. Ohio and Michigan argued over this valuable harbour until President Jackson settled the issue. The Toledo Museum of Art's collection of crystal reflects the city's claim to be 'the glass capital of the world'. Amtrak's Central Union terminal at 415 Emerald Ave opens 0830-1230 and 2245-0045, with trains connecting to Detroit and Ann Arbor.

The Lake Shore Limited leaves on a 68½-mile straight of track.

Holland (12/38)
Neat farms replace industry.

BRYAN (50/70)
A distribution point for agricultural produce, Bryan is also famous for its artesian wells. On your right is WBNO — the world's first solar-powered radio station.

You cross the St Joseph River and the Ohio/Indiana State Line.

Kendalville (25/45)
The highest point on this route, being 995ft above sea level and 400ft above the Great Lakes.

Elkhart River (50/20)
After crossing you follow the river's leisurely course through rolling country.

ELKHART (70/22)

Headquarters of Miles Laboratories, makers of Alka-Seltzer. The Michigan Southern Railroad had repair shops here and Elkhart was a division point on the New York Central (later the Penn Central). At one time this was the world's chief producer of brass musical instruments and mobile homes. Amtrak at 131 Tyler Ave opens 0930-1330 and 2015-2145. Shiny New York Central trains wait alongside a steam locomotive across the tracks to your left.

Amish and Mennonite Christian communities nearby include Goshen, five miles to the southeast.

You leave Elkhart between factories and warehouses and approach South Bend, with the old Studebaker car factory on your left. This plant closed in 1963 but classic Studebakers are featured at the Discovery Hall Museum.

SOUTH BEND (22/60)

Located on a bend of the St Joseph River, where settlers negotiated a treaty with Indians under the Council Oak that still stands in Highland Cemetery. Look for the gold dome of Notre Dame University above trees to your right.

As you pass from Eastern to Central Time, watches go back an hour (forward when travelling east).

La Porte (20/40)

The town was established in 1832 as a trading centre for farmers.

Gary (45/15)

This has long been one of the country's great steel producers. Plants on both sides reveal a mass of complicated pipelines, pylons and storage tanks. Gary was the birthplace of Michael Jackson, Karl Malden and the astronaut Frank Borman.

The train continues via Pine Junction and Indiana Harbor.

Indiana Harbor Canal (50/10)

Crossed on a drawbridge. The canal joins the Calumet River to Lake Michigan, a short distance to the right. On the left are a Standard Oil refinery and a Lever Brothers factory.

HAMMOND-WHITING (60/25)

Hammond-Whiting's modern yellow brick station on the right is Amtrak's usual stop for trains approaching Chicago from the east. Oil storage tanks can be seen on both sides before you leave via freight yards and cross the Calumet River on a steel lift bridge. Look for grain elevators and ships being loaded.

Cross the now-closed Rock Island Line, then the south branch of the Chicago River. Chicago's Skyway is to the left. The city comes into view on the right, featuring the 110-storey Sears Tower, and after crossing the Dan Ryan Expressway you see the El track overhead.

Roby (10/15)

Chicago's first black mayor opened the New Regal Theatre on your right as a centre for Afro-American culture. Mayor Washington was buried in the cemetery to your right. Interstate 90 (the Indiana Toll Road) is on the left.

Comiskey Park (15/10)

On the right is a car park where the legendary White Sox baseball stadium used to be. A new Comiskey Park rises alongside.

Extensive Conrail loading facilities are seen to the left before Amtrak's 21st Street yards appear on the right. Trains are set up here to travel to every corner of the land.

The train concludes its journey by easing into Chicago's Union Station through a tunnel under the Post Office building.

CHICAGO

For Chicago, see *The California Zephyr*.

22 The Capitol Limited

Washington—Chicago

As well as West Virginia, Harpers Ferry, and the Potomac and Shenandoah valleys, this train takes you to the Allegheny Mountains, a revitalised Pittsburgh and the corn fields of Ohio and Indiana. Some views on this 780-mile journey can only to be experienced by train.

Frequency: Daily. The westbound Capitol Limited leaves Washington late afternoon, arriving in Cumberland early evening and Pittsburgh by late evening. You reach Toledo early next morning and Chicago mid-morning.

Travelling east, trains leave Chicago late afternoon to reach Toledo mid-evening and Pittsburgh during the night. You arrive in Cumberland early morning and Washington mid-morning.

One through coach travels between Chicago and Miami, connecting with the Silver Star in Washington. The complete journey takes almost two days, arriving in Miami around midday. A return through coach leaves Florida mid-afternoon.

Reservations: All reserved.

Equipment: Heritage coaches. Dome and lounge car.

Sleeping: Heritage bedrooms, roomettes.

Food: Complete meals, snacks, sandwiches, drinks.

Baggage: Check-in service at most stations.

WASHINGTON
For Washington, DC, see *The Northeast Corridor*. The Capitol Limited slowly leaves with the tiled dome of the Shrine of the Immaculate Conception (America's largest church) visible on the left. The train follows Baltimore & Ohio tracks as far as Pittsburgh.

ROCKVILLE (20/40)
This 18th Century Maryland town is now a Washington suburb. Commuter trains wait on the left next to a spartan station building.

As you shake off suburbia to join the Potomac valley, look for a steam locomotive in sidings to the left.

Monocacy River (18/22)
Cross the river which flows into the Potomac away on your left, with tall chimneys in the distance. The train eases over to accompany the Potomac along the Maryland/Virginia border. Between the tracks and the river are traces of a neglected Chesapeake & Ohio Canal, where trees now grow from the hollows. This engineering feat dates from the middle of the last century, when it carried traffic between Cumberland and Georgetown.

You travel through two short tunnels and lose touch with the river for 15 minutes. Watch for Seaboard trains on the left before you cross the canal, then the rocky Potomac River before Harpers Ferry. Crossing takes you into West Virginia's eastern panhandle, with the Shenandoah River to your left.

HARPERS FERRY (40/20)
Where Virginia, West Virginia and Maryland meet. After the railroad built a wooden bridge in 1836 the ferry which gave the town its name went out of business. John Brown, together with 18 supporters, on the night of October 16 1859 seized the government arsenal at Harpers Ferry, which was one of the important events leading up to the Civil War. The national park has museums, monuments and buildings from before the Civil War. Visitors centre: Shenandoah Street (535-6371). The Harpers Ferry hostel (301-834-7652) is in Knoxville, Maryland, on the other side of the canal. Bus transport is available to and from Amtrak's station on Potomac Street.

To your right as you leave are the remains of an early hydro-electric plant, which was fed by water from a dam. Wind-powered irrigation pumps can be seen on the left. Near Martinsburg is a large cemetery on the hill to your right.

MARTINSBURG (20/85)
After being a railway town for 150 years, Martinsburg still has its original brick station. The country's biggest ever rail strike began here in 1877 among Baltimore & Ohio personnel. As you leave, note the two 1860s roundhouses beside neglected railroad buildings on the right. One roundhouse has been partly demolished.

Continue past villages, farms, woods and orchards, with mountains and a tree-lined ravine on the right.

Potomac River (15/70)
Seen to your right. Much of this largely unpopulated part of the route can only

be enjoyed from a raft on the Potomac or by travelling Amtrak. You follow the river for over an hour, with fine views all the way (apart from a few tunnels).

Watch for deer among the wooded cliffs to your left. Sometimes the rock face rises sheer from the river, which you cross three times before finally leaving West Virginia on the approach to Cumberland. Coal wagons and trailer trains feature on the left.

CUMBERLAND (85/130)
Also known as Washington Town. In 1755 General Braddock led a force 220 miles from the fort here towards Fort Duquesne. A thousand men died in the battle which started the French and Indian war. George Washington also made expeditions from here but his log cabin is all that remains of the fort.

Cumberland was the eastern terminus of the Cumberland (National) Road and western terminus of the Chesapeake & Ohio Canal. The Baltimore & Ohio Railroad arrived in 1842. Look for a miniature fir plantation on the left as you leave.

The Narrows (5/125)
This passage through the Alleghenys provided access for early traders and the military. Later the railway came, then the first federal highway (US 40).

Maryland/Pennsylvania State Line (10/120)
You enter the most central of the original 13 colonies. The Capitol Limited climbs laboriously into the mountains, travelling through Falls Cut Tunnel and the small community of Glencoe.

Wills Creek (40/90)
The stream on the left is popular with anglers.

Sandpatch Tunnel (47/83)
Almost a mile long, this tunnel is the longest on the Capitol's route.

Sandpatch (49/81)
The pinnacle of the Allegheny Mountains and the Capitol's highest point (2,258ft). You travel under tracks of the Western Maryland Railroad, often busy with freight traffic.

Meyersdale (52/78)
Famous for its maple sugar festival.

Blue Lick (57/73)
The train passes beneath a disused Western Maryland bridge.

Casselman River (60/70)
The river is immediately to the left, with old quarry workings on the right.

Rockwood (65/65)
A bridge across the river takes a section of the Baltimore & Ohio to Johnstown.

Pinkerton Tunnel (75/55)
After this short tunnel you emerge briefly before entering Shoefly Tunnel, then the longer Brook Tunnel.

Confluence (83/47)
The Casselman River is joined on the left by the Youghiogheny, which you follow to McKeesport before crossing Laurel Creek.

Sugar Loaf Mountain (90/40)
You can see this distinctive shape off to the right as you continue beside the river. Look for canoeists, fishermen, deer and (possibly) beaver.

Ohiopyle (95/35)
Home of Ohiopyle Falls, which are out of sight to your left. Adjacent Laurel Highlands park includes the state's highest mountain, Mount Davis (3,213ft), and this region is especially beautiful in autumn. The architect Frank Lloyd Wright built Fallingwater at nearby Bear Run.

Indian Creek (120/10)
The train crosses by means of an old stone bridge.

CONNELLSVILLE (130/90)
Connellsville is surrounded by coal fields which produce the raw material for Connellsville Coke. It was an important railroad town where service trains paused during the Second World War and hundreds of female volunteers served food to the troops. Amtrak's station is at Front and Water.

Leaving town you pass beneath a railway bridge that crosses the river to your left.

Interstate 70 (30/60)
After travelling under the highway you begin to meet industrial scenes near Pittsburgh. Approaching McKeesport the train crosses then recrosses the Youghiogheny River amid an increasingly urban landscape.

McKeesport (60/30)
Where the Youghiogheny joins the Monongahela and heavy industry predominates. The Capitol Limited passes a number of steel processing mills.

Pittsburgh's striking outline gradually comes in view ahead to the left.

University of Pittsburgh (74/16)
The Cathedral of Learning's 42-storey Gothic tower is on the left, with Carnegie Mellon University to the right. You proceed through Schenley Tunnel and officially enter the city.

PITTSBURGH (90/100)
The birthplace of Gene Kelly and Perry Como. Renaissance City is the country's busiest inland port, where the Allegheny and Monongahela Rivers join to become the Ohio. In the 1750s this strategic position led to the establishment of a fort named after the British Prime Minister William Pitt. The

Iron City eventually became so industrial it was labelled 'hell with the lid off'. In an 1877 riot 60 people died after soldiers fired on striking railroad workers.

Lately the steel mills have been tamed and slag heaps eliminated as Pittsburgh acquired high-tech industry, smart skyscrapers and clean air. Now the smoke has cleared, even outsiders are impressed.

Transport: Amtrak's station is at Liberty and Grant. Information: 324-3033. Ticket office open 0830-1300, 1400-1715, 2230-0300 and 0400-0715. Waiting room 24 hours. Lockers, vending machines.

Port Authority buses run throughout the city. For details of routes, a free map and off-peak deals contact PAT's Wood Street headquarters (231-5707). *Taxis:* Diamond (824-0984) and Yellow (665-8100).
Car Rental: Budget, 700 5th Ave (261-3320).
Greyhound: 11th and Liberty, near Amtrak's station (391-2300).

The airport is 15 miles west by taxi and Airline Transport (471-2250).

Tours: Port Authority (231-5707) and Lenzner (761-7000). River cruises are available (April-October) with the Gateway Clipper Fleet at Station Square Dock (355-7979). Cable railway inclines take you to an observation deck and restaurants on Mount Washington, from where you can see the Golden Triangle formed by the junction of three rivers. The Monongahela Incline is near Smithfield Bridge, and the Duquesne Inclined Plane at Fort Pitt Bridge.

Visitors Bureau: 4 Gateway Center (281-7711). Open daily.

Telephone Code: 412.

Accommodation: Point Park (AYH) Hostel opens May-August at 201 Wood (392-3824). Members only, $8.

Hotels include the Westin William Penn at 530 William Penn Way (281-7100); Hyatt Pittsburgh, 112 Washington Pl (471-1234); Hilton, Gateway Center (391-0927); Sheraton, 7 Station Square (261-2000); Parkway Center-Best Western, 875 Greentree Rd; Red Roof Inn, 6404 Stubenville Pike (787-7870) — singles $34, doubles $40.

University of Pittsburgh: At Bigelow Blvd, Fifth Ave and Forbes Ave (624-6000). The Cathedral of Learning tower has 18 nationality rooms, tours and a 36th floor observation area.

Point State Park: Off Interstate 279 near Fort Pitt Bridge. Featuring the city's oldest building, Fort Pitt Blockhouse, which was built in 1764 by Colonel Henry Bouquet. Fort Pitt Museum (281-9285) shows the Point's history up to 1800. Fife and drum parades take place on summer Sundays. Open Wed-Sun, admission.

Old Post Office Museum: 1 Landmarks Square, Allegheny Center. Classic clothes and toys are housed in a domed building which was once the North Side Post Office. Open daily.

Industrial Transportation Museum: In Station Square, across the Smithfield Bridge. The collection includes steam engines, railroad cars and trolleys. Nearby P & L E Railroad buildings house a restaurant.

You depart Pittsburgh and continue in darkness.

ALLIANCE (100/70)
The home of Mount Union College, this industrial city on the Mahoning River makes steel and electrical machinery. The station on the corner of Main and Webb is Amtrak's nearest stop to Canton, seven miles southwest.
  The Capitol travels on through northeastern Ohio.

CLEVELAND (70/110)
For Cleveland and the rest of the route to Chicago, see *The Lake Shore Limited*. The Capitol Limited stops at Elyria, Toledo, Waterloo, Elkhart, South Bend and Hammond-Whiting.

23 The Broadway Limited

New York—Chicago

After travelling from New York through some of the country's most densely populated areas, the Broadway Limited turns due west at Philadelphia into Pennsylvania Dutch country, home of the Amish people. You follow the Juanita River to the Allegheny Mountains, climbing spectacular Horseshoe Curve. From Pittsburgh you accompany the Ohio before crossing flat Indiana farmlands to Chicago.

The first Broadway Limited ran on November 24 1912. It was re-equipped as a streamliner in 1938.

Frequency: Daily. The westbound service leaves New York mid-afternoon to reach Philadelphia late afternoon, Harrisburg early evening and Pittsburgh towards midnight. You arrive in Chicago early morning.

Travelling east, trains leave Chicago mid-evening to reach Pittsburgh early next morning and Harrisburg early afternoon. You arrive in Philadelphia mid-afternoon and New York late afternoon.

Reservations: All reserved.

Equipment: Heritage coaches.

Sleeping: Heritage bedrooms, roomettes, slumbercoach.

Food: Complete meals, snacks, sandwiches, drinks.

Baggage: Check-in service at most stations.

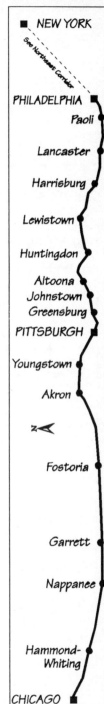

NEW YORK

See Northeast Corridor

PHILADELPHIA

Paoli

Lancaster

Harrisburg

Lewistown

Huntingdon

Altoona
Johnstown
Greensburg

PITTSBURGH

Youngstown

Akron

N

Fostoria

Garrett

Nappanee

Hammond-
Whiting

CHICAGO

NEW YORK

For New York and the route to Philadelphia, see *The Northeast Corridor*.
Broadway Limited trains leave New York with coaches facing backwards. At
Philadelphia, diesel replaces electric power and coaches travel facing
forwards.

PHILADELPHIA

You leave 30th Street Station with apartments on the right and commuter
trains to the left, as you continue to Paoli through suburbia.

Overbrook (10/15)

Victorian buildings feature on the left beyond the wooden station.
 Pass more commuter halts, some with elaborate carvings.

Travellers' Tales
Broadway Limited

by John Ainsworth

When booking our tickets in Britain, we chose to travel overnight on two
occasions by slumbercoach, cheaper than the "first class" sleepers, which include
free meals in the price, but offering the opportunity to lie down. So after a couple
of journeys on the *North East Corridor*, we found ourselves in the grand waiting
hall — with the most elegant McDonalds we'd experienced — of Philadelphia
station late one afternoon awaiting the *Broadway Limited*, en route from New York
to Chicago. No doubt in its pre-war and immediate post-war heyday it carried
some notable personalities but the line in the station was mostly of "middle
Americans" with a fair number of students too for the coach class.

We were welcomed aboard the car by Blaise, our steward, who showed us our
cabin and then explained how everything worked.

The seats were comfortable and private although our view was restricted to one
side of the track. But a lovely fall evening winding through rural Pennsylvania
from Philadelphia to Harrisburg, with its steel mills — or at least what was left of
them after the recession — with an occasional glimpse of an Amish buggy as we
crossed Lancaster County, was relaxing enough. After Harrisburg the darkness
fell and we sampled the dining car; the couple opposite us immediately
introduced themselves and told us of their trip to Oregon which would take them
three days.

With a trip to the lounge car and a few games of cards to pass the time till we
attempted sleep, the evening passed pleasantly enough. We were to alight at
Garrett, Indiana, at 6.30am and Blaise ensured we were ready to leave.
Disembarking just before dawn at the single platform of a small town in the Mid
West — the station at the end of the main street just as in the movies — felt
romantic and we were met by a bus which seemed to appear from nowhere and
took us (with a detour to a truck stop for the driver to get coffee) to the all-
American city of Fort Wayne, or at least a shopping centre on the outskirts of it,
which is what Amtrak has to offer now its trains have been rerouted from the
town's own station.

We could have flown in a couple of hours or taken the Greyhound but we felt
like we had travelled from the big city to the plains in some sort of style.

PAOLI (25/40)

Called after the Corsican revolutionary Pasquale Paoli. Just to the north is Valley Forge, where George Washington's army spent a hungry winter during the Revolution. You can visit Washington's headquarters and the Memorial Chapel. This area is particularly attractive when the dogwoods bloom in spring. Amtrak's utilitarian depot at Lancaster Pike and S Valley Rd opens 0545-1845 (Mon-Fri), or 0830-1245 and 1345-1730 (weekends).

You leave through residential areas into leafy hills.

Coatesville (10/30)

This industrial sprawl can be seen to the left before the train enters fertile Pennsylvania Dutch country — actually settled by Germans (*Deutsch*). Amish people hold to strict religious beliefs and run their tidy farms much as they have done for 300 years. Peter Weir filmed *Witness* among these white farmhouses, where Amish men dress in black and the women wear bonnets.

LANCASTER (40/40)

Founded in 1718 as Hickory Town, it was renamed after Lancaster, England. It's the oldest inland city in the US and was the nation's capital for a single day on September 27 1777. Walking tours are available from the Association of Commerce at 100 Queen.

Lancaster is where the Amish come to market, and you can get information on Amish life from the Pennsylvania Dutch Visitors Centre, 501 Greenfield Rd (717-299-8901). Amtrak's station at 53 McGovern Ave opens 0550-2130 (Mon-Thurs), 0550-2400 (Fri), 0650-2000 (Sat) and 0715-2400 (Sun).

The Railroad Museum of Pennsylvania at nearby Strasburg has one of the best collections in the world (717-687-8628). Locomotives, passenger cars and freight cars date from 1825 to 1970, and the Pennsylvania Railroad Weekend in May is one of many special events. Open daily, admission. The Strasburg Rail Road runs daily steam trains (March-November).

You leave via factories and refineries, with an attractive park on your left, and between here and Harrisburg follow the path of the first telegraph wires. A short distance to the north is Hershey, founded by Milton Herschey in 1903 and still dedicated to chocolate.

Three Mile Island (25/15)

This nuclear energy plant was the scene of an accident in 1979. Two of the four cooling towers show plumes of white vapour away to your left.

Harrisburg Airport (28/12)

Seen immediately on the left, along with rolling hills beyond the river.

HARRISBURG (40/65)

Pennsylvania's capital is on the east bank of the Susquehanna River. The Pennsylvania Canal arrived in 1834 and the first trains two years later. The main Pennsylvania Railroad line linked the city with Pittsburgh in 1847.

Harrisburg's Capitol has bronze doors, stained glass and a marble staircase similar to that in the Paris Opera House. Its 272ft dome resembles the one in St Peter's, Rome. The William Penn Museum is next to the Archives Tower, which has records going back to 1681. Tourist bureau: 416 Forum Bldg (787-5453). Amtrak's atmospheric station at 4th and Chestnut opens 0510-2115. Buses connect to Scranton, Reading and Pennsylvania State University.

Look for the Capitol's green dome (lit at night) amid the offices and car parks on the left as you leave.

Susquehanna River (3/62)
The train crosses on Rockville Bridge — the longest (3,820ft) and widest (52ft) stone-arch bridge in the world.

Duncannon (20/45)
For the next 100 miles you accompany the Juanita River and ascend the Alleghenys. The Susquehanna River disappears to the right as farmland gives way to mountains.

LEWISTOWN (65/35)
This manufacturing centre has a neglected-looking station on the right.

As the Broadway Limited moves deeper into the Alleghenys, look for Jack's Mountain on your right and Blue Mountain to your left.

HUNTINGDON (35/45)
A modest factory town situated on the Juanita.

Spruce Creek (15/30)
You cross a creek fished by President Jimmy Carter and continue through a short tunnel to a land of streams, hills, small towns and rivers. Wooded cliffs feature on both sides.

ALTOONA (45/60)
Founded in 1849 by the Pennsylvania Railroad, Altoona was a supply base for railway construction over the mountains. It still provides maintenance facilities, and you arrive amid extensive yards. Amtrak's station at 1231 11th Ave opens 0700-2145.

The Railroaders Memorial Museum to your left has engines, cars and models associated with the Pennsylvania Railroad (814-946-0834). Almost 7,000 steam locomotives were made in these shops, which now rebuild diesels for Conrail. The museum features the *Loretto*, a private car belonging to Charles M Schwab. Open daily, admission.

As you pass through Altoona centre, note the domed cathedral on the right.

Horseshoe Curve (15/45)
A 2,355ft landmark carved out of the Logan valley hillside in 1854, helping trains cope with the steep gradient. The central curve measures 220 degrees. Look for an old Pennsylvania loco on the left.

Gallitzin Summit (25/35)
You pass through a tunnel to the other side of the Alleghenys. Travelling over these mountains was more laborious in the early 19th Century, when the Allegheny Portage Railroad lifted canal boats across between the Juanita and

Conemaugh Rivers (a distance of 30 miles). This unique engineering system is explained at Altoona's Portage Museum.

JOHNSTOWN (60/50)
In 1889 a dam burst on the Conemaugh, killing several thousand people and destroying property. Since the steel industry's decline, Johnstown has suffered considerable unemployment.

The train continues through industrial scenes for 15 minutes. Forests and mountains return as it follows a sinuously curving river below on the right.

Latrobe (45/5)
A mostly residential town used as a training base by the Pittsburgh Steelers football team.

GREENSBURG (50/42)
The Indians were defeated in 1763 at Bushy Run battlefield close by to the northwest.

You travel among attractive green hills with occasional houses and factories, including the Westinghouse Brake Company. The train slows down as it approaches Pittsburgh, seen to the right.

PITTSBURGH (42/130)
For Pittsburgh, see *The Capitol Limited*.

You travel on through the night across northeastern Ohio.

YOUNGSTOWN (130/60)
Amtrak's station at 528 Mahoning Ave opens 2330-0700.

AKRON (60/110)
German immigrant Ferdinand Schumacher began selling homemade oatmeal in 1854 and his business eventually became the Quaker Oats Company. Akron's Quaker Square features historic mills and silos. The Depot Restaurant and Museum at 120 Mill (216-253-5970) has a solarium car from the Pennsylvania Railroad along with semaphore signals and telegraph equipment. A 1940s Broadway Limited dining car houses 800ft of model railway track.

The National Football League was founded in nearby Canton, home of the NFL Hall of Fame.

FOSTORIA (110/90)
Amtrak's station at 500 S Main also serves the city of Lima.

You cross the Ohio/Indiana state line an hour from Fostoria.

GARRETT (90/35)
The two-storey red brick and tile station on the left at 300 N Randolph also serves Fort Wayne, named after the Revolutionary war general 'Mad' Anthony Wayne. Freight yards extend on the left. As the day gets lighter you continue among fields, streams, trees, ponds and marshes. Look for cattle, mansard-roofed barns and a few small towns.

A mobile home factory on the left signals the approach of Nappanee.

NAPPANEE (35/70)
The train stops across a road, with Nappanee's neat station on your right.
   You pass a Brunswick Marine plant on the left as you re-enter farm country. Watch out for Amish people riding horse-drawn buggies.

Bremen (7/63)
Large factories accumulate on the left.
   You change from Eastern to Central Time, so watches go back an hour (forward when travelling east).
   The train passes beneath a rare highway bridge just before Walkerton.

Walkerton (22/48)
A small town with its cemetery is seen to the left as you leave. Giant irrigation machines appear as the fields get bigger, and pine trees are grown as wind breaks.

Gary (65/5)
Freight yards, smoking chimneys and steel plants gather on both sides.
   Church spires feature on the left as you approach Hammond-Whiting through residential areas, glimpsing Lake Michigan to the right.

HAMMOND-WHITING (70/25)
For Hammond-Whiting, see page 247.

Roby (10/15)
For Roby, see page 247.

Comiskey Park (15/10)
For Comiskey Park, see page 248.

CHICAGO
For Chicago, see *The California Zephyr*.

24 The Maple Leaf
New York—Toronto

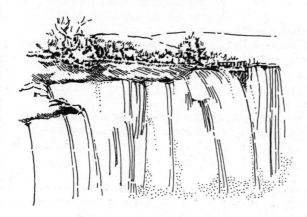

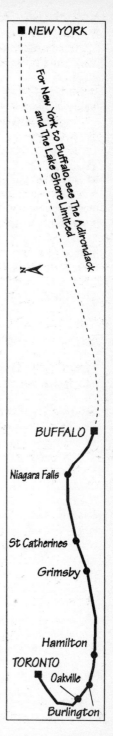

This train starts in New York and travels more than 500 miles before reaching Canada's equivalent city, Toronto. A route that takes in the Hudson River, the Mohawk valley, Niagara Falls and Lake Ontario. Travelling almost entirely in daylight gives you maximum viewing opportunities.

US citizens crossing into Canada do not need passports but should carry documents, such as a birth certificate or voter registration papers, showing proof of identity. A driving licence is not enough. Non-US citizens not resident in America require a valid passport or acceptable travel papers (in some cases a visa).

Frequency: Daily. The northbound service leaves New York early in the morning to reach Albany late morning, Buffalo late afternoon and Niagara Falls early evening. You arrive in Toronto mid-evening.

Travelling south, trains leave Toronto mid-morning to reach Niagara Falls (Ontario) by midday, Buffalo early afternoon and Albany early evening. You arrive in New York late evening.

Reservations: All reserved.

Equipment: Amfleet coaches.

Food: Snacks, sandwiches, drinks.

Baggage: No check-in service.

NEW YORK

For New York and the route to Depew station, Buffalo, see *The Adirondack* and *The Lake Shore Limited*. Leaving Depew station, the Maple Leaf picks its way carefully through a mass of tracks. The clock tower of New York Central's station can be seen on your right, a disused evangelical church home to your left. The city skyline is ahead. You cross Highway 90 before continuing among industrial parks and residential areas.

As you near Exchange Street station, the eclectic buildings of downtown are on your right.

BUFFALO (10/30)

For Buffalo, see page 243.

Amtrak's Exchange Street station at Ellicott and Washington opens 0700-2400. Freight trains gather on both sides. Older, more elegant buildings are seen in the Victorian Allentown area beyond a derelict factory to the right.

You leave with houses on the left and high-rise apartments to the right, before travelling through tunnels to emerge with Lake Erie on your left. The lake soon starts to close in as it forms the Niagara River.

Peace Bridge (8/22)

The bridge on the left connects the USA with Fort Erie, Canada.

Squaw Island (13/17)

Look for this island linked to the mainland by a drawbridge.

The train loses touch with the river for a while to travel through Tonawanda before crossing the Erie Canal.

Niagara (20/10)

The airport on your left lands honeymooners from around the world. As the Maple Leaf nears Niagara Falls it curves right through ragged-looking yards. Unromantic pylons on the right show how much hydroelectricity is produced.

NIAGARA FALLS, NY (30/11)

Two cataracts pour 600,000 gallons of water per second into the Niagara River below, creating awesome sights and sounds. The American Falls reach 184ft. The Canadian (Horseshoe) Falls are a few feet lower but have a longer, sweeping crest of 2,200ft. You can walk to Canada across the Rainbow Bridge. Visitors bureau: 345 3rd (285-2400). The Frontier (AYH) Hostel is at 1101 Ferry Ave (282-3700). Members only, $9.

Previous visitors were tempted to cross the falls on a high wire or go over the rim in a barrel. Such stunts are illegal and not recommended. Enjoy safer thrills by cruising on the *Maid of the Mist* or travel under the falls on a Cave of the Winds tour (rented rain gear provided). Not quite so exciting — but less damp — is the Prospect Point observation tower, rising 100ft above the falls. Amtrak's station opens 0600-1530 at 27 Lockport Rd, several miles from downtown and the falls. Take Metro bus No 52.

US/Canada Border (9/2)

Cross the Niagara on a high bridge with the falls away to your left.

NIAGARA FALLS, ONTARIO (11/20)

Before you can leave the train or continue your journey the Maple Leaf pauses for a customs check. VIA Rail crews replace Amtrak staff.

Like its US counterpart, Canada's town of Niagara Falls makes it easy to see the main attraction. Most people prefer the view from this side, and the 520ft Skylon tower provides a high vantage point. Don't miss the falls by night, when coloured lights create hypnotic effects. Information bureau: 110 Park E. The Art Gallery and Museum on Queen Elizabeth Way has films and a Canadian Pioneer mural.

After leaving past the Canadian National rail yards you proceed towards Lake Ontario through a land of farms and vineyards.

Welland Canal (15/5)

Cross above one of the lock systems which enable ships to move between Lakes Erie and Ontario. Just before St Catherines you cross the Old Welland Canal. This did the same job as the new one but took longer to negotiate.

ST CATHERINES (20/15)

The Garden City is surrounded by orchards and vineyards, with some wineries open to visitors. The Historical Museum has photographs and models explaining the Welland Canal's construction.

The Maple Leaf continues through pretty, rolling countryside and crosses Sixteen Mile Creek nearing Jordan.

Jordan (4/11)

Lake Ontario appears for the first time on the right, and your train stays in touch with the lake for most of the next 70 miles to Toronto.

GRIMSBY (15/22)

Note the picturesque station building. In the late 18th Century Grimsby acquired Canada's first town government.

Ivor Wynne Stadium (17/5)

On the left is the home of Hamilton's Tigercats football team. The scene becomes more industrial as you approach Hamilton.

HAMILTON (22/12)

Canada's steel capital produces half the country's output. It developed as a rail centre and port (Canada's third largest) after the Burlington Canal linked it with Lake Ontario in 1830. The city makes railroad equipment and is a financial centre. Places of interest include the Royal Botanical Gardens and the Canadian Football Hall of Fame.

You leave and travel alongside the harbour, where leisure craft mingle with merchant ships.

BURLINGTON (12/10)

A residential town, Burlington has many preserved houses. Mohawk Indian Joseph Brant's museum can be visited in a reproduction of his home. When the Anglophile chief travelled to England he was feted, presented at court and met James Boswell.

Continue through suburban areas until industry returns near Oakville, where the train crosses Sixteen Mile Creek.

OAKVILLE (10/25)

Situated at the mouth of Sixteen Mile Creek, Oakville grew as a harbour for exporting oak timber. It now makes cars, chemicals and machinery. Look for attractive Victorian houses before you leave past a Ford Motor factory and extensive rail yards on the left.

Port Credit (10/15)

Cross the Credit River, then the Etobicoke and Humber Rivers as the train nears Toronto. The skyline ahead to your right features the CN Tower (1,815ft).

Ontario Place (15/10)

In a park beside the lake on the right are an amphitheatre and the world's largest movie screen.

Fort York Park (21/4)

A historic British garrison can be seen on the right.

TORONTO

Ontario's capital claims to be 'the most livable city in North America'. Explored by the French in 1615, it became a trading post and later a British colonial town called York. Toronto officially began in 1834, when it was named after the Indian word for 'a place of meetings'.

Once scorned as infinitely boring, Toronto has transformed itself into an exciting city. New York without the problems. Three million people live in the metropolitan area, and among 70 ethnic groups is the largest Italian community outside Italy.

Freezing temperatures are likely from November to March and mid-winter gets very cold, but snow is less frequent than in many US cities. Summer heat is refreshed by lake breezes.

Transport: Clean, efficient and attractive Union Station at Front and York reflects Toronto's character. Opened by the Prince of Wales in 1927, this splendid structure boasts 40ft pillars and an Italian tile ceiling. Reservations and information: 800-426-8725 (or 800-4AM-AMTRAK). Ticket office open 0645-2335. Waiting room 0630-2335. Lockers, newspapers, Red Caps, restaurants, shops, taxi stand, subway.

TTC buses and subway trains allow fast travel throughout the city, with day and monthly passes (393-4636).

Taxis: Metro (363-5611) and Diamond (366-6868).

Car Rental: Thrifty (868-0350).

Greyhound: 610 Bay (367-8747). The terminal is also used by Voyageur Colonial and Gray Line.

Pearson Airport is 10 miles west by bus and taxi. Airport Express buses (393-7911) connect with downtown.

Tours: Gray Line (979-3511) and Happy Day (593-6220). Toronto Tours (869-1372) offers sightseeing by trolley. Gray Line boat tours (April-October) leave from Queen's Quay Terminal (364-2412).

Visitors Bureau: 207 Queen's Quay (368-9821). Other centres are outside the Royal Ontario Museum and at Eaton Centre Galleria, 220 Yonge (979-3143). Open weekdays.

Telephone Code: 416.

Accommodation: Contact Toronto Bed & Breakfast, PO Box 269, 253 College Street, Toronto M5T 1R5 (461-3676). Call 596-7117 for the Hotel Association advice service.
International Youth Hostel: 223 Church (368-0207). Members $15, non-members $18.
Central YMCA: 40 College (921-5171).
YWCA Woodlawn Residence: 80 Woodlawn Ave (923-8454).
  Hotels include the Sutton Place at 955 Bay (924-9221); Admiral, 249 Queen's Quay (364-5444); Windsor Arms, 22 St Thomas (979-2341); Hampton Court, 415 Jarvis (924-6631); Journey's End, 111 Lombard (800-668-4200); Ibis, 240 Jarvis (593-9400).

CN Tower: 301 Front W (360-8500). This is the world's tallest free-standing structure (1,815ft 5in), where outside elevators rocket you to the Skypod two-thirds of the way up. Even better views can be had from the Space Deck another 33 storeys on (highest observation platform in the world). On a clear day you can see Niagara Falls. Open daily, admission. Avoid the weekend queues if possible.

Eaton Center: On Yonge, from Queen to Dundas. More than 300 stores and services operate inside this glittering building, which has glass elevators and a 17-screen cinema. Open daily.

New City Hall: Queen (392-9111). Curved towers enclose the circular council chamber, completed in 1965. Free tours on weekdays. Next to City Hall is a favourite meeting place, Nathan Phillips Square, where residents and tourists relax by the lake (in winter a skating rink).

Forst Post Office: 260 Adelaide E (865-1833). Dating from the 1830s and still in use. Costumed guides return you to a world of quill pens and sealing wax. Open daily.

25 The Lake Cities
Chicago—Toledo

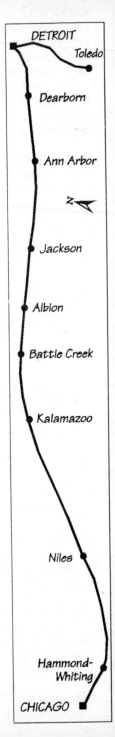

This is a fast trip between Chicago and two of the country's great industrial cities. En route are lakes, orchards and vineyards, plus manufacturing plants belonging to the likes of Kellogg and Ford. It's a cross-section of middle America.

Frequency: Daily. The eastbound service leaves Chicago mid-afternoon, reaching Battle Creek early evening, Detroit mid-evening and Toledo late evening.
   Travelling west, trains leave Toledo mid-morning to reach Detroit just before noon, Battle Creek mid-afternoon and Chicago late afternoon.

Reservations: Unreserved.

Equipment: Amfleet coaches.

Food: Snacks, sandwiches, drinks.

Baggage: No check-in service.

CHICAGO
For Chicago, see *The California Zephyr*. The Lake Cities begins by easing out of Union Station through a tunnel under the Post Office building. In Amtrak's 21st Street yards on the left trains are set up to travel to every corner of the land. Conrail loading facilities can be seen on the right.

Comiskey Park (10/15)
On the left is a car park where the old White Sox baseball stadium used to be. A new Comiskey Park rises alongside.

Roby (15/10)
For Roby, see page 247.
   You see the El track overhead, then cross the Dan Ryan Expressway. Chicago's skyline back to your left features the 110-storey Sears Tower. The Skyway can be seen on your right before you cross the south branch of the Chicago River and the now-closed Rock Island line.
   Cross the Calumet River on a steel bridge, with grain elevators and ships being loaded below.

HAMMOND-WHITING (25/65)
The modern yellow brick station on your left at 1135 Calumet Ave is Amtrak's usual stop for trains approaching Chicago from the east. Open 0645-2130 (Mon-Sat) and 0645-2200 (Sun). Oil storage tanks are seen on both sides of the track.
   Your train continues via the towns of Indiana Harbor and Pine Junction.

Indiana Harbor Canal (10/55)
Crossed on a drawbridge. The canal joins the Calumet River with Lake Michigan, a short distance to your left. On your right is a Standard Oil refinery and the Lever Brothers factory.

Gary (15/50)
For Gary, see page 260.
   As you move from Central to Eastern Time, watches go forward an hour (backward when travelling west).

Michigan City (35/30)
Look for a colourful marina on Lake Michigan to your left just before you cross the Indiana/Michigan State Line. You progress inland through countryside famous for wine and fruit.

NILES (65/45)
This small railway town serves local farmers. A Michigan Central station and clock tower are seen on the left.
   As you continue through grape-growing country look also for cherry trees, strawberries, plums and cider orchards.

Dowagiac (18/27)
This is a scheduled stop for the Twilight Limited trains.

KALAMAZOO (45/30)

The name is Indian for 'place where the water boils', and there are bubbling springs in the river. Look for 19th Century houses on the right. Amtrak at 459 N Burdick opens 0800-2130.

The Kalamazoo, Lake Shore & Chicago Railway operates out of Paw Paw, 15 miles west of Kalamazoo (616-657-5763). You can take diesel-powered rides among orchards, woods and vineyards, travelling next to Lake Cora on a Pere Marquette/Chesapeake & Ohio branch line.

Cross the Kalamazoo River as you leave the city.

BATTLE CREEK (30/28)

The Kellogg Brothers invented flaked cereal in 1894 and made Battle Creek's fortune. The Kellogg Company, Post Cereals and Ralston Purina's production facilities can sometimes be scented as well as seen. A festival in June features 'the world's longest breakfast table'. Amtrak's modern station on the left at 104 Capitol Ave SW opens 0800-2230. Thruway buses connect with East Lansing and Flint to the north.

You leave with Post and Kellogg plants to right and left, then join the Kalamazoo River on your right, following its meandering path through waterlogged terrain.

ALBION (28/22)

The Albion College campus is on your right before you continue among peaceful farming scenes beside the Kalamazoo.

Jackson Airport (18/4)

Runways are to the left.

JACKSON (22/35)

An interesting old brick-built station on the left at 501 E Michigan Ave opens 0815-2245. A stone tablet in Jackson marks where a meeting of Free Soilers, Democrats and Whigs founded the Republican Party in 1854. The 500ft Cascade Falls — America's biggest man-made falls — were built here in 1932.

Leave via Conrail yards and travel through the communities of Michigan Center and Leoni.

Grass Lake (10/25)

Fire destroyed the station building on the right.

You continue via Chelsea and cross the Huron River for the first of many times as it winds from here to Ypsilanti.

ANN ARBOR (35/33)

In 1824 two settlers named the settlement after a grape arbor and their wives, Ann Rumsey and Ann Allen. The Michigan Central Railroad arrived in 1839, linking the town to Detroit. The Art Museum can be found at State and University. Visitors bureau: 211 E Huron (995-7281). The YMCA is at 350 S 5th Ave (663-0536) — singles $20, weekly $75. Amtrak's station at 325 Depot opens 0700-2330.

The University of Michigan — one of America's oldest and largest — moved here from Detroit in 1837. Situated mostly downtown, it saw the first anti-Vietnam war teach-in. Watch for a spacious 19th Century Central Michigan building on the right as you leave town and cross the Huron River again.

Ypsilanti (10/23)
Home of Eastern Michigan University.

Just before crossing the River Rouge near Dearborn, look right for the Henry Ford Museum and Greenfield Village. A million visitors a year come to see historic cars, a letter from Clyde Barrow and the chair in which Abraham Lincoln was assassinated. Greenfield Village's 80 buildings include the Wright Brothers' workshop, Edison's laboratory and the court-house where Lincoln practised law. All were brought from their original sites and reconstructed. Also on display are a locomotive built by Ford in 1876 and an 1893 replica of the *DeWitt Clinton*. Steam train rides are available April-October. Take SMART bus No 200 from Detroit.

DEARBORN (33/25)
This was originally a stage-coach stop on the Sauk Trail. Henry Ford built his Fair Lane mansion on 72 acres next to the river. Amtrak at 16121 Michigan Ave opens 0630-2330.

Soon after Dearborn you see the Ford Company's factory on your right. From here to Detroit the Lake Cities travels a landscape dedicated to the motor industry (Chrysler and General Motors), with manufacturing plants, loading docks and rail yards.

DETROIT (25/100)
This has been the birthplace of Joe Louis, Motown Records (derived from Detroit's nickname 'Motor Town') and countless automobiles. Founded by the French in 1701 as Fort Pontchartrain d'Etroit ('of the strait'), Detroit is strategically located between Lakes Erie and Huron. Fought over by French, British and US forces until 1813, it later became a staging post on the Underground Railroad for slaves escaping to Canada.

Over four million people live in the metropolitan area and their 150 ethnic backgrounds provide a rich cultural experience. Efforts have been made to repair the city's image since the 1960s race riots, but you should still take care in depressed neighbourhoods.

As a rather independent-minded train enthusiast I sometimes yearned to break the rules. I once stood in the lobby at the end of the carriage and was reprimanded for breaking safety rules; the doors there are "stable doors" and I recall in Canada in 1967 travelling with the window at the top open — I like some fresh air when travelling — but this is strictly taboo. I did surreptitiously open one to take photos at a neat country station in Mississippi and felt really naughty. And getting off to stretch one's legs even at long stops is difficult as the train staff only open selected carriage doors. Standing on station platforms too is a British pastime, not an American one.

John Ainsworth

Transport: Amtrak's station is at 2601 Rose (not a safe area). Information: 964-5335. Ticket office open 0630-2330. Waiting room 0630-0100. Lockers, newspapers, luggage trolleys, taxi stand.

The 'people mover' monorail (224-2160) stops at many hotels and attractions. The Trolley (933-1330) and DOT buses (833-7692) operate downtown. SMART buses (962-5515) serve outlying regions.

Taxis: Lorraine (582-6900) and Unity (834-3300).

Car Rental: Call-a-Car, 877 E Eight Mile Rd (541-2700).

Greyhound: 130 E Congress (961-8502).

The airport is 20 miles west by Kirby Tours bus (963-8585).

Tours: Kirby (963-8585) and Gray Line (341-6808) operate during summer. Cruises on the *Star of Detroit* (May-October) leave from 2 E Atwater.

Visitors Bureau: 100 Renaissance Center (259-4333). Open daily. Free visitors guide. Call 567-1170 for an update.

Telephone Code: 313.

Accommodation: Special rates are available for downtown hotels at weekends.

Motor City (AYH) Hostel: 16901 Burgess, 11 miles from downtown (533-9597).

Country Grandma's Home (AYH) Hostel: 22330 Bell Rd, New Boston (753-4901). Members $7, non-members $10.

Hotels include the OMNI International at 333 E Jefferson Ave (222-7700); Pontchartrain, 2 Washington Blvd (965-0200); St Regis, 3071 W Grand Blvd (873-3000); Dearborn Inn, 20301 Oakwood Blvd (271-2700); Days Inn, 231 Michigan Ave (965-4646); Shorecrest, 1316 E Jefferson Ave (568-3000).

Rivertown: This area between Jefferson Ave and the river developed in the last century as a centre for railroads, ship building and lumber yards. The old warehouses have lately been turned into restaurants, shops and nightclubs. Woodbridge Tavern is an atmospheric speakeasy at 289 St Aubin (259-0578).

Detroit Cultural Centre: On Woodward Ave, two miles from downtown. The Institute of Arts (833-7900) has Van Gogh pictures and African sculpture (closed Mon, donation). The Science Center features spacecraft (closed Mon, admission). The Italianate Public Library houses a million books and has murals showing transport history (closed Mon, Fri and Sun, free).

Fort Wayne: 6325 W Jefferson Ave, Livernois (297-9360). The fort was constructed in 1843 to protect the US border. It now has tours by costumed guides and incorporates the Great Lakes Indian Museum. Open Wed-Sun, May to Labor Day. Admission.

Belle Isle: An island park three miles from the city centre, reached via Grand River Blvd and the Douglas MacArthur Bridge (267-7115). Granted to French settlers by Detroit's founder, Antoine de la Mothe Cadillac, the park was designed by Frederick Olmsted. It has a half-mile beach, a zoo, an aquarium and a nature centre (open Wed-Sun, free).

As you leave Detroit look left for the Ambassador Bridge linking the Motor City with Windsor, Ontario. A quirk of geography puts Canada south of the USA at this point.

Cross the River Rouge and, a few minutes later, the Ecorse River.

Trenton (35/65)
A major steel plant and other industry can be seen on the left.

Monroe (65/35)
Cross the River Raisin and the Michigan/Ohio State Line.

Nearing Toledo you pass through rail yards and cross Swan Creek before pulling into the Central Union terminal.

TOLEDO
For Toledo, see page 246.

26 Other Trains

No reservation or check-in baggage services operate except where stated. All trains run daily unless otherwise indicated.

The Ann Rutledge
Chicago-Kansas City. Travels via St Louis. Tray meals.

The Atlantic City Express
Philadelphia-Atlantic City. Several round-trips from Philadelphia and some long distance trains from New York, Washington and Boston. Other direct services run from Harrisburg, Richmond, New Haven and Springfield. All reserved. Club class service on certain trains. The Atlantic City Express connects with the beaches, casinos and boardwalk of New Jersey's answer to Las Vegas. Some casinos give bonuses (coins or food vouchers) to Amtrak passengers.

The Auto Train
A service between Lorton in Virginia and Sanford, Florida, for cars and their passengers only. Sleeping accommodation, dome car, movies and buffet meals (dining car meals for first class passengers). No check-in baggage except in vehicles. Reservations are essential, and you should allow two hours before departure for boarding.

The Carolinian
New York-Raleigh. Follows the Silver Meteor route. All reserved.

The Gulf Breeze
New York-Mobile. Accompanies the Crescent to Birmingham before continuing south through Montgomery to Mobile. All reserved. Check-in baggage. Sleeping accommodation as far as Atlanta.

The Hoosier State
Chicago-Indianapolis. Follows the Cardinal route.

The Illini
Chicago-Carbondale. Follows the City of New Orleans route.

The Illinois Zephyr
Chicago-West Quincy. Follows the Southwest Chief route as far as West Quincy.

The International
Chicago-Toronto. Follows the Lake Cities route to Battle Creek, then continues over the Canadian border before crossing southern Ontario. Tray meals.

The Loop
Chicago-Springfield. Daily except on Sundays.

The Mount Rainier
Seattle-Portland. Follows the Coast Starlight route.

The Niagara Rainbow
New York-Niagara Falls. Travels via Albany and Buffalo, following the Maple Leaf route. All reserved.

The Palmetto
New York-Jacksonville. Follows the Silver Meteor route. All reserved. Check-in baggage. Tray meals.

The Pennsylvanian
New York-Harrisburg. Travels via Philadelphia.

The Pere Marquette
Chicago-Grand Rapids. Travels between Chicago and Michigan's second largest city.

The State House
Chicago-St Louis. Follows the Texas Eagle route.

The Tidewater
Newport News-New York. A northbound service only (on Sundays) along the Colonial route. All reserved. Club class available.

The Twilight Limited
Chicago-Detroit. Check-in baggage service when travelling east.

The Virginian
Boston-Richmond. Follows the Colonial route as far as Richmond. All reserved.

The Wolverine
Chicago-Detroit. Check-in baggage service when travelling west.

Chapter 5

Steam Trains Today

The number of American steam locos peaked at 72,000 just after the First World War. Something like 180,000 steam engines would be built in the USA altogether, culminating in the Union Pacific's *Big Boys* of the 1940s. These (4-8-8-4) monsters weighed 600 tons, had a capacity of 7,000 horsepower and burned 20 tons of coal an hour. In the end lower maintenance costs made the change to diesel inevitable, and no more steam engines were put into service after 1953.

The Norfolk & Western Railroad, centred on Roanoke, was the last steam-powered class one line. Photographer O Winston Link lovingly recorded its culmination over a period of six years, publishing his pictures in *Steam, Steel and Stars*. The last main line steam trains ran on the Norfolk & Western on April 4 1960, and most of the engines were scrapped and exported to Japan.

Steam locomotives served America well and earned the people's affection. They were given nicknames like calliope, hog, jack, mill, pig, pot or smoker. If small they were known as coffee-pot, dinky, kettle or peanut-roaster. Drivers were hog-jockeys, grunts or eagle-eyes. To pick up water from between the rails was to 'jerk a drink'. A head-on collision was a 'cornfield meet'.

The Golden Age of steam lives on thanks to the efforts of volunteer enthusiasts, around 40,000 of whom are actively involved. It can take 30,000 hours work to restore a single locomotive. More than 200 engines function today out of 1,875 remaining in the US and Canada. Most are between 100 and 150 tons, though the largest in working order is the Union Pacific *Challenger* (313 tons). Some reproductions have been imported from Europe and China.

You can ride a steam train at many locations throughout the country, especially during summer. Five million people a year enjoy main line excursions, scenic railways, dinner trains and museums. For more information you should obtain a copy of the Steam Passenger Service Directory, available by mail from Locomotive & Railway Preservation, PO Box 599, Richmond, VT

05477. Or call 802-434-2351.

The following are among the most scenic and interesting railways, all standard gauge except where indicated.

Boone & Scenic Valley
A 15-mile round-trip from Boone, Iowa, over the Dodge, Des Moines & Southern route, crossing the Des Moines River valley on a 156ft high bridge. It uses a modern steam loco made in China. Boone has the world's largest and highest double track rail bridge and is home to Iowa's Railway Museum. Steam trains run May-October, diesels daily. Call 515-432-4278. Nearest Amtrak stop is Osceola.

California Western
Day and half-day trips among California's redwoods, from Fort Bragg on the coast to Willits on Highway 101. Contact PO Box 907, Fort Bragg, CA 95437 (707-964-6371). Amtrak Thruway buses link Oakland with Willits.

Cumbres & Toltec
64 miles of Denver & Rio Grande Western narrow gauge track that crosses the continental divide at Cumbres Pass (10,000ft) and goes through Toltec Gorge. The Colorado Limited travels from Antonito to Osier, Colorado, via the gorge. The New Mexico Express leaves Chama, New Mexico, for Osier via Cumbres Pass. Daily, May-October. Dress warmly. Contact PO Box 668, Antonito, CO 81120 (719-376-5483) or PO Box 789, Chama, NM 87520 (505-756-2151).

Deadwood Central
The highest steam trip east of the Rockies. Trains leave Deadwood, South Dakota, for a 10-mile journey over the Burlington & Black Hills Highline Branch, travelling out of Deadwood Gulch through mountain scenery. Daily, May-September. Contact PO Box 48, Deadwood, SD 57732 (605-578-2255).

Durango & Silverton
479 Main Ave, Durango, Colorado (303-247-2733). Travel through the Rockies along a 36in-gauge line built in 1881 to transport miners to Silverton. It follows the Animas River among the San Juan National Forest. Daily, May-September.

Eureka Springs & North Arkansas
Four miles through the Ozark Mountains, leaving from the 1913 Eureka Springs depot. Daily, May-October. Weekends during April. Contact PO Box 310, 299 N Main Street, Eureka Springs, AR 72632 (501-253-6774).

Grand Canyon
518 E Bill Williams Ave, Williams, Arizona (602-635-4000). Trains travel 65 miles through forest and desert between the Williams depot (a former Harvey House) and the 1910 South Rim station on the edge of the canyon. Restored 1920s Pullman cars operate February-December. Amtrak's Flagstaff stop is 30 miles east.

Heber Creeper

Starts from the 1899 Denver & Rio Grande Western depot (now a museum) in Heber City, Utah, for a 32-mile journey through the Heber valley among mountains, rivers and canyons. Daily, May-September. Contact PO Box 103, Heber City, UT 84032 (801-654-2900). Amtrak's Desert Wind stops at Provo, 11 miles west.

New Hope & Ivyland

From New Hope's picturesque station to Lahaska along a branch of the Reading Railroad. Narrated trips take you through Pennsylvania countryside by way of Pauline's Trestle and part of the Underground Railroad route. Daily, May-October. Weekends in March, November and December. Contact PO Box 634. New Hope, PA 18938 (215-862-2332). Nearest Amtrak stops are New York, Philadelphia, Princeton and Trenton.

Ohio Central

Steam and diesel trains operate out of Ohio Central Station, 111 Factory, Sugar Creek (216-852-4676). This is Amish country, and an area known as Ohio's Switzerland. Hour long trips (except Sun and holidays) between May and October.

Travellers' Tales
For Train Buffs

John Ainsworth

One of the fascinations for train buffs is the number of freight lines left, even after the amalgamations of the last 20 years. You can spot the number of different companies operating freight cars. I bought Rand McNally's *Handy Railroad Atlas* for $11.95, which has maps of the lines in each state and a list of all the companies and their mileages.

There are also plenty of tourist lines and even steam operated excursions on main lines. *Trains* is the monthly magazine which includes a checklist of special events. The annual *Steam Passenger Service Directory* published by Locomotive and Railway Preservation Limited of Richmond, Vermont (1991 edition was $8.95) lists not just steam but preservation projects state by state. They vary from the spectacular 45 mile long steam hauled Durango and Silverton Railroad in Colorado (a day trip by steam through mountains to a restored gold rush town) to descriptions of what to find in static museums. There are discount vouchers for many of the attractions.

In London you can get these and many other North American train books at Motor Books, 33 St Martin's Court, near Leicester Square. In the USA Heimburger House publishes a good selection of specialist railroad books. Address: 7236 West Madison St, Forest Park, Illinois, 60130. A selection of their books follows:

Rio Grande Narrow Gauge Recollections by Kenody Charlton
Rails Across the Land by Kenody Charlton
Spirit of the South Shore by William Raia
Trains of America by Donald Heimburger
Wabash by Donald Heimburger

And if you really want to experience rail travel as it used to be, get to know somebody who owns a private railroad car. There are several still about.

Railtown

A museum at 5th Ave and Reservoir Road, Jamestown, California (209-984-3953). The 1897 Sierra Railway buildings are kept as they originally operated. Excursions take place to Sonora, Keystone and Fassler on most weekends, March-October. Nearest Amtrak stops are Stockton and Riverbank.

Reader

The oldest steam standard gauge railway in the country, with open wooden coaches drawn by historic logging engines, providing seven-mile round-trips out of Reader, Arkansas. Contact PO Box 9, Malvern, AR 72104 (501-624-6881). Nearest Amtrak stop is Arkadelphia.

Roaring Camp & Big Trees

Trains leave the 1880 South Pacific Coast depot at Felton, California, for a six-mile trip on 36in-gauge track between Roaring Camp and Bear Mountain. You go via the state's first preserved redwoods and Spring Canyon into the Santa Cruz Mountains. Daily, June-September. Contact PO Box G-1, Felton, CA 95018 (408-335-4484). Nearest Amtrak stop is San Jose.

St Louis, Iron Mountain & Southern

From Jackson, Missouri, along a Missouri Pacific branch line. Journeys last one and a half hours (to Gordonville), two hours (Dutchtown) or four hours (Delta). Weekends, April-October. Contact PO Box 244, Jackson, MO 63755 (314-243-1688).

Texas State

One train a day goes in each direction between Rusk and Palestine over part of the Texas State Railroad (completed in 1896). Trains operate Thurs to Mon (May-August) and on weekends (March-May). Contact PO Box 39, Rusk, TX 75785 (903-683-2561). Nearest Amtrak stop is Longview.

Valley

A 10-mile round-trip through Connecticut countryside between Essex and Chester on a New Haven Railroad branch line, stopping at Deep River for optional boat trips on the Connecticut River. Daily, June-August. Contact PO Box 452, Essex, CT 06426 (203-767-0103). Nearest Amtrak stop is Old Saybrook.

Virginia & Truckee

At Washington and F, Virginia City, Nevada (702-847-038). A half hour ride along part of the Virginia & Truckee line through the Comstock mining area, with commentary from the conductor. Daily, May-September. Weekends in October. Amtrak's nearest stop is Reno.

Western Maryland

Leaves Cumberland's station (a transport museum) to travel over Western Maryland and Cumberland & Pennsylvania tracks. You pass through the Cumberland Narrows, stop at the historic Frostburg depot and negotiate spectacular Horseshoe Curve. Operates mostly Tues-Sun (May to

November). Call 1-800-TRAIN-50 or 301-759-4400. Amtrak's Capitol Limited stops at Cumberland.

Whitewater Valley

Indiana's longest scenic railway runs between Connersville and Metamora, next to the old Whitewater Canal. Mostly weekends and holidays, May-October. Contact PO Box 406, Connersville, IN 47331 (317-825-2054). Amtrak's Cardinal stops in Connersville.

Wilmington & Western

At Greenbank Station, four miles southwest of Wilmington (302-998-1930). Trips to Mount Cuba over part of the Baltimore & Ohio Landenberg branch line (Sun, May-October) or to Hockessin (Sat, June-August). Amtrak's nearest stop is Wilmington.

Yosemite Mountain-Sugar Pine

South of Yosemite National Park through California's Sierra Nevada, this 36in-gauge line once hauled logs for the Madera Sugar Pine Lumber Company. Trains reach 5,000ft before descending via Lewis Creek Canyon and Cold Spring Crossing. Narrated tours on weekends (May-October) and some weekdays (June-September). Contact 56001 Yosemite Hwy 41, Fish Camp, CA 93623 (209-683-7273). Amtrak's nearest stop is Merced.

Yreka Western

A 15-mile trip between Yreka and Montague, California, along the Yreka Railroad which connected with the California & Oregon in 1889. You travel via lumber mills and the Shasta valley with views of Mount Shasta to the south. Wed-Sun (June to September). Weekends (May-June). Contact PO Box 660, Yreka, CA 96097 (916-842-4146). Amtrak's nearest stop is Dunsmuir.

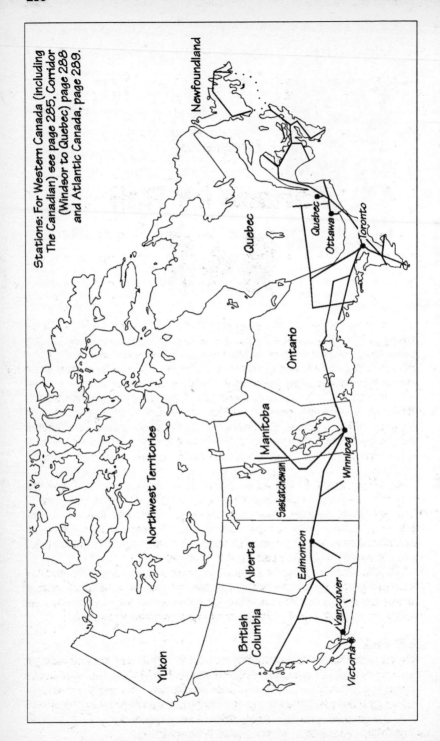

Stations: For Western Canada (including The Canadian) see page 285, Corridor (Windsor to Quebec) page 288 and Atlantic Canada, page 289.

Chapter 6

Canada by Rail

Canada may be the only country in the world with a written constitution linking its formation to the building of a railway. In 1867 a parliamentary act proclaimed the construction of the Intercolonial Railway 'essential to the consolidation of the Union of British North America', and trains have been part of Canada's economic and political history ever since.

In 1836 the first railroad — the Champlain & St Lawrence — opened a 14-mile route between St Johns on the Richelieu River and La Prairie on the St Lawrence. The success of companies in the USA encouraged further development, including the Grand Trunk Railway from Montreal to Toronto. In 1857 the Great Western Railway built the world's first sleeping car, inspiring the American Pullman design two years later.

The transcontinental Canadian Pacific route opened in 1885 and the following year the first train ran 3,000 miles from Montreal to British Columbia. The Canadian Northern, later to become the Canadian National, soon followed. These trains and others opened up the land, created a sense of nationhood and brought development along the way. More than 40,000 miles of track existed when the First World War ended.

The 20th Century brought competition from airlines, highways and the automobile. The Canadian Pacific's last steam trains ran in 1960 and annual passenger miles fell to around 20 million (one third of the peak figure). Like its US counterpart, the Canadian government was compelled to act.

VIA Rail

Canada's equivalent to Amtrak began in 1977, taking over most passenger services. VIA has its own locomotives and service personnel but uses tracks belonging to Canadian Pacific and Canadian National. The equipment, though generally older than Amtrak's, remains comfortable and has been refurbished. VIA Rail joins Amtrak in running trains that connect with US cities (the Adirondack, Montrealer, Maple Leaf and International).

Sleeping: Pillows and blankets are not provided for overnight travel in coach accommodation (except for dayniters). All necessary bedding is supplied in sleeping car accommodation, which includes bedrooms and roomettes on long distance trains.

Reservations: Required for all first class seats and sleeping cars, as well as for dayniters between Ontario, Quebec and the Maritimes. Coach seats are automatically guaranteed on purchase of your ticket.

For reservations, information and tickets by mail you should call the following numbers —

Newfoundland	:	1-800-561-3926
Prince Edward Island	:	1-800-561-3952
Halifax, NS	:	902-429-8421
Elsewhwere in Nova Scotia	:	1-800-561-3952
Moncton, NB	:	506-857-9830
Saint John, NB	:	506-642-2916
Elsewhere in New Brunswick	:	1-800-561-3952
Montreal, Que	:	514-871-1331
Quebec City, Que	:	418-692-3940
James Bay, Que	:	514-871-1331
Elsewhere in Quebec	:	1-800-361-5390
Hamilton, Ont	:	416-522-7533
Kingston, Ont	:	613-544-5600
London, Ont	:	519-672-5722
Ottawa, Ont	:	613-244-8289
Toronto, Ont	:	416-366-8411
Windsor, Ont	:	519-256-5511
Elswhere in Ontario	:	1-800-361-1235
Other provinces	:	1-800-561-8630

If you have hearing or speech problems, you can communicate through TDD (telecommunication devices for the deaf) on 368-6406 in Toronto and 1-800-268-9503 elsewhere.

For Amtrak train information or reservations call 1-800-426-8725.

Information on VIA Rail is available from Amtrak at 400 N Capitol Street, Washington, DC 20001, or the following in Canada —

Alberta
VIA Rail, 10004 104 Ave, Edmonton, Alta T5J 0K1.

Manitoba
VIA Rail Travel Centre, Room 101, 123 Main Street, Winnipeg, Man R3C 2P8.

Nova Scotia
Call VIA Rail Canada (24 hours) on 800-561-3952 or 800-361-7773.

Quebec
VIA Rail Canada, Rail Travel Bureau, Central Station, Montreal, Que H3C 3N3.

Tickets: You can get advance reservations and tickets up to six months in advance, either from authorised travel and sales agents or from a VIA sales office. See Appendix for agents abroad.

Train conductors will issue a cash fare to a passenger not travelling beyond the end of the train run.

People over 60 or full time students get 10% discount, and reductions of 40% are available for many routes on 'discount days'. Children under two accompanied by an adult (one child per adult) travel free. Children aged 2-11 pay half the adult fare. Children under eight are not allowed to travel unaccompanied, but those aged 8-11 can travel with written permission from a parent or guardian.

VIA Rail is not normally liable for lost, stolen or destroyed tickets, though you can apply for reimbursement by completing a lost ticket indemnity bond obtainable at VIA Rail offices.

Connections: Published connections with other trains, buses or ferries are not guaranteed and are subject to change without notice. Effort is made to keep to schedule but VIA doesn't accept responsibility for delays or inconvenience.

Payment: Credit cards can be used for buying tickets, meals and upgraded accommodation. Personal cheques must be drawn on a Canadian or US bank. Fares and accommodation prices are subject to a 7% goods and services tax.

Smoking: Coaches are divided into smoking and non-smoking areas. Smoking is only permitted in designated coaches or sections of coaches, enclosed sleeping cars and lounge cars. Pipes and cigars are prohibited and there is no smoking in dining cars.

Baggage: Up to 100lbs of personal luggage may be checked in for each adult fare, and half that amount for each child. Extra luggage is subject to surcharge. Bags must be checked at least half an hour before departure. Carry-on luggage is limited to two pieces, for which VIA does not accept liability.

Free baggage carts are available at stations in Halifax, Quebec City, Ottawa, Winnipeg, Edmonton and Vancouver.

The Amtrak and VIA Rail (Canada) experiences are essentially different from travel in Europe and to me they have more similarity to air travel; the exception being the frequent services in the North-East Corridor between Boston, New York and Washington. But on the long-distance journeys you are looked after from beginning to end. Your baggage can be checked, you are escorted onto the platform and to a specified seat or sleeper, and if in the latter you may have vouchers for free meals. There seems to be an abundance of staff.

John Ainsworth

Canrail Pass

Canrail and Youth Canrail passes can only be bought by residents of countries outside Canada. A valid passport must be shown. For the Youth pass, available to those aged up to 24, proof of your birthdate is required.

All passes allow unlimited VIA Rail coach class travel for 30 days on a system or regional basis. System passes cover the entire network. An eastern pass covers the Quebec-Windsor Corridor and destinations east of Montreal.

Canrail passes are not valid for other Canadian railways and are not sold in Canada, so get one before leaving home. The following prices apply (high season runs from June to September) —

System: Adult $299 (low season) and $439 (high season)
         Youth $249 (low season) and $399 (high season)

Eastern: Adult $179 (low season) and $269 (high season)
          Youth $159 (low season) and $219 (high season)

Tickets must be obtained before boarding.

The Trains

Reductions in government subsidies have meant major changes in VIA Rail operations. The Canadian, which used to make one of the world's great journeys between Montreal and Vancouver, ceased running in January 1990. For the latest information and schedules call 1-800-665-0200.

The following passenger services are among those currently operating.

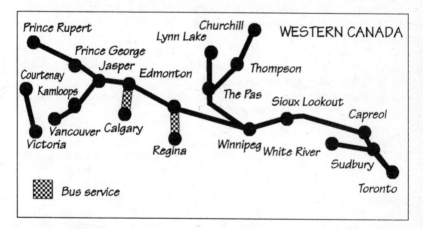

The Canadian

Previously called the Super Continental, running three days a week between Vancouver and Toronto. The complete trip takes three days and four nights. You see the farms and prairies of Saskatchewan, Jasper National Park, mountains, plains and river gorges.

Trains leave Vancouver mid-evening each Mon, Thurs and Sat to reach Jasper mid-afternoon on the second day and Edmonton late evening. You reach Saskatoon early morning and Winnipeg mid afternoon on the third day, then Capreol late on day four. You arrive in Toronto mid-evening on Thurs, Sun or Tues.

Travelling west, the Canadian leaves Toronto just after midday on Tues,

Thurs and Sat to reach Capreol mid evening. You arrive in Winnipeg early evening next day and Saskatoon during the second night. Edmonton is reached early morning on day three and Jasper mid afternoon. You arrive in Vancouver early in the morning on Fri, Sun or Tues.

Trains connect in Jasper with the Skeena to Prince Rupert, British Columbia.

Check-in baggage at major stations. Complete meals service, lounge car, bedrooms and roomettes.

VIA uses the following stations —

Vancouver: 1150 Station Street. Information: 604-669-3050. Reservations: 1-800-561-8630. Ticket office open 0900-1700. Waiting room 0700-1700. Buses connect with the Amtrak network in Seattle, Washington.

Winnipeg: 123 Main. Reservations and information: 1-800-561-8630. Lockers, newspapers, luggage trolleys, taxi stand.

Saskatoon: 11th and Chappel Drive, four miles west of downtown. Reservations and information: 1-800-561-8630. Lockers, vending machines, taxi stand.

Edmonton: 104th Ave at 10th. Reservations and information: 1-800-561-8630. Ticket office and waiting room open 0900-1730. Lockers, newspapers, taxi stand.

Jasper: 607 Connaught Drive. Reservations and information: 1-800-561-8630. Ticket office and waiting room 0730-2230. Lockers, newspapers, Red Caps, restaurant, shop, taxi stand. For Jasper Park contact PO Box 98, Jasper, Alberta T0E 1E0 (403-852-3858).

The Skeena

A 529-mile journey among mountains, ski resorts and river valleys, this route follows the Fraser River to Prince George, then the Skeena River to Prince Rupert ('halibut capital of the world'). Look out an hour from Jasper for Mount Robson, the highest point in the Canadian Rockies (12,972ft).

Before the Grand Trunk Railway arrived in 1914 Prince Rupert was an isolated settlement on Kaien Island. Ferry services now operate from Prince Rupert north to Alaska or south along the British Columbia coast to Seattle.

The Skeena leaves Jasper mid-evening on Sun, Wed and Fri to reach Prince George during the night and Prince Rupert mid-afternoon (Mon, Thurs or Sat).

Travelling east, trains leave Prince Rupert late morning on Sun, Tues and Fri to reach Prince George just after midnight and Jasper early next morning (Mon, Wed or Sat).

Check-in baggage at main stations. Complete meals service, bedrooms and roomettes.

VIA uses Prince George's First Avenue and Quebec station, close to downtown. Reservations and information: 1-800-561-8630. Lockers, vending machines, luggage trolleys, taxi stand.

Prince Rupert station closes Sun. Reservations and information: 1-800-561-8630.

The Rocky Mountaineer

A two-day, 600-mile journey among the mountains, rivers, waterfalls and forests of the Canadian Rockies, this route from Vancouver to Calgary was part of the now defunct transcontinental Canadian's. You travel via Banff, Yoho and Glacier National Parks as well as the country's longest rail tunnel.

Trains depart Vancouver early in the morning to reach Kamloops late afternoon. After an overnight stop you leave Kamloops early next morning for either Jasper (arriving late afternoon) or Banff and Calgary (mid-evening).

Travelling west, the Rocky Mountaineer leaves Calgary early morning (or Jasper mid-morning) to reach Kamloops mid-evening. After an overnight stop you leave Kamloops early next morning to arrive in Vancouver late afternoon.

You can book on a one-way or round-trip basis and a single fare starts at $435. Prices include breakfast, lunch and non-alcoholic drinks on board, plus hotel accommodation in Kamloops. Reduced fares for children aged 2-11.

You should check in at least an hour before departure. Checked baggage (maximum 66lb) can not be reclaimed before your final destination so take a small bag on board for the overnight stop.

Rocky Mountaineer trains are operated by the Great Canadian Railtour Company, 345-625 Howe Street, Vancouver, BC, V6C 2T6 (604-669-1939). Information and reservations: 604-984-3315 (in Vancouver) or 800-665-7245 (Canada/USA).

Calgary's station is at 9th Avenue and Centre. Lockers, newspapers, Red Caps, restaurant, taxi stand. Reservations and information: 1-800-561-8630.

The Corridor Services

VIA's busiest route is between Quebec City and Windsor, Ontario, via Montreal and Toronto. Additional services link with Ottawa (three times daily in each direction) and Niagara Falls (one train daily in addition to Amtrak's Maple Leaf). Many trains offer first class service with at-your-seat meals, complimentary drinks, newspapers and telephones.

VIA uses the following stations —

Quebec City: The refurbished Gare du Palais at 450 rue Saint-Paul. Reservations and information: 418-692-3940.

Montreal: Gare Centrale (Central Station) on Rene Levesque Blvd at Mansfield. Also used by Amtrak and commuter trains. Reservations and information: 871-1331. Ticket office open 0700-2330. Red Caps, restaurants, shops, taxi stand. The Canadian Railway Museum at Saint Constant just south of Montreal features historic locomotives in two large train sheds (514-632-2410).

Toronto: Clean, efficient and attractive Union Station is at Front and York. Opened by the Prince of Wales in 1927, this splendid structure boasts 40ft pillars and an Italian tile ceiling. Reservations and information: 366-8411 (or 1-800-426-8725 for Amtrak). Ticket office open 0645-2335. Waiting room 0630-

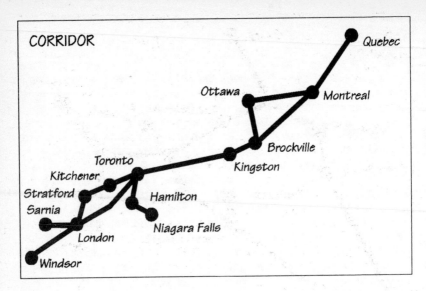

2335. Lockers, newspapers, Red Caps, restaurants, shops, taxi stand, subway.

Ottawa: A modern station at 200 Tremblay, two miles from downtown. Reservations and information: 613-238-8289. Ticket office and waiting room open 0600-2400. Lockers, newspapers, Red Caps, restaurants, shops, taxi stand. The National Museum of Science and Technology at 1867 St Laurent Blvd has steam engines and vintage rolling stock (613-991-3044).

The Atlantic
Over 750 miles along the 'short line' route between Halifax, Nova Scotia, and Montreal, Quebec, via Moncton and St John, New Brunswick. As well as Halifax's beautiful harbour and a good deal of New Brunswick countryside, the Atlantic crosses northern Maine in the USA. The usual customs and immigration regulations apply.

Westbound trains leave Halifax soon after midday on Mon, Thurs and Sat to reach Moncton early evening and St John mid-evening, arriving in Montreal early next morning (Tues, Fri or Sun).

Travelling east, the Atlantic leaves Montreal early evening on Mon, Thurs and Sat to reach St John early next morning, Moncton towards midday and Halifax late afternoon (Tues, Fri or Sun).

Check-in baggage at main stations. Complete meals, bedrooms and roomettes.

VIA uses the following stations —

Halifax: 1161 Hollis. Ticket office and waiting room open 0800-1830. Reservations and information: 902-429-8421. Lockers, vending machines, newspapers, Red Caps, restaurant, taxi stand.

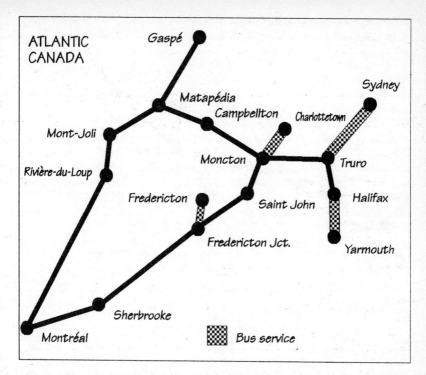

ATLANTIC CANADA

Gaspé
Matapédia
Campbellton
Charlottetown
Sydney
Mont-Joli
Moncton
Truro
Rivière-du-Loup
Fredericton
Saint John
Halifax
Fredericton Jct.
Yarmouth
Sherbrooke
Montréal
Bus service

Moncton: 1234 Main. Ticket office and waiting room open 0930-2200. Reservations and information: 506-857-9830. Lockers, newspapers, Red Caps, restaurant, taxi stand.

The Ocean

This follows the old Intercolonial Railway (ICR) route between Halifax and Montreal via the port of Campbellton, NB. Unlike the Atlantic, the Ocean does not enter the USA and so avoids customs checks.

Trains leave Halifax soon after midday on Wed, Fri and Sun to reach Moncton early evening, Campbellton late evening and Montreal early the following morning (Thurs, Sat or Mon).

Travelling east, the Ocean leaves Montreal early in the evening on Sun, Wed and Fri to reach Campbellton early next morning, Moncton mid-morning and Halifax mid-afternoon (Mon, Thurs or Sat).

Check-in baggage at main stations. Complete meals, bedrooms and roomettes.

The Chaleur

Operates three days a week, following the Ocean's route between Montreal and Matapedia before continuing to Gaspé along the beautiful Gaspé Peninsula.

Trains leave Montreal early on Mon, Thurs and Sat evening to reach Matapedia early next morning and Gaspé just before midday.

Travelling south, the Chaleur leaves Gaspé mid-afternoon on Mon, Thurs

and Sat to reach Matapedia mid-evening and Montreal early next morning.
Check-in baggage. Complete meals, bedrooms and roomettes.

The Hudson Bay

Over a thousand miles from Winnipeg north to Churchill and polar bear
country on Hudson Bay. The Hudson Bay Railroad opened in the 1920s to
move grain from the Canadian prairies for export.

Trains leave Winnipeg late evening on Sun, Tues and Thurs to reach The
Pas early next day and Thompson late afternoon. Gillan is reached around
midnight and you arrive in Churchill early morning on Tues, Thurs or Sat.

Travelling south, the Hudson Bay leaves Churchill mid-evening on Tues,
Thurs and Sat to reach Gillam early morning and Thompson mid-morning.
The Pas is reached mid-evening and you arrive in Winnipeg early morning on
Thurs, Sat or Mon.

Book well in advance, especially during summer. Check-in baggage.
Complete meals, bedrooms and roomettes.

Churchill's station is at 74092 Churchill, on the western edge of town.
Reservations and information: 1-800-561-8630. Left luggage room.

Travellers' Tales
The Canadian-Pacific from Montreal to Vancouver
A nostalgic recollection

by Susan Bishop

Back in the early 70s, when Amtrak was only a gleam in a corporate eye, the train
that everyone talked about was the coast to coast Canadian Pacific between
Montreal and Vancouver. It took three days and four nights (I think) and seemed
as good a place as any to spend a honeymoon. Not, perhaps, the most direct
route between Boston (where we lived) and Florida (where we were heading) but
never mind. We needed time to relax. As hand-luggage I carried a small weaving
loom and my new husband brought a huge plastic bag full of old copies of the
New York Sunday Times which he hadn't had time to read. We booked a single
cabin with a single narrow bunk; I seem to remember some disapproval over
these arrangements, but not an outright refusal.

We were blissfully happy. I set up my loom and trailed bits of wool all over the
place and Peter spread out his newspapers and got to grips with Watergate. The
woods and farms, prairies and lakes floated past the windows, changing slowly
over the days, lulling us into a state of semi-pupation, so that it took considerable
effort to emerge once a day to eat a civilised and sociable meal in the dining car
(we had copious supplies of wine, cheese and crackers for the other meals).

When we reached Edmonton in the evening, with the ride through the Rockies
ahead of us, the whole train was buzzing with excitement. It was early spring, had
snowed recently, and everyone hoped for a clear night. We knew the moon was
full, having made our plans around it. So had other passengers. At midnight
people were standing in little groups by the windows, gazing up at the blue-white
snow-fields and black crags, glistening under a cloud-free moon. Magic!

Other VIA Rail Trains

On Vancouver Island, services run daily between Victoria and Courtenay via Malahat Pass and the Cowichan Valley. You leave Victoria early morning or Courtenay early afternoon for a 140-mile journey lasting four hours.

The Hudson Bay connects at The Pas, Manitoba, with trains to Lynn Lake. You leave The Pas mid-morning to reach Lynn Lake mid-evening on Mon, Wed or Fri. Trains leave Lynn Lake early morning on Tues, Thurs and Sat, reaching The Pas by early evening.

Trains depart Sudbury on Tues, Thurs and Sat mornings for a 301-mile journey to White River, Ontario, arriving early evening. Travelling east, trains leave White River on Sun, Tues and Thurs morning to reach Sudbury mid-evening.

British Columbia Rail Limited

The British Columbia Railway operates daily passenger services between its own stations at 1311 W 1st Ave, Vancouver, and 1108 Industrial Way, Prince George.

Trains leave Vancouver early morning to reach Lillooet by early afternoon. On Sun, Wed and Fri you can continue to Prince George (arriving mid-evening).

Travelling south, trains leave Prince George early on Mon, Thurs and Sat to reach Lillooet mid-afternoon. From Lillooet, trains depart daily to reach Vancouver by mid-evening.

Services to and from Prince George operate daily from mid-June to mid-September. Reservations are required for trains north of Lillooet. Check-in baggage, snacks and complete meals are available.

In summer the company runs steam train excursions between Vancouver and Squamish, travelling along the coast of Howe Sound. For informaton contact the British Columbia Railway, PO Box 8770, Vancouver, BC, V6B 4X6 (604-631-3500).

The Algoma Central

Trains run 296 miles between Sault Ste Marie and Hearst in Ontario, travelling a land of forests, mountains, lakes and rivers, with terrific views of the Agawa Canyon. During the popular foliage season (September-October) you should plan a weekday trip if possible. Services are less frequent during winter.

For information contact the Algoma Central Railway, 129 Bay Street, Sault Ste Marie 26, Ontario P6A 1W7 (705-254-4331).

The Northlander

Operates between Toronto's Union Station and Cochrane via North Bay. Trains leave Toronto at midday every day except Sat, reaching North Bay late afternoon and Cochrane late evening.

Travelling south, the Northlander leaves Cochrane early morning to reach North Bay mid-afternoon and Toronto early evening.

Reservations are required. Complete meals. For information contact the Ontario Northland Railway, 555 Oak Street E, North Bay, Ontario P1B 8L3 (705-472-4500).

Other Railways in Canada

The Cartier Railway: Gaganon, Quebec G0G 1K0.

The Quebec Central Railway: 780 CP Rail Terrace, Sherbrooke, Quebec J1H 1T8.

The Quebec North Shore and Labrador Railroad: 100 Retty, Sept-iles, Quebec G4R 4L5 (418-968-7805) and Airport Road, Labrador City, NF, A2V 2K5 (709-944-8205).

No passenger trains run in either the Northwest Territories or the Yukon.

Appendix

Useful Addresses

Amtrak Customer Relations Office: 400 N Capitol Street, NW, Washington, DC 20001.

VIA Rail Canada Inc: C P 8116, 2 place Ville-Marie, Montreal, Quebec, Canada H3B 2G6.

Locomotive & Railway Preservation: PO Box 599, Richmond, VT 05477.

US Bureau of Customs: 1301 Constitution Ave, NW, Room 6303, Washington, DC 20229.

Canada Customs and Excise: Ottawa, Ontario, Canada K1A 0L5.

Greyhound International: 625 Eighth Ave, New York, NY. Also at 785 Market Street, Suite 1100, San Francisco, CA.

American Bed & Breakfast Association: PO Box 23486, Washington, DC 20024.

Bed & Breakfast Registry: PO Box 80174, St Paul, MN 55108.

Tourist House Association of America: PO Box 355A, Greentown, PA 18426 (717-857-0856).

American Youth Hostels National Office: PO Box 37613, Dept USA, Washington, DC 20013-7613 (202-783-6161).

YMCA National Council: 101 N Wacker Drive, Chicago, IL 60606.

YWCA National Council: 135 W 50th St, New York, NY 10020.

US Immigration and Naturalisation: 425 I Street NW, Washington, DC 20536 (202-633-1900).

US Customs Service: 1301 Constitution Ave NW, Washington, DC 20229 (202-566-8195).

Camp America: 37a Queens Gate, London SW7 5HR (071-589 3223).

BUNAC: 16 Bowling Green Lane, London EC1R 0BD (071-251 3472).

Council Travel: 205 East 42nd Street, New York, NY 10017 (212-661-1450).

State Information Bureaux

Alabama: 532 S Perry St, Montgomery, AL 36130 (205-261-4169).

Arizona: 1480 E Bethany Home Road, Phoenix, AZ 85014 (602-255-3618).

Arkansas: One Capital Mall, Little Rock, AR 72201 (501-371-7777).

California: 1121 L St, Suite 103, Sacramento, CA 95814 (916-322-1396).

Colorado: 5500 S Syracuse Circle, Suite 267, Englewood, CO 80111 (303-779-1067).

Connecticut: 210 Washington St, Hartford, CT 06106 (203-566-3385).

Delaware: PO Box 1401, Dover, DE 19903 (302-736-4271).

Florida: Collins Building, 107 W Gaines St, Tallahassee, FL 32301 (904-487-1465).

Georgia: PO Box 1776, Atlanta, GA 30301 (404-656-3590).

Idaho: State Capitol Building, Room 108, Boise, ID 83720 (208-334-2470).

Illinois: 310 South Michigan Ave, Suite 1000, Chicago, IL 60604 (312-793-4732).

Indiana: One North Capitol, Suite 700, Indianapolis, IN 46204 (317-232-8860).

Iowa: 600 E Court Ave, Des Moines, IA 50309 (515-281-3100).

Kansas: 503 Kansas Ave, Topeka, KS 66603 (913-296-3487).

Kentucky: Capital Plaza Tower, 22nd Floor, Frankfort, KY 40601 (502-564-4930).

Louisiana: PO Box 94291, Baton Rouge, LA 70804-9291 (504-925-3860).

Maine: 97 Winthrop St, Hallowell, ME 04347 (207-289-2423).

Maryland: 45 Calvert St, Annapolis, MD 21401 (301-269-3517).

Massachusetts: 100 Cambridge St, Boston, MA 02202 (617-727-3201).

Michigan: 100 Renaissance Center, Suite 1950, Detroit, MI 48243 (313-259-4333).

Minnesota: 240 Bremer Building, 419 N Robert St, St Paul, MN 55101 (612-296-5029).

Mississippi: PO Box 849, Jackson, MS 39205 (601-359-3414).

Missouri: Truman State Office Building, PO Box 1055, Jefferson City, MO 65102 (314-751-4133).

Montana: Helena, MT 59620 (406-444-2654).

Nebraska: PO Box 94666, Lincoln, NE 68509 (402-471-3796).

Nevada: Capitol Complex, Carson City, NV 89710 (702-885-4322).

New Hampshire: PO Box 856, Concord, NH 03301 (603-271-2666).

New Jersey: CN 826, Trenton, NJ 08625 (609-292-2470).

New Mexico: Bataan Memorial Building, Santa Fe, NM 87503 (505-827-6230).

New York: One Commerce Plaza, Albany, NY 12245 (212-309-0413).

North Carolina: 430 N Salisbury St, Raleigh, NC 27611 (919-733-4171).

North Dakota: Liberty Memorial Building, Capitol Grounds, Bismarck, ND 58505 (701-224-2525).

Ohio: PO Box 1001, Columbus, OH 43213 (614-466-8844).

Oklahoma: 215 NE 28th St, Oklahoma City, OK 73105 (405-521-2409).

Oregon: 595 Cottage St, NE Salem, OR 97310 (503-378-3451).

Pennsylvania: 416 Forum Building, Harrisburg, PA 17120 (717-787-5433).

Rhode Island: Seventh Jackson Walkway, Providence, RI 02903 (401-277-2601).

South Carolina: PO Box 71, Columbia, SC 29202 (803-758-8735).

South Dakota: Box 1000, Pierre, SD 57501 (605-773-3301).

Tennessee: PO Box 23170, Nashville, TN 37202 (615-741-2138).

Texas: Box 12008, Capital Station, Austin, TX 78711 (512-475-4326).

Utah: Council Hall, Capitol Hill, Salt Lake City, UT 84114 (801-533-5681).

Vermont: 134 State St, Montpelier, VT 05602 (802-828-3236).

Virginia: 202 N Ninth St, Suite 500, Richmond, VA 23219 (804-786-4484).

Washington: 101 General Administration Building, AX-13, Olympia, WA 98504 (206-753-5600).

Washington, DC: 1575 Eye St, NW Washington, DC 20005 (202-789-7000).

West Virginia: Building 6, Room B564, 1900 Washington St. E, Charleston, WV 25305 (304-348-2286).

Wisconsin: 123 West Washington Ave, Room 950, Madison, WI 53702 (608-266-2147).

Wyoming: I-25 at College Drive, Cheyenne, WY 82002-0660 (307-777-7777).

Amtrak International Sales Agents

ARGENTINA/PARAGUAY
Organfur, SA: President Peron 725-Piso, 6, 1038 Buenos Aires, Argentina. Tel: 46-1193. Tlx: 17557.

AUSTRALIA
Destination Holidays: 34A Main Street, Croydon, Victoria 3136. Tel: 725 4655. Tlx: 33317.

Walshes World: 92 Pitt Street, GPO Box 51, Sydney, NSW 2000. Tel: 008-221452. Tlx: 70655.

Thomas Cook: 175 Pitt Street, Sydney, NSW 2001. Tel: 229-6666. Tlx: 122169.

Thomas Cook: Myer Centre, Elizabeth & Albert Streets, Brisbane, Queensland 4001. Tel: 221-9749. Tlx: 122169.

Thomas Cook: 257 Collins Street, Melbourne, Victoria 3000. Tel: 650-2442. Tlx: 32628.

Thomas Cook: 45 Grenfell Street, Adelaide, SA 5000. Tel: 231-9532. Tlx: 82151.

Thomas Cook: Wesley Centre, 760 Hay Street, Perth, WA 6000. Tel: 321-2896. Tlx: 93665.

Thomas Cook: Star Village, Smith Street Mall, Darwin, NT 5794. Tel: 814 088. Tlx: 85479.

Thomas Cook: 21-23 London Circuit, Canberra, ACT 2601. Tel: 57 2222.

Thomas Cook: 40 Murray Street, Hobart, Tasmania 7000. Tel: 34 2699. Tlx: 32628.

AUSTRIA
Austria Reiseservice: Hessgasse 7, 1010 Vienna. Tel: 3445 16. Tlx: 115264.

BAHAMAS
R H Curry Freeport Ltd: Regent 2, Explorers Way, (PO Box F-453), Freeport, GB. Tel: 809-352-7234.

New Providence Travel: PO Box N 8160, Nassau. Tel: 322-8409.

BELGIUM/LUXEMBURG
Wirtz Travel/Top Snacks: De Keyserlei 44, B-2018 Antwerp, Belgium. Tel: 220-18-11. Tlx: 31484.

Wirtz Travel/USA Snacks: 66 Raventein, B-1000 Brussels, Belgium. Tel: 5100011.

BERMUDA
L P Gutteridge Ltd: Gutteridge Bldg, Bermudiana Road, (Box HM-1024), Hamilton 5. Tel: 295-4545. Tlx: 3397.

BRAZIL
De Luxe Destinations: Ave N S Copacabana, 500-Gr. 505, Rio de Janeiro 22020. Tel: 255-6466 or 800-1535 (toll-free). Tlx: 2133449.

De Luxe Destinations: Ave Paulista 807, SAL 1914/1915, Sao Paulo 01311. Tel: 277-0585. Tlx: 1138488.

CAYMAN ISLANDS
International Travel: PO Box 925, Trans-National Bldg, West Bay Road, Grand Cayman, BWI. Tel: 947-4323. Tlx: 4380.

COSTA RICA
Travelmar, SA: PO Box 1864-1000, Ave Central y Calle Uno, San Jose. Tel: 21-6695. Tlx: 2491.

DENMARK
T P S Travel Promotion Services: Vermundsgade 38, Dk-2100 Copenhagen. Tel: 39 27 27 20. Tlx: 19901.

DOMINICAN REPUBLIC
Turinter: Leopoldo Navarro 4, (PO Box 20202), Santo Domingo. Tel: 686-4020. Tlx: 4536.

ECUADOR
Kleintours: Ave Shyris 1000 y Holanda, PO Box 617A, Quito. Tel: 548-910. Tlx: 21378.
Kleintours: Avda 12 de Octubre 1721 y 6, Baquerizo.

FINLAND
United Travel/Finam Tours USA Dept: Mechelinkatu 10, SF-00100 Helsinki. Tel: 90-441-961. Tlx: 123615.

FRANCE
Wingate Travel: 19 bis Rue Du Mont Thabor, F-75001 Paris. Tel: 42 60 39 85. Tlx: 680229.
Loisirs, SA: 38 Rue du Mont Thabor, F-75001 Paris. Tel: 42 96 20 61. Tlx: 680229.
Loisirs, SA: Bureau du Ruhl, 1 Promenade Des Anglais, F-06000 Nice. Tel: 87 19 79.
Loisirs, SA: 53 Cours de L'Intendance, F-33000 Bordeaux. Tel: 445290.
Loisirs, SA: 11 Rue Boileau, F-44000 Nantes. Tel: 891092.
Loisirs, SA: 48 Rue du Vieux Marche Aux Vins, F-67000 Strasbourg. Tel: 329022.
Loisirs, SA: 6 Rue Stella, F-69002 Lyons. Tel: 422162.
Loisirs, SA: 41 La Canegiere, F-13003 Marseille. Tel: 916634.

GERMANY
D E R (Deutsches Reiseburo): Eschersheimer Landstrasse 25-27, D-6000 Frankfurt 1. Tel: 1566474. Tlx: 415292-32.
F & G Reise Gmbh: Landwehrstrasse 31, D-8000 Munich 2. Tel: 597643. Tlx: 522034.
F & G Reise Gmbh: Klosterstrasse 47, D-4000 Dusseldorf. Tel: 162197. Tlx: 8587520.

F & G Reise Gmbh: Waldschmidstrasse 127, D-6000 Frankfurt 1. Tel: 490292. Tlx: 414267.

GUATEMALA
Aire Mary Y Tierra: Plaza Los Arcos, Calle 5-36, Zona 10, (PO Box 1048), Guatemala City. Tel: 370149. Tlx: 5141.

HONG KONG
Travel Advisers Ltd: 1105 Swiss House, 11 Chater Road, (GPO Box 8136). Tel: 225-181. Tlx: 44430.

INDIA
Sita World Travel: F-12 Connaught Place, New Delhi 110001. Tel: 3311122. Tlx: 3165141.

Shree Raj Travels & Tours: 27-B/C Panchratna, Ground Floor, Mama Parmanand Marg Opera House, Bombay 400004. Tel: 8117000. Tlx: 1173473.

IRELAND
Eurotrain: 34 Lower Abbey Street, Dublin 1. Tel: 741777. Tlx: 33579.

ISRAEL
Tal Aviation Ltd: Migdalor Bldg, 1 Ben Yehuda Street, 68801 Tel Aviv. Tel: 652163. Tlx: 33574.

ITALY
Viaggi Kuoni SRL: Via Boncompagni 14, I-00100 Rome. Tel: 4746051. Tlx: 623304.

Tabb SRL: Piazza della Republica 28, I-20124 Milan. Tel: 657-1141. Tlx: 322561.

JAPAN
Japan Travel Bureau: 1-6-4 Marunouchi, Chiyoda-ku, Tokyo 100. Tel: 284-7371. Tlx: 28648.

Travel Plaza Intl: Fuji Bldg, 5-30-9 Shiba, Minato-ku, Tokyo 108. Tel: 591-4237. Tlx: 2223613.

Kintetsu International: 19-2 Kanda-Matsunga-Cho, Chiyoda-ku, Tokyo 101. Tel: 255-7111. Tlx: 2226896.

Nippon Travel Agency Co Ltd: Shimbashi-Ekimae Bldg No 1 6F, 20-15 2-Chome Shimbashi, Minato-ku, Tokyo. Tel: 25223795.

Flex International Tours Inc: Kawabe Bldg, 3-7-9 Shimbashi Minato-ku, Tokyo 105. Tel: 501-7478.

KOREA
AJU Tourist Service Co Ltd: Hyosung Bldg, 21-1 Seosomun-dong, Chung-ku, Seoul. Tel: 753-5051. Tlx: K24103.

MEXICO
Viajes Ancho Mundo SA de CV: Dante 14-8th Floor, Col Anzures CP 11590,

Mexico City, DF. Tel: 574-9325. Tlx: 1773401.
Asesora Public Turistica SZ: Bruselas 904 Col Mirador, Monterrey NL. Tel:
432666. Tlx: 382932.

NETHERLANDS
Incento BV: Stationsplein 1, 1400 AM Bussum, (Correspondence address:
PO Box 457, 1400 AL Bussum). Tel: 2159-48586. Tlx: 43157.

NEW ZEALAND
Carefree Holidays Ltd: 44-48 Emily Place, (PO Box 557), Auckland. Tel: 797-
105. Tlx: 60152.
Atlantic & Pacific Travel: Parnell Place, 164 Parnell Road, (PO Box 3839),
Auckland 1000. Tel: 770-660. Tlx: 2401.
Walshes World: Dingwall Bldg, 87 Queen Street, Private Bag, Auckland 1000.
Tel: 793-708. Tlx: 21437.
Thomas Cook (NZ) Ltd: 96/98 Anzac Avenue, (PO Box 3595), Auckland
1000. Tel: 796-800. Tlx: 2236.

NORWAY
NSB Reisebyra: Stortinsgt 28, N-0161 Oslo. Tel: 83 88 50. Tlx: 71725.
A/S Nordmanns-Reiser: Radhursgt 23B, N-0158 Oslo. Tel: 416582. Tlx:
72782.

PANAMA
Agencias Giscome: Eusebio A Morales, Edif Atlantida, Panama City. Tel: 64-
0111. Tlx: 3678.
Margo Tours, SA: Calle 51 Bella Vistra No 24, Panama City. Tel: 69-6704.

PERU
Lima Reps SA: Ave Juan de Arona 883, San Isidro, Lima. Tel: 815-8157. Tlx:
63621.

PHILIPPINES
PCI Travel Corp: 2nd-3rd Floors, PCCI Bldg, 118 Alfaro Street, Salcedo
Village, Makati, Metro Manila. Tel: 815-8157. Tlx: 63621.

PORTUGAL
Pinto Basto Tours: Praca Duque Da Terceira 20-1200, Lisbon. Tel: 3460091.
Tlx: 12169.

PUERTO RICO
Star Tours: 1035 Ashford Ave, (PO Box 13321), San Juan, Puerto Rico
00908. Tel: 724-6660. Tlx: 2907.
Viajes Caribe: J Augusto Rivera Esq Canals URB, Roosevelt Hato Rey,
Puerto Rico 00918. Tel: 756-6720. Tlx: 0736.

SINGAPORE/MALAYSIA
Diners World Travel: 7500 E Beach Road, The Plaza 02-201, Singapore
0719. Tel: 292-5522. Tlx: 50566.

Diners World Travel: 6-4 Wisha, Lorong ABU-SITI, Penang 10400, Malaysia. Tel: 27175. Tlx: 40118.

Diners World Travel: 6th Floor, East Block, Wisma Selangor Dredging, 142-B Jalan Ampang, 50450 Kuala Lumpur, Malaysia. Tel: 261 3522. Tlx: 32998.

SOUTH AFRICA
World Travel Agency: PO Box 4568, 111 Commissioner Street, 13th Floor, Johannesburg 2001. Tel: 29-7234. Tlx: 483595.

SPAIN
Expomundo: Sta Cruz de Marcenado 31, 1st Floor, Oficina 10, 28015 Madrid. Tel: 542-1348. Tlx: 44585.

Expomundo: Xucla 8, 08001 Barcelona. Tlx: 99748.

SRI LANKA
Mercantile Tours (Ceylon) Ltd: 51 Janadhipathi Mawatha, Colombo 1. Tel: 549-994. Tlx: 21138.

SWEDEN
Reso Travel Agency: Dalagatan 7, (PO Box 139), S-101 21 Stockholm. Tel: 11 81 56. Tlx: 19693.

Trivselresor Resebureau: Vagagatan 4, (PO Box 6420), S-113 82 Stockholm. Tel: 24 86 40. Tlx: 11829.

Tour America: Balzartgatan 25-5th Floor, (PO Box 4438), S-203 15 Malmo. Tel: 72426. Tlx: 32812.

SWITZERLAND
Kuoni Travel Ltd: Neue Hard, Neugasse 231, CH-8037 Zurich. Tel: 277-444. Tlx: 823052.

SSR-Reisen: Backerstrasse 52, Postfach, CH-8026 Zurich. Tel: 242-3000. Tlx: 812171.

UNITED ARAB EMIRATES
Al-Tayer Travel Agency: B-65 Sheikh Rashid Bldg, Al Maktoum Street, (PO Box 2623), Dubai. Tel: 236000. Tlx: 47662.

UNITED KINGDOM
Albany Travel: 190 Deansgate, Manchester M3 3WD. Tel: 061-833-0202. Tlx: 667174.

Destination Marketing: 2 Cinnamon Row, Plantation Wharf, York Place, London SW11 3TW. Tel: 071-978-5212. Tlx: 27231.

Explorers Tours: 222 Coppermill Road, Wraysbury TW19 5NW. Tel: 0753-681999.

Long-Haul Leisurail: PO Box 113, Peterborough PE1 1LE. Tel: 0733-51780. Tlx: 57-269006.

Thistle Air Ltd: 22 Bank Street, Kilmarnock, Ayrshire, KA1 1HA Scotland. Tel: 0563-31121. Tlx: 51-77-9082.

Trailfinders: 42-50 Earls Court Road, Kensington, London W8 6EJ. Tel: 071-938 3366. Tlx: 919670.

VIRGIN ISLANDS
Southerland Tours: Chandler's Wharf, Christiansted, St Croix. Tel: 773-9500 or 800/524-2022 (toll-free).

VIA Rail International Sales Agents
ARGENTINA
Canadian Airlines International: Avenida Cordoba 656,1054 Buenos Aires. Tel: 392-3632.

AUSTRALIA
Walshes World: 92 Pitt Street, GPO Box 51, Sydney, NSW 2000. Tel: 02-232-7499. Tlx: 71/70655.

AUSTRIA
Reiseburo Intropa: Karntner Strasse 38, 1015 Vienna. Tel: 515-14-0. Tlx: 112521.

BELGIUM
Topsnacks (Wirtz-Air NV): Appelmansstraat 12-14, B-2018 Antwerp. Tel: 03 222-1870. Tlx: 31-484.

BRAZIL
Canadian Airlines International: Rua da Ajuda 35, 29 Andar, 20040 Rio de Janeiro. Tel: 220-5343.
Canadian Airlines International: Av Sao Luiz 50, 7 Andar, Sao Paulo, CEP 01046. Tel: 259-9066.

CHILE
Canadian Airlines International: Huerfanos 669, Suite 311, PO Box 9252, Santiago. Tel: 39-3058.

COLOMBIA
Atturs Ltda: Calle 100, No 14-15 Apartado Areo, 075609 Bogota. Tel: 257-0220/218-1381.

DENMARK
Topdanmark Rejsebureau: Lautrupvang 3, Dk-2750 Ballerup. Tel: 45 44686688. Tlx: 35398.

GERMANY
Canada Reise Dienst: Rathausplatz 2, D-2070 Hamburg/Ahrensburg. Tel: 04102 51167. Tlx: 41-2189857.

HONG KONG
Japan Travel Bureau: Room 1709, One Pacific Place, 88 Queensway. Tel: 5-261117. Tlx: 68840 JTBAD HX.

INDIA
Raj Travel & Tours Ltd: 27-B Panchratna, Ground Floor, Mama Parmanand Marg Opera House, Bombay 400004. Tel: 811-0415. Tlx: 81-1176645.

ISRAEL
Tal Aviation Ltd: Migdalor Building, 1 Ben Yehuda Street, 68801 Tel Aviv. Tel: 03-652163. Tlx: 33574.

ITALY
Gastaldi Tours: Viali Restelli 5/A, 20124 Milan. Tel: 02/ 668-121. Tlx: 333071.

JAPAN
Japan Travel Bureau Inc: 1-6-4 Marunouchi, Chiyoda-ku, Tokyo 100. Tel: 03-3284-7382. Tlx: 72-28648.

MALAYSIA
Diners World Travel Pte Ltd: 6th Floor, East Block, Wisma Selangor Dredging, 142-B Jalan Ampang, 50450 Kuala Lumpur. Tel: 036-261 3522. Tlx: 32998 DINKUL MA.

MEXICO
VIAJES Crucero SA: Division Del Norte No 421, 1 Col Del Valle, DF 03100 Mexico City. Tel: 687-5056. Tlx: 1760226.

NETHERLANDS
Incento BV: Station/plein 1, 1404 AM Bussum, (Correspondence address: PO Box 457, 1400 AL Bussum). Tel: 2159-48586. Tlx: 44-43157.

NEW ZEALAND
Walshes World Ltd: 2nd Floor, Dingwall Building, 87 Queen Street, PO Box 279, Auckland 1. Tel: 09 793 708. Tlx: 74-21437.

PERU
Canadian Airlines International: Paseo de la Republica 138, Casilla 812, Lima. Tel: 24-9262.

SINGAPORE
Diners World Travel Pte Ltd: 7500 E Beach Road, No 02-201, The Plaza, Singapore 0719. Tel: 292 5522. Tlx: 87/ 50566.

SWEDEN
Tour Canada of Sweden: Box 311, S-791 27 Falun. Tel: 23-20681. Tlx: 54-74150.

SWITZERLAND
Touring Club Suisse: Rue Pierre Fatio 9, CH-1211 Geneva. Tel: 046-054140. Tlx: 45-22488.

TAIWAN
Ken Shin Travel Services Ltd: Capitol Building 308, No 158 Sung Chiang Road, Taipei. Tel: 536-5115. Tlx: 25888.

UNITED KINGDOM
Long-Haul Leisurail: PO Box 113, Peterborough PE1 1LE. Tel: 0733-51780. Tlx: 57-269006.

Thistle Air Ltd: 22 Bank Street, Kilmarnock, Scotland KA1 1HA. Tel: 0563-31121. Tlx: 51-77-9082.

USA
Amtrak, Union Station: 60 Massachusetts Ave NE, Washington, DC 20002. Tel: 202-906-3000.

Canadian Airlines International: 212-2222 Kalakaua Avenue, Honolulu, HI 96815. Tel: 808-922-0533.

INDEX OF PLACE NAMES

For train names and other subjects, see Table of Contents